S0-BOW-444

From Ah Q to Lei Feng

From Ah Q to Lei Feng

FREUD AND REVOLUTIONARY SPIRIT IN 20TH CENTURY CHINA

Wendy Larson

STANFORD UNIVERSITY PRESS
STANFORD, CALIFORNIA

Stanford University Press
Stanford, California

Printed in the United States of America on acid-free, archival-quality paper

Library of Congress Cataloging-in-Publication Data

Larson, Wendy.
From Ah Q to Lei Feng : Freud and revolutionary spirit in 20th century China / Wendy Larson.
p. cm.
Includes bibliographical references and index.
ISBN 978-0-8047-0075-7 (cloth : alk. paper)
1. Chinese literature—20th century—History and criticism. 2. Psychoanalysis and literature—China. 3. Psychoanalysis and motion pictures—China. 4. China—History—Cultural Revolution, 1966-1976—Literature and the revolution. 5. China—History—Cultural Revolution, 1966-1976—Motion pictures and the revolution. 6. Literature and history—China. I. Title. II. Title: Freud and revolutionary spirit in 20th century China.
PL2303.L365 2009
895.1'09353—dc22
2008011827

Typeset by Bruce Lundquist in 10.5/14 Adobe Garamond

In Memory of
Donald Martin Larson
1957–2002

Contents

Illustrations

Acknowledgments

I would like to extend my gratitude to the following organizations for directly supporting the research in this project: the Stanford Humanities Center, which supported the crucial final year of a ten-year project with a Marta Sutton Weeks senior fellowship for the 2005–6 academic year; the Oregon Humanities Center, which supported a term of research in 2001; the Freeman Foundation, which funded a trip to China in 1999. With Bryna Goodman, I received support from the Association for Asian Studies, the Chiang Ching-kuo Foundation, the Center for the Study of Women in Society at the University of Oregon, and the Center for Asian and Pacific Studies at the University of Oregon, all of which helped fund a conference on Gender in Motion: Divisions of Labor and Cultural Change in Late Imperial and Modern China, where I first presented my work on film director He Jianjun. My thinking on the topics included in the book was expanded and improved through presentation of my work at conferences and individual talks, many of which were supported by groups and organizations at the following universities and institutes: the Institute of Chinese Literature and Philosophy at Academia Sinica in Taiwan; the University of California, Davis; Stanford University; Beijing University; the University of Chicago; Saint Petersburg State University; Nanjing University; Harvard University; University of California, San Diego; Institute of Far Eastern Studies at the Russian Academy of Sciences; University of Washington; University of British Columbia; Colorado College; and the University of California, Berkeley. Various talented people working in the libraries at Academia Sinica (Taiwan), Stanford University, and Harvard University assisted me in locating a number of difficult-to-find articles and books.

Because the work for this book progressed over a such a long period, it is impossible to thank each individual who has contributed to the development of its ideas. I have been the beneficiary of discussions with so many people that a list would be little less than a who's who in Chinese literary studies. Several recent conversations—often where I was invited to present an individual talk or I presented at a small conference—stand out, however; in that regard, I would like to thank Xiaomei Chen, Marian Galik, Michel Hockx, Liu Jihui, Kang Liu, Hsiao-yen Peng, Lisa Rofel, Carlos Rojas, Xiaobing Tang, Ailing Wang, Michele Yeh, Xueping Zhong, Sheldon Hsiao-peng Lu, and Theodore Huters. My fellow fellows at the Stanford Humanities Center in 2005–6, especially those who participated with me in the Interrogating Modernity and Postcoloniality Workshop—Johannes Fabian, Purnima Mankekar, and Sabine Frühstück—provided detailed critique of my work. Stephen Yao, Ya-Chen Ma, Judith Lichtenberg, and Marinés Fornerino also were frequent conversation partners during that year. At the University of Oregon, I want to credit my recent graduate students Rui-hua Shen, Eileen Vickery, Hongwei Lu, Daniel Baird, and Xin Yang for their contributions in and out of class. And finally, I would like to thank my colleagues at the University of Oregon for providing a stimulating intellectual environment and ready opportunity to discuss and debate issues in the Chinese studies field. Especially, I have benefited from talking over my work with Bryna Goodman, Stephen Durrant, Tze-lan Sang, and Richard Kraus. I am deeply grateful to them for their continued friendship and support.

Parts of this book were previously published as articles or book chapters, although in some cases they have been significantly revised and further developed. Chapter 6 (pp. 197–221) was originally published as Chapter 9 of *Gender in Motion: Divisions of Labor and Cultural Change in Late Imperial and Modern China*, eds. Bryna Goodman and Wendy Larson, Rowman and Littlefield, 2005, 211–38, with the title "He Yi's *The Postman*: The Workspace of a New Age Maoist." The part of Chapter 5 concerning Anchee Min (pp. 183–96) was originally published as "Never This Wild: Sexing the Cultural Revolution," *Modern China*, Volume 25, Number 4, October 1999, 423–50, although the work has undergone extensive revision for this book. The part of Chapter 4 on Wang Xiaobo (pp. 132–53) was originally published as "Okay, Whatever: Intellectuals, Sex, and Time in Wang Xiaobo's *The Golden Years*," *The China Review: An Interdisciplinary Journal on Greater China*, Volume 3, Number 1, Spring 2003, 29–56. I am grateful to these publications for permission to use this work here.

From Ah Q to Lei Feng

Introduction

This project began in 1995, when I saw Jiang Wen's (1963–) then-newly released film *In the Heat of the Sun* (Yangguang canlan de rizi) in Beijing. Although stories that revised the earlier Cultural Revolution narrative of a youthful idealism betrayed by corruption and violence were not uncommon in the work of Wang Anyi (1955–), Zhang Xianliang (1936–), Wang Xiaobo (1952–1997), Mang Ke (1950–), Anchee Min (1957–), and others, I had never before seen the Cultural Revolution period visually represented with such sexual innuendo and sensual abandon in image, sound, and story.

While eventually coming to believe that these narratives did not substitute sexual for revolutionary excitement in any simple sense, I initially wondered whether this representation simply modernized the revolutionary past through an imaginary discursive alliance with European and North American sexual modernity—projected in literature, media, advertisements, and cultural theory—that privileged what we have come to call "sexuality," valorizing the importance of sexual desire and behavior. After all, interpreting the explosion of sexual representation in post-Mao culture as reaction against an excessively repressive Confucian and Maoist past was common in China. Marking the poles of this debate, the popular media tended to regard stories and films about sex as either emancipatory or decadent. To investigate these issues, I began researching authors and filmmakers who set their stories during the Cultural Revolution but delved into the sexual relations of their characters. My initial working hypothesis was that representing the Cultural Revolution as a sexually interesting or exciting time updated or modernized it through the imagined alliance and, by extension, modernized the entire revolutionary past. Within this interpretation, writers and film directors recognized the important 20th-century historical development of a Euro-American discourse that emphasized sexual identity within modern subjectivity and constructed their characters on this basis.

The project immediately ran into problems. Although these stories and films featured a great deal of sexual desire and activity, a deeply sexual subjectivity was not established in the characters. If writers and directors were not merely renovating their cast-off revolutionary past through an imagined sexual modernity, then what were they doing? The immense popularity of a film like *In the Heat of the Sun* and the cultish intellectual following behind the work of Wang Xiaobo, as well as clues in the films and novels themselves, suggested that this was no simple failure to execute. Perhaps I had yet to identify the motivation behind this seemingly familiar combination of revolution and sex, and needed to look more carefully at the way in which subjectivity was described, represented, and imagined. While sexual desire and behavior were significant aspects of these stories, other important concepts of the mind and mentality also appeared to be at work.

These two areas—theories of the mind and theories of sexual desire—led me to the work of Sigmund Freud (1856–1939). Although Freud was not the first person to theorize an unconscious, he endowed it with dynamic productivity as a site where repressed sexual desire continually maintained a controlling influence on nearly every aspect of life. This combination of repressed sexual desire and the unconscious proved itself a powerful theory, a perspective that assumed a crucial position within American, French, and more generally Western cultural life. Over the 20th century, a psychotherapy that sought explanation—often sexual in nature—for difficulties or problems not in the social environment or in social relationships, but in early life experience, developed rapidly and was institutionalized in medicine and popular culture. Freud became a household word in terms such as the "Freudian slip," and psychoanalytical terminology and methodology entered cultural theory, for a time (and even to some extent today) dominating film theory and postcolonial studies. Psychoanalytical concepts such as the "return of the repressed," "sublimation," "transference," "denial," and "desire"—often with the implication or direct statement that all desire was at root sexual desire—proliferated in literature, history, film, anthropology, cultural studies, and other academic fields. Recognition and release of so-called repressed desire were linked to political progressivism and enshrined as an ideology with potential far exceeding the realm of the sexual. Models of the mind, self, sexual desire, and social life related to Freudian sexual subjectivity assumed a central position in the West; criticisms of "belated modernity" notwithstanding, they provided and continue to provide a potent example for other modernizing countries.

In literary and film studies, this Freudian influence was most obviously expressed in psychoanalytical criticism, which also has been popular in studies of modern Chinese literature, where unquestioned assumptions about the universal existence of a sexualized unconscious and a whole set of psychological mechanisms have flourished. Although scientists have long debunked Freudian theory and the last thirty years also saw increasing critique of Freud's ideas within cultural studies, these very ideas often appeared in explanations of Chinese culture and social life under revolutionary conditions. Scholars argued or implied that the socialist state channeled sexual desire into controllable behavior and expression and that it was therefore logical to regard revolutionary passion as simply sublimated sexual passion. In this teleological model, Chinese society was inexorably moving toward a sexual modernity already ubiquitous in the West. Often underlying this critique was the implication that sexual liberation would lead to political liberation, that once an individual was "free" to express and enact sexual desire, society would follow with increased democratization and choice, and totalitarian mentalities and approaches to governing would disappear. But revolutionary discourse developed its own theories of the mind and social life, desire and emotion. Could the sexualized unconscious and its associated ideas of repression, denial, and sublimation, which were not concepts circulating in revolutionary culture, satisfactorily elucidate subjectivity at the time? Did these concepts possess a modern universality sufficient to explain mental life under revolutionary culture? Privileging sexuality as a thematic and aesthetic focus was an interpretive strategy that failed to recognize the full creative conditions of these films and novels, I eventually realized.

Thus this book is structured through the identification of two powerful discourses, one a Freudian approach that centers sexual desire within modern subjectivity and identity, the other a revolutionary epistemology that conceptualizes subjectivity and identity as socially developed and yet also informed by a passionate wellspring of emotion and intellect. Sexual desire did not occupy a privileged spot in revolutionary subjectivity, which projected its own unique structure and unfolded according to its own assumptions. The pervasive influence of psychoanalytical sexual theory in cultural studies and a corresponding tendency to center sexual desire within literary investigation—especially in European and American research but increasingly in work on Chinese literature coming out of China today—turned this simple and seemingly obvious position into a hard-won victory.

My initial task, then, was to historically trace and deconstruct Freudian sexual theory, with the goal of fully illustrating the naturalized discursive environment behind researchers' proposition of sexuality as an overarching explanatory concept or uncritical use of concepts such as repression or sublimation. This effort both develops the theoretical structure of my argument and, as I will later explain, responds to one aspect of my critique of the field. In my first chapter, I show how Freudian sexual and mental theory ascended within the cultural field (and within psychology, psychoanalysis, and psychotherapy) over the century, as well as present Western historical alternatives and recent attacks on the influence of Freudian thought within cultural theory. This history has been documented in a rich body of scholarship and should be well known. Even so, the authority of Freudian ideas in cultural studies—film, literature, history, anthropology, psychology, and more—brought me to the conclusion that despite the existence of this fierce dismantling and critique, Freudian ideas are firmly naturalized and therefore continue to exert tremendous explanatory power. In this chapter I demonstrate how a Freudian model of the mind, replete with a richly productive sexualized unconscious, became central to our convictions about what made us modern. I rely on a wide range of sources to historicize and dismantle any claim on behalf of universality or naturalness in Freudian theory.

In Chapter Two, I investigate the introduction of modern psychology and Freudian theory in China, making several points about the conditions under which this new "science" was understood. First, because modern psychology first came into China through a context of educational reform, it was closely allied with the sweeping changes and implications of new educational systems that were rapidly developing at the end of the Qing dynasty. The work of Joseph Haven (1816–74), Harald Höffding (1843–1931), Ruric Nevel Roark (1859–1909), Kubota Sadanori, and Hattori Unokichi (1867–1939) established influential frameworks within which the mind was studied and understood. This organization placed psychology—as a discipline as well as a more general emphasis on subjectivity as something that must be carefully cultivated if one is to be modern—in a tight relationship with discourses of national health and power. It also dovetailed with traditional concerns about education and self-cultivation. Second, I evaluate the entry of Freudian psychoanalysis into China, with special emphasis on the unconscious, sexual desire, and related ideas. China's most famous psychological researcher, Gao Juefu (1896–1993), rejected the primacy of both sexual desire and the unconscious in Freud's theories, and was especially critical of their combination in the sexualized unconscious. His arguments provide the outlines of an epistemology that imagines the mind quite differently than did Freud. Third, I closely read a debate between "Dr. Sex" Zhang Jingsheng (1889–1970) and Zhou Jianren (1888–1984), interpreting it as a refusal on the part of Zhou Jianren and other cultural intellectuals to center sexual desire as the crux of modern mentality. And finally, I examine the translation of Freudian ideas about the mind and sexual desire into literary texts of the 1920s and 1930s, ending with a brief discussion of post-Mao "Freud fever." Overall, in this chapter I trace the difficult negotiations and explosive confrontations between, on one hand, the new subjectivity-emphasizing psychology and the Freudian centering of repressed sexual desire as the most important aspect of modern mentality and, on the other, a more socially oriented concept of the mind in which environment and relationships generate subjectivity. Within this system, sexual desire is but one of a number of desires, and, like the others, it must always be socially contextualized. It does not become the linchpin of "identity."

Chapter Three focuses on the development of theories of the mind in revolutionary culture, beginning with the late Qing and early Republican periods. Lu Xun's fictional character Ah Q (A Q) was known for his "spiritual victory method" (jingshen shenglifa), a strategy that turned defeat into victory. After his 1921 debut, Ah Q became an icon countrywide through which concerns about national, ethnic, and personal qualities and ways of thinking were hotly debated. While rejecting "bourgeois" emphasis on subjectivity and personality, the 1930s–40s essays and talks of Mao Zedong stressed the importance of human will, and in the 1950s, psychology was one discipline charged with theorizing this focus. Revolutionary Chinese psychology valorized the Leninist notions of reflection and recognition, both of which demanded a keen awareness of position, and also consciousness as opposed to the unconscious, social contextualization as opposed to the isolated interior mind, and *jingshen* (often translated as "spirit") as opposed to the sexual. Although often essentialized as a quality, *spirit* for the revolutionary subject is the significant concept or orientation through which one negotiates one's social position or one's relationship to power. While the modern Westerner may find him- or herself in endless psychotherapy designed to probe the hidden unconscious and locate sexual motivation behind seemingly unrelated problems, the revolutionary Chinese subject can easily suffer from an improper spirit, or a refusal to internalize and exemplify, through attitude and behavior, his or her correct social position. The discourses of spirit in revolutionary popular culture, philosophy, psychology, and medical psychiatry range from romantic to punitive, from overtly ideological to normative, overall forming a tight web of signification that positioned revolutionary spirit in a spot as important as was sexual desire within the Freudian model.

Yet there is more to spirit than simply position, power, and social relationships. Just as the privileging of sexual desire in the unconscious requires significant personal attention and emotional investment, so the centering of revolutionary spirit in subjectivity demands a passionate embodiment of its underlying suppositions. Although not a fictional character as was Ah Q, the historical Lei Feng is also enveloped within an extensive discourse of spirit that captures the most significant aspects of mentality as it was envisioned at the time. From Ah Q to Lei Feng, this discourse of spirit—social positioning, radical embodiment of oneself in relation to power, and profound emotional and intellectual identification with that position and the structure of relationships it implies—outlines the construction of revolutionary subjectivity.

Therefore, not only the familiar story of a deep interiority and a sexualized unconscious but also the revolutionary discourse of social position and embodied spirit must be taken seriously. From this historical perspective, it would be naïve to imagine that writers and filmmakers who use a sexual focus to depict the Cultural Revolution are simply updating a repressive sexual past or replacing one way of envisioning the mind with another that they view as more modern. Two important discourses exist within these stories. In the rest of the project, I return to the stories and films that sparked my interest in this topic, analyzing their themes and literary aesthetics with an eye to the particular aspect of revolutionary subjectivity that each writer or director is highlighting, and an ongoing query about the representation of sexual desire and behavior as set up against, as part of, or in combination with revolutionary culture.

To avoid turning my project into the dreaded literary survey, I narrowed its scope to include only stories and films in which the setting is the Cultural Revolution period, and a primary focus is sexual desire, relationships, and behavior. These stories provided a context within which I could evaluate the two discourses, and also opened my investigation to subtle foci and meanings that creative aesthetic imagination can reveal. A second concern about the field of modern Chinese literary studies in the United States also directed my restraint. New historicism, cultural studies, and postcolonial studies brought questions about the value of New Criticism and its methods of textual analysis, encouraging scholars to recognize literature as a social product and to integrate our discipline with intellectual currents outside the field. While this process was not without important benefits, the question of how literary aesthetics produced meaning withered, expanding the logic of historical investigation by turning literature into an example to be mined for "larger" trends. In this project, the texts and films directed my historical research, not the other way around, and I wanted not merely produce a survey of novels and films that fit the history I had unraveled, but to carefully tease out and interpret their aesthetic meanings. Because I wanted to do a closer, tighter, and deeper analysis including not only meanings produced through theme, plot, and character but also aesthetic strategies, I decided to sharply limit the number of texts and films. Clearly many more could have been included.

In the next three chapters, therefore, I interpret the work of three writers and two filmmakers: Mang Ke, Wang Xiaobo, Jiang Wen, Anchee Min, and He Jianjun (1960–). With the exception of He Jianjun, they all set their stories during the Cultural Revolution, and all five express a strong thematic interest in sexual desire and behavior. In other words, these five storytellers bring to bear the dual discourses I identified. That is where their similarities end, however. Each takes on a seminal concept—or dynamic myth—of revolutionary consciousness, identifying and deconstructing it to produce a new direction. It should not surprise us that Chinese writers and filmmakers profoundly intuit the deepest historical and contemporary meanings of the society in which they live and work, or that they direct their abilities toward understanding, critiquing, and creatively reworking these meanings.

Even in the case of He Jianjun's film *The Postman*, which does not mention the Cultural Revolution, revolutionary subjectivity is the primary target of aesthetic investigation, I argue.

Chapter Four concerns the novels *Wild Things* (1994) by Mang Ke and *The Golden Years* (1991) by Wang Xiaobo, and begins with the recognition that as semi-autobiographical stories about sent-down youth, they participate in a far-reaching reconstruction of the evocative 20th-century discourse of the countryside. In both cases, however, the stories do not merely dismantle this legacy of meaning under revolutionary culture; they also investigate the way in which it determined revolutionary subjectivity. Mang Ke thematically and aesthetically flattens the countryside, disallowing it as a site of intellectual rejuvenation and anti-civilization symbolism. His protagonist Maodi skips across the landscape, forming sexual relationships in the city and the countryside with no regard to locale, creating a web-like configuration of nodes or links that structures the logic of his existence. Mang Ke's novel spatially reworks the spiritually embodied countryside, gutting it of significance. Just as the material reality of the countryside always was much more than the discourse in which it was embedded, so is this gutting meaningful beyond its deconstruction of a potent revolutionary idealization of rural life, in addition pointing to spatial idealization as a formative element of consciousness. Like Mang Ke, Wang Xiaobo also zeroes in on one aspect of revolutionary discourse, replacing the progress-based, clear, directed, and deterministic temporal consciousness of the revolutionary spirit with a sense of time passing that is more detached and philosophical. Although Wang Xiaobo's protagonist Wang Er is ever interested in sexual intercourse, he is not enervated by emotion or passion but meanders gently, gaining greater perspective through ageing than through political movements or concerns. Because the story is narrated by an older Wang Er who knows of the damage time can inflict, the melancholy of this passage of time infects and alters the present moment. Brilliantly establishing—but never directly representing—revolutionary time as an abstract notion and a precondition to his work, Wang Xiaobo seeks an ontological revision that thoroughly alters a fundamental aspect of existence. His essentially temporal vision complements the spatial orientation of Mang Ke's writing.

The focus of Chapter Five, the work of filmmaker Jiang Wen and expatriate writer Anchee Min, also is on revolutionary subjectivity, the more mystical approach of these two artists signaling an underlying concept of transcendence. Both extract the revolutionary spirit from its material and ideological environment, allowing it to soar free from contaminating pretense and the corruption of bureaucratic life, or the disintegration of the revolutionary vision. *In the Heat of the Sun* (1994), directed by Jiang Wen, shows that even though a revolutionary heroism fueled by the imagined superiority of socialism is false, it contains a kernel of forward-directed movement that can be abstracted and recouped. Although in the late years of the Cultural Revolution the film makes youthful curiosity and playful sexual desire the most obvious indications of this unfixable spirit; they are significant almost entirely as the means through which something very good about the revolutionary past may once again come to life, even under conditions of capitalist consumer culture. In *Red Azalea* (1994), Anchee Min more forcefully mines the revolutionary spirit from deadened social forms, concocting a magical force with orgasmic qualities. Because she writes in English and publishes in the United States, where tales of sexual awakening are readily published and absorbed, her vision comes close to implying that sexual desire is at the core of revolutionary passion. Although in this way she falls victim to the Freudian myth of overarching sexual significance, Min nonetheless distinguishes her story by attributing to this quality a mass characteristic devolved from revolutionary culture and expressed most directly by the radical female leftist Jiang Qing, the wife of Mao Zedong. Jiang Wen shows revolutionary spirit to be largely a mass experience and sexual desire as alienating the individual from the social group, but for Anchee Min an overarching mysticism unites and expresses both revolutionary spirit and sexual desire. This quality of "for the masses" reiterates one of the primary directives of revolutionary culture: serve the people. Echoing Jiang Wen's approach, Min separates Maoism into cultural and spiritual Maoism, which can be imaginatively productive for the future, and political Maoism, which is dead.

In Chapter Six, on He Jianjun's (He Yi) 1995 film *The Postman*, we leap into post-Mao culture in actual film time, violating my guideline of evaluating only fiction and film with plots set during the Cultural Revolution. Yet although the society that He Jianjun portrays cannot by any stretch of the imagination be called revolutionary, his protagonist nonetheless is a character that grasps the logic of revolutionary spirit and tries to actualize it through his work. Xiao Dou turns his job as a letter carrier into a spiritual endeavor when he secretly opens letters and intervenes to rectify relationships that fall outside an imagined social norm. The filmic representation of a depressed and fragmented society where Xiao Dou lives and works indicates, I argue, a dispersion of cultural and ideological authority into space and spatial relationships. Literally a node through which hundreds or thousands of communications pass, the inarticulate and bumbling Xiao Dou fixes on unorthodox relationships involving marital infidelity, drug use and homosexuality, prostitution, and suicide, doing his best to reorient these relationships in a positive way. Xiao Dou's hidden optimism, completely unrepresented in his personality, combines with his singular effort, turning him into an uncanny laborer, a heroic Lei Feng transported into a decidedly unheroic postmodern world. Although he carries on an incestuous relationship with his sister and gets involved with a co-worker, Xiao Dou's deepest interest is not sexual satisfaction but the rectification of social relationships and the reestablishment of a positive orientation. In this regard, He Jianjun has distilled the good out of the revolutionary ethos, robbing it of sentimental melodrama and re-inserting it into the nearly catatonic Xiao Dou.

Through analysis of these literary texts and films, I came to the conclusion that my initial assumption of an unproblematic modernizing shift from a revolutionary to a sexualized subject was even more simplistic than I originally thought, and basically incorrect. By depicting characters with expressed sexual desire and behavior, these novels and films pay credence to a Western-developed cultural field in which interest in or representation of sexuality is an important marker of modern consciousness. However, even in novels and films that clearly are in some way "about" sex, their primary inquiry is not Freud's profoundly sexual mind or the sexually saturated unconscious. What turn out to be significant are the qualities and the very definition of subjectivity or consciousness developed over the 20th century in Chinese revolutionary culture. These writers and filmmakers aim their efforts at the construction and deconstruction, strength and weakness, and potential power to revise the past, build the present, and imagine the future of revolutionary mentality. Attuned to the most salient and pressing myths and concepts of the culture in which they live and work, the writers' and directors' apprehension and understanding of these concepts, creatively reworked in their novels and films, is at least a large part of what appeals to their readers and viewers, many of whom grew up when revolutionary concepts of the mind were in full force. The fact that revolutionary subjectivity has continued to attract attention and has remained a topic of concern in the face of radical social change indicates that it may be more central to contemporary consciousness than we have recognized.

The methodology of this book was developed in response to my concerns about the study of modern Chinese literature in the United States. In my Conclusion, I examine the conditions that encourage derivative, repetitive research and mark the field as auxiliary. This is not an anti-theory polemic or a claim on behalf of essentialized Chinese knowledge or experience, but a self-critical discussion of our failure to imagine that theory could emerge from the Chinese intellectual environment, or that Chinese literary (and film) studies could be a significant player in the larger field. Despite our success in reconfiguring modern Chinese studies as different from its supposedly isolated, nostalgia-based parent Sinology, our research exists largely as subsidiary knowledge produced within a secondary field. To put it bluntly, we read scholarship in Western literary studies for its theoretical concepts, but scholars working in Western studies read our work only because they are required to know a little about "the other," to express and ally themselves with a global perspective, or to pay respect to deconstructions of Western knowledge supposedly emerging from non-Western cultures, but often coming directly out of their own framework of knowledge. In literary and cultural studies, one central methodological stratagem of this failure is an overly historical logic that encourages us to disregard fundamental ontological or epistemological meanings that may underlie the work we analyze, instead inserting it into themes and approaches that we glean from scholars in Western studies. The conditions of pedagogy, where we teach to an audience ignorant of even basic facts about Chinese life, contribute to this tendency.

Perhaps global economic and social relations determine this derivative status, and there is nothing we can do to change it. However, there may be ways to realize the independent theoretical potential of our research, where no contradiction between aesthetics, theory, and ideology should necessarily be at work. Now that our former faith in the power of aesthetics has been tempered by an understanding of exclusion and social power, we should recognize that aesthetic and creative texts and films may unravel their own unique and imaginative logic, and may point us toward more deeply theoretical understanding.

ONE

Freudian Obsessions

> Enduring grief was widespread after the war among both veterans and civilians. The millions of deaths from the influenza epidemic piled on more losses: Europe was a continent in mourning. . . . Freud did not want to know about the effects of these terrible traumas and immense losses. Lou Andreas-Salomé wrote to him in 1919 about a young woman patient who had lost her twin brother in the war, and suffered from a number of serious somatic and obsessional symptoms. Neither she nor Freud paid the least attention to the brother's death, discussing, instead, the usual sexual factors: repressed homosexuality, father fixation, phallic symbols, and the Oedipus complex.
>
> BREGER *2000, 262*

The epigraph references many of the important concepts of psychoanalysis that have become well-known and accepted in contemporary popular culture in the United States even as Sigmund Freud's (1856–1939) work has undergone increasing academic critique. Central to Freudian psychoanalysis are the ideas that the real cause of anxiety and trauma lies not on the surface of phenomena or in recognized daily-life experience but below, at a depth not readily visible or accessible, in the unconscious; that in order to deal successfully with loss, one should consult experts, who are trained to see and interpret the invisible depth; that each individual occupies a special spot informed almost entirely by his or her unique experiences and history (even if those are largely dictated by the unconscious mind); and that at the root of most mental problems or anxiety one will find a core of sexual dysfunction and unexamined sexual desires and experiences. In this deep sexual core is where the real resides (Horrocks 2001).[1]

Emphasis on sexual desire as a crucially important aspect of human behavior did not begin with Freud but was well under way by the 19th century. Erasmus Darwin (1731–1802), the grandfather of Charles Darwin, set sexual love at the center of his theories as "not merely the basis for the creation of the race but also the focal point for all psychological feelings of unity and harmony with others and with the world," and a similar approach was picked up by Percy Shelley (1792–1822), who believed every experience of the soul was erotic (Reed 1997, 55). The German / Austrian psychologist Richard von Krafft-Ebing (1840–1902) published his massive study *Psychopathia Sexualis: With Especial Reference to Contrary Sexual Instinct: A Clinical-Forensic Study* in 1886. Although von Krafft-Ebing's early work aimed to provide understanding of and practical solutions for the problems of caring for the mentally ill, it also was part of a general interest in sexuality that developed rapidly in the second half of the 19th century. English sexologist Havelock Ellis (1859–1939) published *Man and Woman: A Study of Human Secondary Sexual Characters* in 1883, and began publishing what became a seven-volume set, *Studies in the Psychology of Sex*, in 1897.[2] German sexologist Iwan Bloch's (1872–1922) *Sexual Life of Our Time in Its Relations to Modern Civilization* appeared in 1908. Austrian psychologist Albert Moll (1862–1939) published *The Sexual Life of the Child* in the same year. Others, including Karl Heinrich Ulrichs (1825–95), Magnus Hirschfeld (1868–1935), and Edward Carpenter (1844–1929) expanded the study of sex through their work on homosexuality and other topics. As Arnold I. Davidson argues, it is

> not because we became preoccupied with our true sexuality that a science of sexuality arose in the nineteenth century; it is rather the emergence of a science of sexuality that made it possible, even inevitable, for us to become preoccupied with our true sexuality. Thus our existence became a sexistence, saturated with the promises and threats of sexuality; the biggest change of the nineteenth century in terms of sexual discourse is a changing of the "rules" in which sexual identity became separated from anatomical structure, becoming "a matter of impulses, tastes, aptitudes, satisfactions, and psychic traits. (Davidson 2001, 35)[3]

For Freud, sexual desire was not just one aspect of human life, but a basic quality of the unconscious to which all form of experience were linked. Freud's interest was not so much in evaluating actual sexual behavior, but in constructing a *theory* of sexuality. David Seelow explains: "Freud creates fiction as a way to reach a truth that must, being psychic in nature, remain hidden from the scientific eye, the microscope, and the laboratory" (Seelow 2005, 23). Sexual desire lurked in the unconscious, metamorphosing through repression into a powerful, not-to-be ignored instigator of everyday problems. As an ever-elusive yet potent cause of almost any kind of anxiety, trauma, or despair, sexual desire could be endlessly represented, manipulated, excavated, and brought into the light, if never for the final time. Freudian psychoanalysis, with its mixture of a hidden unconscious, a productive sexual desire, and a pathology of daily life, translated three centuries of interest in sexual desire into a pseudo-medical and cultural system. It laid out important guidelines about the modern person: how s/he must think and feel, and what could and should be acted upon. It mandated sexuality at the core of human identity and demanded significant, life-long attention to this "truth." Freud's sexually rich unconscious was not just a theory of sexuality but also a theory of the mind. Interpretation of Freud's work, psychoanalysis, psychology, and psychiatry spawned a massive field that expanded rapidly over the century in many locales. It became an arena populated not only by medical professionals but also by philosophers, theorists of popular culture, literary critics, film critics, historians, biographers, and more.

The story of Freud's development of his sexual theories, which posited hidden sexual motives behind psychological problems, has been studied extensively. Freud first worked with hysterical patients (meaning those whose symptoms had no obvious physical cause) in his collaborations with Josef Breuer (1842–1925). Breuer published his early work on the subject in 1893 and 1895, with Freud as joint author. Most of the patients he sent to work with Freud were women, and the first case presented in the latter volume was that of "Frau Emmy von N.," in real life Baroness Fanny Moser. In his evaluation of this case, Freud began to move away from materialist explanations of Moser's mental distress—which focused on the actual events that had caused her pain—toward emphasis on sexual abstinence as the cause of her problems. Although Breuer believed sexuality was only one area among many where psychological trauma could be located and thereby cautioned against over-reliance on sexual explanations, Freud pushed ahead with his approach and eventually broke off relations with his former collaborator (Breger 2000, 111–25).

Freud then met and eventually formed a tight friendship with Wilhelm Fliess (1858–1928), a nose doctor who developed theories out of his observation that nasal tissue and genital tissue were similar. Fliess published *The*

Relationship Between the Nose and Female Sexual Organs in 1897. In a series of letters dating from 1887 to 1904, Freud discussed his ideas on hysteria, neuroses, the interpretation of dreams, and the psychopathology of everyday life with Fliess (Masson 1985).[4] It is apparent in these discussions as well as in his other writing that although Freud initially credited real sexual events with motivating power, he eventually came to believe that sexual trauma was imagined by children, who were held in the grips of the Oedipus complex. Freud's view that neuroses resulted from sexual conflicts at the unconscious level was further developed in his *Three Essays on the Theory of Sexuality*, published in 1905. Here he expanded the power of sexuality by showing how it determined not only mental illnesses but also personality and character (Breger 2000, 163). Homosexuality, bisexuality, masochism, sadism, and fetishism—many behaviors that supposedly emerged during infancy—were theorized in terms of an individual's lifelong identity, and Freud argued that in their lifetimes, human beings passed through several stages of sexual desire and expression.

Freud gained and lost important disciples, some of whom supported and developed his theories and others who rejected them, going in new directions. Karl Abraham (1877–1925), who published the Freud-approved essay "The Experiencing of Sexual Traumas as a Form of Sexual Activity" in 1907, proposed that in the case of children who had been raped, sexual trauma was "desired by the child unconsciously" (Breger 2000, 214). Abraham also furthered Freud's focus on sexuality by insisting that soldiers traumatized in battle were merely suffering from impotence or frigidity; fear, the stress of violence, watching their friends die, and questioning the morality of killing those like them on the other side all were irrelevant. Carl Gustav Jung (1875–1961), a one-time Freud supporter who eventually became estranged, asked Freud where a 6-year-old girl supposedly "seduced" by her foster father could have found the story of her abuse. Freud assured him that the child, preoccupied with sexuality, was under the influence of a fantasy and had not been abused at all. In 1919, Freud published *Beyond the Pleasure Principle*, where he elaborated on a natural aggression that accompanied the sexual drive inherent in all human beings (Breger 2000, 223–59).

Although Freud developed a comprehensive system for imagining the new sexual modernity as a profound psychic reality, there was no guarantee that his vision would be widely accepted. Yet Freud's sexual theories became particularly influential in the United States, where their popularity, largely limited to New York intellectuals in the 1920s and 1930s, became widespread after World War II. E. Fuller Torrey explains:

> Following the war Freud's theory began to spread, first sending roots westward under the Hudson River and eventually extending tendrils into every American city and town. The transformation of Freud's theory from an exotic New York plant to an American cultural kudzu is one of the strangest events in the history of ideas. (Torrey 1992, 104)[5]

Torrey traces Freud's ascending trajectory to efforts to discredit the racially motivated theories that lay behind the Holocaust. Before the Holocaust, a discussion on race and immigration, and its accompanying debate on nature versus nurture, raged throughout the late 1800s and the first half of the 20th century in the United States, with most well-known figures arguing that immigration from eastern and southern Europe, as well as from Asia, was ruining America. Racial determinism was all the rage, and it was promoted by famous figures in all walks of life. From MIT president Francis A. Walker in his 1896 article "Restriction of Immigration" to Madison Grant, with his *The Passing of the Great Race* on Nordic superiority in 1916; from Harvard president Charles W. Eliot to Stanford president David Starr Jordan; from Alexander Graham Bell to Charles Davenport in the Eugenics Records Office, leading intellectuals jumped on the eugenics bandwagon. The Ku Klux Klan, which peaked at 5 million members in 1915, led attacks against all immigrants, but especially African Americans, Jews, and Catholics. American xenophobia and racism was widespread in the middle class, and it was given even more credibility through Kenneth L. Roberts's 1922 best-seller *Why Europe Leaves Home*, in which he portrayed the newcomers as stupid, vermin-laden animals (Torrey 1992, 39–59).

According to Torrey, the anthropologist Franz Boas (1858–1942), who taught at Columbia, should be regarded as a central figure not only in the fight against racism but also in Freud's ascendancy. Boas's research empirically discounted the eugenicists' arguments; through published debates, scientific research, and congressional testimony, Boas warned against attempts to "raise a race of supermen" (Torrey 1992, 54). In *The Mind of Primitive Man* (1911), he laid out the principles of cultural relativism, which denied the value of universals in evaluating culture; instead, he championed a deep investigation into the specificities of each culture. He thus changed the meaning of the term *culture* from a singular to a plural (Stocking 1996). Boas believed in the importance of collecting data about every aspect of human behavior and focused on language as a window into any particular culture. He clashed with many leading eugenicists, whose sexual conservatism led them to oppose birth control and sexual liberation. Although Boas was impressed by Freudian sexual theory, two of his students—Ruth Benedict (1887–1948) and Margaret Mead (1901–78)—picked up the connection between early childhood sexuality and cultural nurture in earnest, deploying Freud's sexual theories to further their mentor's fight against racism and their own claims on behalf of culture over genes. Mead in particular, with her research emphasis on sexual mores, corroborated Freud's theories in her 1928 *Coming of Age in Samoa*, which Boas cited in claiming that "where sexual life is practically free sexual crimes do not occur" (Torrey 1992, 71–72). According to Mead—whose research gained such canonical status that it was not challenged or thoroughly debated within the field of anthropology until a half century after it appeared—the absence of cultural taboos on sexual relations in Samoa produced a neurosis-free society.[6]

It was the Holocaust, however, that shocked people into realizing that eugenics could become genocide; without the Holocaust, Torrey argues, New York intellectuals would have lost interest in Freud. Freud's emphasis on childhood experience and its amalgamation in the unconscious was an appealing alternative to racial determinism, and when Marxists finally came to recognize Stalin's atrocities, they too joined the sexual liberationists and nurture proponents, shifting their allegiance from Marx to Freud. Although in the 1930s Freud was "a Viennese physician promulgating an unusual theory about the importance of childhood sexual experiences," by the 1950s he had become a "quasi-religious figure sent to redeem His children by confession and transference" (Torrey 1992, 111).

Next came the discovery of Freud by the media, beginning with *Life* and *Time* magazines, which was quickly followed by Benjamin Spock's (1903–98) adoption of Freudian principles in his widely read books on childcare; the popularization of Freudian sexual theory through articles and films (including Margaret Mead's monthly column for *Redbook* in the 1960s); the New Left's inflation and expansion of sexual theory into a theory of social and political liberation through the work of Herbert Marcuse (1898–1979), Paul Goodman (1911–72), and Norman O. Brown (1913–2002); and the elevation of mental health as a national goal by John F. Kennedy. Psychoanalytical sexual theories penetrated nearly every discipline in the social sciences and humanities, and the New York intelligentsia, which was closely allied with the publishing industry, made certain that Freud-positive works were published. The personal growth movement, begun in the 1960s but still alive and kicking in the next century, was based to a large extent on Freudian theories (Torrey 1992, 128–213).[7]

Although over the course of the 20th century research on Freud had been done in many European countries, Freud's name became a common word in France only after the student revolt of May and June 1968, resulting in a "dramatic reversal of the relationship between psychoanalysis and French society and culture" (Turkle 1978, 4).[8] Freud himself had despaired over the ease with which Americans accepted psychoanalysis; in France, resistance to his theories, as well as their location within the high culture of literature and art, indicated to him that its subtlety and difficulty were recognized. And cultural and historical differences did result in different emphases: in the United States, Freud's theories lent weight to the optimistic belief that individuals could change through their own efforts; in France, however, Freudian thought was more linked to the political and intellectual left, forming a "complex knot" of French Marxism, French feminism, French antipsychiatry (which looked to psychoanalysis as its ally), and French psychoanalysis, reversing the left's pre-1968 premise that Freudian psychoanalysis was a reactionary tool for "psychologizing away social problems" (8). What emerged in France was a reading of Freud that bridged activist politics and a politics of the person, a trend further developed through the work of Jacques Lacan (1901–81), who emphasized the relationship between the unconscious, language, and symbolic behavior. May 1968 slogans, such as "Take your desires for reality. . . . A policeman dwells in each of our heads, he must be killed. . . . Liberate psychoanalysis," speak to the personal and political transformation that underlay the French psychoanalytical movement (65). The personal-political link was strengthened by the writing and speaking of Philippe Sollers (1936–) and Julia Kristeva (1941–). Sollers demanded the integration of psychoanalysis and Marxism, while Kristeva wanted a confrontation of the "symbolic order" through a novel politics of language. Even more popular was the writing of Gilles Deleuze (1925–95) and Félix Guattari (1930–92), whose *Anti-Oedipus: Capitalism and Schizophrenia,* which was published in 1972, attacked—and yet in the very process of attack, expanded—the Freudian concept of the Oedipus complex and privileged the schizophrenic, whose very existence challenged the notion of an integrated self. In promoting the politics of schizophrenia or "schizoanalysis," Deleuze and Guattari constructed a vast system leading from desire out into every facet of social organization, a modern-day healing process that necessitates a "political, social, and economic analysis of the community and its neighbors" rather than the small structure of "Daddy-Mommy-me" (Turkle 1978, 80–82; 152).

In France, then, Freudian theory came to express a melding of the personal and the political that was supposed to thoroughly reform both spheres, effecting epoch-changing epistemological, metaphysical, and structural transformations. This new regime was to shatter the conventions of bourgeois society, and the free-association method of saying whatever comes to mind was supposed to liberate thought and discourse about sexual behavior. By focusing on female subjectivity, feminine writing / language, and multiple sexual identities, Julia Kristeva sought to recuperate Freudian theory for women. The work of Kristeva, Lacan, Deleuze, Guattari, and many others catapulted the French Freud into a powerful theoretical position, from which it came to influence almost every aspect of humanistic work in Europe and the United States, including art and art criticism, literature and literary theory, history, anthropology, and linguistics. A century after the publication of Freud's *The Interpretation of Dreams*, the practice of psychoanalysis still flourishes in France (Quinney 2004, 114–26).

The combination of American, French, and, more generally, Western fascination with the personal and social liberation implicit in Freudian theory presents a 20th-century trajectory that has had profound implications for intellectual and everyday life. Whether in favor or against, virtually all critics today recognize the importance of Freud, not only within the academy but also in beliefs and practices with broad relevance outside the university and research institute. Despite the existence of hundreds of vigorously publishing sexologists, philosophers, and psychologists at work in the late 19th and early 20th century, it was Freud whose ideas had the most far-reaching effect, influencing thought, behavior, culture, and institutions. In carving out the powerful sexual unconscious as essential to what it means to be human and modern, Freud sexualized and psychologized the mind, in the process setting up a demand for a lucrative practice for psychoanalysts and therapists.[9] In combining deep sexual motivation, the unconscious, and the notion that psychological problems are not limited to the pathological but form a hidden web of connections within daily life, Freud imaginatively constructed a person who since has appeared so extensively in novels and films, advertisements and descriptions, psychological texts and cultural critiques, that s / he has become not just one, but *the* most normal and acceptable example of a modern subject.

OTHER WAYS OF BEING: FREUD'S CRITICS AND SELVES OF A DIFFERENT NATURE

As many have pointed out, the theory of the unconscious did not originate with Freud, and the centering of sexuality as one (and perhaps the most important) aspect of identity for a modern individual was promoted through literature and art as well as through psychological theory and sexology (Goodheart 1997, 136; Reed 1997, 127–43; Ellenberger 1970).[10] However, Freud's name has become ubiquitous, not only in academia but also in popular culture, and his theories of the unconscious, dream interpretation, and sexual repression are so omnipresent, at least in the United States and France, as to have entered the oft-unquestioned territory of *common sense*.[11] As psychoanalysis and psychotherapy gained a solid foothold in medical circles and popular culture, one's visits to the psychoanalyst or psychotherapist became nothing more than part of a normal weekly schedule. Indeed, Dana L. Cloud argues that the United States has become the therapeutic society par excellence, with literature and art aimed at illustrating therapies for life problems, and self-care replacing political engagement. Cloud elucidates the development of psychotherapy in the United States after World War II, offering a criticism from a material and political perspective:

> Psychotherapy is a politically contradictory phenomenon that sometimes helps suffering people even as it can reinscribe individuals into the very social relations that produced their "illnesses." This contradiction, however, also makes the therapeutic persuasive: It can admit to the existence of suffering in modern society without having to transform the society publicly or structurally. (Cloud 1998, xvii)

While not claiming that all psychological problems have sociopolitical roots, Cloud argues that "therapy as a practice housed in the disciplines of psychology, psychiatry, and social work" is part of a structure "substituting self-care justified in therapeutic terms for political engagement" (Cloud 1998, 51).[12]

Freud's influence may be waning, however, as numerous detractors have aggressively gone after his findings. Also, neurology has shifted focus onto the biological causes of behavior, and pharmaceutical companies have developed new and more powerful drugs to alter mental states and behavior. Former adherents of Freudian approaches to cultural analysis, such as Frederick Crews (1933–), have broken rank and published passionate and scathing denunciations in intellectual journals and newspapers (Crews 1998).[13] In 1993, Crews published a controversial critique of Freud in the *New York Review of Books*. In the introduction to his 1998 edited volume of anti-Freud essays, Crews recounts the fiery 1995 controversy over a major exhibit on Freud that was to be held by the Library of Congress in the fall of 1996 in Washington, D.C., and was then moved to Vienna. When he learned that only Freud's supporters would be involved in the exhibit, historian Peter J. Swales (1948–) circulated a petition asking the Manuscript Division of the Library of Congress to ensure that various viewpoints were represented. Fifty signatures were collected, among them three anti-Freudians—Adolf Grünbaum (1923–), Frank Cioffi (1928–), and Malcolm Macmillan (1929–). When a shortage of funding and an indefinite delay was announced, rumors began to fly. Elisabeth Roudinesco (1944–), the biographer of (semi-) Freudian theorist Jacques Lacan, wrote in to criticize the critics as puritans, inquisitors, and possibly anti-Semites and presented a petition of her own, signed by 180 people (Crews 1998, xx–xxi). Eventually the exhibit was held under the direction of the original group, with an outside panel as monitor. The passions aroused in this controversy give witness to the high cultural stakes involved in the reinterpretation of Freud's ideas and importance.

The academic debate on Freud has been ongoing, with critics of the critics also publishing counter-attacks (Robinson 1993, 126–50; Goodheart 1997; Kurzweil and Phillips, 1983). Todd Dufresne (1966–), author of *Killing Freud: Twentieth-Century Culture and the Death of Psychoanalysis*, humorously attacks the excesses of the pro-Freudian camp with chapter titles such as "Freud and His Followers, Or How Psychoanalysis Brings Out the Worst in Everyone" (53–71).[14] Dufresne believes Freudian influence in the humanities is slowly dying out, although post-structuralism at large has been a "handmaiden of psychoanalysis," and film studies and postcolonial studies are still holdouts (155, 176). Thomas Szasz (1920–) has gone a step further in his research, tirelessly criticizing the very notion of "mental illness" and the related fields of psychology, psychoanalysis, psychotherapy, and psychiatry.[15] The ever-productive Szasz, whose signature work was the 1960 "The Myth of Mental Illness: Foundations of a Theory of Personal Conduct," believes that too often the most basic life problems related to relationships, work, and social norms are erroneously medicalized within psychiatry and psychology. In his 1978 *The Myth of Psychotherapy: Mental Healing as Religion, Rhetoric, and Repression*, Szasz demolishes the practice of psychotherapy historically, attacking not only Freud but also his precursors in mesmerism and repression theory such as Franz Anton Mesmer (1734–1850), Johann Christian Heinroth (1773–1843), Wilhelm Erb (1840–1921), and Julius Wagner-Jauregg (1857–1940). Szasz treats psychoanalysis as a discipline that has conquered through a powerful form of near-religious rhetoric. Szasz's critique, which has spanned decades and produced hundreds of articles and books, boldly attacks Freud's role in the medicalization of consciousness and daily life and the overall psychologization of subjectivity.

Freudian theory is now under siege in France, just as it has been for decades in the United States. In 2005, the publication of the 800-page *The Black Book Of Psychoanalysis—How to Live, Think and Get On Better Without Freud*, which presented Freudian critiques by some forty authors from ten countries, resulted in a flurry of debate (Meyer, Borch-Jacobsen, Cottraux, and Pleux 2005). The authors argue that the prevalence of Freudian methodology in psychology has set the field back by decades, ruined thousands of lives—quite literally in the case of heroin addicts, who were treated with Freudian analysis to address the "inner cause" of their addition rather than being given methadone—and enforced an oppressive ideological thought regime.

Disagreement with Freud's sexual theories predates the contemporary period, however. Because Freud demanded strict loyalty to his vision of sexual centeredness and psychoanalysis, he lost disciples, many of whom went on to form their own groups and develop their own approaches.[16] Throughout the 20th century, psychologists and psychiatrists such as Karen Horney (1885–1952), Harry Stack Sullivan (1892–1949), and Erich Fromm (1900–1980) disagreed with Freud's sexual focus and developed dissenting theories of human mentality, sexual desire, and human behavior. Horney rejected Freudian penis envy, instead analyzing social change and work conditions for women. For Horney, sexual problems were "an effect, not a cause, of emotional distortions" and "personal conflicts do not arise internally but are the product of cultural determinants from industrialization" (Brennan 2003, 232–34). Fromm regarded the modern world as inherently alienated and the modern individual as lonely, helpless, and seeking escape; for him, the search for freedom is more important than biological needs such as hunger, sexual desire, or thirst.

Harry Stack Sullivan developed the notion of interpersonal psychiatry in the 1940s, arguing that historical social reality, not universal and ahistorical psychic structure, is what determines the nature of the mind. For Sullivan, the self was an "open system interacting with the environment" (Brennan 2003, 234–35). He believed that racial injustice, poverty, class, ethnic discrimination, labor, war, and other social problems were the environment in which study and treatment of the human psychology should take place. This approach does not assemble a deep unconscious interior fraught with sexual secrets and repression but instead focuses on social interactions and relationships. It also shifts emphasis away from the romantic and unique individual, said by Sullivan to be an illusion, a cultural artifact of the 20th century. Sullivan's work highlights the cultural context of any concept of the self and any therapy or healing method that claims universality.[17] Although not nearly as famous as Freud, Sullivan was not an unknown figure in American psychological circles; he organized conferences, helped in the creation of the Washington School of Psychiatry and the William Alanson White Institute, and founded the journal *Psychiatry* (Cushman 1995, 173). Railing against the collusion of psychotherapy with social inequity, Sullivan criticized its practitioners as failed doctors who had accepted the bourgeois ideal and "found for themselves a useful function in sheltering society from those whom it has destroyed" (Cushman 1995, 185).[18]

Philip Cushman ranks Melanie Klein (1882–1960) as the most important Freudian in the United States. Despite differences, Klein follows Freud in locating a sexually motivated mind that is basic to human emotion and behavior, even at a young age. Cushman recounts Klein's analysis of her son Erich's fear of going outside:

> For instance, in response to his phobia about venturing outside, she asked him to describe a street that was particularly frightening to him. He answered that the street was one that was filled with young toughs who tormented him. Klein ignored this fact and realized that the street was lined with large trees. She interpreted the trees as phalluses and explained to Erich that this meant that he was desiring his mother, and his anxiety was no doubt caused by the castration anxiety that inevitably followed this desire. It was only many years later that Erich's brother Hans (a reluctant adolescent analysand of his mother) explained this scene and many others to Erich. Hans told Erich that the bullies were an anti-Semitic gang that routinely attacked Jewish children. Erich, in fact, was never told by his mother that he was Jewish; he discovered it accidentally when he was ten. (Cushman 1995, 201–2)

As Cushman puts it, Sullivan's was the road not taken in the United States, where psychotherapy was a full participant in the development of the empty self unsituated in any sociohistorical context, dedicated to self-liberation through consumerism, isolated, lonely, and individualistic; this was the self developed to perfectly support the capitalist state.[19]

Following Freud, the emphasis on desire—with any desire often considered but a pale flicker of the primary sexual instigator—has produced great deal of contemporary research. Michel Foucault (1926–84) set out to trace what he called not a "history of sexual behaviors and practices . . . but to dwell on that quite recent and banal notion of 'sexuality'" (Foucault 1990a, 1990b; Laqueur 1990). Foucault's investigation of "the ways in which individuals are able, are obliged, to recognize themselves as subjects of this sexuality" became a larger, more influential study when he defined it as a *genealogy*, or an analysis "of the practices by which individuals were led to focus their attention on themselves, to decipher, recognize, and acknowledge themselves as subjects of desire" (Foucault 1990a, 4–5). Although Foucault chose to abandon a strictly historical approach in favor of a more philosophical endeavor, his work was based on the premise that the sexualized subject did not suddenly appear but developed over some three hundred years. According to Foucault, by the 19th and 20th centuries, people did not merely have sex or experience sexual desire but actually viewed themselves, deeply and fundamentally, as sexual creatures.

However, even as it historicized, denaturalized, and made transparent the notion of *sexuality*, Foucault's work endowed this latter-day concept with near-transcendent qualities, further extending the implications of Freud's sexual theory. This tendency has not been ignored by feminists, who fault Foucault for his failure to recognize and critique the gender implications of Freudian sexual theory, or by materialist theorists, who demand a more meaningful interpretation of class and material relations. In a sharp counterattack on the discourse of desire in postmodern culture, Teresa L. Ebert criticized feminist theory and Marxist feminists for "substituting discursive determinism for an economic determinism" (Ebert 1996, 25; 139–40).[20] According to Ebert, the work of Michel Foucault, Jacques Derrida (1930–2004), Judith Butler (1956–), and Donna Haraway (1944–) is emblematic of a shift away from economics and class toward discourse, and she strongly criticizes the neo-Marxist Fredric Jameson for his segregation of the sexual from the material.

FREUDIAN SEXUAL THEORY AND MARXISM IN RUSSIA AND THE SOVIET UNION

The debate on Freudian sexual theory in early 20th-century Russia and the Soviet Union, where revolutionary theory was fast forming, is an interesting case to consider in relation to China. Russian intellectuals, as opposed to their counterparts in China, were quite involved with Freud and his circle; some even participated in his weekly discussion sessions in Vienna and established psychoanalytic practices when they returned home. Speaking of Russia and the Soviet Union in the teens and twenties, Arthur Petrovsky writes: "The theory of Freud spread like wildfire, going far beyond its initial borders—psychology and psychiatry—to embrace ethics and aesthetics, the theory and history of literature and arts, and eventually created its own philosophy of history, its own pedagogy and sociology" (Petrovsky 1990, 153). The new sexology studies from Europe were actively translated into Russian and in general came out earlier in Russia than they did in China. Richard von Krafft-Ebing's work appeared in 1887, only a year after its publication in German, and Havelock Ellis's *Man and Woman* came out in 1887. Iwan Bloch's work came out in Russian in 1908.

The concept of the unconscious was not new in Russia: it had been investigated within the context of religious and philosophical thought much earlier, within the spheres of science and education in 1895, and shortly after by psychiatrists, who were moving in the conceptual direction of psychoanalysis as early as the 1880s. In the early 1900s, Russian psychoanalysts participated in meetings that took place at the home of Freud, whose *Interpretation of Dreams* was translated into Russian in 1904. The Russian psychiatrist Nikolai Osipov (1877–1934) published an early review article on psychoanalysis in 1908, praising Freud's therapeutic approach and subsequently organizing a group to study psychoanalysis. In his application of psychoanalytical principles to his case work, Osipov followed Freud in emphasizing the sexual problems and motivations of his patients (Miller 1998, 21–26, 29).[21] The psychoanalytic movement in Russia continued to develop through the work of N. A. Vyrubov (1869–1918), Moshe Wulff (1878–1971), F. Berg, M. M. Asatiani, and others, and the journal *Psychotherapy* was founded in 1909.

Some Russian psychiatrists joined their European colleagues in criticizing Freud's work, expressing perspectives that are echoed in later critiques by Chinese intellectuals. In 1909, O. B. Fel'tsman published a paper arguing that the search for unconscious motivations was generally ineffective, whereas a reeducation and reorientation of the patient more often produced results. He also shifted away from claiming that sexual issues motivated other problems, instead finding that they frequently masked difficulties that themselves were producing symptoms. Interest in psychoanalysis continued to grow in Russia, however, and in 1922 the Russian Psychoanalytic Society was formed, followed by the Institute for Psychoanalysis. In the same year, Freud proposed to the International Psychoanalytical Association (IPA) that the Russian group be accepted as a member, but some members objected to excessive inclusion of non-medical personnel (psychologists, social scientists, humanists, and even a vice president trained as a mathematician). In Russia, however, psychoanalysis as a field included not only therapists but also people active in history, art, and philosophy (Miller 1998). It is precisely in these areas, along with their daily life spheres, that Freud's theories exercised their most stunning influence in the 20th century.

In these early times, it was not at all clear that Marxism eventually would totally reject the premises of psychoanalysis. Russian psychoanalysts worked not only theoretically but also in social projects that they hoped would convince the new government of the importance of their approach. One of these projects was a school for disturbed children that opened in 1921 with government support. The school was run on Freudian principles, and a great deal of "attention was devoted to the sexual life of the children," for whom "it was assumed that many of their actions were motivated by the unconscious quest for sexual gratification" (Miller 1998, 64). Because of rumors of sexual excess, the school was almost closed down, but in the end a government commission appointed to study the issue recommended that the school merely reorient itself toward "the study of the social origins of child development" (66). Shortly after this time, the government decided to close the school.

Even after the closing of the school, it was not certain that those in favor of and those opposed to Freudian psychoanalysis would develop irreconcilable positions, since many psychoanalysts believed they could work out a materialist approach. The contradiction between Marxism and psychoanalysis was only part of a larger debate about the appropriate context through which to apprehend and analyze the human mind. In psychology at large, discussions on the value of the field began in the early 1920s, and several psychologists were forced to resign from their positions.[22] Psychoanalysts and those interested in psychology continued to publish articles arguing for the importance of Freudian methods and their relationship to Marxism. In late 1923 Bernard Bykhovskii (1898–) a philosopher working in dialectical materialism, published "On the Methodological Foundations of Freud's Psychoanalytical Theory" in the official party journal *Under the Banner of Marxism*. This article, which argued that Freud's ideas, in particular that of the unconscious, did not contradict Marxism and could even enrich it, initiated a debate on "Freudian Marxism." In an article on the psychology of religion, constitutional law expert M. A. Reisner (1868–1928) argued that Marxism was not forthcoming on the issue, and that Freud's insights on the "sexual mentality" of social development could be extrapolated into a general idea of the displacement of individual social conflicts into culture and society. By this means, childhood sexual fantasies transformed themselves into religious commitment, for example. A. B. Zalkind (1888–1936), a psychotherapist and party member, published "Freudism and Marxism" in 1924, arguing in it that the human mind reflected social existence biologically, and could be effectively deployed in Marxism's fight against the concept of the soul. Zalkind mentioned high-level party members who had spoken and written favorably about Freud's work; at the same time, he criticized Freud's focus on the individual and on sexual motivation (Miller 1998, 73–77).

Another article by the same name was published shortly after Zalkind's article. Written by party ideologue V. Iurinets (also W. Jurinetz), it criticized Freud as an idealist who had no basis for his claims. The debate continued with contributions from both sides.[23] A negative assessment of Freud's emphasis on sexual motivation attributed to Vladimir Lenin (1870–1924) was published after his death, but it came from the memoir of Lenin by the German writer Klara Zetkin (1857–1933) (published in 1925 in German), and was never substantiated through any original written material by Lenin. Nonetheless, the importance of Lenin's critique of Freud was noted in *Pravda* in 1925 (Petrovsky 1990, 160–61). Leon Trotsky (1879–1940) believed Freud's work and dialectical materialism could be reconciled; he argued that although psychoanalysis should not be rejected, it also did not necessarily have to be accepted.

A serious attack on the Freudians came out in V. N. Voloshinov's (1894/5–1936) book, *Freudianism*, in 1927. Voloshinov criticized the subjective nature, individual context, and lack of consideration of social space in Freud's theories, all of which, he argued, culminated in excessive focus on the sexual, itself nothing more than an indication of the values of the capitalist classes (Miller 1998, 88–89). When Vienna Psychoanalytic Society member Wilhelm Reich (1897–1957) arrived in Moscow for a series of lectures in 1929, it was clear that his disagreement with Freud over a number of issues was the precondition of his invitation. In identifying the Soviet attack on Freud as an attack not on psychoanalysis as a discipline but on the "psychoanalytic view of the world," Reich put his finger on the basic conflict between Freudian theory, which had come to mean much more than just a medical approach to mental illness, and Marxism, which also came to be much more than just an economic theory.[24]

In the 1920s, a discussion of the new sexual morality was under way in the Soviet Union, with articles by women's activists and others who attempted to lay the groundwork for sexual relations under the conditions of revolutionary culture. Nadezhda Krupskaya (1869–1939) is one example of a woman critic who found Freud's sexual theories to be overblown and discriminatory to women: "Freud does not just take into account the role of sexual attraction in our actions. He inordinately exaggerates that role, while explaining all subconscious actions by sexual attraction. Many of his explanations are artificial, stretched out and besides are permeated by a bourgeois-philistine attitude towards women" (Petrovsky 1990, 160). "Sexual depravity," a term that at this time also included homosexuality, was attacked as part of bourgeois capitalist culture, and legislated against. By 1930, when A. Stoliarov's *Dialectical Materialism and the Mechanists* came out, few were willing to stand up and defend Freud's theories. Stoliarov criticized Freud as excessively individualistic, anti-social, bourgeois, and completely in contradiction with materialism. In a 1932 article, a central figure in psychoanalysis in the 1920s, Alexander Luria (1902–77), wrote an article clearly separating Western psychology and Marxism. By the mid to late 1930s, Freud was essentially discredited within Soviet psychology, which continued to exist in departments at major universities.[25]

Freud's downfall in the Soviet Union caused intellectuals in Europe and the United States to rethink his contribution within the context of theoretical Marxism. Notable among them was Wilhelm Reich, who eventually was thrown out of Freud's group for attempting to unify Marxism and Freudism.[26] Alfred Adler (1870–1937), who focused on social orientations to the point that Freud found his work a serious trend away from his own emphasis on the sexual and the unconscious, represented another approach (Cushman 1995, 146). Otto Rank (1884–1939), who once said that he was in Freudian theory "deepest of all," developed the idea that the trauma of birth was what produced psychosis. Although his single-cause methodology was similar to that of Freud, Rank elevated the mother in importance and virtually dismissed the father (Breger 2000, 194–207). Later scholars like Reuben Osborn (also Osbert) (1908–?), Louis Althusser (1918–90), and Herbert Marcuse tried to synthesize psychology and Marxism. As Marcuse explained in his classic text *Eros and Civilization*,

> For example, productiveness—proclaimed as the goal of the healthy individual under the performance principle—must normally (that is, outside the creative, "neurotic," and "eccentric" exceptions) show forth in good business, administration, service, with the reasonable expectation of recognized success. Love must be semi-sublimated and even inhibit libido, staying in line with the sanctioned conditions imposed on sexuality. This is the accepted, "realistic" meaning of productiveness and love. (Marcuse 1966, 259)

Behind these efforts lay the conviction that although Marxism could explain economic structures, labor history and movements, and related social issues, it was insufficient when used to explain human desire or how social reality is understood by and expressed through the mind (Osborn 1965; Althusser 1996; B. Brown, 1973). From the perspective of the New Left, the combination of Freud's sexual theories, which imagined and expanded true sexual freedom, and Marxist theory, which explained class exploitation and projected liberation, could revamp personal, social, and political relations on radically egalitarian terms. The stale, outmoded dregs of religion and civilization, which refused to allow true human essence to flower, would be washed away. The entire globe, many of the New Left believed, would be transfigured through this transformation.

TWO

Psychology and Freudian Sexual Theory in Early 20th Century China

As in Russia and the early Soviet Union, Freudian ideas entered the Chinese cultural world at a time when revolutionary social and political theory was developing rapidly (Jingyuan Zhang 1992).[1] However, Russians interested in psychoanalytic theory had a ready-made context for those interests within the field of applied psychology as well as in culture at large, where ideas about a modern self were developed by Russian intellectuals in contact with their counterparts in Europe. Although Freud's "talking cure" was introduced in China, unlike in Russia there was no link to practicing clinicians in Europe, and only limited application in institutions for the mentally ill.[2] In China, Freudian sexual theory was almost immediately understood as a possible new science of the mind and a way of thinking about the characteristics of the modern person, especially the modern mind and its relationship to sexual desire. Along with the attack on the extended family, arranged marriage, and Confucian values in general, the Freudian centering of sexual desire became one perspective from which to dismantle the past and imagine a new future. As David Der-wei Wang (1997) has noted, "gendered and psychologized subjectivity" is one aspect of the Western imperative that asserted that "Chinese literature could not accomplish the task of modernization without borrowing western cultural and literary capital" (6).[3]

In this chapter, I analyze several contexts where Western theories of the mind and subjectivity, as well as Freudian theory, were actively introduced, debated, and discussed. First, I examine the entry of modern psychology through translations and pedagogy. In China the earliest introductions to psychology were undertaken in missionary schools, and these were quickly followed by educational reforms that turned the discipline into a required class for teachers. This pervasive educational framework had implications for the way in which psychology was understood, emphasizing its value as a tool of modernization and socialization. At the same time, these introductions enlarged the significance of subjectivity, or one's sense of mental properties and qualities, and mentality, or the social interpretation of mental properties and qualities, thus feeding into expanding discourses of national, ethnic, and racial essence, spirit, and "soul."

Second, I take a close look at early references to Freud and his theories, which, like psychology in general, often were contextualized within the national improvement trends underlying education. One significant aspect of the new learning was sex education, and many interested in Freud debated his writings from that perspective. However, sex education was viewed as part of modern science, not as training that could help students realize a more sexually fulfilling existence. In terms of social class, those interested in this new science marked themselves as cosmopolitan intellectuals who were a step above the "masses" (Shih 2001, 97).[4] As in the case of psychology in general, Freudian theory was channeled for specific uses, thus muting its more radical prospects for a new subjectivity.

Third, I examine the early articles of Gao Juefu (*ming*: Gao Zhuo, 1896–1993), one of China's most well-known scholars of psychology. His work provides another clue as to why Freudian sexual theory—although often debated and deployed over the 1920s and 1930s—did not become widely accepted. Gao's essays on Freud, along with those of a few other early critics, indicate a strong cultural resistance to accepting sexual motivation as the basis of pathology, and a tendency to neutralize the implications of Freudian sexual theory by enveloping it within a social framework. As for the unconscious as a concept, although Gao initially had a mixed evaluation, he came to question its importance, and eventually its existence.

Fourth, I examine the conflict between Zhang Jingsheng (1889–1970) and his critics Zhou Zuoren (1885–1967), Zhou Jianren (1888–1984), and Zhang Xichen (1889–1969) over the publication and reception of Zhang Jingsheng's book *Sex Histories* (Xingshi) in 1926. In requesting that contributors to his book conceptualize and recount their lives from a sexual perspective, Zhang Jingsheng (perhaps unwittingly) took a step closer to Freudian psychoanalytical principles. The debate that followed, I argue, was a pivotal moment when the potentially far-reaching reorientation of subjectivity and social life offered through sexual modernity was decisively and directly rejected by leading intellectuals.

Finally, I briefly discuss Freudian theory with reference to Chinese literature in the 1920s and 1930s and in post-Mao China. In individual stories or poems, some writers successfully created characters that manifested the isolated mind and sexual angst implicit in Freud's sexualized unconscious. Overall, however, May Fourth literature balanced this approach with attention to social relationships and economic realities. Although the modernists and New Perceptionists of the 1930s were fascinated with Freud, their interest diminished as the civil war escalated, eventually almost vanishing when the Communists took control and branded Freud's work as bourgeois and typical of capitalist society. In the 1980s, however, a "Freud fever" broke out again, with some replay of ideas and interpretations that had been popular in the 1920s.

In all of these histories, moments, and events, Freud's most original and influential invention—the sexualized unconscious—fails to take hold. Conditioned through the moral and educational context of modern psychology's introduction into China in the late 19th century and through a cultural tendency to view the subject as socially embodied, Freudian theory becomes part of the discourse of enlightenment, science, and modernity. The story does not stop there, however, as this discourse alone cannot fully address the emotional and "spiritual" aspect of the developing revolutionary subject. That is the topic of Chapter Three.

INTRODUCTION OF PSYCHOLOGY IN LATE 19TH- AND EARLY 20TH-CENTURY CHINA

When Freudian theory entered China in the early 20th century, it came on the heels of a general introduction to psychology or "mental philosophy," supposedly a newly developing science from the West. Three important conditions determined the way in which the field of psychology took shape in China.[5] First, because the earliest introduction of psychology occurred through the teaching and translation of missionaries, it initially appeared as an adjunct to or expansion of modern moral education, and thus it was easily absorbed into a long-standing Chinese concern with moral development. Second, because most early psychology texts were translated as textbooks, the educational structure, with its accompanying notions of socialization, personal cultivation, and responsibility to society and nation, framed the entry of psychology into China.[6] And third, exactly at the time when psychology was being introduced in missionary schools and through translation of textbooks, educational psychology—rapidly developing as a field in the United States—was quickly picked up as a subject for normal schools in Japan, which provided a model for the modernization of Chinese education (Blowers 2000). Through this confluence, psychology became inexorably connected to education, with the first departments of psychology in Chinese universities established in education schools.[7] These three conditions, I argue, combined with a Confucian cultural bias toward constructing and imagining the subject as fundamentally social, eventually constrained the development of the alienated, isolated sense of trauma rooted in frustrated sexual desire that was implicit in Freud's work.[8] Yet the conditions of its emergence in China did not merely constrain psychology. In the curricula established by late Qing educational reformers, and in the textbooks they chose to translate, we can identify the strong emphasis on subjectivity and mental processes that becomes a mark of the modern subject. We also can see a simultaneous attempt to interpret the mind within the context of relationships, educational process, moral value, and national and ethnic characteristics. In this regard, the early texts and curricula both set the stage for Freudian theory and simultaneously drew the boundaries within which it could function.

In Europe and the United States, psychology was often taught as part of religious training, emerging as an independent field of study only slowly and picking up steam in the mid to late 19th century.[9] Writing in 1879, G. Stanley Hall (1844–1924) criticized psychology and philosophy for their exceedingly close ties to religion in the United States, a situation that, he argued, bred dependence of thought and a tendency to accept orthodoxy rather than to cultivate "openness and flexibility of mind" (90). As Hall put it, the "great open questions of psychology and metaphysics are made to dwindle in number and importance as compared with matters of faith and conduct," and the religious bent of philosophy in the United States meant that the temptation to "criticize or instruct rather than to add to the sum of the world's intellectual possessions by doing original work" was difficult to counteract (90, 104). American psychology broke off from its European roots between 1890 and 1910, a time when it also was in the process of pulling away from its ties to religion and philosophy (Berliner).

The connection between psychology and religion was evident in its introduction to China through the work of missionaries, who set up Western-style schools that introduced philosophical and early psychological thinkers, arranged for Chinese students to go abroad to study, and translated key texts into Chinese (Yang and Zhao 1999, 98–144). One of the earliest and the most famous Chinese students to study in the United States, Yung Wing (also known as Rong Hong, 1828–1912), entered the Morrison Educational Society (Malisun xuetang), set up by the American Christian missionary Samuel Robbins Brown (1810–80) in Macao and Hong Kong, at age 13 in 1841, and left the school with two other students in 1847 to travel with Brown to study in the United States. Wing Hung studied some psychology at the Monson Academy in Massachusetts, and graduated from Yale College in 1854. Curricula that included psychology were first established in China at schools such as the Mengyang Educational Society (Mengyang xuetang), established in 1864 in Shandong by the Presbyterian missionary Calvin Wilson Matteer (in Chinese, Di Kaowen, 1836–1908). According to records from 1876, the curriculum included psychology in the final year of a nine-year period of study. Other schools run by missionaries also introduced psychology—or "mental philosophy"—with the strong emphasis on moral development and religious thought that G. Stanley Hall had condemned.[10]

Teachers at missionary schools in China also learned Chinese and translated textbooks for classroom use. Amherst professor Joseph Haven's (1816–74) *Mental Philosophy: Including the Intellect, Sensibilities, and Will*, published in 1857 and used as a textbook in the United States, was the first book on philosophical psychology to be translated into Chinese, in 1889. *Mental Philosophy* was used as a textbook at the famous St. John's College (Shengyuehan shuyuan), which initiated its psychology curriculum in 1879 with a class taught by Yan Yongjing (1838–98). Yan had assisted Samuel Isaac Joseph Schereschewsky (in Chinese, Shi Yuepi, 1831–1906), the Episcopal bishop of Shanghai, in establishing the school the year before. Yan entered missionary school as a student in 1848 and at age 15 traveled to the United States, where he studied linguistics at Columbia University and graduated from Kenyon College in 1861. In either the fall of 1860 or the spring of 1861, Yan took Joseph Haven's course on mental philosophy. He returned to China in 1862 to take up various church-related duties, and published the first volume of Haven's book in 1889, in Chinese titled *Xinling xue*. The second volume, which apparently was completed in draft, was not published.[11]

As the first book introducing psychology to be translated into Chinese, Haven's study lays out the basis of understanding and investigating the relationship between mind and body. For the purpose of my study, there are four important aspects of this foundation, which builds on the work of earlier theorists of the mind. The first is Haven's establishment of "mental philosophy" or "psychology" as a subject that must be studied as part of the emerging modern intellectual field. Haven separates psychology from the earlier metaphysics and establishes it as a natural science:

> *Mental Philosophy not properly Metaphysics.* Neither in its wider nor in its stricter sense does this term properly designate the science of the mind. Mental Philosophy neither embraces every thing not included under physics, nor is it the science of abstract being. . . . To designate the science of mind in distinction from these other sciences [logic, ethics, politics, ontology, metaphysics], some more definite term is required. The word *Psychology* is now coming into use as such a term. (Haven 1862, 16)

A second important aspect is Haven's effort to compare the study of the mind to the study of natural phenomena using the technique of learning through observation and experience: "A careful induction of particulars will place us in possession of general principles, or laws, and these, correctly ascertained and stated, will constitute our science, whether of matter or mind" (Haven 1862, 18). Following quickly on this definition of psychology as a natural science, Haven points out the difference between the science of nature and the science of the mind:

> While both matter and mind can be known only by the observation of the phenomena which they present, in mental science the field of such observation lies in great part within ourselves—the phenomena are those of our own present or former consciousness—the mind is at once both the observer and the object observed. This circumstance, which at first seems to present a difficulty, is in reality a great advantage which this science possesses over all others. (Haven 1862, 18)

Third, Haven valorizes introspection as a scientific methodology that can lead directly to an understanding of not only the self, but also the mind. Noting that the mind has the power to "know itself," Haven states that in psychology, "the observer has within himself the essential elements of the science which he explores; the data which he seeks, are the data of his own consciousness; the science which he constructs is the science of himself" (19). Looking back from a later Freudian perspective, this emphasis on introspection as the basis of both self-knowledge and knowledge of the mind as an entity—and the fact that both are presented as scientific knowledge—is significant. Fourth, Haven includes within psychology as a discipline all aspects of mental processes as well as their relationship to the body in sense, perception, and desire. In the second chapter of his first division, Haven addresses "Mind as affected by certain states of the brain and nervous system," including sleep, dreams, somnambulism, and insanity (342–76). He also covers emotions, affections, and desires that arise from the body and the mind (happiness, knowledge, power, society, and esteem). Haven goes on to define psychology as important to natural science, the arts, self-understanding, oratory, education, freedom, and mental discipline.

Mental Philosophy may have been limited in its use as a text to missionary institutions, but as the first full translation of a psychological textbook into Chinese, it established psychology as a modern endeavor touching every aspect of life, underscored the importance of introspection as a means of attaining knowledge, and brought psychology under the validating aegis of science. These principles were repeated in many texts translated and written after this time, especially as China set out to modernize its educational institutions. In 1901, the Empress Dowager, Zi Xi (1835–1908), suggested a number of relatively drastic measures: revising the content of the civil service examination to include testing not only on the classics, but also on the history of China, the government of China and foreign countries, and modern science; banning of the eight-legged essay; and the development of a new curriculum (Bonner 1986, 23–25). Within a few years, the reformation of the Chinese educational system was announced, and in 1905, the examination system was abolished and a Ministry of Education created. Students were sent abroad to study in greater numbers. Following the model of Japan, the Qing government decreed that psychology would be a mandatory class for students in teaching colleges, setting for psychology a supporting role that buttressed the larger goals of education (Yang and Zhao 1999, 122–27). The massive educational reforms undertaken after

1901 coincided with development of educational psychology in the United States and Europe, a concurrence that further strengthened the relationship between psychology and education.[12]

To feed the rapidly changing educational system, Western books and textbooks on educational psychology were translated into Chinese, often via an earlier Japanese translation; alternately, they were introduced through lectures in Japan or China. In 1902, the Japanese historian Hattori Unokichi (1867–1939) began to teach a psychology class at the newly founded Teachers Training Institute (Shifanguan) of Beijing Teachers Academy (Beijing shifan xueyuan), which was the precursor to Beijing Teachers University (Beijing shifan daxue). The materials he used, *Psychology Lectures at [Beijing shifan] University* (Jingshi daxue xinlixue daxue xinlixue jiangyi), lay out his approach. Hattori defined psychology as a science because of its methodology of seeking objective rules and principles, emphasizing the location of the psyche in the brain (rather than the heart) and the importance of the nervous system's relationship to the psyche. He valued child psychology and ethnic psychology (minzu xinli), as well as experiments and psychological measurements. Hattori also brought in relevant sources from Chinese traditional theories of the mind / heart (xin) and nature / essence (xing), attempting to show how Chinese and Western theories of the mind could resonate and playing to the fact that his audience was composed of Chinese students. *Lectures in Psychology* was a teaching volume, a mandatory textbook for normal colleges, and an introduction to psychology that sold well in both China and Japan (Yang and Zhao 1999, 122–26).[13]

Most or all psychology books translated from Japanese around the turn of the century were related to education. Four such translations are still in existence, including the influential *Psychological Education* (Xinli jiaoyu xue) by Kubota Sadanori, which was published in 1902. Approaching education from the perspective of psychology, Kubota's introduction makes the social Darwinian argument that survival of the fittest is a direct result of education: "Those with education survive, those without die out; those with the most complete education are strong, those without are weak. Those who observe the countries of the world all recognize this" (Yang and Zhao 1999, 128). The book also emphasized the foundational contribution of education to national strength in terms of training the mind and "soul" (hun) of the people. Three other books translated from Japanese around this time also emphasized the absolute importance of mental or spiritual development as the basis of education. First, the 1903 *Light of Civilization in the Mental/Spiritual World* (Xinjie wenming deng), introduced the concept of the unconscious and also devoted a chapter to social psychology, stressing its significance (Yang and Zhao 1999, 127–34).

Second, in 1905, Chen Huang's (1872–1931) *Easy Explanations of Psychology* (Xinli yijie), a compilation designed for students like himself who were studying in Japan, laid out a religious and moral framework within which to understand the mind. Chen had not studied psychology in any formal context but took advantage of a period of illness to put the book together. He consulted the third, *Psychology: Empirical and Rational* (1900) by the Reverend Michael Maher, S.J. (1860–1918), a book also used extensively by the modernist writer James Joyce (1882–1941) (Rickard 1999). Maher, a Jesuit, argued on behalf of a soul that resisted change and was expressed through memory (Rickard 1999, 24–29). Chen altered some of the terms from the translation to make them more palatable to Chinese readers, changing, for example, "instinct" (benneng) into a term that is now used in philosophy to mean "intuitive ability" (liangneng). He made use of concepts from Harald Höffding's work (see below) as well as other materials available at the time. Two other books on psychology, based on notes from lectures given by Japanese professors in Hubei and Jiangsu, were published in 1905 and 1906 (Yang and Zhao 1999, 134–36).

Wang Guowei's (1877–1927) immersion in Western philosophy, psychology, and aesthetics produced a number of important translations, including the 1882 work by the Danish philosopher Harald Höffding (1843–1931) *Outline of Psychology* (in Chinese, Xinlixue gailun), the first book written with the express goal of providing students with a general introduction to the field of psychology (Wozniak).[14] Wang's goal of using the book as a text in teacher-training academies, where psychology was a government-mandated course after 1903, expanded the reach of Höffding's work into new geographical and cultural territory. The book saw around ten printings in Chinese, with editions in 1907, 1915, 1926, 1931, and 1935 (Yang and Zhao 1999, 112–18).

Outline of Psychology is organized into seven chapters. Höffding rejected philosophy's emphasis on metaphysics, turning to a dynamic view of consciousness and stressing the importance of the unconscious, as well as elaborating on the relationship between the two. In chapter 3, "The Conscious and the Unconscious," Höffding argued: "Psychology is on secure ground only when it confines itself to the clear and certain phenomena and laws of consciousness. But starting from this standpoint, it discovered the unconscious, and sees to its astonishment that psychological laws prevail beyond the province of conscious life" (73).

Referring to the work of William Benjamin Carpenter (1813–85), who in his 1855 *Principles of Mental Physiology, With Their Applications to the Training and Discipline of the Mind and the Study of its Morbid Conditions* contended that because thought and emotional reaction frequently operated outside of the conscious, the unconscious was often powerfully at work, Höffding too underscored the unconscious and placed it at the basis of learning: "All education rests on the possibility of the intermediate links thus sinking below 'the threshold,'" a principle that he argued was as true for nations and races as it was for individuals (74–75). Höffding stated: "In the history of individuals and of the race, inner connection is preserved by means of this unconscious growth, which determines a great part of the content and of the energy of conscious life" (77). For Höffding, dreaming was the intermediate stage between consciousness and the unconscious, and the relationship between the two states could sometimes be grasped at the moment of awakening.

Höffding followed his predecessors in emphasizing the significance of subjectivity in cognition, feelings, and will. He also linked the unconscious to characteristics within not only the individual but also the nation and the race, a theme that was to have its own trajectory of development in China. For Höffding, important internal events fed off this murky relationship between the conscious and the unconscious, and the unconscious was powerful not because it was the site where sexual repression could be located, but because of its key role in the learning process. Höffding's vision locates the origin of learning within the unconscious; the unconscious becomes significant only when it is thus contextualized within learning.

Through another translation, Ruric Nevel Roark's (in Chinese, Lu Erke, 1859–1909) 1895 *Psychology in Education; Designed as a Text-book, and for the Use of the General Reader* (Jiaoyu xinli xue), Wang Guowei directly introduced the developing field of educational psychology (Roark 1895).[15] Translated by Wang from the Japanese version in 1910, Roark's work championed the importance of psychology in all aspects of education and medicine, and of psychological understanding in guiding students toward deeper knowledge. Many areas covered by Joseph Haven and Harald Höffding such as emotions, imagination, judgment, sense perception, desire, and will were now put into the context of teaching, training, and personal development, where they became seminal concepts of the modern educational system.

The principles introduced in this book are in use to the present day (Yang and Zhao 1999, 118–20).

In Roark's view, "Psychology sustains the same relation to the science of education that anatomy, physiology, and pharmacy sustain to the practice of medicine. It is as necessary that the teacher should know something of the mind's activities as it is that the physician should know the bodily organs and their functions, their normal and their abnormal conditions" (1895, 7). Promoting a combination of introspective, observational, comparative, laboratory, and classroom methods, Roark brought psychology completely into the socializing process of education, treating it as a tool through which the teacher would have direct access to the mind of his or her students, and through which s/he could expertly guide them toward intellectual and moral development. In a description that was bound to find resonance within Chinese culture, Roark moved from the brain and nerves through the physical senses and memory to the emotions, which included pity/sympathy, reverence, awe, and conscience. He divided the affections into two categories, the benevolent and the malevolent. The benevolent desires included "love of family, the basis of society," "love of country, patriotism," "love of mankind, philanthropy," and "love of God, the basis of real religion" (134–37). Although his focus on love would have been considered unusual, otherwise Roark could easily have been speaking of Chinese society when he wrote,

> [Love's] first manifestation is the love that is the basis of the family, and through the family is the basis of society . . . The family is the social unit, and influences brought to bear upon the child in the home will very largely determine what he shall be as a member of that organism we call society. (134–35)

Roark's emphasis on family, society, and country meshed perfectly with Chinese concerns with nation building, personal improvement, and the development of civic society. He divided desires into the physical, the intellectual, and the moral, and limited them to three: for food, air, and water, for rest and exercise, and for sleep, easily dismissed in less than a page, although his discussion of intellectual desires took far more space and culminated in the "desire for society." The effectiveness of isolation as a punishment, even "by the toughest criminals," indicated to Roark "the strength of the social feeling even in its instinctive form in the very young"; therefore, he did not recommend this method of discipline (144).

He also spoke out on behalf of culturally specific "mental peculiarities—the ways of thinking, the ethical standards, the expression of the inner life in literature and art—that marked one nation as different from another," noting that there was "a psychology of the nation as well as of the individual" and, even more significantly, "a psychology of society as an *organism*" (247). He provided a set model of the progress of civilizations on the road from a "rude and savage state" to the methods of "pure science," a path that he said all nations must follow (276). Overall, Roark presented a strikingly social, group-oriented, nationally significant vision of human mentality and life.

The psychological treatises of Haven, Höffding, Kubota, Hattori, and Roark cross at various points in their valorizing of subjectivity and psychology for the individual, society, ethnic group, and nation, in their claim that psychology is a science, in their emphasis on the moral right of trying to understand the mind, in their expansion of the significance of the unconscious to include national and racial characteristics, and in their foundational argument on behalf of education, or the training of the mind as more than a repository of content. A more mystical strand of thinking about the mind and society was at work in the efforts of New Text Confucianism, which tried to bring together Confucianism, Buddhism, and Christianity (Sun 1992, 237). Lung-kee Sun argues that at this time Chinese intellectuals "no longer saw human spirit as continuous with the forces permeating a moral universe; instead, it became 'psychology,' governed by its own amoral, naturalistic laws." However, I find in educational psychology an ongoing concern with morality that was woven into the discourses of eugenics, nation-building, and the importance of modern mental characteristics such as independent will and a strongly developed sense of self.[16] Tracing the emergence of social psychology, Sun highlights Yan Fu's definition of psychology as "sympathy among people," various early articles on national psychology published in student newspapers, and the discourse of national psychology by leading intellectuals such as Liang Qichao (1873–1927). Liang's claim—that the "world is produced by the psychologies of all of mankind in the world, a society is produced by the psychologies of all its members"—shows not only an emphasis on psychology as a tool through which to evaluate society but also a "bias toward mentalism" or subjectivity similar to that expressed in the texts I examined above (Sun 1992, 242). The debate on national psychology, national soul (guohun), and ethnic spirit (minzu jingshen) brought together issues of knowledge, feeling, will, and desire at the individual, social, and national level, laying a strong foundation for the emphasis on the mind that underlies Freudian theory, while simultaneously directing the trajectories of its interpretation.

FREUD AND THE NEW SEXUAL CULTURE IN CHINESE CRITICISM

Articles mentioning Freud began to appear in China during the teens, scattered in journals devoted to general intellectual culture and modern life, the evolving field of psychology, and education. Many of the earliest articles, which were written by the most well-known cultural figures, simply mentioned or briefly introduced Freud's work, without taking a position on his theories. In 1914, *Eastern Miscellany* (Dongfang zazhi) editor Qian Zhixiu (1883–1948) published "Research on Dreams" (Meng zhi yanjiu), in which Freud's work is mentioned for perhaps the first time in a Chinese context. Chen Daqi (1886–1983) set up a lab for work in experimental psychology in 1917 at Beijing University, the following year publishing the textbook *Outline of Psychology* (Xinlixue dagang) for the use of university students. During 1918 and 1919, Chen's lectures on psychology were published in the *Beijing University Gazette* (Beijing daxue rikan) (no. 111) beginning on April 15, 1918.[17] Chen starts out by establishing psychology as a science and its scope as covering not only human beings, but animals as well—a significant statement in terms of traditional Chinese ideas about the mind and human nature. Chen points out that the new psychology differentiates itself from philosophy by looking at mental process in the ordinary person, thereby departing from the restrictions of philosophy. He adds that it also focuses on the mind-body relationship, uses scientific methods, and has a body of experts—Ernst Heinrich Weber (1795–1878), Gustav Theodor Fechner (1801–1887), Wilhelm Wundt (1832–1920), and William James (1842–1910)—who have produced a distinctive body of research material (Qian Zhixiu, N.114, April 18, 1919). Chen introduces various branches of psychology and argues against the traditional beliefs that the heart rather than the brain is the site of mental / psychic function (xin zuoyong) and that the spirit can leave the body. Chen discusses abnormal psychology, dream analysis, hysteria, and the subconscious (xia yishi). Chen's lectures on instinct attack the ideas that animals function instinctually and humans logically, and that animals have no consciousness. He severely criticizes

Chinese education for driving out good instincts such as the child's desire to play, noting that in Europe and the United States—where he believes the instinctual is not constrained and eliminated—even old men like to go out and kick a ball for fun. The virtue of education, Chen argues, is that it can direct instincts toward the good or the bad.[18] In his 1919 lectures, Chen introduces spiritualism, noting that since Chinese materials on ghosts and supernatural phenomena are not reliable, researchers in this area have no option but to use foreign sources. Although Chen is critical of spiritualism as experimentally unproven, he notes that foreigners seem to take it very seriously.[19] Chen mentions a spiritualist society (xinling hui) in Shanghai, and goes into a deeper critique of spiritualism in his 1918 article "Rebutting Spiritualism" (Guan "xinling") (Chen Daqi 1918).[20] Here Chen argues that the hallucinations of the mentally ill should not be understood as anything more than that, and introduces and defines the subconscious (xia yishi). In a critical comment typical of the times, Chen argues that because the Chinese glorify following the ancients, their subconsciouses are filled with slavishness, and thus they believe they can invoke the spirit of the ancients through planchette writing (a method of divination). Chen is skeptical of such claims.

After John Dewey (1859–1952) spoke in China from 1919 to 1921, and Bertrand Russell (1872–1970) lectured there in 1920, interest in psychology and the unconscious grew. Several of Freud's pieces were translated into Chinese, and secondary sources that presented and critiqued his work also were translated and discussed. Key books and articles were translated from German, English, or Japanese. In May 1920, Wang Jingxi (1898–1968) published "The Most Recent Trends of Psychology" (Xinlixue de zuijin de qushi) in Beijing University's new journal *The Renaissance* (Xinchao). In it, Wang states that Wilhelm Wundt's psychological theories are outmoded, but he gives Wundt credit for proving the existence of the unconscious (wu yishi), thereby challenging other branches of psychology. Freud's approaches, Wang notes, are not only an extremely effective alternative to hypnosis for the treatment of the mentally ill but also help explain everyday psychology, and he includes a discussion of a number of methods, concepts, texts, and names in the field. In 1921, Zhu Guangqian (1897–1986) published the introductory "Freud's Unconscious and Psychology" (Fuluode de yin yishi yu xinlixue) in *Eastern Miscellany*; the year before, a certain "Y" had published "A Few Words on the New Psychology of Freud" (Fuluote xin xinlixue zhi yiban) (Zhu Guangqian 1921; Y 1920).[21] Zhang Dongsun

(1886–1973) published two articles on psychoanalysis in 1921, and by 1924, articles introducing various aspects of Freudian theory had been published in intellectual journals (Jingyuan Zhang 1992, 167–69).

The *Journal of Chinese Psychology* (Xinli) introduced Freud's sexual theories in a series of articles from 1922 to 1924. The most bizarre of these contributions was by a German educator, Alfred (Daniel) Westharp (in Chinese, Wei Xichin or Wei Zhong, 1882/3–?), who published several articles on male-female sexual relations between May 1922 and April 1924.[22] Westharp imaginatively invokes Freud's sexual theory to support a mystical system of male-female relations. Bringing in Chinese *yin-yang* cosmology and representing male-female sexual essence and relations through strange graphs and drawings, he argues that a correct understanding of sexual relations is the basis of social order.

The first issue of the *Journal of Chinese Psychology* (Xinli), contained a two-part series by Yu Tianxiu (1887–?) called "Psychoanalysis" (fenxi xinlixue); it was published under the category "abnormal psychology" (biantai xinlixue). In it Yu notes that psychoanalysis is a science dealing with various abnormal

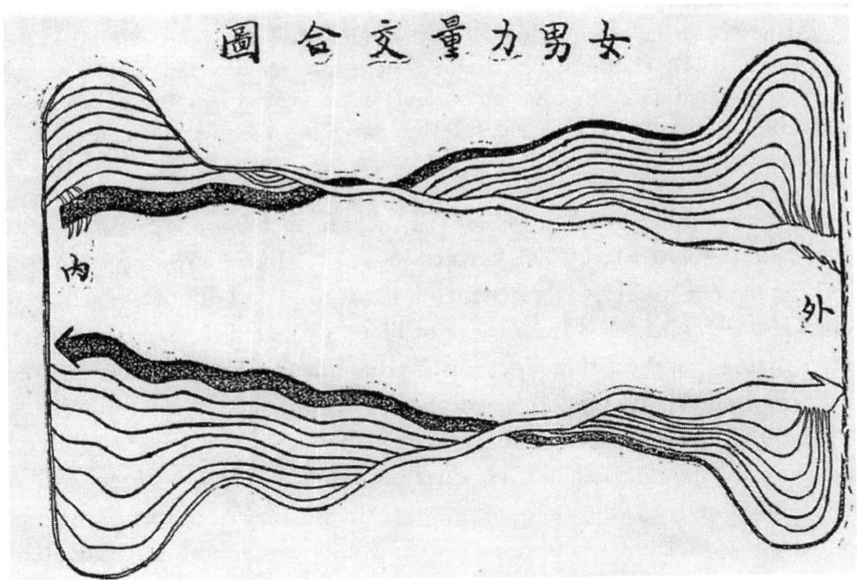

FIGURE 1. Alfred (Daniel) Westharp, "Female-Male Power Intercourse Chart" (Nünan liliang jiaohe tu) "New Psychoanalysis of the Relations Between Man and Woman" (Nannü xin fenxi xinlixue) *Xinli* 4:1 (October 1922): 1–29; 13. On left is "inner," on right is "outer."

psychologies, such as extreme addiction, insanity, neurosis, etc. (Yu Tianxiu 1922a).[23] According to Yu, psychoanalysis also includes the study of "abnormal social phenomena" such as herd psychology, mob psychology, revolutionary psychology, strikes, xenophobia, the severing of nation-to-nation relations, war, and illicit sexual relations. In his description of the process of psychoanalysis, Yu simply states Freud's conclusion as fact: "Early on, [Freud] discovered the relationship between sexual desire and neurosis (shenjing bing)" (84). After describing a few of Freud's clinical cases, Yu explains:

> Based on many experiences such as these, [Freud] invented his new theory, which states that most neurosis originates from irregularity / lack of harmony in sexual desire (xingyu bu tiaohe). When sexual desire is not regulated, it is because this instinct was disturbed in childhood. [Freud] thinks that sexual desire for the most part is expressed in early youth. For example a girl may adore her father and not love her mother; a boy may adore his mother, and not love his father. This is one kind of disturbance in sexual desire. Sexual desire originally is a kind of energy, and we can alter the direction of this energy's development and use it for socially useful endeavors. Otherwise, sexual desire could become the [patient's] normal state of affairs, and it would turn into mental illness, becoming harmful for the self and for society. Because individual heredity and environment are not the same, the potency and frequency of sexual desire also will differ. These are things we should know when teaching children. The origin of neurosis generally comes from an excess of sexual desire that has no outlet. If we don't redirect it so as to gratify its desire, its power will smolder in the heart / mind (xin) and become illness (Yu Tianxiu 1922a).

In the second part of the series, Yu introduces the work of Boris Sidis (1867–1923), Pierre Marie Félix Janet (1859–1947), Morton Prince (1854–1929) (with reference to Hippolyte Bernheim, 1840–1919) and discusses their conclusions, which differed from those of Freud (Yu Tianxiu 1922b).[24] While recognizing that these three specialists were critical of Freud, Yu accepts the idea that repression could appear in healthy people just as in the mentally ill, and that dreams, errors, and slips could show the repressed thought and emotions of the unconscious. He does not take a position on Freud's centering of the sex instinct, but emphasizes the possibility of turning sexual desire toward socially useful tasks, which would benefit both the individual and society.

In the early 1920s interest in sex education was growing, with articles published in many of the same journals that introduced Freud as well as in specialized journals that focused on education. Intellectuals who published in general cultural journals such as *Eastern Miscellany* or *New Youth* (Xin qingnian) also published in specialized journals, especially those in the field of education. The educational context, which positioned Freudian sexual theories within the framework of self, family, and national improvement, was considered a prime target for modernization, one that thus was especially valuable in illustrating the way in which these theories were interpreted. Over time the education context became even more important as the crucial socializing structure within which Freudian sexual theory was interpreted.

In August of 1923, *The Educational Review* (Jiaoyu zazhi) featured a special issue on sex education. The year before, in the same journal, Zhou Jianren (1888–1984) had published "The Theory and Actuality of Sex Education" (Xing jiaoyu de lilun yu shiji), in which he mentions Freud's work on the ego, which works to protect and preserve the individual, and the sex instinct, which works to protect and preserve the race (minzu) (Zhou Jianren 1922). In daily life, Zhou argues, understanding these concepts and the value of sex education can have an important function, that of nurturing "the basis of morality and hygiene." In another article in the special issue on sex education, "Some Principles of Sex Education" (Xing jiaoyu de jitiao yuanli), Zhou states: "Modern psychologists tell us that human beings are animals of two sexes whose lives in every movement are related to sex," and adds that sexual desire can be transformed into art (Zhou Jianren 1923, 2). Zhou promotes a more open discussion of sexuality, so that young people will not end up searching for information in places where they may learn falsehoods (for example, in novels or in discussions with friends); this could lead to perverse sexual practices such as masturbation or sex with animals. Zhou describes sexual intercourse from a scientific perspective, and ends by affirming the value of sex education in school. His emphasis on sex as scientific knowledge—an idea he repeats in his later debate with Zhang Jingsheng (1888–1970)—shows the powerful influence of scientism in modern Chinese culture at the time, as well as Zhou's tendency to insert the discourse of sex into a socially oriented intellectual framework (Kwok 1965).

Zhou Jianren's brother, Zhou Zuoren (1885–1967), also participated in the discourse on sex education. In a 1926 article called "Some Problems in Sex Education," published in *The Educational Review*, he advocates sex education in the home as well as in school. Zhou breaks home-education efforts into five stages depending on the child's age and emphasizes the early use of scientific terminology and the need for a positive attitude toward sexual organs for very young children. Believing that it is an error to hide sex from children, Zhou ends his article by claiming that lack of proper sex education—the most pressing problem in education at large—produces angst and melancholy. This statement is quite different, of course, from claiming that lack of a sufficiently developed sexual identity produces angst and melancholy.

One important early translation was Barbara Low's (1877–1955) 1920 *Psycho-Analysis: A Brief Account of the Freudian Theory*, which was published in 1927 (Zhao Yan 1927). Low argues that because it uses the scientific method of observation, theory development, and testing, psychoanalysis should be treated as a science (although Low herself believed psychoanalysis fell somewhere between philosophy and science). More important, however, Low expresses a near-worship of Freud and a messianic appreciation of his ideas:

> His work may be roughly described as the provision of new keys by which we can now unlock doors in the human personality hitherto impassable, through which doors we may pass into areas unguessed at formerly. By the use of the instruments he has forged, we shall in the future be able not only to prevent, to a very large extent, the creation of the neurotic and mentally diseased, but also to set the feet of the new generations on a more desirable path, leading to a destiny more splendid and satisfying than we yet dream of. (Low 1920, 16–17)

In a nutshell, Low captures the visionary aspect of Freudian theory, which had more to do with imagining a new human life than with curing mental illness, an endeavor that still brought to bear the old categories of normal versus abnormal. The abandonment of these categories of meaning proved difficult for Chinese thinkers; in their overwhelmingly social perspective, the primary space open for eccentricity and sexual excess was decadence.

Despite all the early interest, reservations about the sex drive, the unconscious, child sexual desire, and other aspects of Freudian theory remained. In 1934, psychologist Chen Derong translated John C. Flugel's (1884–1955) article "Theories of Psycho-analysis (Chen 1934). This article is significant because it discusses Alfred Adler's disagreement with Freud on the importance of sexual motivations. Later in the 1930s, work by Wilhelm Reich and W. Jurinetz (also V. Iurinets) that synthesized Marxism and Freudianism also was published, and in 1940 Reuben Osborn's 1937 *Freud and Marx:*

A Dialectical Study was translated and published (Chu Zhi 1940). Jingyuan Zhang concluded that "Osborn's picture is that psychoanalysis is the science of human desires and drives, whereas Marxism can be defined as the science dealing with external conditions that either fulfill or frustrate those desires" (Jingyuan Zhang 1992, 21). Marxists (and later Maoists) were not amenable to Freud or other "bourgeois" psychology, eventually completely repudiating Freudian theory in all respects.

From the very beginning of Freud's introduction into China, there were questions about his sexual focus, although opinion was not consistent. Some critics supported what they viewed as Freud's help in "liberating" sexual desire, while others found it excessive.[25] Ultimately, however, Freudian sexual theory failed to take root in early modern China, a reality also recognized by Liu Jihui (2004, see below), who deplores this "lack" as an overarching cultural failure. Although questions about Freudian theory could be linked first to the influence of behaviorists trained in the United States, who were unlikely to admire Freud, and then to the politically motivated condemnation of Freudian theory as bourgeois idealism, the work of Freud's early introducers and scholars indicates that they persistently positioned the human mind and human behavior within the social sphere—or, in other words, interpreted the human being as first and primarily a social creature. In the next section I examine the writing of Gao Juefu, who provides a more directly articulated example of this tendency.

GAO JUEFU AND FREUDIAN SEXUAL THEORIES

One of the most well-known and prolific commentators on Freud and his sexual theories was Gao Juefu. Gao's work stands apart not only for its deep and systematic understanding of Western psychological theory, which is comprehensively introduced, but also for his willingness to critically evaluate the theories he encountered. Over his long career, Gao studied not only, or even primarily, Freud, but scores of other famous psychologists and theoreticians. He was an expert on social psychology, introducing and critiquing the work of William McDougall (1871–1938) and Kurt Lewin (1890–1947).[26] However, Gao devoted considerable time to Freud, publishing several articles on his work and translating key texts. Gao's approach reveals careful selection of some aspects of this oeuvre, and critique or rejection of other aspects. In his early work, Gao was favorably disposed toward the theory of sublimation (usually translated as "shenghua," but first given as "hualian"); but even as he recognized the value of thinking about "instincts" such as self-preservation and sexual fulfillment, he was critical of Freud's pan-sexualism (fanxing zhuyi). Whereas one might imagine that Freud's insistence on the central position of sexuality would be a necessary precondition for accepting the concept of sublimation, Gao's discussion in effect shrinks the Freudian emphasis on sexuality and expands the notion of sublimation; repression conceptualized as a problem disappears, to be replaced by a positive socially oriented direction that will flourish if educational and social conditions are right.

Gao Juefu contributed to educational journals, where he published articles on psychological problems relevant to education and child-rearing. Two months after the special issue on sex education in *The Educational Review,* Gao published "The New Psychology and Education" (Gao Juefu 1923). Basing his term "new" on A. G. Tansley's (1871–1955) use of the word to describe Freudian psychology, Gao picks out the concept of the "complex" (yixu) as the most meaningful.[27] Gao interprets the complex as something that develops in the child through "the influence of experience, education, and environment, which gradually nurture various complexes," adding that these often conflict in the adult. Following Tansley, who added the "herd instinct" to the Freud's two instincts of sex and self-preservation, Gao recognizes three basic complexes: the ego (ziwo), sex (xing), and the herd (qun).[28] Following this line of reasoning, he implicitly takes a position on an important debate about the relative influence of inherited instinct and environment.[29] Gao introduces repression (zuyi) as the psychological way to avoid conflict, and he also discusses mental censorship, rationalization, the meaning of dreams, word association, sublimation (hualian), the Freudian slip (koushi), and psychoanalysis (xin zhi fenxi). Gao's synthesis assimilates Freudian sexual ideas into a theory that is fundamentally social, emphasizing "experience, education, and environment." He adds:

> For example, if the sex instinct is excessively indulged, it cannot help but harm the individual's health and break down the moral excellence of society. If it is excessively restrained, one cannot avoid holding it in the unconscious (qianxin shi), where it will become the precondition for mental illness. So the best thing to do is to sublimate the power of sex into literature, music, art, etc. The emotion of sex is approximately the same as the emotion of literature, music, art, and so on. It is much better for this feeling to seek satisfaction in literature, music, and art than in sex. The poets, musicians,

> and artists since ancient times all were successful because of the sublimation of sexual power. (Gao Juefu 1923, 6)

A main goal of education, Gao notes, should be the building of excellent and harmonious "complexes." Furthermore, "the nurturing of excellent complexes and the sublimation of primitive instinctual drives is a good way to prevent the emergence of illness" (Gao Juefu 1923, 8).[30]

Gao takes on the question of instinct versus environment more directly in his 3-part series, "An Outline of Social Psychology" (Shehui xinlixue gaishuo) (1926a, 1926b, 1926c). In the third installment, he argues against conflict (zheng) as a basic instinct; while he accepts sexual desire as innate, he simultaneously argues that the concept should be narrowly understood and not generally applied. Noting that "in a broad sense, sexual behavior is something adults and children both possess alike," Gao argues on behalf of a conservative definition: sexual awakening comes only when one reaches puberty (Gao 1926c, 8). While this change is biological and thus sexual desire is innate, the interpretation of what that "fact" means within any actual environment is not straightforward; the influence of the environment is powerful and perhaps even primary:

> First we have the individual and then society, or first we have society and then the individual—naturally the first theory seems more reasonable. But if we add some explanation to the second, it can also be said to not be without logic. When a child is born, he has parents, brothers, and sisters, and these parents, brothers, and sisters have a number of habits. As the child grows up, therefore, the basis of all of his actions comes from this. But because those in his family already have habits, his basic actions will in all times and places be corrected by his parents . . . This is enough to see that our basic actions develop into different habits because we are influenced by society. And society influences individuals the most in thought, especially in customs, organization, institutions, law, and traditional social thought. Customs, organization, institutions, law and so on all exist before the birth of the individual, so the individual cannot but be influenced by them . . . Therefore, except for a tiny few with extreme independence, the people of a given society will largely have similar behavior. This common behavior will be even more obvious in the military, which is disciplined. It should not be thought unusual that each soldier, receiving the same order under the same conditions, will tend to behave the same way. If because of that, we hypothesize a "military psychology" or "group psychology," we cannot but be met with scorn. (Gao Juefu 1926c, 10–11)

Finally, in another important statement, Gao concludes "to explain behavior, we do not need to hypothesize the unconscious" (Gao Juefu 1926c, 12).

Because for Freud the site of sexual repression is the unconscious, Gao has effectively blocked the most radical of Freud's sexual theories, limiting the influence of the sex instinct and shrinking the site of its power within the individual.

In a much later article in *The Educational Review*, Gao (1934) more thoroughly critiques Freud's sexual theories, providing charts to show the various appearances of Freudian theory in the work of scholars. He tracks the basic approaches and references to different aspects of Freudian theory, identifying the main categories as: history, disciples, focus on slips, jokes, psychoanalysis, memory, repression, sexual instinct, dreams, the unconscious, and critique. Gao finds no consistent approach to analyzing Freudian theory but recognizes Freud's contribution in that his emphasis on the unconscious overturned the centrality of reason as a prime motivation in human behavior, just as Darwin overturned the belief that humans were at the center of the universe. After going through Freud's contributions (the critique of reason, the elevation of cause / effect, promoting the close relationship between psychologists and human life), Gao notes: "And his explanations are not unreasonable. No matter who they are, people cannot fail to have personal / private desires (siyu), and these desires cannot always be satisfied. If these unsatisfied personal / private desires cannot openly seek satisfaction, they cannot help but stealthily become errors / slips, dreams, or mental illness in order to gain expression" (6).

When Gao moves on to problems with Freud's theories and the necessity of approaching them critically, however, he begins with pan-sexualism, which he again does not accept in either its inevitability or its broad application: "His emphasis on instinct is not without considerable logical basis, but going from instinct to the promotion of pan-sexualism is not something with which we can agree" (6). Gao begins his critique of Freudian sexual theory in section 3 by raising questions about the unconscious, which he feels Freud has overemphasized. In section 4 of his article, Gao directly criticizes Freud's pan-sexualism:

> If Freud's theory of the unconscious is mystifying, his pan-sexualism is especially preposterous. He affirms that dreams and neuroses all are for the purpose of satisfying unconscious desires, and that the desires of the unconscious cannot help but be sexual. So as he sees it, dreams are the implementation / practice (shijian) of the satisfaction of sexual desire, and neuroses are a substitution for sexual satisfaction. If we ask him to analyze a dream, he always finds a means to resolve it by way of the sexual drive. If we have a neurosis

> and ask him to cure it, he won't stop until he has investigated our sexual life. If you say that the dreams and neurosis of someone on the surface all arise from the censoring sexual desire, how can this be seen as the satisfaction of sexual desire? Then he tells you that in the case of dreams and neurosis, censoring desire and indulging desire originally are the same. . . . (8)

Gao also finds Freud's theories of sexual symbolism excessive: "So according to Freud, our lives are simply surrounded by sexual symbolism. When a writer lifts a pen to write an essay, when a female worker takes up a needle to sew clothes, when a farmer picks up a hoe to till the ground, when a doctor injects a needle into a patient's arm—these actions are all symbolic of sexual intercourse. And the electric poles by the side of the road, the Dragon Well of Dragon Well Mountain, and in fact everything is the symbol of male or female reproductive organs. What kind of talk is this!" (9).

Gao asks how it is possible to know that symbols in dreams are all sexual, and attacks Freud's theories of sexuality in children as overblown. Although he is less sure in his interpretations of the unconscious, he basically rejects the sweeping transformation of the human being into a comprehensively sexualized person.

In the next section I examine the debate over Zhang Jingsheng's *Sex Histories* that occurred in 1926–27. Although Zhang himself may have been as focused on science, knowledge, and education as most intellectuals were at the time, his publication of *Sex Histories* releases some of the radical potential of Freud's sexual theories, I argue. In *Sex Histories*, Zhang asks his respondents to imagine a sexual identity and from that position write their history. Yet the fate of this bold move reiterates the rejection of the radical sexual potential that Gao Juefu and others had expressed a few years before. As my discussion of their earlier articles shows, two of the central players in this debate, Lu Xun's (1881–1936) brothers Zhou Jianren and Zhou Zuoren, like Gao Juefu understand sexual desire and behavior as significant primarily within a social environment. While Zhou Jianren, Zhou Zuoren, and Gao Juefu all accept Freud's underlying theme of a basic sexual drive, they differ in their emphases. Like Freud, Zhou Zuoren sees a relationship between angst and sexual desire but locates the damaging possibilities associated with sexual desire in lack of understanding about it, enveloping it within the modern search for knowledge that is part of scientific rationality. Zhou Jianren also focuses on modern sexual knowledge as scientific, but he goes farther than his brother in treating that context as foundational and mandatory. Gao Juefu incorporates Freud's sexual theories into a model of socialization and rejects theories of the mind that contradict this connection. For Gao especially, Freudian repression is an excellent way to turn instinct into a socially beneficial force, although by the mid-1930s he was casting serious doubt on all Freudian sexual theory. Although these three intellectuals are unanimous in supporting sex education, they minimize or reject the overarching sexual theory that Freud advocates. This is the ground on which the debate over *Sex Histories* takes place.

ZHANG JINGSHENG AND THE DEBATE OVER SEX HISTORIES

Zhang Xichen, the Zhou brothers, and Zhang Jingsheng belonged to an intellectual cohort of cultural liberals at Beijing University. Zhou Zuoren had once expressed guarded approval of Zhang Jingsheng's promotion of an aesthetic and sensual life, although he also worried about the connection between Zhang Jingsheng's sexual proposals and the decadence of traditional Chinese sexual culture. Despite some disagreements, until *Sex Histories* was published in May of 1926, Zhang was viewed as a member of the Beijing group. Afterward, however, Zhang's status changed radically. He was attacked in articles featured in several journals and newspapers—most significantly, *Thread of Talk* (Yusi), *The New Femininity* (Xin nüxing), and *In Common* (Yiban) (Leary 1994, 241–43).

In this falling out we see an apparent conundrum: although the Zhou brothers and Zhang Xichen (1889–1969) had long promoted sex education and worked to change negative attitudes about sex, they now spoke up against "Dr. Sex," who had campaigned persistently in favor of the aesthetic and sensual life. Why would these cultural liberals suddenly speak out so harshly against a member of their group? In his study of Zhang Jingsheng's life and thought, Charles Leary (1994) points to the scientism of the three intellectuals, in contrast to what he sees as Zhang Jingsheng's aesthetic mission. Leary argues that the three critics simply failed to understand the basically aesthetic nature of Zhang's work, instead regarding him as a failed scientist. Hsiao-yen Peng (2002), however, disagrees with Leary's emphasis on the aesthetic and literary, instead bringing in Zhang's embedded commentary in *Sex Histories* to show that his approach is similar to that of early sexologists; in other words, like his critics Zhang Jingsheng also regarded himself as working within a framework of scientific rationality and enlightenment.[31] Yet we also can see, I argue, the critics' rejection of *Sex Histories* as a protest against the elevation of the personal experience of sexual desire above other kinds of experience and knowledge. In effect, Zhang Jingsheng's project—if not necessarily Zhang himself—took Freud's mandate to heart, asking that the respondents to the survey not only take stock of and report on their sexual behavior but also in the process reconceptualize themselves as primarily sexual beings. Like the Zhou brothers and Zhang Xichen, Zhang Jingsheng may have envisioned sexual liberation as meaningful mostly within the context of national liberation, eugenics, and social modernity—that is, within the enlightenment paradigm. Yet although he may not have tailored *Sex Histories* after Freudian sexual theory on purpose, it was in some respects a more authentically Freudian project than the psychological studies or even, in most cases, the literary experimentation of his contemporaries. Thus *Sex Histories* elicited a strong reaction from Zhang Xichen and the Zhou brothers, who rejected the far-reaching implications of Zhang's framing of sexual desire and behavior. I will focus on the quarrel between Zhang Jingsheng and Zhou Jianren, which most succinctly demonstrates the line that *Sex Histories* seems to have crossed.

What Charles Leary calls the anti-mysticism, pro-science position of Zhang Jingsheng's critics is the most obvious aspect of their critique. When we consider the educational context within which psychology had been framed over the last three decades, we can readily see that *Sex Histories* was also more autobiographical and personal than any earlier treatise claiming scientific credentials. The request to consider one's life from the beginning from the perspective of sexual desire, the autobiographical form or self-representation of one's sexual life, and the significant act of remembering and recounting all connect *Sex Histories* with the methods and goals of sexologists in general, and Freudian psychoanalysis in particular.[32] As Harry Oosterhuis (2000) relates it, in his case histories von Krafft-Ebing published the letters and autobiographies of his patients without censorship, and in psychoanalysis a sexual self was created and established through the telling of stories about the past (212). Von Krafft-Ebing used autobiographical material empirically, and these autobiographical case histories were "directed toward the discovery of one's authentic personal being"—in other words, toward constructing a sexual identity (215).

Although Zhang Jingsheng knew about Freud and even translated some of his work, my argument does not rely on this direct link.[33] Neither does it rely on Zhang's explicit positioning of his theories within the Freudian sexual sphere. As Liu Jihui (2004) and Hsiao-yen Peng (2002) have argued, Zhang Jingsheng and the Zhou brothers all generally worked within the familiar categories of national salvation and modernization.[34] By thinking about the implications behind *Sex Histories*, however, we can see that this work functioned quite differently from the articles on sex education written by Zhou Zuoren and Zhou Jianren. What Zhang Jingsheng did in *Sex Histories* was to take a general social interest previously enveloped within the institutions of education, medical practice, science, and literature, and demand that his respondents conceptualize their entire lives from this perspective. Because it encourages not just the presentation and discussion of sexual information but the construction of a sexual identity, *Sex Histories* is an exemplary Freudian document.

Zhou Jianren's (1926a) "A Few Words About *Sex Histories*," which appeared in the first issue of *In Common*, began the debate. Zhou's main point is that *Sex Histories* is "not a systematic, scientific work, but a few bits of data," which must be synthesized, interpreted, simplified, and organized by experts into basic principles to be intelligible to the population at large (114). The collection of data and its synthesis into principles for the average person are important, Zhou asserts, because reality is too complex to be understood by the non-scientist, who would be quickly overwhelmed. This claim on behalf of the scientifically trained intellectual goes a step further when Zhou adds the parenthetical comment that although data alone are not useful, the parts of *Sex Histories* that are "like description in novels" do not even count as data (114). He follows with a deeper critique of the novel-like structure of the book:

> As for the self-recounting of those sexual experiences, they almost all are unspecific [vague and general] narrative, and the parts about the various sex lives are all novelistic and emotional descriptions. This adds little to the explanation of sex, especially considering that the book's goal is to be reading material for the average adult. If one reads a scientific book, one's attention should be focused on its tendencies toward application, and that is also the case with scientific books about sex. So if the book ignores deep discussion and the scientific attitude, relying instead on emotional, novelistic descriptive styles, it will not give rise in the reader to the desire for knowledge, instead becoming merely a target for his enjoyment. (115)

Zhou goes on to elucidate scientific errors in the book, and ends by stating that the book's value is not in its scientific contribution, but perhaps has to do with the "art of love" (118).

What Zhou objects to in this revealing short article is the propriety of someone's regarding his or her self as sexually embodied and narrating the self in this way. Although *Sex Histories* is scientifically lacking in the information it provides, Zhou states, it also is based on emotion and is excessively novelistic. That an individual should speak out about his or her sexual experiences as if that recounting had any true meaning or relationship to reality does not, for Zhou, seem useful or revealing, nor does it expand scientific knowledge. Furthermore, it allows sexual behavior to veer dangerously close to the image of the old literati, with their leisure at brothels in the company of educated, poetry-writing prostitutes.

Zhang Jingsheng responds by insisting that this recounted, embodied sexuality be taken seriously. In "A Response to Mr. Zhou Jianren's 'A Few Words on *Sex Histories*,'" Zhang Jingsheng (1926a) calls Zhou Jianren's request for scientific results "exactly opposite what we are trying to do!" (434). This approach, Zhang argues,

> . . . is of a kind of abstract nature, a dry, boring summary that surely cannot give rise to "the average person's" interest. The material used in *Sex Histories* is very different from this, its purpose is to give the reader the interesting "data itself," allowing the reader to follow along, grasping and examining it. The reason it has become something today's readers like to read is that it does not rely on presenting sexual rules, such as the time period of women's sex desire, which is something that would interest the average scientist. (434–35)

The debate continues with Zhou Jianren's response, which even more revealingly illustrates his rejection of Zhang's subjectively experienced "sexuality." This time centering his comments on the issue of truth, Zhou argues:

> First, Mr. Zhang states that his objective is to infuse sexual knowledge through narration of the individual's sexual past, written in an interesting way. From beginning to end, I can't agree with this. I believe that it is fine for scientific writing to be interesting, but it doesn't matter if it isn't interesting as long as what is said is true. If it isn't true, even though it is interesting, it is useless. . . . If we go according to Zhang's method of asking people to understand sexual science, they must go and read each person's "sex history." China's population is 400 million, which means for one generation there must be 400 million records, and many more "sex histories" will come with the next generation. If Mr. Zhang feels that reading abstract scientific results is not as good as reading data, in the future Chinese people won't

> even have time to eat or sleep. . . . Second, Mr. Zhang believes that only by changing the word "unspecific" into "real," and "novelistic" into "literary," do we see the true situation. This is quite confusing. "Unspecific" is a modifier of "real," not its opposite. "Novelistic" means describing and narrating the way a situation is. Mr. Zhang believes this is not just an error, but also an exaggeration. So can he produce proof that what is recounted in *Sex Histories* is not unspecific [vague and general], and that the descriptions are not novelistic? (Zhou Jianren 1926b, 436–37)

The international context of national reputation also frames Zhou's comments, as he ends this short essay by commenting on how upset he feels when he hears Westerners mention the "pseudo-science" of China (440). The unscientific elevation of individual experience cannot, he argues, produce the real, nor is it in practical terms possible to grasp a reality produced through description of such experience. One should seek understanding not in the recounting of his or her experience, but in the voice of experts who have filtered and synthesized the impossibly complex reality. The debate continued with other participants throughout 1926 and 1927, and into the next two years. Zhang Jingsheng's work was eventually banned, and he was arrested in 1929 for "disseminating sex education, inciting youth" (Leary 1994, ii).

Like Gao Juefu, the Zhou brothers tended to disallow sexual absolutism and to distrust the truth-value of subjective experience. By taking the question of sexuality to the people, so to speak, and by asking for a personal recounting of each person's sexual past, *Sex Histories* put into practice two of Freud's most important concepts. Although the volume does not envision a "talking cure," it both highlights sexual desire and asks for a personal telling, coming a step closer to the sexually centered mentality imagined by Freud. Because *Sex Histories* ambitiously took the Freudian sexual imperative one giant step further, the very people who strongly supported sexual education and liberation ultimately rejected it. Whereas Gao Juefu was willing to consider many of Freud's theories, he too ultimately rejected Freud's pan-sexualism, shifting emphasis to the social sphere that is the result of sublimation. Later, as I have discussed, Gao became more critical of sublimation and also threw doubt on the need for the theory of the unconscious.

Both Gao Juefu's filtering of Freudian sexual theory and the criticism of *Sex Histories* represent critical points in the debate on psychological theories—that is, theories about the fundamental nature of mind and behavior.

These points reveal many things. Perhaps the ethos of national salvation was so great as to squash any approach that elevated personal experience over the value of the larger group, whose directives must always be visible. Such an interpretation would support Fredric Jameson's (1934–) much-criticized contention that all third world literature is national allegory (Jameson 1986).[35] Perhaps, as proponents of neo-Confucianism argue, the Confucian insistence on the group framework is a value that can and did stand up to an individualistic, self-centered Western model (Du 1989). Undoubtedly, the enlightenment paradigm placed subtle demands on new knowledge, which was almost always filtered through the lens of national improvement. However, I also read these two occurrences as markers indicating that we, as cultural readers, should not jump too readily to conclusions about how a powerful model of modernity was absorbed, remolded, or rejected, however obvious they might seem. First, Gao Juefu's efforts in understanding and selectively accepting or dismissing Freud's sexual theories, along with Zhou Jianren's spirited argument against the publication of *Sex Histories,* bespeak if not a totally open field, at least a lack of fixed or pre-determined meaning for sexual modernity in China. Second, the trajectory of Freudian theory in China, especially in the early 1920–27 period, when political positions were under heavy negotiation and ideological interpretations were flexible, could help us put into perspective the 20th century in the United States. From the viewpoint of the Chinese experience—and perhaps not only China—the American Freudian century appears as an extreme anomaly, a perverse confluence of conditions, beliefs, and historical development that may never be repeated. The reach of sexual modernity may be shorter than we imagined.

FREUD AND CHINESE LITERATURE

During the May Fourth period, many well-known writers knew about Freud and experimented with his ideas in their writing, creating characters with "abnormal" psychologies, unusually strong sex drives, "perversions" that often were sexual in nature and involved sex out of marriage, homosexuality, masturbation, incest, obsession, and a wildly active dream life. Depicting sexual desire and centering it as the primary motivator behind human behavior and thought turned out to be a slippery issue, however, and writing in a "modern" way about sexual desire and the unconscious presented writers with a web of treacherous links and possibilities. Although the depiction of sexual desire could be a strategy through which to critique traditional ideas of family and relationships, it also could push the fragilely modernizing Chinese society dangerously closer to an imagined bestiality associated with so-called primitive societies, and attributed by some non-Chinese critics to Chinese culture. Writing about sexual indulgence also ran the risk of invoking traditional practices such as arranged marriages, concubinage, and prostitution, as well as liaisons developed through, for instance, the opera, whose patrons were known for their sexual escapades with young male stars. If the new psychology demanded a sexually fertile unconscious, it had to be somehow distinguished from these discredited social habits of the past, and placed into characters whose minds and behavior were clearly different from these premodern sensibilities.

In an impressive study of the influence of Freudian ideas on 20th-century Chinese literature, Yin Hong (1994) argues that Freudian influence on May Fourth writers, whose work was heavily romantic, and on the modernists and New Perceptionists of the 1930s, was fairly strong until the League of Leftwing Writers gained power and "realism suppressed romanticism, themes of political revolution suppressed themes of enlightenment" (34). Yin Hong states: "We should say that in May Fourth romantic literature, most description of sex, sexual desire, sexual psychology, and sexual relationships, as well as the expression of various kinds of abnormal behaviors, sexual psychologies, and incestuous relations, the representation of dream illusions, movement of the conscious and unconscious, etc. actually all have myriad connections to the influence of Freudism" (43). At the same time, the emergence of sexual desire and behavior as a theme in May Fourth fiction is not only because of Freudian psychoanalysis, according to Yin, who believes that some writers' depictions had little relationship to Freud.[36] Yin Hong also describes the rationale behind Chinese writers' 20th-century interest in Freud as an interest in a dialogue with the West, a perspective that emphasizes the importance, for Chinese writers, of figuring out how to be modern:

> Of course, any historical interest is rooted in the passions of the time. As we "return to the origin" and reconsider the historical connections between Freudism and 20th century Chinese literature, we see that its most important significance is in its search for a dialogue with modern Western culture; its search for a way to develop the future of Chinese national literature in the broader global cultural and literary connections; its search for the direc-

> tion and road to literary modernity; and its search for understanding the possibilities for relationships between Freudism and contemporary literary thought, critique, and creation. (39)

Although the social, political, and philosophical transformations taking place during the May Fourth period far exceed the realm of Freudian theory or psychoanalysis, a novel sexual subjectivity was part of many literary experiments, and sexual issues were actively debated in intellectual journals. Within the overall racial improvement and nation-building effort implicit in eugenics, sexual modernity included profound changes in the position of women, transformations in the basic structure and meaning of marriage, modifications of the extended family with reference to the model offered by the nuclear family, changes in the structure and content of educational institutions, the entry of women into professions from which they were previously barred, and countless adjustments that influenced thought, behavior, and daily life, especially in urban areas and among the elite. The idea of sexual liberation and its initial fundamental demand—personal choice of a marriage partner unrestricted by family or social demands—is well developed in 1920s fiction. Except when it is a clear indication of old-fashioned literati decadence, a modern fictional character's claim on relative freedom in sexual life is usually a marker of distance from traditional culture. Although as Yin Hong (1994) states, it is certainly theoretically possible to write about sexual desire without the benefit of psychoanalytical theory, I am less convinced that the same holds true for the unconscious; without anchoring the unconscious and larger implications for subjectivity, Freud's sexual theories may not have been as radical as many others in circulation at the time, including women's participation in politics through voting and election (Barlow 2004).[37]

Although Freud did not explicitly promote sexual liberation, his weighting of sexual desire within the unconscious lent support to Chinese reformers who both promoted sexual freedom and regarded sexual liberation as a fundamental right. His emphasis on the sexual deeply within the unconscious demanded a novel subjectivity to anchor a new way of being, seeing, thinking, and feeling. Yin Hong also recognizes this situation:

> I feel that the most important influence of Freudism on May Fourth romantic writing is in its provision of a narrative technique and method to recognize and express the self, subjectivity, and individuality. Freudism did not alter but rather encouraged the romantic artistic search of Chinese

> writers. Whether in dreams or stream-of-consciousness, they expressed relatively less Western mysticism and symbolism; the romantic May Fourth writers did not hope to use the forms of anti-logic with which to construct subjectivity, but more precisely hoped to reconstruct the psychological essence of the human image in a deeper register. In this significant area, Freud allowed them to locate a method by which they could pierce through the deep roads of the mind and express the spiritual world. . . . For the writers of the new literature, Freud offered a new "modern" vision that brought human sexual life and sexual psychology into the vision of literature. . . . (1994, 65–66)

Although some traditional Chinese novels freely describe sexual desire and activity, there are significant differences between the sexual focus of May Fourth novels and traditional fiction such as *Jin Ping Mei*. Even in a novel so closely focused on sex, the idea that sexual desire is evil is a framework through which the characters and plot are constructed. The narrative perspective toward the central male character, Ximen Qing, is one of condemnation; in additional, we do not view sexual desire or intercourse from the perspective of Ximen Qing's mind, imagined as a deep and troubled wellspring. Furthermore, the overarching moral framework that characterizes traditional fiction is in full effect despite the salacious sexual content (Yin Hong 1994, 52–53). Freud, however, by linking sexual desire to an unconscious that cannot be readily accessed, proposed that sexual desire is a masked motivator lurking beneath and exerting its influence in ways the subject does not recognize.

Recently many scholars—Yin Hong (1994), Liu Jihui (2004), Wu Lichang (1987), Wang Ning (2002), Liu Jianmei (2003), and others—have tried to make sense of the theme and representation of sexual desire in May Fourth literature. I have made extensive use of Yin Hong's research, and I refer to Wu Lichang's work in the last part of this chapter. Wang Ning covers much of the same material and is less critical or comprehensive in his approach. Because the methodology and conclusions of both Liu Jihui and Liu Jianmei are almost directly opposite mine, I will discuss their work in some detail.

In her 2004 *Perverted Heart: The Psychic Forms of Modernity*, Liu Jihui charts interest in Freud in 1920s/1930s China and 1960s/1970s Taiwan in criticism and literature, as well as discussing a variety of cultural events, situations, and productions such as the art of the Taiwan bodily-horror photographer Chen Jieren (1960–); the relationship between the New Life Movement, the Society for Vigorous Practice (Lixing she), and the Blue Shirts Society (Lanyi she); Ye Lingfeng's (1905–75) artwork; the "self-alienation" of the Creation Society (Chuangzao she) with special emphasis on Guo Moruo (1892–1978); the two politically motivated 1930s films *The Mainland* (Dalu) and *Mood of the Nation* (Guofeng); utopian movements of the 1930s; and so on. Liu's theoretical basis lies in the work of Georges Bataille (1897–1962), whose 1943 *Inner Experience* (L'expérience intérieure, 1988 in English), 1957 *Eroticism* (L'Erotisme), and 1961 *The Tears of Eros* (Les larmes d'Éros, 1989 in English) sketch out a mystical aesthetics of sacrifice, physical revulsion, and bodily transgression. Bataille's aesthetics have influenced some of the biggest names in Western theory: Jacque Derrida, Philippe Sollers, and Michel Foucault. Figuring largely in Liu's study are Freud, Foucault, Jacques Lacan, Louis Althusser, and Julia Kristeva. She argues that not only the modern West but also China and Taiwan have experienced the alienation, fascist aesthetics, and totalitarian political control (along with revolutionary utopian thought and visions of the power of the masses) that characterized modernity (219).

Liu nonetheless chastises Chinese culture for refusing to engage fully with radical transformation in subjectivity. For Liu, Freudian psychic history is not merely one absolute aspect of modernity; rather, history itself must be investigated with a Freudian methodology that looks for hidden fragments, or symptoms that can reveal the psyche (xin), physicality or corporalization (shenti hua), and formation (xingshi hua) of the national culture. Whereas Yin Hong's research is largely historical, Liu Jihui's approach toward Freudian theory—in particular the unconscious and pansexualism—is to take it as a universal, real, and essential tool through which to identify and critique the most important intellectual trends of 20th-century culture in China, Taiwan, and the West.[38] On the one hand, Liu investigates the actual entry of Freudian ideas into China, tracing the popular intellectual idea of "spiritual / mental illness" at a national level and showing how writers and critics understood, accepted, and rejected various ideas. In this aspect of her research, Liu also works historically, showing how Freudian theory—often through the translation of scholars who wrote in Japanese or English—conveniently provided a vocabulary through which Chinese intellectuals could express their despair. Obviously, this language was attractive for other reasons as well, since we cannot assume that despair went unexpressed in earlier times. On the other hand, Liu normalizes the larger structure of psychoanalytical theory, regarding Freudian psychic mechanisms such as repression or resistance as natural and true, and as underlying, overarching, and universal symbolic principles.

Liu's research on the early entry of psychoanalytical theory into China supports my claim that a cultural bias against accepting without question Freud's pan-sexualism and his theory of the unconscious is one reason why his theories were not as influential as they could have been. However, for Liu, this rejection represents a massive national / cultural failure to recognize and unearth psychic, ontological, and epistemological truth at the national and cultural level:

> We should ask: during the phase of modernist literary movements in China and Taiwan, on what symbolic system, mechanism of identification, or structure of defense does the rejection of psychoanalytic "deep unconscious mechanistic function" rely? Or from what site does this rejection or repression depart from the immersion into desire, and to what site does it turn and devote itself? Perhaps we can consider the theory proposed by Chen Fuxing. Chen Fuxing believes that rejection of psychoanalysis is a kind of "ethnic discourse": "It reveals 'difference' and the 'rationality of the Other,' the 'violence of excluding the Other,' and so on." The rejection of psychoanalysis actually is related to the violent exclusion of the Other by ethnic opposites.
>
> Therefore if we continue with this theory, we will face the condition of refusing self-alienation in Chinese and Taiwanese modernity. The discourse of psychoanalysis developed in China and Taiwan could never accept concepts such as "the unconscious," "sexual desire," and so on, and used a utilitarian, practical way of translating the mechanism of "repression," illustrating the special pattern of this rejection. The violent exclusion of the "Other" in the process of Chinese and Taiwanese modernity is precisely a move that pushes away self-alienation, similar to the "*unheimliche*" (uncanny) and "the return of the repressed" that Freud explained. We can explain this phenomenon thus: through exposure to the "Other" inside, and through the recurring and extensive image of perversion that appears and reappears in modernist literature, the subject confronts the un-*heimliche*, un-*native alien* that frightens and elicits defense. It is through this external "illness" that the subject suddenly notices an internal attraction to "the obscene." The subject cannot bear this and therefore abruptly departs, turning and investing itself, while the "eyes turn another direction, not watching," taking an "*un-heimliche*" negating action. What the subject turns and invests itself into, then, is a concern with the completely healthy and pure, the normal, the familiar, the *native* place, the place of the home. The internal *enclave* of this *phobic structure* expands into every corner of the arteries and veins of culture and society, in various forms developing a tight system of defense. In the purges and revolutions in China of the mid and late 1920s, and the 1930s' move toward the war in the Pacific, or the way in which Taiwan was gradually isolated from international political links, the national body was threatened, making

> the acts of "repression," "denial," and "return home" even more necessary. The change of direction of late 1920s modern Chinese literature emerged from within this mechanism, as did the modernist-nativist debate of 1970s Taiwan. (156–57)[39]

In a way that resonates with my project, Liu Jihui studies the work of a number of critics and writers who worked with Freudian theory in the 1920s, and identifies the points of conflict and debate. Otherwise, our approaches could not be more different. Liu radically expands psychoanalytical theory, not evaluating it merely historically, or in terms of content, but ahistorically turning it into a methodology that will reveal the deep and universal structure of society. She completely accepts the existence not only of the sexually determined unconscious, but also of concepts such as "repression" and psychological "defense," transforming them into psychic mechanisms with vast implications for Chinese culture across national borders. By contrast, I regard the suspicion toward Freudian theory as well-justified, and as indicating the presence of ideas of the mind, social life, the body, and discourse that vary considerably from what Freud proposed. As I will show in my next chapter, in China these ideas developed into a model of the person within society that differed considerably from that proposed by Freud.

In her *Revolution Plus Love: Literary History, Women's Bodies, and Thematic Repetition in Twentieth-Century Chinese Literature*, Liu Jianmei (2003) purports to understand Freudian sexual theory as completely historical:

> However, we should regard the pervasive representation of the repressed individual, sexual repression, and the autonomous transformation of a repressive society as historical phenomena rather than omnipresent facts of existence, invoked by Freudian psychoanalytical theory. After the transformation from literary revolution to revolutionary literature, sexual relations became much more closely assimilated with social relations than during the previous historical periods. (15–16)

However, she also argues that Chinese revolutionary culture was built on the foundation of sexual desire, which it channeled into revolutionary passion—an omnipresent idea that I hope to counter in this study. For example, Liu chides the cultural critic Li Tuo for refusing to see that the "cultural destruction brought by revolution is not based on 'social rationalization' but on libido-charged revolutionary passion," and she regards the May Fourth quest for love and intimacy as "an unfinished project interrupted by the Maoist discourse" (7). From Liu's perspective, revolutionary romanticism is nothing more than "a positive romantic spirit that is able to mobilize and sublimate individual sexuality into the higher goal of political culture," and she invokes Herbert Marcuse's theories to support this viewpoint (22, 23). The Cultural Revolution "resulted from an aggrandizement of sexual instinct and sensuousness" that was "catastrophic for personal identity," Liu argues, and the "repression of personal feeling and sexuality corresponds to the myth of Mao's nation building" (23).

By contrast, Shu-mei Shih (2001) recognizes the implied universality of psychoanalysis, fingering it as a welcome theory for semi-colonized Chinese intellectuals, whose interest indicated their desire to become modern and cosmopolitan through alliance with Western ways of conceptualizing the mind. Yet although Shih's project is based on a thorough deconstruction of Eurocentric cultural universalism, she still invokes Freud's "anxiety neurosis" to explain the condition of the colonized: "Anxiety neurosis as a psychological condition resulting from sexual frustration parallels the condition of the colonized man, who occupies a feminine role because of colonial domination" (137–38). Freud's definition of melancholia works perfectly, Shih argues, to show how the West has become the object of desire, transforming itself into a psychological category in a way that "the landscape of the self's libido becomes structured in its image" (139–40).

Although Shu-mei Shih implies that in some cases, at least, Freud succeeded in locating and describing universal mental functions, in general she is critical of the implied and invasive universality of psychoanalytical categories and psychology and / or psychoanalysis as a way of conceptualizing the mind. By contrast, Liu Jianmei's approach to analyzing the representations and discourses of revolution and sexual desire is almost directly opposite to mine. Her viewpoint, along with that of Liu Jihui, recognizes the 20th-century power of sexual modernity, or the privileging of sexual desire and behavior within identity and culture. In addition, however, her analysis naturalizes this historical development, interpreting all desire as fundamentally sexual. This perspective is also adopted by Ban Wang (1997), who argues—accurately, in my opinion—that "in a way Communist culture courts exuberant passions rather than rejects them" (123). For Wang, however, these exuberant passions are the "recycling of the individual's libidinal energy for revolutionary purposes," a politico-libidinal act through which "politics . . . assumes sexual connotations" (124). The emotion invested in the desires and behaviors associated with revolutionary culture and society is, according to Wang, merely sublimated sexual desire that is based in the "pure biological needs" illustrated by the sucking infant who derives more pleasure from "fantasizing over the finger, a substitute for the mother's breast, than from physical contact with it" (134). The "deep psychic roots of Communist culture" can be understood, then, as long as one recognizes "sexuality in the guise of politics" (134). Wang deserves credit for recognizing the importance of emotion and passion in the ideal revolutionary subject. Even so, interpreting this emotion and passion as at root libidinal disregards the extensive conceptual and theoretical development of revolutionary emotion over 20th-century China, participates in a pervasive and unwarranted privileging of sexual modernity—especially in its identity-building components—as universal and ubiquitous, and, most important, fails to adequately recognize or interpret the complexities of revolutionary subjectivity. This is the topic of my next chapter.

CHINESE WRITERS AND FREUDIAN THEORY

Lu Xun, the most famous of the May Fourth writers, knew about Freud and at least to some extent made use of Freudian theories in his fiction, although Lu Xun balanced subjectivity and social justice, sexual liberation and decadence. In his 1922 collection *Buzhou Mountain* (Buzhou shan), Lu Xun noted that he "adopted Freudian theories to explain the origins of creativity—of humans and literature"; the story "Mending the Sky" (Butian) shows his experimentation with Freudian sexual theory (Yin Hong 1994, 30; Wu Lichang 1987, 145–46, 156–65). In 1924 Lu Xun published his translation of Kuriyagawa Hakuson's (1880–1923) *Symbols of Anguish* (Kumen de xiangwei), which introduced Freud (Tsau 2001; Liu Jianmei 2003, 15–16; Shih 2001, 66–68). Although Kuriyagawa directly criticized Freudian sexual theories and Lu Xun remarked favorably on this position, the Chinese author did not reject off-hand ideas such as sublimation or repression. Despite the fact that Kuriyagawa was not well known in Japan, he became famous in China among intellectuals and writers, and Lu Xun's translation of *Symbols of Anguish* was reprinted twelve times between 1925 and 1935 (Wu Lichang 1987, 158–59; Liu Jihui 2004, 125–26).[40]

Despite his interest in Freudian sexual theories, Lu Xun clearly recognized the risk of confusing the modern sexually obsessed character with the corrupt, pleasure-seeking literati of the past, a stock character thoroughly repudiated in May Fourth iconoclasm and often mocked in his stories. In his 1924 story "Soap" (Feizao), which came out in the same year that he translated Kuriyagawa's book, he creates a damning portrayal of a Confucian gentleman whose apparent concern for the well-being of a young beggar girl masks his desire to turn her into a sexual plaything (Carolyn Brown 1988b).[41] The bar of soap Siming gives to his wife embodies his subliminal desire and becomes a symbol that is both literally and figuratively slippery. While "Soap" indicates that Lu Xun toyed with the centering of sexual desire and with Freudian ideas of the unconscious, his positioning of sexual desire in the body of an old-fashioned hypocritical Confucian scholar rather than a modern, forward-looking youth suggests his skepticism about deploying Freudian sexual theories as foundational or emancipatory. Under Lu Xun's pen, the masking function inherent in the idea of the unconscious becomes a form of corruption and debasement related more to social class and situation than to any underlying psychological motivation. If "Soap" can be a guide, Lu Xun associated the expression of sexual obsession with the traditional past; he also worried about the connection between reproductive desire and racist critiques of the Chinese as animal-like, a fear that would or could not be allayed through adherence to psychoanalytic theory.[42] This fear was shared by Lu Xun's brothers Zhou Jianren and Zhou Zuoren, who, as I have discussed, criticized Zhang Jingsheng for his positive invocation of traditional Chinese sex practices. Lu Xun argued against Yasuoka Hideo's 1926 description of Chinese people as sex-loving, lustful, or lascivious (haose) and therefore barbaric.[43] Although he did not completely reject either the theory of the unconscious or the existence of the sex drive, and some of his most famous stories turn on the significance of psychological mechanisms, ultimately Lu Xun's fiction depicts a world in which poverty, hunger, and other social factors are much more important than sexual desire in determining human behavior; the anguish to which Kuriyagawa Hakuson refers comes more from unfavorable social conditions than from repressed sexual desire.

In their early work, Creation Society members Guo Moruo, Yu Dafu (1896–1945), and others often wrote stories that featured characters with profound sexual repression and mysterious unconscious motivation. They also expanded the importance of subjectivity and psychology by bringing out a character's motivations and thought processes. For example, in a 1921 essay on the classical tale "Story of the Western Wing" (Xixiang ji), Guo experimented with Freud's pan-sexualism, placing sexual repression at the center of the characters' motivation; he also argued that the power of his famous story "Late Spring" (Canchun) comes not from its description of events, but of what was in the characters' minds (Wu Lichang 1987, 167–71; Shih 2001, 96–109). Guo was interested in the idea of "sweeping out the chimney" promoted by Josef Breuer (who used the metaphor to indicate the curing process in psychoanalysis) not only as a technique for literary criticism but also as a revolutionary strategy that could encourage the nation to spit out its weakness and despair. Liu Jihui argues that Guo's role in the Creation Society and transformation from decadent individualism to a focus on revolution, society, and the collective link him closely with evolving Chinese cultural modernity, and from his approach we can see the underlying structure that motivates debate and social change at the time. Guo's conceptual model was always repression-liberation, Liu claims, and he transformed this dyad from a personal metamorphosis into a form of social awakening and revolution (Liu Jihui 2004, 140, 172–73, 193–200). Because Liu Jihui criticizes the Chinese cultural propensity to reject psychoanalysis and a focus on sexuality in favor of a social or national context, she mentions Guo Moruo as yet another example of this trend. From my perspective, however, Guo's inclination to direct the reader beyond an isolated subjectivity toward the national or social issues shows a fundamental rejection of the basic tenets of Freudian theory, a rejection that became more pronounced under late 1920s political influences.

Yu Dafu claimed that the most powerful, dangerous, and important emotion of inner life was the sex drive, and he often created characters suffering from the inability to reach sexual satisfaction. The main character of his 1921 story "Sinking" (Chenlun), which "shocked the world," is a young Chinese student studying in Japan, tormented by the sexual desire he experiences when around Japanese women and when alone (Wu Lichang 1987, 49, 190). However, even in this tale of heightened sexual angst, the student blames his suffering on the weakness of the Chinese nation. Ding Ling's (1904–86) famous 1927 novella *Sophia's Diary* (Shafei nüshi de riji), with its sexually tormented main character, attracted special attention at the time (Barlow 2004; Kubin 1982; Liu Jianmei 2003, 18). Other writers such as Zhang Ziping (1893–1959), Ye Lingfeng (1904–75), and Zheng Boqi (1895–1979) wrote stories featuring sexual repression, taboos, and homosexuality. In 1928 the journal *Huanzhou*, edited by Zheng Boqi and Pan Hannian (1906–77) put out a special issue entitled "On the Spirit and the Flesh" (Ling rou hao) in which Pan, under the penname Ye Ling, wrote "Our Concepts on Sexual Love" (Women de xing'ai guannian), arguing that social life emerged from the need for sexual intercourse.[44]

With their "art for art's sake" theory, members of the Creation Society were more likely than others to make use of psychoanalytical theory in their fiction, but the lack of social factors motivating human behavior in Freud's theories did not impress members of the Literary Research Society, which emphasized "art for life's sake." Some, such as Zhou Zuoren and Xu Jie (1901–93), used Freudian sexual theory in their work nonetheless. Zhou Zuoren credited Havelock Ellis (1859–1937) with influencing his early thought; while he did not refer to Freud often, he praised Freud for his development of useful ideas in child psychology. Wu Lichang (1987) argues that though Zhou believed the idea that "the higher social civilization goes, the broader sexual morality and the healthier sex life will be," was a daydream, Zhou's emphasis on sexual education and use of Ellis's theories to attack traditional morality indicates his debt to Freudian psychoanalysis. Xu Jie, whose fiction generally featured rural life, tended toward decadence when he wrote about urban youth, according to a critique by Mao Dun; with his friend Wang Yiren (1908–33), Xu Jie admired the work of Creationists such as Yu Dafu, and the Freudian theories of repression, dream analysis, and sublimation (Wu Lichang 1987, 184–93). Even controversial ideas such as sexual desire in children found expression in May Fourth literature, in the writing of Guo Moruo, Chen Xianghong (1901–69), and Tao Jingsun (1897–1952). Freudian dream theory appeared in Guo Moruo's writing, as well as in stories by Xiang Peiliang (1905–61), Ye Lingfeng, Xu Qinwen (1897–1984), Yu Dafu, Xu Jie, and others. Stream-of-consciousness, a modernist technique, was used in writing by Wang Yiren, Lin Ruji (1902–76), and Lü Yin (1899–1934) (Yin Hong 1994, 51, 61–65).

In the late 1920s and 1930s fiction of the New Perceptionists (Xin ganjue pai), which was modeled after that of its forerunners in Japan, Freudian sexual theory often appeared, especially in the work of Shi Zhecun (1905–2004). Through his journal *The New Art and Literature* (Xin wenyi) and publications out of the Shuimo ("froth") Bookstore, Liu Naou (1900–1940) introduced the work of the Japanese New Perceptionists and the writing of Chinese New Perceptionists, including his own work and that of Mu Shiying (1912–40) and Shi Zhecun. These authors used the modernist aesthetic method, which formed the core of publications in the 1932–35 journal *The Modern* (Xiandai). Much of this work showed interest in the Freudian ideas of the dream wish, the unconscious, and especially the sex drive; and produced works with an emphasis on the bizarrely erotic that was unprecedented in modern Chinese literature. Although a discussion by characters in Mu Shiying's story "Pierrot" (original title in French) about Freud and sexual desire shows that the author was familiar with Freudian sexual theory, he did not use this theory as a foundation for his writing as much as did Shi Zhecun, who became strongly interested in Freud in the late 1920s and purposely deployed Freudian theories of sexual desire, dream wish fulfillment, and the unconscious in his stories (Wu Lichang 1987, 195–98; Shih 2001, 302–39).

Wu Lichang (1987) analyzes three themes in Shi Zhecun's writing that relate to psychoanalysis: the conflict between flesh and spirit, dreams as erotic wish fulfillment, and abnormal sexual desire (201–18). Yet Wu insists

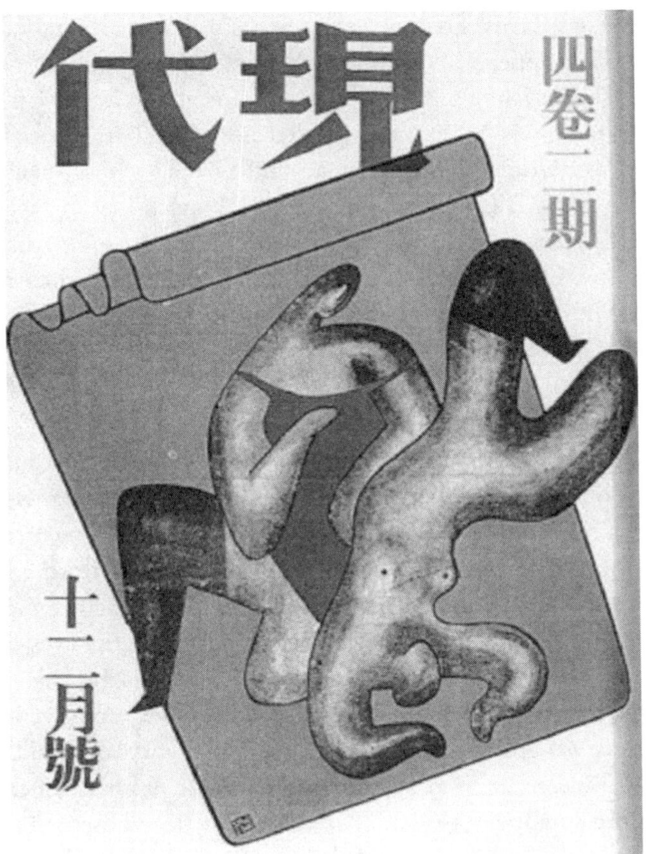

FIGURE 2. *The Modern* (Xiandai) cover, 4:2:12 (1931).

that even in the story that best expresses the Freudian claim of motivating sexual desire—Shi's "Spring Sun" (Chunyang)—the author did not repudiate the importance of social environment. Yin Hong (1994) goes further, arguing that because Chinese society had not sufficiently modernized in the 1930s, the experimentalists of that time made use of modernist techniques only superficially, diluting their vision with realist works published concurrently (81). Although Shi Zhecun and others looked to Freudian theory for support for their literary experiments, some argue that the realist connection between observed life and writing was nonetheless basically respected—a position that would be difficult to defend in the case of all stories by Shi (Yin Hong 1994, 82–83).[45] Neither is a long-standing, fully developed modernist literary aesthetic sustained through their writing. Especially in the case of Shi Zhecun (and also Li Jinming), who desired to query the unconscious, Freudian ideas of abnormal psychology and sexual repression often appear, but fictional characters do not exhibit psychological depth, and psychological probing remains at the level of phenomena (Yin Hong 1994, 94–99).[46] Although traces of Freudian theories are present in works of writers of the late 1930s and 1940s such as Shen Congwen (1902–88), Zhang Ailing (1920–95), Qian Zhongshu (1910–99), Lu Ling (1921–94), Li Jianwu (1906–82), and Xiao Qian (1910–99), Zhang Ailing shows the most serious engagement with Freudian ideas before the late 1970s and 1980s, when Freud fever broke out.

This brief literary survey indicates two things. First, Freudian sexual theory offered a profoundly new way of imagining human life that attracted a great deal of interest among writers. Every aspect of the newly imagined sexual being became grist for literary experiment, interacting with and playing off the widespread and significant social change informed by the ideas and concepts of sexual modernity. Because it centered sexual desire within a hidden unconscious, Freudian theory offered a novel way of thinking about the body, mind, and "spirit," dangling the promise of a radically modern subjectivity and way of being before the eyes of the new writers. Second, although the prospects tendered in Freud's deeply sexual modern person were taken seriously and considered, disagreements, recognized or unrecognized, with some of the basic tenets of Freud's thought prevented Chinese writers from fully realizing the promise inherent in his work. Failing to appear are fictional characters like those of D. H. Lawrence (1885–1930), who are saturated with sexual desire and derive almost every imaginable meaning from that desire. Yet I view this "failure" as extremely promising. From Lu Xun's lustful, poetic Confucians to Yu Dafu's references to national weakness, from the failure of Ding Ling's Sophia to embody and project the delights of sexual liberation to Shi Zhecun's superficial psychological probing, from Guo Moruo's transformation of psychological theory into national metaphor to a general awkwardness about expressing sexual desire—even before the political demands of Marxism branded psychoanalysis as idealist and bourgeois, Chinese writers working in the 1920s and 1930s were unwilling to completely accept the fully sexualized, fully psychologized person as the only way to be modern.

FREUD FEVER

Freud's theories were increasingly criticized in the 1930s and 1940s and were eventually totally repudiated in the 1950s, when Freud's and other "bourgeois" branches of psychology were replaced by a Soviet-based system. I will discuss this development in Chapter Three. Before going on, however, I should note the "Freud fever" that broke out in the 1980s, when interest in Freud's work reached a high point and many articles and translations were published. Yin Hong (1994) regards it from a broad perspective: "Without the influence of modern Western philosophy, aesthetics, psychology, ethics, literature, and art, the scope, nature, and appearance of today's contemporary Chinese literature is unimaginable" (113).[47] Freud's work became quite influential in literature and literary studies, providing new ways of thinking about aesthetics, ethics, and representation. Although Yin Hong may be overly adulatory in saying that Freud and other psychological theorists—Carl Jung (1875–1961), Alfred Adler (1870–1937), Herbert Marcuse (1898–1979), Karen Horney (1885–1982), Erich Fromm (1900–1980), and Jacques Lacan (1901–81)—"liberated" Chinese thinking from the revolutionary "dark period of cultural ignorance," he is accurate when he describes the deep influence of these thinkers from the mid-1970s to the mid-1990s (114). Yin does not accept the protestations of writers such as Wang Anyi who claimed they had never read Freud, arguing that the influence of his ideas was so widespread and profound as to be unavoidable (116; 121–23; 136).

While my project works within the framework of the two discourses of Freudian and revolutionary mentality and therefore includes discussion only of cultural works that combine these two trends, many examples of a more single-minded focus exist. On the side of revolution, the late 1970s and the early 1980s are full of stories that criticized various aspects of society while continuing to hold dear many of the cherished notions of revolutionary culture. The fiction and poetry of Zhang Jie (1937–), Wang Meng (1934–), Shen Rong (1936–), Bai Hua (1930–), Ai Qing (1910–96), and many others made use of the themes, styles, and language of the socialist period. While implying that socialist society did not live up to its egalitarian goals, they often expressed continued hope for what once would have been called "social rectification." On the other end of the scale, younger experimental writers such as Yu Hua (1960–), Can Xue (1953–), Mo Yan (1956–), Ma Yuan (1953–), Liu Suola (1955–), Hong Feng (1957–), Su Tong (1963–), and Ge Fei (1964–) picked up the new consciousness and subjectivity rapidly, peppering their writing with unconscious motivation, repression, dream theory, sexual love, perversion, and illogic. The entire experimental movement could hardly have existed without the influence of the new interest in Western psychological theories and the translation of literature by Franz Kafka, argues Yin Hong (1994, 116–23). Popular also were magical realists such as Gabriel Garcia Marquez and Jorge Luis Borges.

Cultural researchers, too, participated in Freud fever, with famous scholars such as Qian Zhongshu and Yue Daiyun (1931–) publishing on Freud, and others seeking ways to find ways of thinking in traditional Chinese culture that fit with Freud's ideas. The basic approaches in this effort were, first, to find ways in which art and literature emerged from the unconscious, and, second, to recognize art and literature as expressing unconscious motivation through symbolic processes. Although there was theoretical interest in the sex drive, often scholars were more interested in the unconscious or the nature of the mind. Li Zehou's (1930–) much-studied work on subjectivity was one indication of the attention bestowed on the mind or mental functions, which were investigated at least in part to explain Chinese ways of thinking that had produced the Cultural Revolution and authoritarianism in general. Li blamed the lack of a dualistic mind-matter concept, for example, and the corresponding emphasis on harmony between nature and humans within traditional Chinese philosophy for China's failure to develop science and technology, which demand the conquest of nature. By contrast, because it had no ontological opposition between mind and matter, Chinese philosophy placed great emphasis on the ability of the exceptional man to transform the world, leading to the voluntaristic approach characteristic of Mao Zedong (1893–1976) (Woei Lien Chong 2002).

As Yin Hong points out, the energetic surge of interest in the unconscious almost immediately produced a backlash criticizing it as overemphasis and demanding that equal attention be given to the functions of the conscious mind (1994, 173–79). Studies in psychology also started to change during this time. Scholars whose careers began before 1949, such as Gao Juefu and Yang Xinhui (1935–), began to publish widely, and compilations of their earlier work began to appear. Psychological perspectives that had been abandoned in the 1950s came into vogue again, and traditional ideas about the mind were studied from these "new" vantage points. Rather than spanning the entire spectrum of psychological thought, this reconstruction of the field included but was by no means limited to studies of Freudian theory (Yang Xinhui 2002).

The Freud fever of the post-Mao period is a significant immediate environment for the writers whose work I analyze in the second half of this book. Even more important, it speaks to the powerful influence of psychological and sexual modernity as it was conceived, expanded, and established in the West. Despite decades of revolutionary disavowal, the models of modern subjectivity provided through literature and theory as developed in the West do not seem to have lost their allure. In their consistent revision of the revolutionary past through representation of sexual desire, the novels and films of post-Mao writers and directors illustrate this attraction. Yet we also must consider what effects the long discourse of revolutionary consciousness had on the understanding and experience of subjectivity in the post-Mao period. This revolutionary discourse, with its own theories of the mind—fully articulated discursively and through extensive daily practice—must be fully understood if we are to recognize and appreciate the aesthetic and thematic contributions of these writers. Just as ignoring the earlier entry into China of the new psychology and Freudian sexual theory will not give us a comprehensive picture of either theories of the mind or of sexual desire in modern China, so jumping from the early 20th century to the post-Mao period as if revolutionary culture left no mark will erase from view important themes and aesthetic strategies. In the next chapter, I turn to this revolutionary discourse, which has been highly influential in developing distinctive and effective ways of thinking about the mind, emotions, and spirit.

THREE

Revolutionary Discourse and the Spirit

From Ah Q to Lei Feng

Lu Xun's 1921 novella *The True Story of Ah Q* (A Q zhengzhuan) gained lasting fame through its portrayal of Ah Q, a day laborer who lives as a squatter in a room of an unused temple. Ah Q's "method of spiritual victory" (jingshen shengli fa), which he puts into play whenever he is beaten or bested, became a key term denoting an unsavory aspect of the Chinese character. In the story every nuance of social life comes to life under Lu Xun's critical pen, but at the basis of the most satiric scenes lies the relationship between the powerful and the powerless, and its accompanying self-positioning or jockeying for power. Whether it is Ah Q fighting with the also-powerless Xiao D, in his encounters with the better educated and wealthier village leaders, with the police, judiciary, and military, with religious institutions, or in his imagined role as a revolutionary, spiritual victory indicates a deception of the self in the power struggles that make up social relations. The many references to foreigners, foreign learning, and foreign customs, coupled with the setting of revolutionary political and cultural change, imply that the author is not simply speaking of one person's defects. His critique—which centers on Ah Q but is relevant for every person in the story—situates China within a global context, taking aim at those who continue to proclaim the superiority of Chinese culture in the face of multiple defeats on many fronts.

The "spiritual" value around which Lu Xun develops the plot is, I argue, positionality essentialized as a profound and ubiquitous quality. In Ah Q's case, whether the quality is indispensable to the so-called Chinese character or simply attached to anyone functioning under the semi-colonial conditions of the times, and whether it is temporary or long-lasting has been an ongoing topic of debate.[1] Like personhood (renge), this quality refers to mental traits that transcend individual differences; however, whereas personhood can exist or not exist (as in the example of Chinese women, who were thought to have been denied personhood by traditional culture), this spiritual quality has a far greater normative range. By coining the term "spiritual victory method" to point to the subjective understanding and expression of loss of national and personal power, Lu Xun establishes *spirit* as a key translational point that interpolates between the person, power at large, and power as it exists in various social actors. In the case of Ah Q, spirit also becomes that point abstracted as a quality, a representation with far-reaching effects across the 20th century. Lu Xun's imaginative construction of spirit in Ah Q defines it as an intersection for multiple transecting meanings related to position and power. Probably the most famous, widely discussed, and important of 20th-century Chinese literary texts, *The True Story of Ah Q* in particular captures the centering of spirit as a crucial point of negotiation between the person and the state, one of the many spheres of transaction for the fictional character Ah Q.

In this chapter, I analyze the Chinese discourse of revolutionary spirit, arguing that this 20th-century focus set up a mentality that differed radically from that of the Freudian subject, with its deeply sexualized unconscious. In terms of the structure of the mind, however, the person with a revolutionary spiritual core was in some ways similar to the Freudian subject. Like the unconscious, the spirit-as-node was deeply situated within the mind and had significant intellectual and emotional implications. Just as the unconscious demanded a never-ending effort to uncover its secrets, the spirit also required constant self-critique and a push for greater awareness. Both the sexualized unconscious and the revolutionary spirit anchor comprehensive systems that imply normative attitudes, reactions, and behaviors, and both are enacted through cultural institutions and strategies developed to bring the errant into line through example, persuasion, and coercion. When the theory of the sexualized unconscious mind is normalized in cultural thought and behavior, its extreme application or abuse is endless psychotherapy, obsession with sexual relationships and "identity," and the recovery of memories—frequently of sexual abuse, but also of other traumatic experiences—that may or may not be linked to anything that actually happened.[2] When the theory of the spiritual core is normalized in cultural thought and behavior, its extreme application or abuse is endless self-criticism—which may or may not be accepted by the authorities—and the imprisonment of those who do not sufficiently recognize their bad attitude or lack of spiritual awareness. The importance of the proper spirit—that is to say, of appropriate positioning of the self in relation to power—has implications for many aspects of mental life, from the emotional to the intellectual, the "individual" to the social.

To argue that existence revolves around social relations, or the positioning of the self in regard to those with power, may not appear to tell us much new about a society with Confucian roots. The revolutionary emphasis on spirit is certainly a theory of sociality concerned with relationships and their necessary outward expression of proper position. Yet by envisaging the negotiations as a quality that can inspire the most fiery, explosive emotions as well as the most pedestrian, drudge-like loyalty, this emphasis also theorizes an abstract essence that extends from the core to the exterior, is intellectual as well as emotional, and is both deeply felt and sincerely expressed. Revolutionary spirit could be a tremendous source of inspiration, a tool of self-knowledge, and a guide on how to live one's daily life. It also could be a rationale for violence, a stick to hold over someone's head, or a reason to despair of life and opt for suicide. I hope to show, however, that as a point of mediation between the self and power or those in power, revolutionary spirit occupies a position of importance within the mind that is every bit as crucial as the position of the sexualized unconscious for the Freudian subject.

One reason, therefore, that the character Ah Q became such a potent, productive icon is that it captured and expressed the crucial mental pivot point of relational power, linking it to or translating it into questions of class, gender, language, revolution, and national sovereignty. As we know, Lu Xun experimented with psychoanalysis and Freudian theory, and in this story he manages to have it both ways: a psychological mechanism is at the heart of the tale, but its tentacles stretch not inward, toward hidden unconscious desire, but rather outward, toward Ah Q's arbitration with those around him. Although Ah Q is attracted to the Zhao family servant Wu Ma and torments the young nuns with sexual taunts, these scenes are in no way separated out from the other scenes of the story; nor are they granted any overarching interpretive function. Sexual desire is seen as simply one aspect of human life, and it unfolds strongly located within the social environment.

By the late 1920s, as the May Fourth period waned, critics began to object to Ah Q's cowed image:

> No matter how much Lu Xun writes, no matter how much some readers worship Lu Xun, no matter how stylish and biting his words are, in the final analysis, Lu Xun is simply not representative of this era. The ideas in his works cannot represent this decade of Chinese literary thought. . . . *The True Story of Ah Q* hides within it the sick national character of the past, and this is worthy of our consideration. . . . [But] first, the peasants of today are not as immature as those of Ah Q's time. Most of them are part of well-functioning organizations and have a good understanding of politics. Second, the revolutionary nature of Chinese peasants already has thoroughly been expressed. They oppose landlords, participate in revolution . . . and revolt, certainly without the spirit of cowing before the aristocracy like Ah Q. Third, Chinese peasants have more knowledge than did the peasants of Ah Q's time. They don't scurry about like uncomprehending insects as Ah Q did, they have purpose and goals, they don't just spout off angrily, but rather [work] for political struggle. . . . These are revolutionary times that can be expressed only by writers who possess an exuberant, thunderous revolutionary spirit. Only writers who burn with sincere and earnest emotion, have an intimate understanding of politics, and stand at the front of revolution can express it! The techniques of *The True Story of Ah Q* simply cannot do it! The era of Ah Q has long been dead and gone! We need no longer suffer from it beguiled, let us bury Ah Q's skeleton and spirit, let us bury Ah Q's skeleton and spirit! (Qian Xingcun 1993, 81)

However, the revolutionary years did not provide a satisfying answer to the questions posed by *The True Story of Ah Q*, and Ah Q's skeleton and spirit survived, taking center stage as over the 20th century, article after article and book after book came out about Lu Xun and this novella. *The True Story of Ah Q* was repeatedly made into films and plays and taught in university classes across the country, attracting the attention of successive generations of intellectuals and students. It was discussed and dissected in journals, magazines, and newspaper articles, becoming a literary and cultural phenomenon. Withstanding many attempts to declare the character Ah Q—weak of mind and yet devious enough to forge for himself a method of spiritual victory—dead, gone, and useless, the story continued to capture interest over the course of the century (Davies 1991; Foster 2006; Kuoshu 1999; Junhua Lu 1981; M. Huang 1990).[3]

In general terms, Lu Xun was interested in matters of the spirit, especially in his early work. One of his earliest articles from 1908, "On the Power of Mara Poetry" (Maluo shi lishuo), asks of China "Where are the warriors of the spirit?" and his 1922 preface to *Call to Arms* (Nahan) proclaims that nothing is more important than changing the spirit of the people. Interested in thinkers such as Nietzsche and Kierkegaard, Lu Xun was an insistent voice on behalf of spiritual renewal (Huters 2005, 252–74; Mills 1977). Although his thinking changed over time, his initial intellectual attempts privilege subjectivity, elevating it over any material transformation (Huters 2005, 255–56). Most of his stories express an intricately woven environment in which subjectivity, the physical, the material, and the social interact in a complex way, altering and redefining their relationships moment-by-moment.[4]

I have made use of *The True Story of Ah Q* to initiate this chapter because it so succinctly illustrates the important role of spirit in forging the revolutionary mind. Ah Q surely lacks the proper spirit, but, crucially, he well understands the vital position that spirit occupies. Ah Q's spiritual deficiency comes to stand in for the failure of the nation and its people, expressing in one fictional character an idea that is henceforth concrete, full of interest, easy to represent in writing and image, and eminently deployable in polemical conversation. Mao Zedong's canonization of Lu Xun, who from the grave stubbornly refused to accompany his colleagues in their free fall from power over the 1950s and during the Cultural Revolution, assured the author's place in the pantheon of revolutionary writers. Yet as Paul B. Foster's ambitious study clearly documents, official deference alone cannot account for Ah Q's seemingly perpetual ability to fascinate. And though Lu Xun may have most pithily captured and expressed the idea of spirit, he was not alone in finding it to be a noteworthy topic. A brief glance at the many notions of spirit circulating in the late Qing and early Republic reveals a field rife with competing ways of thinking about the mind. The Freudian unconscious was merely one of many early 20th century ideas about the mentality, spirit, psyche, and soul that circulated among intellectuals and evolved into a focus on a mental quality that was very different from what Freud proposed.

MIND AND SPIRIT IN TRADITIONAL, LATE QING, AND EARLY REPUBLICAN CHINESE CULTURE

The mind / heart, or *xin*, was an important concept in Confucian philosophy, which also emphasized the position of human beings within the social order. The "belief that the social order is embedded in the cosmic order"—an idea that lent a transcendent quality to the philosophy—was also significant, although there is a great deal of debate about the relative weight of these concepts in any one philosopher's work or at any given time (Hao Chang 1993, 11).[5] Generally, Confucianism required that human beings improve themselves through effort, or self-cultivation, thereby contributing to the improvement of the social order. Moral / spiritual qualities such as faith in an inner essence and the sense that all people were cosmically united in harmony with the natural world lay behind this Confucian directive toward self-improvement.

From the Song dynasty (960–1279) on, the relationship between the heart / mind and the social order was often at the center of philosophical writing. The neo-Confucian thinker Zhang Zai (1020–70) argued that the heart / mind could realize two kinds of knowledge, sense perception and moral-spiritual intuitive knowledge, although the "mystic oneness" that could be achieved also was generally expressed in the form of an ideal social order (Hao Chang 1993, 14–15). For Zhu Xi (1130–1200), self-cultivation had a strong spiritual component in Confucian moral education, even though its ultimate goal was improvement within the social world. Importantly, the various aspects of cultivation of the heart / mind were ontological rather than psychological. Thus, according to Hao Chang, "*xin* serves as an essential link between heaven and the individual person, a sort of sensorium of transcendence in the individual self" that resulted in an "order of the soul" (16–17).[6] Another way of describing *xin,* under the Confucianism of Song philosophical giants Cheng Yi (1033–1107), Cheng Hao (1032–1085), and Zhu Xi, is as "the operation of the subjective consciousness, or the location where the operation of the subjective consciousness takes place" ("Wang Yangming [1472–1529 CE]"). Wang Yangming, who used the term "substance of the mind / heart" (xinti), increased the transcendence inherent in the heart / mind and the process of self cultivation and crafted a distinction between the heart / mind in itself and the human heart / mind, lending the concept of *xin* greater abstraction. Yet Wang's seminal concept of the unity of knowledge and action (zhixing heyi) implied that knowledge should not be conceptualized separately from its expression in action. Li Zhi (1527–1602) heightened the possibility of transcendence and the autonomy of the heart / mind even further. The Cheng-Zhu Neo-Confucians fought an ongoing battle with followers of Wang Yangming because they feared excessive concern with inner or personal cultivation and lack of interest in political service (Bol 2003, 38; Ivanhoe 1990).

In addition to the philosophical discourse of *xin*, other spheres also contained their own spiritual or quasi-spiritual concepts. Confucius asked for respect for ghosts, but insisted that they be kept at a distance. Confucian scholars often had a tense relationship with Daoist and Buddhist spiritualism, philosophy, and practice, although at different times these traditions exerted influence on Confucian ideas. Shaman (wu) subculture was strongly rejected by neo-Confucians, with Zhu Xi denouncing spirit mediums as socially destructive. Although cults of spirit mediums existed even in urban areas with populations of scholars, those who had commerce with spirit mediums were widely criticized in Ming and Qing publications. Especially during the Qing dynasty, popular religion's fascination with spirit mediums was attacked for its tendency to contribute to the confusion of social categories, which Confucians despised. Even so, in their most extreme examples, concepts such as filial piety also expressed an element of magic, for example when the devotion of a son or daughter and his or her self-mutilation on behalf of an ill parent could produce a cure (Sutton 2000).

Madness, another area in which the mind was imagined, theorized, and addressed, was generally called *dian* or *kuang* in the earliest Chinese medical text, the *Inner Canon of the Yellow Emperor* (Huangdi neijing), which is thought to be a compilation of writings ranging from the 5th century B.C.E. to the 1st century C.E. Other terms for madness were *xian* and *feng* (Chen Hsiu-fen 2003).[7] Although the traditional treatment for madness was herbal medicine or acupuncture, in some cases various "psychological" methods were invoked for a cure (Chen 2003, 6–7).[8] The *Inner Canon* describes madness as an excess of *yin* or *yang*; but spirit possession, the Six Excesses (liuyin), heteropathy (xie), or disturbances of *qi* also could cause madness (4, 23). Under influence from Jesuits in the Qing dynasty, however, madness came to be regarded as a spiritual illness, at least in some cases and most likely in a limited context (Vivien Ng 1990, 25–28).

There is no strict body-mind separation in traditional Chinese medicine but rather an interrelation between concepts such as the Five Intents (wuzhi) and the Seven Emotions (qiqing) and the body; the concept of *xin* is used not only in Confucian philosophy but across medical texts as well.[9] According to the *Inner Canon*, Chen Hsiu-fen relates,

> each of the Five Viscera—the Liver, the Heart, the Spleen, the Lung, and the Kidney—is regarded as the organ that stores each of the Five Intents—*hun*-soul (hun), spirit, will, *po*-soul (po), and intent. Moreover, the Five Viscera are also said to be corresponding to the different emotions—anger, joy, worry, sorrow, and fear—respectively. Accordingly, when a visceral organ experiences change, the mental state and emotion that it corresponds to will be changed or disturbed, too. By the same token, any imbalance of a certain kind of emotion will also injure the organ in which it lodges. It should be noted that traditional Chinese medicine's conceptions of the functions of some of the visceral systems are basically similar to those of western medicine, but some other conceptions differ greatly. *Xin* of the Five Viscera is an example. On the one hand it is regarded as "the Heart" in which "spirit" is conceived of being stored. On the other hand, however, *xin* is also viewed as a general name for human mental activities and thus can be interpreted as "the Mind." In Chinese medical doctrines *xin* is an "organ of master" in which "divine intelligence" (shen ming) originates. The case of *xin* as "heart-and-mind" precisely explains the holism of mental and physical functions. (2003, 607)

As a concept, therefore, *xin* spanned a wide field that included what we now think of as physical, physiological, psychological, spiritual, and emotional conditions.

The immediately pre-modern Qing dynasty (1644–1912) is generally regarded as a time when philosophical thought pulled away from metaphysics in favor of practical or concrete studies (shixue) or statecraft, a turn that emphasized the importance of action and deemphasized internal musings. Chen Hongmou (1696–1771), an influential Qing official, is a good representative of the trend, although he also supported moral training. While Chen was a conservative who valued social order, he also championed the innate good that could be nurtured and released, the importance of saving the world through individual effort, and the significance of personal drive. For Chen, who valued education that centered on social benefit, "the routine process of civilizing others gave meaning to one's own existence"; literary education for male and females, Chinese and "barbarians," was for the purpose of helping them understand and fulfill social roles (W. Rowe 2001, 323–24, 406, 416, 428).

In the early 19th century, some scholars responded to China's internal and external problems by emphasizing statecraft proposals that would improve the imperial bureaucracy, seen as under attack from various quarters, including its own corruption. These writers found their inspiration in early Qing writers such as Gu Yanwu (1613–82) and Huang Zongxi (1610–95), who rejected both metaphysical speculation and the textual focus of 18th century evidential scholarship (kaozheng) (Elman 2001, 274–75). Gong Zizhen (1792–1841) made use of the *Spring and Autumn Annals* and the *Gongyang Commentary* to support statecraft and moral reform, and Fang Dongshu (1772–1851) criticized the "useless erudition" of the Han Learning movement, supporting concrete learning instead. Even those who defended evidential scholarship tended to think of it from the perspective of statecraft. After the mid-19th century Taiping rebellion, a great deal of intellectual effort went into the reconstruction of libraries that had been destroyed, and the debate centered even more on statecraft, along with the pressing problem of westernization (Elman 2001, 276–92).

Despite this apparent focus on the practical and useful, around the turn of the century interest in the mind and spirit grew stronger among reformist intellectuals, who blamed Chinese mental or spiritual qualities for the political, military, and economic quandaries China was in, as well as for the nation's seeming inferiority to the West. Yan Fu (1853–1921), Liang Qichao (1873–1929), Tan Sitong (1865–98), Wang Jingwei (1883–1944), and others wrote extensively about various aspects of the mind and spirit, delving anew into older ideas such as sympathy or benevolence, and adopting new concepts such as the national soul (guohun) and the ethnic spirit (minzu jingshen). The idea of ethnic psychology (minzu xinlixue), which assigned essential characteristics to roughly differentiated ethnic groups or races, was also widely discussed. Liang Qichao picked up the idea of historical and non-historical races—from writing on Gustave Le Bon (1841–1931), Emile Durkheim (1858–1917) and others—in 1902, when he was working in Japan and had access to texts on Western history and philosophy through Japanese translations. Liang classified the "yellow" races with the "white" as historical, but also urged the Chinese toward constant character improvement. In 1904, he used a spiritual or psychological interpretation to reformulate a Confucian way of looking at the relationship between the person and the world: "The world is produced by the psychologies of all mankind in the world, a society is produced by the psychologies of all its members, just as an individual is produced by his individual psychology" (Sun 1992; Tang 1996).[10] Although Liang's notion of heredity may have been more cultural than biological in nature, it expressed a clear preference for a mentalist understanding of world order (Sun 1992, 242–46). The racial qualities and national characteristics of the unique spirit that Liang promoted are indications that although he may have been concerned with problems of the mind or spirit, this emphasis had a great deal to do with the position of the person or nation in relation to those around, or the context of political power under which the mind functioned. In the debate over national psychology, soul, and spirit that took place in 1902–3, the "national spirit and national soul were often treated as two sides of the same coin," both being part of the national psychology, which could be improved through education (Sun 1992, 250). Despite the tendency of May Fourth intellectuals to emphasize a Chinese spiritual sickness at the expense of national unity and revolution, "one thing remained constant: the continuous use of 'psychology' in a collective context," notes Lung-Kee Sun.[11]

The "collective context" of spiritual or mental concerns was expressed in many ways and using a range of vocabulary that included older terms as well as new inventions; some of the new terms disappeared while others became part of the modern Chinese language. For example, a series of articles on the "spirit of the people" (minqi) appeared in *Eastern Miscellany* in 1904–5. Although *qi* and *xin* were different concepts in traditional Confucian medicine and philosophy, where *qi* is a term for a vital material force, here the term also indicates an essential spiritual quality that, like "national spirit" or "national psyche," can be improved.[12] The overall context in which the "spirit of the people" is discussed in these articles is that of national strength: "The nation (guo) is the unity of the people. If the people are strong, the nation is strong, if the people are weak, the nation is weak. Those looking at the national situation do not consider the strength or weakness of the nation, but rather the vigor or decline of the people's spirit (minqi)" (Chong You 1904).[13]

In the view of these authors, an improperly developed spirit led to a host of woes: the weakness of education, stunted development of democracy, absence of national unity, fawning on foreign nations, military defeat, poverty, ignorance, selfishness, physical illness, and so on.

The question of China's position in the world and its relationship to the West, and to what extent its position defined the intellectual discourse of the late Qing and early Republican era, has been a topic that has produced as much scholarship as *The True Story of Ah Q*. As Theodore Huters notes, the dominant historiography of the early modern (jindai) period divides it into three segments. The first, before 1895, is characterized by the belief that limited and superficial technological borrowing from the West would be sufficient. In the second, from around 1895 to 1917, the focus was on reform of economic and political institutions. Sometime after 1910, however, these approaches were replaced by a "realization that only the most thoroughgoing modification of traditional mentalities would suffice to salvage China and bring it into the realm of modernity" (2005, 9).[14] The built-in contradiction between modernity and the nation-state lies in the simultaneous demand that not only continuity with the past be strongly proclaimed but the past be rejected and alternatives to the dominant culture be eliminated. Literature—which had already taken on a special importance as a way to change thinking and improve the national character—was a site within which to imagine how these negotiations could play out, and one common strategy was to posit an "indigenous spirituality" in contrast to the fundamental materiality of the West (16, 203–28). Liang Qichao used this tactic when he noted that in "customs, habits, literature, and the fine arts, all have an independent spirit that has been passed down from father to son" (62). We must note, therefore, that part of the mentalism to which Lung-kee Sun and others refer is at least to some extent a strategy that emerged as a product of the semi-colonial encounter.

Whether viewed from a positive or negative perspective, as either the necessary kernel or contaminating core of traditional culture, *spirit* occupied a crucial spot. The discourse of the weak spirit, expressed so well in the character of Ah Q, was carried on throughout the May Fourth period, and was later both deployed and attacked by revolutionary leaders. When Lu Xun compared Chinese culture to a hereditary syphilis, and Zhou Zuoren assigned the four qualities of paralysis, ulceration, insanity, and gonorrhea to it, they brought together an emphasis on spirit that extended into the body, the material world, political relations, and every aspect of life (Sun 1996). From a similar critical perspective, Chen Duxiu (1879–1942), the founder of *New Youth* (Xin qingnian) magazine—a journal noted for its emphasis on transforming consciousness—and early communist leader, wrote that "loyalty and filiality represent the morality of a patriarchal (*zongfa*) society in the feudal period and comprise the persisting spirit of the semicivilized (*ban kaihua*) Eastern peoples" (Huters 2005, 210, 258). Huang Yuanyong (1885–1915), who wrote about the clash between Chinese and Western culture, proclaimed that Chinese scholars "consider it our most urgent task to research and seek out the particular malignancy that is universal among us," expressing the "sick man of Asia" theory common at the time (212). Huters terms Huang's description of the problem thus: as "without system, without substance, without character, and without distinctions," giving rise to "arbitrariness, despotism, stagnation, corruption, and following weakly along," and as "empty formalism" (213). It also could simply be called spirit, clearly an issue of both position and essence. Considering the productivity of this abstraction, it is not at all strange that Huang developed a mental or spiritual structure through which to analyze the important aspects of Western culture, a culture which, according to his system, begins with an unconscious period and moves through subsequent eras of critical thought and theoretical synthesis.

As Huters explains, Huang's approach allows for significant voluntarism. It also opens the door to a common perspective—as in Du Yaquan's (1873–1933) implicit claim that the excessively instrumental West cannot easily negotiate the balance between the material and the spiritual—that as I have noted has resonance in the work of many others (Huters 2005, 215–21). The violence and social disintegration of World War I cast a grim shadow on so-called mechanistic and overly scientific Western values and gave some credence to the ideal that Eastern spirituality could trump Western materialism (a view supported by Bertrand Russell [1872–1970] in his Chinese tour of 1920–21); however, the biggest obstacle to the claim that Chinese culture was inherently, and for the better, more spiritual than Western culture came from the challenge of science (Kwok 1965, 16). In 1923, a full-fledged debate pitting science against metaphysics broke out, with Qinghua University professor Carsun Chang (Zhang Junmai, 1887–1968) leading the anti-science charge, and V. K. Ting (Ding Wenjiang) picking up the cause of science. Chang promoted a return to spiritual values and a "philosophy of life that was marked by its stress on subjectivity, intuitiveness, synthetic outlook, freedom of will, and uniqueness of personality," while Ting called his rivals "metaphysical ghosts" (141–42). As D.W.Y. Kwok explains,

> The basic contention was that of the priority of mind over matter. A corollary to this was the less philosophical contention that Eastern civilization was spiritual, while Western civilization (molded by science) was materialistic. The philosophers and metaphysicians argued strongly in favor of the existence of another world beyond the immediate world of the senses . . . In order to survive, the national heritage with its highly spiritual development needed to be kept intact. (157–58)

Although we should take care when reducing the many discourses of spirit and mind of the late Qing and early Republican periods to the Hegelian dialectic between the ideal and the material, by 1923 the importance of communist ideology was becoming apparent within the intellectual debate, and the logic of Chen Duxiu and other participants in the discussion increasingly followed its contours.

Even earlier, the writings of Wu Zhihui (1865–1953) express a radical materialism, illustrating the sphere where the pro-science faction could—but did not always—find resonance with the materialism of the Chinese communist party. Working with Cai Yuanpei (1868–1940), Wu founded the Society of Patriotic Scholars (Aiguo xueshi she) and the newspaper *Subao*, fleeing to Japan when his articles angered the government. Wu traveled and studied in Japan, England, and France, and in 1905 met Sun Yat-sen in England and joined Sun's Tongmeng hui; he also collaborated on the establishment of the weekly *The New Century* (Xin shiji), which was first published in 1907 and ran articles sympathetic to anarchists. Wu began to develop his own world view in a series of articles beginning around 1907. While not completely sympathetic to communism or socialism, he promoted a scientific materialism in which consciousness is the by-product of matter and spiritual issues are secondary to the material and the scientific. In Wu's view traditional spiritual approaches were an amalgamation of Confucian and Buddhist ideas, promoted idealist thought, and should be avoided. Echoing Marx on religion as the opiate of the masses, Wu clearly states: "I firmly believe that there is no spirit beyond matter. Such things as spirit or soul are merely terms to cloud reality; they have a narcotic effect on man" (Kwok 1965, 56).

This brief foray into traditional, late Qing, and early Republican ideas, along with the developing discourse of education and psychology discussed earlier, shows a lively intellectual field in which new theories of the mind, matter, and spirit circulated with older notions. The relationship between scientific materialism, Marxist materialism, and various ideas of spirit, and the way in which these spheres blended and crossed, was frequently debated. While vocabulary was mutable and under revision, the political and cultural discourse of the spirit, which saw it as a collective expression of national / ethnic / cultural weakness developed into a powerful social perspective; it existed sometimes comfortably, sometimes uneasily with scientific or Marxist materialism. From this angle, spirit was indeed a quality or perspective through which the person perceived and which oriented the self in relation to power. In literature, perhaps Lu Xun's famous pessimism, which implied that a state of mind was the most accurate indication of historical times, expressed this focus with the greatest subtlety. Considering the fertile background out of which it emerged, it should come as no surprise that revolutionary discourse developed a powerful theory of the spirit as a quality and a site of negotiation between the person and the state, the nation and the globe, the mind and its environment.

REVOLUTION, MIND, AND SPIRIT

Reformist and revolutionary thinkers of the early 20th century wanted to change the way people think; that does not mean, however, that they all emphasized mental or spiritual qualities as the only or even the most seminal transformation that had to take place. In journals such as *New Youth*, treatises on science and institutional reform stood side by side with those that emphasized changes in thought and consciousness. Any number of thinkers and politicians attended to identifiable institutions, traditional, discriminatory social practices, and so on, asking readers to shift their attention to political policies, government bodies, social welfare, education, and other areas where structural transformation could improve China. Yet putting these changes in effect inevitably demanded changing the way people thought. Beyond that, it was not unusual for some writers to assign great importance to a powerful abstraction, a mentality or spirit that would allow for and promote personal and social transformation. For these writers, the issue was not only traditional customs or ways of thinking but, in addition, an intangible quality that was and remains difficult to define. To some degree, many or perhaps most revolutionary thinkers at one time or another expressed a conviction that there was something inherently wrong with the fundamental mental attributes of the Chinese people, and that it was essential that this quality be recognized, addressed, and renovated. The extent to which this property could be extracted and disconnected not only from material or social life but also from a focus on specific ideas or conventional ways of thinking indicates the extent to which it was considered transcendent, sublime, or spiritual.

While used in many situations in daily life, the term "spirit" became highly ideological in China over the revolutionary period, and to some extent it remains so today.[15] However, the discussion of spirit within revolutionary discourse predates the post-Mao period and may be linked to earlier discourses of the national spirit or soul that can be traced at least to the late Qing dynasty. Those in both the Nationalist party and the Communist party invoked it frequently.[16] As I have mentioned, spirit and revolution are not unfamiliar bedfellows.[17] An emotional appeal that encourages people to identify with a cause and to sacrifice their comfort, their well-being, and even their lives in times of intense struggle—or more simply, a demand that someone position him or herself "correctly" vis-à-vis the revolutionary leaders and group—is not uncommon. Yet as the fight against easily identifiable enemies moved into a period of "permanent revolution" or continued revolution under conditions of relative peace, the position of spirit in Chinese revolutionary thought and culture was enhanced. What revolutionary spirit captures, develops, and expresses in China from the 1950s through the 1970s is the emotive and mental aspect of a full understanding of position and relationship from the perspective of recognized state authorities and cultural figures, and within the mind of the revolutionary subject. It also opens a space where transcendence can flourish and be tapped for use within that scheme, forming a unified system where spirit, from its most ordinary to its most sublime meanings, can anchor an entire discourse.

For my investigation into the concept of revolutionary spirit, I regard various aspects of socialist Chinese culture to be relevant for analysis: its populist tendencies, the development of the leadership cult, the celebration of backwardness, the emphasis on heroism, messianic language, and romanticization of the peasantry and countryside. Especially relevant is Mao's development and promotion of a voluntaristic ideology, in which spirit and will played a strong role in actualizing the series of leaps toward communism that characterized the post-1949 era. Maurice Meisner's 1982 *Marxism, Maoism, and Utopianism* outlines evidence for his view that Maoism went further than any other widespread revolutionary movement in valorizing the spirit.[18] Meisner traces the utopian elements and ambiguity of Marxism, noted by many researchers, and discusses the utopianism that seems to be a necessary part of revolutionary movements.[19] Remarking that "Maoist utopianism" or the "Maoist vision" generally refers to "politically abnormal or economically irrational behavior," Meisner shows how Mao's constant elevation and romanticization of the rural became the concrete structure of his emphasis on the spirit, providing both a cultural memory of ideal agrarian life and a physical site of transformation (17). Also, Meisner recognizes that Mao's tendency toward voluntarism to some extent illustrates his theorization of China's position under imperialist attack in the early 20th century. In order for China to assume a vanguard position in the global revolutionary struggle against imperialism, Maoists needed to "deny that China's socialist future rested on the social and materials results of modern capitalist forces of production" (54). A peasantry supposedly untouched by modern industrialization therefore assumed a prominent role in the intellectual imagination of Chinese leadership on the global revolutionary stage, and often was partially defined through a Chinese and communist essence that was historically and fundamentally revolutionary.

In Meisner's view, Maoism "replaces the Marxist belief in objective laws of history with a voluntaristic faith in the consciousness and the moral potentialities of men as the decisive factor in sociohistorical development" (1982, 61). Socialism under Mao, Meisner argues, had two identifying qualities: an anti-urban, pro-rural focus, and an "extraordinary emphasis placed on the role of human consciousness and moral qualities . . . and the spiritual transformation of the people" (68, 70). Taking off from a combination of a Leninist focus on mental qualities and a populist disregard for historical inevitability, this approach, common in populist movements, in China became the dual development and deployment of two crucial concepts: revolutionary consciousness in the intelligentsia and "spontaneity" in the masses (84, 99, 103). The doctrine of permanent revolution was to continually transform the popular mentality at all levels. According to Meisner, the historical circumstances of China over the first half of the 20th century—imperialism, an alien capitalism with no indigenous bourgeoisie, and an intelligentsia that wished to distance itself from tradition—contributed to the creation of Maoist voluntarism as much as populist and Leninist ideology did.[20] Under Maoism, spiritual values such as selflessness, sacrifice, courage, discipline, honesty, and frugality were elevated and were especially attached to youth (112–20). This imbuing of youth with spirit should alert us to the special qualities of the spiritual mentality imagined and enacted during the Maoist times, especially the imagination of the future as we see it embodied in literature and film.

Meisner locates an early voluntaristic emphasis in the ideas and practice of early Chinese communists such as Li Dazhao, who in 1919 called on Chinese students to leave the corrupting cities and re-educate themselves through labor with the peasants (Meisner 1982, 95).[21] The *mentality* of being revolutionary, Meisner implies, became increasingly important over the years; in the late 1930s and early 1940s, Mao's literary and philosophical lectures and essays, especially "On Practice" (Shijian lun), "On Contradiction" (Maodun lun), and the "Yan'an Talks on Art and Literature" (Zai Yan'an wenyi zuotanhui shang de jianghua), set the stage for the excesses of the 1950s and the Cultural Revolution. The "red and expert" theory helped hone this focus and encouraged each person to use the weapon of self-criticism to delve into his or her own consciousness, with the goal of carrying out a lifelong revolution of the mind (128). Faith was not enough, however; the new consciousness had to be expressed through behavior. Meisner and other scholars have noted the pan-religious quality of Maoist society, a quality eventually implicitly criticized even by Mao (169–70). As K. K. Yeo comments, the "selfless sacrifice in Maoist teaching was honored as heroic martyrdom and seen as human power equated with divine power. The 'regeneration' process of *pi-dou-gai* criticism, combat, and revolution, does show its religious function of the inner and spiritual transformation of humanity" (2002, 145).[22]

Arif Dirlik (2005) agrees with Meisner that Maoist ideology must be regarded as specific to Chinese historical circumstances, so specific that it should be regarded as a vernacular version of Marxism (75–104).[23] The crucial historical elements are, Dirlik argues, the global, third-world, and national dimensions, three spheres of mutual interaction and influence upon which Mao's Marxism is most properly considered a reflection (80–81). It is the "irreducibility of the national and the global in this practical discourse, and the centrality to resolving its contradictions of the reflecting subject" that led to deep contradictions in Mao's thought vis-à-vis relative versus absolute truth and theory versus practice; Mao's solution was an attempt to restore the "direction of history" through revolutionary will (95). Much earlier, Dirlik (1983) analyzed the predicament of Marxist revolutionary consciousness, tracing the various interpretations of Mao's emphasis on consciousness and defending Mao's focus on his own unique interpretation.[24] Unwilling to agree that Mao's faith in consciousness is a result of his obsession with will or simply an inherited Chinese cultural legacy, Dirlik speaks out against a purely economistic Marxist approach that denies the significance of consciousness for social change and revolution. Noting that Frederic Wakeman and Li Rui have traced Mao's preoccupation with subjective will since his early days, Dirlik (2005) nonetheless claims "Marxism tamed Mao's subjectivism, and taught him the constraints placed on revolutionary will by social circumstances" (128–29). Mao's seeming assertion of the power of revolutionary will to alter material reality during the Cultural Revolution can only be understood if we realize that Mao juxtaposed not consciousness against social or material reality, but revolutionary consciousness against consciousness in general, Dirlik argues. Whereas consciousness in general is shaped both by material/social reality and inherited culture, revolutionary consciousness is shaped by class considerations. This problematic then constitutes Mao's contribution to Marxism; Mao realized that revolution "would have to be made, and a revolution in consciousness and culture was the precondition to, rather than an expression of, a revolution in material existence" (132). Through this theoretical understanding, Mao turns consciousness into an "agent of change," while the essay "On Contradiction" affirms the possibility of "revolutionary transcendence" (135). While confirming Mao's subjectivist focus—albeit with his own twist—Dirlik also notes that from 1926 on, Mao was more interested in the hierarchies of power of social groups than in the relationship of class to production.

Kang Liu (1997b) also explains Mao's emphasis on cultural revolution, the superstructure, or consciousness by way of a link to Mao's theory of contradiction, arguing that Mao viewed cultural revolution as a way to establish an alternative modernity. Like Meisner and Dirlik, Liu traces Mao's ideas on cultural transformation to his late 1930s and early 1940s talks and essays, noting especially that his 1942 "Yan'an Talks on Art and Literature" became one of the most important pieces of his thought, especially during the Cultural Revolution, when it assumed "virtually the status of Holy Scripture, inspiring quasi-religious fervor as well as dictating the nature of cultural life" (Kang Liu 2005, 251). Mao's 1940 "On New Democracy" (Xin minzhu zhuyi lun) also turned from economics, which is quickly recognized and disposed of, to a discussion on culture and revolution. Liu states that while railing against ideas of inner laws, subjectivity, and essence, Mao in fact subscribed to such views in his writing, equating cultural revolution with absolute truth (257).

Whether or not one regards Mao as having become too comfortable with a fundamentally idealist ideology, it is undeniable that Maoist thought places a great deal of emphasis on subjectivity and cultural transformation, a focus that peaked during the Cultural Revolution, when political figures like Lin Biao brazenly proclaimed the supremacy of subjectivity. Minimally, in order to understand the mind as it was conceptualized and existed under revolutionary culture, we should recognize and take seriously the way in which subjectivity and consciousness are incorporated into revolutionary thought. Rather than assuming that the mind is universal and, no matter where or when, works in basically the same way—as has been the case in much of Western psychology and psychoanalysis over the 20th century—we should take a close look at the way in which mentalities are described, enacted, and professed in revolutionary times. Thinking or thought with a specific content is important, but so is the discourse of spirit, a quality invoked in articles, films, and fiction, and a key aspect of basic revolutionary practices such as daily self-critique and criticism. Referring to subjectivity under the conditions of revolutionary culture, this discourse of the spirit took on an ideological meaning that far exceeded its former deployment within ordinary language and medical discourse.

The concept of spirit, therefore, is a fundamental aspect of the theory of the mind in revolutionary China. The difference between the discourse of spirit in Chinese revolutionary culture and a more general invocation of spirit under extreme conditions of revolution lies in the normalization of the role of spirit in daily life; this is indicated by its incorporation in a dazzling variety of social practices and representations. Although activists all over the world have called upon "spirit" for the purpose of drumming up an emotional commitment to their cause, in China this concept was fully integrated into the pedestrian. Extensively normalized in the everyday through its invocation in texts and images, theory, and an astounding array of social practices, spirit is the expression and embodiment of a position in relation to other people or institutions in power. When essentialized as a quality, this positionality could be lived, thought, felt, and expressed through passionate emotional declarations.

Below, I delineate two closely linked aspects of the discourse of spirit in revolutionary culture. The first is spirit as a medical concept, codified in the concept of "mental illness" (jingshen bing) within a field where the heart / mind (xinli) and the spirit (jingshen)—both of which were candidates for the translation of the term "psychology" in early 20th century texts—came to refer to very different things. The second is the ideological discourse of spirit as it appears overtly in concepts such as "spiritual civilization" (jingshen wenming) or "spiritual pollution" (jingshen wuran) and covertly in heroic references and images in literature, popular culture, film, and so on. This second arena also includes a regime of confession and self-improvement wherein the correct spirit came to represent the perfect position of the person in relation to power and the powerful, or an inner recognition of social position and role, imagined as an embodied, unified essence. Together, these two discourses form a unified whole, framing a subjectivity that constituted itself through reference to models from daily life, heroic passions, conventional moralities, and punitive guidelines that monitored, directed, and criminalized behavior.

PSYCHOLOGY, PSYCHE, AND REVOLUTION: THE MAOIST DISCOURSE OF SPIRIT

The two characters *jing* and *shen*, which when joined in modern Chinese form a cognate usually translated as "spirit," appear together and are discussed at length in the *Huainanzi* (2nd century B.C.E.). As Sarah A. Queen (2001) explains, however, here *jingshen* is not a cognate but two concepts put together, related but retaining their autonomy:

> Essence [jing] and spirit [shen], both aspects of *qi*, are important terms throughout most *Huainanzi* chapters, especially chap. 6, "Peering into the Mysterious", and 7, "Essence and Spirit". [Chap. 7] describes the two terms as follows: "Essence and spirit are what one acquires from Heaven. Form and Frame are what one receives from Earth." Chapter 21 further describes its discussion of essence and spirit as involving "what vitalizes human beings" and "what brings understanding and awareness to what lies within the form, frame, and nine orifices." (67)

As the "medium through which humans and Heaven achieve mutual resonance," essence and spirit are metaphysical and cosmological concepts that function as a node between two relational entities (67). Other than in the *Huainanzi*, the two characters appear together in the *Hanshu*, the *Chuangzi*, *Shishuo xinyu*, and other classical texts. Their modern use as a cognate meaning "spirit," however, most likely originated as a returned graphic loan word that, although derived from classical Chinese, was borrowed from contemporary Japanese use around the turn of the century.[25] As in the case of other terms used in classical texts and re-adopted into the modern vocabulary, the meaning of *jing* and *shen*, although not completely unrelated to their earlier uses in numerous texts, was reworked to serve the new environment. In this case, the expression became a potential candidate to represent the new discipline of psychology and, as in *jingshen fenxi*, psychoanalysis. The use of the term *jingshen* in the People's Republic of China represents a revealing beginning point from which to query the role of spirit in revolutionary subjectivity.

In the late Qing and early Republican period, *xinli fenxi xue* and *jingshen fenxi xue* were both used within the larger field of mental illness and mind theories. Gao Juefu's explanation for his choice of terms makes it clear that even in the 1930s, there was flexibility in usage and terms were not set:

> In 1930, Mr. Wang Yunwu of Commercial Press asked me to translate Freud's *Introduction to Psychoanalysis* (Jingshen fenxi yinlun). Freud's use of the term "psychoanalysis" was to avoid confusion with Rene Descartes' "psychological analysis" (xinli fenxi). At the time I thought about its difference with "psychoanalysis of the heart / mind" (xin zhi fenxi) popularized by Bertrand Russell, and wanted to get closer to its original meaning, so I translated it as "analysis of the spirit" (jingshen fenxi). Freud was mostly a psychologist, and when J. Strechey edited the standard translation of Freud's 24 volume works, he called it *The Standard Edition of the Complete Psychological Works of Sigmund Freud* (Fuluoyide xinlixue quanji biaojun ban). (Shen Heyong 2000, 194)

Over the course of the first half of the 20th century, *jingshen fenxi* became the preferred idiom for "psychoanalysis," while *xinli xue* came to dominate for "psychology." *Jingshen*, like *xinli*, remained a common term in daily conversation, as well as appearing in two specialized discourses, the first of which was medicine. *Xinli*, in the cognate *xinli xue* or psychology, tended to be used to indicate the study of the mind under the "normal" social conditions of labor and education, whereas *jingshen*, in the cognate *jingshen bing xue* or the study of illness of the spirit, came to refer to the study of abnormality of the mind or psychosis (psychiatry). The role of *jingshen* within psychological discourse after 1949 to indicate severe pathology (*jingshen bing*, mental illness, psychosis) moved it closer to becoming a medical concept with clinical applicability and the implication of illness.[26] In this usage, "spirit" indicates a mental malfunction.[27] In the following paragraphs, I will discuss the crossing nexus of *jingshen* and *xinli*, with the goal of identifying and interpreting the parameters of their use.

Attacks on psychoanalysis and other Western psychological approaches as methods to theorize and understand the mind increased in the 1930s and 1940s, buoyed by Marxist critique of the field as bourgeois. After undergoing a period of American influence through the work of behaviorists trained in the United States, Chinese psychology dropped this emphasis after 1949, when Soviet theories became more popular and the concept of *consciousness* more prominent. The unconscious, not to mention Freudian theory, was completely discredited. Both "consciousness" (yishi) and "active ability / consciousness" (zijue nengdongli) were vital in the approach that developed over the 1950s. Active consciousness, or agency, was thought to be what led to socially desirable action and thereby was inherently linked to a theory of social life. The theoretical basis of this theory was "reflection" (fanshe), a Leninist notion that stated that the "human brain knows the world because it mirrors objective reality" (Chin and Chin 1969, 12–13). In a book published in 1953, Yuan Gongwei lays out the boundaries of the "new psychology":

> What is "psychology" (xinli)? The "psychology" of humankind is a product developed out of the material [world]: inorganic material has no psychological phenomena, and although animals have feelings and other psychological processes, it is no more than a low level psychological phenomenon. Human psychology is relatively complex. . . . In the past, idealist philosophy took this kind of psychological phenomena to have a non-material, formless existence called the "spiritual" (xinling) or the "soul" (linghun). Now our dialectical materialism opposes this theory, recognizing the human "psyche" (xinli) as partially the fundamental biology of the nervous system and brain, and partially a reflection of the outside world. . . . The primary responsibility of a psychology that is Marxist-Leninist and takes on the highest guidance and principles of Mao Zedong thought is to deploy the theories and methods of psychological science to reform anew the psychological consciousness of the Chinese people, and combine the construction and reformation of the objective material world to victoriously enter socialist society and soon arrive at communist society. (Yuan 1953, 1–3)

In Yuan's description, psychology as a discipline mimics the position of the psyche in Marxist-Leninist-Maoist thought: whereas the psyche is a pivot point at which the material world (as it exists in social reality) is reflected into and molds subjectivity, the discipline of psychology is a pivot point through which the material / social world works to produce a certain understanding—or collective subjectivity—of this world.

The job of turning the discipline of psychology into a revolutionary study appropriate for socialist society began with a 1952 call from the party to psychology professionals, who were asked to begin study on Marxist-Leninist-Maoist ideas relevant to the field. The most pressing task in "thoroughly reforming the thought structure of psychology was to first reform the thinking of psychological workers" (Gao Juefu 1986, 385). In 1953 a conference on Pavlovian theory was held, and subsequently mental health professionals were encouraged to study and make use of Pavlov's methodology (Pearson 1995, 13; Gao Juefu 1986, 385). Soviet texts were translated and experts invited from the Soviet Union to teach and do research in China. The journal *Psychology Information* (Xinlixue tongxun) was initiated in 1953–54, to be followed by *Acta Psychologica Sinica* (Xinlixue bao) in 1956 and *Journal of Translations in Psychology* (Xinlixue yibao) in 1956–58. When it was inaugurated in 1955, the Chinese Psychological Society (Xinlixue hui), headed by Pan Shu (1897–1988) and Cao Richang (1911–69), became the premier state psychological institute (Chin and Chin 1969, 39). In 1956, a twelve-year plan (1956–67) for the sciences was developed, in which psychology was included (Gao Juefu 1986, 386–87). A number of problems in defining the discipline continued to be hot topics of debate throughout the 1950s and into the 1960s: the class nature of psychology, the target of psychological study, the nature of individuality and its relationship to class and collective nature, and methods for distinguishing and addressing the social and biological aspects of mental life. In the late 1950s, psychology moved away from Pavlovian methodology, which through Soviet influence had dominated the field in the early 1950s. Although Ivan Petrovich Pavlov (1849–1936) had won a Nobel prize in 1904 for his work on food stimuli and salivary response in dogs—which led to a theory of conditioned response—he later studied not physical input, but the functioning of language as a code. In Pavlov's system, culture was interpreted as belonging to a "second signal system" that makes use of words, symbols, and language and through them influences the nervous system. This approach was picked up by American behaviorist J. B. Watson (1878–1958), who argued that all learning occurred through stimulus and response. Ironically, the theory that dominated much of early 1950s Chinese psychological study also dominated American behaviorist research until around 1960 (Bruner 2004). In China, however, Watson's behaviorism was criticized as the psychological theory of capitalism:

> Behaviorist psychology is rooted in capitalism. To put it simply, behaviorism suited the needs of the capitalist class at that time. We must bear in mind that behaviorism originated in the 1920s in the United States, the greatest capitalist nation in the world, just after the First World War when capitalism was beginning to crumble. The working class at that time was becoming a strong force and the international revolutionary movement was spreading daily. The capitalist forces thus had cause to fear the realisation of a growing revolutionary consciousness. Therefore they resorted to a theory that undermined human consciousness and safeguarded the interests of the capitalists. (Ni 1957, trans. in L. B. Brown 1981, 44–48)

The *Chinese Journal of Scientific Neuropsychiatry* (Zhonghua shenjing jingshen kexue zazhi) was first published in 1955, and the discipline of psychiatry focused on advancing the field, decreasing the number of psychiatric patients, and providing humane treatment that accorded with the ideal of serving the people. According to some sources, psychiatric wards, the capacity of which had been greatly increased after 1949, served "some 73,000 mentally ill persons" by 1957, with about a third "recovering" (Pearson 1995, 14–15). The First National Conference of Psychiatric Specialists, organized by the Ministry of Health, was held in Nanjing in 1958. The main theoretical thrust of the conference was to urge development of indigenous approaches and a simultaneous move away from Western theories, as in psychology (13). Although psychology and psychiatry were separate fields, when it came to questions of the relationship between theory and practice, their interests coincided, as did criticisms of their methods and assumptions. This confluence became more pronounced in late 1950s political movements, when concerns about the theoretical basis of both fields intensified.

By late 1958, there were calls for the complete reconfiguration of both psychology and psychiatry and even the abolition of the disciplines. In August 1958, Beijing Normal University initiated a campaign to "Criticize the Capitalist Direction of Psychology" (Pipan xinlixue de zichan jieji fangxiang), which quickly spread around the country. Doctors who locked up their patients were criticized as capitalistic in their methodology, and the confinement of patients was abolished. The five-year plan was adjusted, to focus on "controlling the rapidly increasing, almost rampant problem of neurasthenia, especially among 'mind (intellectual) workers,' a category that included office workers, teachers, and students, and to a lesser extent, among laborers and in members of the armed forces" (Lin 1985, 13). While attributing mental illness to irregularity in physical nervous activities, the plan also noted consequences to the economy and to social security. Cures were to proceed through four methodologies: Chinese and Western medicine, labor therapy, cultural and sports therapy, and educational therapy (Pearson 1995, 13–19). The so-called Intensive Comprehensive Group Treatment or Speedy Synthetic Method of group therapy was developed and used nationally, "emphasizing 're-education' of the patient to develop 'correct ideas and attitudes' to work and socialist life, especially in fostering the proper relationship of the self to the society, the Party, and the nation" (Lin 1985, 14).

During the same period, psychologists were criticized for abstraction (studying isolated mental processes instead of the whole person), biological reductionism (researching simple physiological processes in place of complex psychological phenomena), and lack of class analysis. Robert Chin and Ai-li S. Chin (1969) list medical psychology (yixue xinlixue), labor psychology (laodong xinlixue), and educational psychology (jiaoyu xinlixue)—with some research on moral character and individuality—as the three subfields of psychology that were formally divided and recognized during the Great Leap Forward (53–59).[28] The new labor psychology was distinguished from industrial psychology (gongye xinlixue), which had followed the practice of F. W. Taylor's (1856–1915) 1911 *Principles of Scientific Management* and was aimed at improving productivity. The focus of labor psychology was the overall psychological condition of workers, but problems such as learning, work speed, and division of tasks also were part of this work (106–12). In 1958, Liu Chengjie, Wang Tianhou, and Zhang Mingjuan, all psychology majors in the Philosophy Department of Beijing University, outlined the mental characteristics that progressive workers should have: "Each progressive worker, no matter young or old, must always be full of vim and vigor and optimism. For those with a proper work attitude, selfless immersion into labor is a natural thing, because what they always desire is to create more wealth for the nation. As production increases, they get happier" (Liu Chengjie, Wang Tianhou, Zhang Mingjuan 1958, 47).

By focusing closely on "spiritual wealth" (jingshen caifu) as indicated by selflessness, clear and complete recognition of the value of work, a feeling of mastery, a well-developed sense of responsibility, self-enforced discipline, and especially optimism, these student authors outline a sphere of subjectivity almost identical to the cultural discourse on spirit I discuss below (Cao Richang 1959). During the Great Leap Forward, "hospital wards were reorganized to provide an atmosphere of 'revolutionary optimism' in order to encourage patients to struggle for their own recovery and restoration to a normal social life as members of the communist society. Self-help and self-regulations were keys in programming the individual and group ward activities of the patients" (Lin 1985, 11–12). The relationship between theory and practice, so actively debated over the 1950s, was decided in favor of the latter, and researchers left their laboratories to go out in society and work with the people.

Government authorities decided to "put the brakes" on leftist radicalism in 1959, when meetings were called for psychological workers in Changchun, Harbin, Guangzhou, Lanzhou, and other cities, with the goal of revisiting and rejecting the more serious attacks from the Anti-Rightist Movement

(Gao Juefu 1986, 388). Articles arguing on behalf of a moderate position appeared. In a 1959 article on the target of psychological study, for example, Cheng Naiyi argued that not all aspects of psychological study are related to class, although they are all social in nature (Cheng Naiyi 1959). However, it was not long before both psychology and psychiatry moved into what Gao Juefu calls its third time period, beginning in 1960. While the overall political direction was toward developing and formulating a distinctively Chinese socialist psychology, according to Gao's account the fields of psychological and psychiatric research were active and exciting. In the early 1960s, some three hundred articles on psychological research were published and several key textbooks written and published (Gao Juefu 1986, 390). Active debate on a variety of topics was encouraged. At Beijing University, the Psychology Major of the Philosophy Department held two meetings to discuss the relationship between the natural and the social in the psyche, with well-known professors putting forward various conflicting views.[29] Substantial criticism echoing Gao Juefu's early work on Freud reappeared, attacking again the theory of the unconscious as a wellspring of repressed desire, as well as other ideas associated with Freudian psychoanalysis, such as the implication that the sane and the insane are different only in degree, the concepts of repression and sublimation, the sexual motivation of culture, and the notion that linguistic slips indicate points of repression (Tang Qian 1960). Tang Qian contrasts Pavlov's notion of the unconscious as simply things of which one is not entirely aware with Freud's unconscious, which is woven through repressed sexual desires, and he also attacks what he calls the "psychological determinism" of Freudian theory as unscientific, while noting that since Freud was "from the capitalist class and located in a capitalist society . . . his theories and approaches on the human psyche reflected the psyche of that corrupt capitalist class" (117–18; 120).

Three areas—labor, education, and medical psychology—continued to be the primary categories through which the mind was conceptualized. Educational psychology was closely concerned with consciousness as it developed throughout the learning process and within the educational institution. In 1962, a special committee on educational psychology was formed and a five-year plan to study psychological development in children was developed (Gao Juefu 1986, 390). Pan Shu listed the aspects of education that should be addressed by psychologists, including moral education and "the training of workers with socialist consciousness and culture," "love of socialist fatherland, love of the laboring masses, love of the Communist

Party, love of the leaders, and love for physical labor, science, and public property." Also included were training for "patriotism and international spirit" and "willingness to support the leadership of the Party and serve socialism and the people" (Chin and Chin 1969, 134).

Because it was concerned with mentalities and thought, the discipline of psychology became tightly connected to political ideology during a time when virtually everything was analyzed for its political meaning. This ideological direction may have not been completely obvious to someone working in the field at the time, although with hindsight, Gao Juefu realized that despite the appearance of a flourishing intellectual sphere, "indications of the obliteration of psychology" had also appeared (Gao Juefu 1986, 390). The death knell was sounded when Gang-of-Four member Yao Wenyun (1931–2005) published two articles on psychology in 1965, branding the field as a "90 percent useless, 10 percent perverse," reactionary, unscientific, antirevolutionary scholarly orthodoxy created and managed by capitalist intellectuals (Gao Juefu 1986, 390–91). This attack ushered in the fourth period for psychology (1966–76), when the discipline was virtually abolished.

Over the revolutionary period, the social sciences in general were criticized as bourgeois and inconsistent with Marxist and Maoist theories of class struggle. Veronica Pearson (1995) argues that in the 1950s, the attacks on and criticisms of sociology, anthropology, and the social study of psychology allowed a "predominantly medical model of psychiatric practice to develop with little input from professionals with a background in the social sciences such as psychologists, social workers and occupational therapists" (13). While Chin and Chin find many social contexts where psychologists worked—predominantly in labor and education—Pearson is correct in stating that

> mental illness is seen as essentially problems in thought, and therapy as thought liberation. The individual expresses this as a rejection of reality and a refusal to accept the design and demands from a social context in which the patient feels alienated. At the same time, all individuals have the ability to learn and change both themselves and the world around them. Thus if the patient is informed of the correct way to view circumstances he / she can be encouraged to arm himself to fight his own illness. (23)

C. Ratner (1970) extends this perspective by noting that

> Chinese psychotherapy does not focus on the patient's emotions or childhood experiences; it does not attempt psychological explanations. The main

> concern is for the patients to develop logical, rational thinking and to develop good social values of cooperation. Then the patients can come to have happy, fulfilled lives through their ordinary social activities. In other words because social life is fulfilling, the point is to participate in it and there is no need to engage in purely psychological, personal analysis. (Quoted in Pearson 1995, 23)

In medical psychology, psychotherapy was an important concept that was defined differently than in the West; it consisted of "everything that goes through the patient's psychological activity which has a curative effect" (Chin and Chin 1969, 87). The Leninist concepts of "recognition" (renshi) and "reflection" (fanshe), two important tools that psychologists in labor and educational psychology used to socially situate and reform their subjects, also were used in medical psychology, where "neurasthenia would be present only when the individual had mistaken recognition (that is, failure to properly 'reflect' the regulations and techniques of work) or when he had faulty responses to a newly awakened sense of responsibility" (101). As the critical literature on Freudian theory indicates, since mental health was seen as the result of a healthy society and proper recognition of one's correct position within that society, capitalist cultures were thought to produce many more mentally ill people.[30]

Although during the 1950s both *xinli xue* and *jingshen bing xue* addressed thought and ideology, in its role within educational and labor psychology *xinli xue* theorized the mind of the socialist subject under normal social conditions. Psychologists working in these areas, as well as reasonably well-adjusted people, all existed under the same ideological regime. It is only when someone becomes seriously disturbed that s/he moves out of the realm of *xinli xue* and into *jingshen bing xue.* This clear distinction echoes one of the main difficulties that scholars in the 1920s and 1930s had with Freud's theory of the everyday, in which the mind of a normal person was essentially the same as that of someone who was abnormal. Within the socialist scheme, medical psychology, or *jingshen bing xue,* is interesting on at least two counts. First, it must both handle and theorize the more severely disturbed subject, for whom therapies that attempt to reestablish social connection or position do not work. Through theories of the mind developed in medical psychology, we can view the edges—or in some cases, the underbelly—of the system. Second, *jingshen bing xue,* straying as it does out of the realm of the normal, provides a more direct link to the cultural discourse of spirit, which opens up a range of passionate identifications that are not part of either regular psychology or medical discourse. It is in this connection that we can perceive an overarching system that centers the spirit as a mental pivot, through which the socialist subject mediates his or her social position and translates that position into thought, emotion, and behavior.

Another related term, used to refer to the nerves or nervous system, also is important in medical psychology. Although they both make use of the character *shen* for "spirit," *shenjing* (nerve) is a more technical and somatic term than *jingshen*, generally referring to the actual nerve circuits of the body. However, just as *jingshen* and *xinli* have some common uses, so do *jingshen* and *shenjing*. Neurasthenia, generally rendered as *shenjing shuairuo zheng*, can also be called *jingshen shuairuo zheng*. Neurosis is put as *shenjing bing*, but psychosis given as *jingshen bing*.[31] In general, however, although "spirit" can be deployed as a medical and technical term in some cases, it often refers to a more abstract, metaphysical, or ideological quality, as in "cultural / intellectual life" (jingshen shenghuo), "mental outlook / spiritual ethos" (jingshen jingjie), or "state of mind" (jingshen zhengtai).

Chinese mental health professionals, like those in other countries, strained to interpret and deal with those who were genuinely psychotic, but they had at their fingers a concept of mental illness—*jingshen bing*—that recognized the inability of some patients to reform within commonly accepted social therapies, and allowed for radical somatic therapies. In 1950s and 1960s China, those who committed a crime but were found to be seriously psychotic submitted to various invasive cures. In this respect, the connection between psychiatry and the judicial system in China is no different than that of many other countries. Yet in China, those who had not committed a crime but simply refused to recognize and accept their proper position within social hierarchies also found themselves entangled within this system. Robin Munro's (2000) research on forensic psychology sheds a light on the inability of the system to deal with social rebellion without psychologizing such acts as mental illness. Throughout the revolutionary period, Munro finds, state-appointed psychiatrists often dealt with "cases of a political nature" that were referred to them by law-enforcement authorities for "forensic-psychiatric evaluation" (sifa jingshenbing jianding) (8–9). In practice this close relationship between psychiatry and law meant that religious, cultural, and political dissenters often were subject to compulsory hospitalization, where surgery, drugs, physical restraint, and torture were common methods of control. Such a practice also existed in the Soviet Union, where, Munro explains, those with "reformist delusions," "litigation mania," "overvalued religiosity," or "an interest in poorly-understood and bizarre foreign fashions and trends in art, literature and philosophy, and discussion of such interests" often were locked up and treated (20). In China, which worked within a similar ideological framework, people who gave "reactionary speeches," put up "posters with absurd content," and committed other anti-social acts also were institutionalized, operated upon, and drugged. Recently, Dutch forensic psychiatry professor B.C.M. Raes and forensic psychiatrist B. B. van der Meer evaluated Wang Wanxing, a Chinese dissident who spent thirteen years in a mental hospital run by the state, finding no mental disorder. Apparently Wang was confined for unfurling a banner critical of the state; he was described as having "delusions of grandeur, litigation mania and conspicuously enhanced pathological will" (Kahn 2006).

Munro's point is not that psychiatric abuses occurred only in socialist countries, although through his work as China research director of Human Rights Watch in Hong Kong from 1989–1998, he is intent on publicizing these abuses and recommending change (Human Rights Watch 2002).[32] As he points out, forced psychiatric treatment in the form of insulin coma therapy, electroconvulsive shock therapy (ECT), and prefrontal lobotomy were once common treatments in Europe and the United States, adding that "tens of thousands of lobotomies were performed in the United States from 1936 until around 1952" (Munro 2000, 23, n. 50). Munro credits Ken Kesey's novel *One Flew over the Cuckoo's Nest* and the film of the same title with changing American opinion about psychosurgery, which lost popularity in the 1970s. Although psychosurgery was banned in the Soviet Union in the mid-1950s, in China insulin coma therapy and ECT are still in use (24). ECT is also still used in the United States, where it has enjoyed a recent resurgence as a treatment for depression, and in several European countries, although it is now administered with anesthesia. Furthermore, in China as in the United States, Europe, and the Soviet Union, psychiatrists often genuinely believed and still hold that these invasive and sometimes forced therapies help or even cure the deeply psychotic.

Over the revolutionary period, argues Munro (2000), Mao's emphasis on will and subjectivity evolved into the belief that incorrect thinking or mentality was a crime. From 1972 to 1978, Chinese psychiatrists debated the "essential nature of mental illness," and eventually hammered out a return to international standards of diagnosis and definition (7–8). Contending that the politicization of Chinese psychiatry went well beyond that of the Soviet Union, Munro claims that the total number of political activists imprisoned during the Cultural Revolution far exceeded the number of violent criminals or violent mentally ill that were imprisoned at the same time (11). One document that Munro translates and publishes confirms the high number of political dissidents branded as mentally ill over the first four decades of the People's Republic of China (13).

Even recognizing that the line between the socially different, the dissident or simply uncooperative, and the mentally ill may not be entirely clear, we see that in cases where diagnosed psychosis consists of political, social, cultural, or religious difference or disagreement, the reigning concept of the mental in Chinese revolutionary culture is based on recognition and embodiment of a social agreement or contract that underlies thought and behavior. Those who refuse to recognize the power relationships of society and their position within these relationships are, by definition, mentally ill. If their mental illness can be addressed through socially oriented therapies that use suggestion (anshi) and reasoning (shuili) to improve recognition (renshi), such people can be reabsorbed into the social body (Chin and Chin 1969, 87). If not, their refusal to improve their mentality—that is, to recognize and live through proper social relations—becomes a form of psychosis, or a disturbance of spirit. Munro's examples show that sometimes mental illness (jingshen bing) is the enforced consequence of a person's failure to recognize and live by the ideological demands of the day—or, in other words, a failure to recognize and embody a correct social position.

In order to understand this point more deeply, we must take a closer look at the deployment of spirit within the cultural and ideological realm, where it refers to an important aspect of the mental processes and subjective and emotional life of the revolutionary subject. In the early 20th century, the word "spirit" often appears in conjunction with "revolution" (geming), although it is by no means restricted to that context.[33] In socialist China, the term *spiritual civilization*, referring to mental life, culture, and spirit, was taken from Hegelian and Marxist philosophy and became both a general concept covering all aspects of culture and a highly ideological term. For example, the *Dictionary of Spiritual Civilization* (Jingshen wenming cidian) lists 887 entries (Gao Qinghai 1983).[34] The editor explains that aside from dictionary items that are part of the emergence and development of "spiritual civilization," the rest are items relevant to the development of culture and thought, "especially terms, technical phrases, and primary theories, people, and texts commonly used in the development of socialist spiritual civilization" (Gao Qinghai 1983, n.p.). Included are population study, natural philosophy, contradictions among the people, Mao Zedong, Marx, fiction, genius, chemistry, public morality, study of oracle bones, psychology (xinlixue), subjectivism, Leninism, sympathy, freedom, social psychology, revolutionary position, myth, theory, nihilism, good and evil, Lei Feng, among many. Twenty-six terms begin with the word "civilization" (wenming), twenty-eight with "society" (shehui), forty-two with "morality" (daode), and five with "spirit." Those five are spiritual civilization (jingshen wenming), spiritual life (jingshen shenghuo), spiritual world (jingshen jingjie), radical idealism (jingshen wanneng lun), and radical anti-idealism (jingshen wuneng lun). After a brief explanation, the phrase "spiritual civilization" directs us to the page explaining the contrast between "material civilization" (wuzhi wenming) and spiritual civilization:

> Material culture is the material result of having transformed the natural world. It is expressed in progress in material production and improvement of material life. Spiritual civilization occurs when simultaneous to the human transformation of the objective world, the subjective world also is transformed. Social spiritual production and spiritual life are developed and expressed as education, science, the development of cultural knowledge, and the elevation of standards of human thought, politics, and morality. The construction of material culture is a foundation that must not be lacking in the construction of socialist spiritual civilization. Socialist spiritual civilization greatly encourages the development of material civilization, and guarantees that it develops along the correct path. Each is the condition of the other, and neither can be lacking . . . Spiritual civilization cannot be detached from material conditions. Historically, no spiritual life or spiritual production has been totally divorced from the limitations of material conditions. (Gao 1983, n.p.)

One year before the publication of this dictionary, spirit and spiritual civilization were given center stage in a political / cultural movement with widespread repercussions. The Anti-"Spiritual Pollution" Campaign (Fan jingshen wuran yundong) of 1983 raised the possibility that the Cultural Revolution, with its extreme emphasis on the subjective and its expression in political action and daily life, might begin again. As was made clear by the targets of the movement, the degradation of spirit was seen as a serious matter that could occur through exposure to pornography, decadent Western customs, or many other things. The term "spiritual civilization" figured largely in the campaign, which through its emphasis on correct thinking and behavior provides insight into the meaning of spirit in revolutionary culture (Larson 1989; Brugger and Kelly 1990, 137–60).

The same focus we have seen in psychological and psychiatric discourse was apparent in a more overtly ideological context from the early 1950s, carried on from its development over the decades of resistance to imperialism, the Anti-Japanese War, and civil war. In 1951, Hu Qiaomu (1912–92) (1952) argued that attitude was the most important thing that cultural workers—artists and writers—must address if they wanted to live a revolutionary lifestyle: "Therefore, in order to allow the literary and art workers to fully put into a leadership role the spiritual life (jingshen shenghuo) of our nation's people, we cannot but strive to stand with the working class, we cannot but strive to establish a close relationship with the working people" (6). Spirit trumped matter in some texts preceding the Cultural Revolution, as we see in this 1964 comment by Cao Zefu: "We can go a step further and state that human life does not only include material life, but also spiritual life. Furthermore, the spiritual life of the human being is loftier than material life. This is because: first, politics are our commander, and are an absolute for human life" (1964, 2).[35] And immediately preceding the Cultural Revolution, although Mao argued for a dialectical relationship between matter and spirit, his aim was to determine "where correct thinking comes from": "Correct recognition often must go through the several back-and-forth movements from matter to spirit (wuzhi dao jingshen), from spirit to matter, from practice to recognition, from recognition to practice, before it can reach completion" (Mao Zedong 1986, 840).

This ideological interpretation of spirit—along with its emotive and behavioral expression—gained perfect incarnation in a figure whose revolutionary spirit flashed across the country in slogan and image. Although Ah Q continued to be evoked as a negative symbol throughout the revolutionary period, his luster was stolen by the upstart Lei Feng (1940–62), who after his death became a culture phenomenon whose influence rivaled that of his "evil twin" from the early 20th century. The so-called Lei Feng spirit (Lei Feng jingshen) came to stand as an embodiment of the spirit in the flesh, someone whose social life was in perfect congruence with his revolutionary spirit. As a symbol for and enactment of the spirit as it was interpreted in revolutionary culture, Lei Feng provided a flawless model of negotiation between the spiritual, material, and social worlds.

THE LEI FENG SPIRIT

Ah Q and Lei Feng can be regarded as two sides of the same coin, as doppelgangers, or as mutual "others." At best a victim, at worst pathetic and conniving, Ah Q appeared in articles, films, woodcuts, and drawings representing either all that was bad about Chinese culture and spirit or all that had been backed into a corner by military and cultural imperialism. This fearful image is the opposite of the heroic presentation of Lei Feng, especially after he was elevated to near sainthood by Mao's March 5, 1963, hand-written proclamation "Learn from Lei Feng" (Xiang Lei Feng xuexi). But both Ah Q and Lei Feng are exemplars of spirit—in Ah Q's case, of the spiritual victory method, in Lei Feng's, the spirit of the cog (literally the "spirit of the screw" [luosiding jingshen]). In *The True Story of Ah Q* and in the relentless cultural activity in creating and disseminating the story of Lei Feng, we see how for the two figures, spirit embodies the negotiation of social stance and position. Ah Q and Lei Feng capture the primary cultural contradiction of their times. For Ah Q, it is the constant and difficult compromise and conciliation with power in the form of the village aristocracy, nunneries and monasteries, the little-understood revolutionaries, the Qing military, the judiciary, and his immediate cohorts, all important as he inches himself toward a seemingly more potent position. For Lei Feng, it is the direct translation of revolutionary culture, in the important Maoist notion of "serve the people," into subjectivity, and the extension of that idea into and through behavior, thought, and emotion.

Ah Q and Lei Feng both react to the environment in which they live, forming their theories and behavior out of minute interactions and split-second decisions. To some extent, both of them transform the social and material world with the unique spiritual resources they develop to survive and actualize their vision. Although neither is politically powerful or materially wealthy, their relationship to the powerful and rich reveals some differences that can help us pinpoint and understand the nature of spirit in revolutionary culture. Ah Q's impoverished life is a struggle toward material sufficiency based on an imagined but unrealized unification of matter and subjectivity; it is because he cannot grasp the benefits of the material world that Ah Q must develop his theory of spiritual victory. This aspect of the Ah Q spirit is given form in the 1958 film *The True Story of Ah Q*, directed by Yuan Yang'an (1905–) in Hong Kong, which contains an extensive scene of a lavishly dressed Ah Q transformed by his imagination into a wealthy official. This scene, which is not in the novel, shows Ah Q as one by one either forgiving or condemning those who had wronged him, emphasizing the way in which the story depicts social relations as determining consciousness.

For Lei Feng, however, no opposition between matter and spirit exists. Lei Feng is the quintessence of the idea of permanent revolution during peaceful times, as he translates the common vocabulary of struggle into his life work:

> When struggle is the most arduous and victory is in the future is the time when it is easiest to waver. So for each person, that is the critical juncture of the ordeal. If you can endure the ordeal and smoothly pass through that critical juncture, you can become a revolutionary soldier; if you cannot bear the ordeal and fail to make it through the juncture, you become a shameful deserter. Whether you become a revolutionary soldier or a shameful deserter depends entirely on whether you have unwavering faith in the face of trouble. (Wang Zengfan 1979, 78, quoting Lei Feng's diary)

A member of the People's Liberation Army, Lei Feng was noted for his willingness to sacrifice personal comfort to help others. After a truck driven by a friend hit and killed him, his diary was discovered and made public. That was the beginning of the Lei Feng myth and the transformation of his life into a narrative and an image with national implications. As did Ah Q, Lei Feng gained wide currency through a story.

Ah Q, the imaginary creation of Lu Xun, struggles against conditions that crush his ideal vision of social life, a vision in which he is recognized for his contributions and lives comfortably, in an ordinary way, with a wife and family (Ah Q worries about his failure to produce descendants). His "spiritual victory" method is a strategy that allows him to continue to exist under conditions of oppression and victimization, and also a tactic that prevents him from fully recognizing the lowliness of his true social position. Lei Feng, a historical figure known through his diary, embodies a world in which subjectivity does not conflict with material and social reality. He has what he wants, and needs only to actualize it, to produce a seamless connection between the subjective and the material. The Lei Feng spirit, or the spirit of the cog, is a true taking on or internalizing of the theory of permanent revolution in every aspect.[36]

Because Lei Feng is an exemplar of revolutionary optimism, it is important to note that although the Lei Feng constructed through story and image recognizes the obstacles produced by material life, with its discomforts in the form of heat, cold, exhaustion, and exertion caused by the resistance of matter, the struggle is almost entirely internal or spiritual.[37] If one can obtain the correct understanding of work and life as a revolutionary, then many real-life situations attain clarity, and decisions about what to do and how to do it come into view. Images of Lei Feng doing battle with material forces are scattered throughout popular culture as posters and woodcuts. For example, one drawing shows him carrying a full bucket and mop while two smiling elderly observers look on. The title tells us how to interpret the scene: "Learn from Comrade Lei Feng—a revolutionary spirit in which speech and actions are unified." Another drawing depicts him mending while a man sleeps behind him, with the caption "Learn from Comrade Lei Feng—his communist style of being selfless and for the greater good." Perhaps most succinctly indicating the spiritual demands of Lei Feng's model is a poster showing him knee-deep in water, surrounded by jagged ice, snow falling as he helps another soldier hook a rope to a truck, in order to pull out a vehicle that has turned on its side. "Learn from Comrade Lei Feng—a proletarian fighting will that does not heed the body," the caption reads, translated literally. Lei Feng is often pictured working, with the implication that he is saving others who are weaker, more tired, or less willing to exert themselves, who are often shown in the background or nearby. At the same time, Lei Feng also is often shown studying Mao's works, reading, lecturing, or teaching, clearly developing and expanding the spirit and theory of selflessness.[38] While Ah Q again became a topic of debate in the 1980s, a new "learn from Lei Feng" movement was initiated in 1990, a fact that speaks to the relevance of the model constructed from his image.[39]

It is these imagined seamless transitions between the subjective, the social, and the material that we need to take seriously and keep in mind as we investigate post-Mao culture, especially those aspects of the culture that directly represent the revolutionary past. Undoubtedly the fictional Ah Q and the idealized Lei Feng are only imaginary constructions that pinpoint the extremes of popular perception. But their wide acceptance as negative and positive cultural models, their persistent popularity, and their power in creating influential images and narratives should alert us to the kind of mentality that was developed under revolutionary Chinese culture. The revolutionary subject was consumed not by a deeply sexualized unconscious, but by a social vision that demanded a keen sense of one's position and one's relationship to power and a well-developed emotional and intellectual expression of this position. This is the central contradiction that is negotiated and mediated through figures like Ah Q and Lei Feng; they struggle on one hand to recognize and realize a position, and on the other to actualize a vision in which subjectivity must passionately embody this theory. For both of them, spirit, or *jingshen*, is the moment and indication of this struggle.

FOUR

The Spirit of the Countryside

Mang Ke's Wild Things *and Wang Xiaobo's* The Golden Years

The long discourse of the countryside in 20th-century Chinese fiction has left a "heavy historical legacy," as one critic puts it, and brought to the fore conflicts between revolution and modernity, two themes that sometimes merged and at other times separated (He Jixian 2004, 8; Yingjin Zhang 1996).[1] The relationship between the countryside and modernity in their many representations and forms was never simple or easy to conceptualize. While the work of some writers implied that the countryside was a site of an ignorant, slave-like mentality that needed to be excised from the new, modern China, others found a poetic land that contained not only the ability to fight the excesses of modernity, but the very nucleus of Chinese—and later revolutionary—values. Writers chose different approaches to the problem of the countryside, their styles ranging from sarcastic mocking to adulatory praise. The countryside became even more meaningful under revolutionary culture, which increasingly injected it with attractive emotional, ideological, and aesthetic qualities. Writers who worked under the demands of revolutionary literature had no choice but to somehow come to terms with the countryside. Although many famous writers have written about the countryside, three of the most well known are Lu Xun, Shen Congwen (1902–88), and Zhao Shuli (1906–70). Along with the later roots-seeking tradition of Han Shaogong (1953–), Ah Cheng (1949–), and others, their work represents four major literary directions in writing about the countryside.

With his oft-repeated theme of educated young men returning to their homes in the countryside, Lu Xun often is given credit for having "discovered" the countryside in modern Chinese literature. His story "My Old Home" (Guxiang) is the most famous prototype for the encounter between the intellectual narrator, with his intensely experienced subjectivity and tentative mentality, and the countryside, bifurcated into a luminous memory and a brutal, unsavory social and material reality, a reality that the relatively privileged narrator never perceived as a child. While recognizing the poverty of peasants and the physical toil of working the land, Lu Xun rarely relinquishes the narrative viewpoint of the intellectual's mind, through which the countryside and its long-term inhabitants are newly observed and experienced. There are few "healthy" peasants in Lu Xun's writing, and stories such as "Soap" and "The True Story of Ah Q" add "country gentlemen" into the mix, usually putting them in a less than favorable light as well. In Lu Xun's fiction, the best thing that can be said about the countryside is that peasants are not responsible for their suffering, although they may be cruel and stupid. In any case, unless one is a child in a privileged family—hardly a long-term position, since the child eventually grows up to become either a doubting intellectual or a corrupt or insensitive country gentleman—Lu Xun's countryside generally takes on a negative hue (Lu Taiguang 2004, 17). As a catalyst for intellectual angst, self-criticism, and social judgment, it also occupies a position of subservience in relation to these more important issues, and thus although it is supremely significant, it is instrumentalized within the narrative structure.

Shen Congwen admitted to being influenced by Lu Xun and his tendency to present the countryside or village life through memories (Chen Zhonggeng 2004, 72).[2] Shen's approach, however, is quite different than that of Lu Xun, as he uses a more lyrical style and expresses more sympathy for those who live in rural areas. Much more than Lu Xun, Shen Congwen portrays a countryside that could be favorably exploited if one were seeking positive attributes of the so-called Chinese spirit. Honesty, purity, local color, and a vibrant daily existence all are part of Shen's portrayal of country life, which also can be tinged with mystery and thereby carry a spiritual quality completely missing in Lu Xun's version. In Shen's work, the inarticulate, numb-minded quality of Runtu, the wretched vulnerability of Xianglin's wife, and the pathetic self-deception of Ah Q are gone, although Shen's stories can recognize brutality and suffering. Shen's name is often associated with the term *nativism* (xiangtu) in modern Chinese literature, a tendency that recognizes his more romantic approach to representing the countryside (Kinkley 1985).

In 1946, Guo Moruo, Mao Dun (1896–1981), Zhou Yang (1908–89) and others began to introduce and promote the work of Zhao Shuli. After 1947, when Chen Huangmei (1913–93) published "Stride Forward in the Direction of Zhao Shuli" (Xiang Zhao Shuli fangxiang maijin) in the *People's Daily* (August 10), Zhao's fiction came to represent a turning point between the individualistic, urban, intellectual fiction of the past and the emerging revolutionary discourse of the countryside. Zhao, however, regarded himself as an intellectual, and his work as an eclectic mix of Chinese and foreign influences (Kuang Xinnian 2004, 16–18). That did not stop his fiction from being regarded as the most authentic voice of the countryside to emerge in the modern period, and his stance as one of "friendship" with peasants (Cheng Zhonggeng 2004, 73). Although he was lauded as a genuine peasant writer by Mao Zedong, Zhao's characters, setting, and plots bore little relationship to the increasingly glorified writing about rural life that emerged from Yan'an and eventually became an important part of the worker-peasant-soldier literary tradition. As Zhao claimed,

> "Xiao Erhei Gets Married" (Xiao Erhei jiehun) did not mention party members at all. In Soviet writing, someone always comes in from beyond, and then you end up with communist thought, which seems to be poured in from the outside. The countryside did not give birth to communist thought, that is for sure. If we want to be more accurate with village characters, it always seems strange to give them communist thoughts. (Kuang Xinnian 2004, 16–17)

Focusing on daily life and customs, Zhao's writing is often regarded as producing a strong "reality effect" that avoids the sharp critique of Lu Xun and the later pumped-up glory of revolutionary romanticism (Yang Kai 2004, 28).[3] The late 1950s criticism of Zhao's writing emphasized his tendency to assign elements of backward, non-revolutionary thought—such as self-interest—to the peasants.

Finally, the roots-seeking writers Han Shaogong, Ah Cheng, and others portray the countryside as a unique site where well-educated Chinese youth can delve into basic principles of Chinese culture that have not been contaminated by excessively stultifying civilization.[4] The soul of the nation once again is a center of concern, and solutions are to be found in the periphery, often in non-Han cultures where, the writers imply, a deep, essentially unchanged spiritual essence still resides. The goal of roots literature is not to represent the day-to-day lives of people in the countryside, but to take advantage of the actual and symbolic distance between the city and the countryside to question modern values and directions.

In this chapter, I analyze two novels that are set during the Cultural Revolution; each has as its protagonist a male sent-down youth (zhiqing, literally "knowledge youth") who gets involved in one or more sexual relationships, a theme highlighted throughout. Each narrative also negotiates with spiritual aspects of the countryside as it was imagined under revolutionary culture, and a consciousness informed by that spirit. The former Misty poet Mang Ke's 1994 novel *Wild Things* (Yeshi), set during the Cultural Revolution, is an example of sent-down youth literature (zhiqing wenxue), a genre that offers its own understanding of the countryside.[5] The encounter between the already cynical sent-down youth and those with whom he interacts is a collision between post-revolutionary sentiments and the discourse of the countryside, which is flattened historically, spatially, and thematically—but most importantly, aesthetically—in the encounter. The novel offers neither a new perspective on the Cultural Revolution nor a proposal on behalf of sexual excess as the ethos of the future or the linchpin of a new subjectivity. The opposition is expressed through the very flatness of experience, sensation, and aesthetics, or the gutting of a once-rich set of references, that exceeds its deconstruction of the rural, expanding into a flatness of consciousness. The main character, Maodi, is opportunistic in his alliances but offers nothing in terms of a positive orientation toward the future. Although Mang Ke's aesthetic imagination contains a temporal aspect in its treatment of history and historical discourse, his vision mostly addresses itself to the spatial implications of revolutionary consciousness.

In Wang Xiaobo's *The Golden Years* (Huangjin shidai), the countryside is even less of an actor in its own right, appearing more as background, or as a site where meaning seemingly disconnected to its existence can be produced. However, in this process, the discourse of the countryside undergoes transformation as its former qualities appear in a new light, even though that change is not the primary target of the author's efforts. Whereas Mang Ke deconstructs the very notion of spiritual embodiment and consciousness through his spatial flattening and oddly disconnected histories, events, and styles, Wang Xiaobo works at the intersection of time and consciousness, evoking a novel temporal sense that both softens and philosophizes the revolutionary time of political movements, with their characteristic expressions of passionate loyalty and historical innocence. For Wang Xiaobo, time expands, infiltrating any forward march with a muffled throb that ends in the aging of the body. The sense of time that becomes Wang's deconstructive tool eats away at the immediacy, fervent and deeply held emotion, clear-cut expression of position, optimism, and drive toward progress that make up the revolutionary spirit. The sexual relationship—never expressed as an all-consuming passion for the protagonist—provides a form through which this temporal revision can work. The narrator's recounting of the story from a detached point in the future, and the aging of the characters are two strategies Wang uses to construct anti-revolutionary time. This philosophical time combines with a quiet immediacy in the sexual encounters to produce a profoundly non-revolutionary sense of life and consciousness.

The two main characters of these novels—Maodi and Wang Er—are each a kind of anti–Lei Feng. The first of these dispassionate creatures jerks across the landscape without taking root, belying over fifty years of rural transcendence. The second distances himself from the lived meaning of the countryside and toys with the passion of emotional involvement. Both stories challenge the revolutionary discourse of the countryside, not only in ideology and theme, but also as it is experienced subjectively. In other words, the way in which revolutionary optimism, well captured and expressed in the figure of Lei Feng, is not merely an attitude but a structuring of time and space is the topic of these novels. Whereas Mang Ke provides very little in terms of an imagined new subjectivity, Wang Xiaobo proposes a gentle, somewhat ironical philosophical detachment that can stand up to and possibly even replace the revolutionary mindset.

MANG KE'S WILD THINGS: FLATTENING THE REVOLUTIONARY PAST

While perhaps seeming to investigate a new binary between the "old" revolutionary values and the "new" opportunistic, libidinal economy, *Wild Things* does not actually offer a simple split or choice, but rather manipulates each so that they play off each other as two equally uninviting ways of being.

Narrator and sent-down youth Maodi flits among the young country women with whom he has sex, alighting only superficially on their bodies, in their families, and within the cultural environment where they live, weaving an aesthetics of flattened perception that displaces the depth-laden, fervor-producing atmosphere of the revolutionary past. The once ideologically charged countryside is thoroughly reformed in this vision; rather than functioning as the mystical center of the national spirit, it is gutted of any particular meaning, degenerating into a series of trivial family disputes, encounters between women and men, and violence uninformed by hope, ideals, or knowledge. In a backward move that inserts the present into the past, *Wild Things* undermines the very idea of revolutionary passion as ever having been a motivating force, fundamentally questioning its veracity and reality. Both country life—potentially rich as a symbolic repository of meaning while remaining materially poor—and the new sexual morality are but tools that the author uses to compress historical time and flatten the fertile spatial distinction between country and city that has informed much of modern Chinese culture.

Wild Things works on at least three levels to demolish the idea of revolutionary passion, in the process deconstructing the countryside and situating itself within and against the long discourse of the rural. Its first method is thematic: a persistent topos is the ongoing sexual relationships between Maodi and various women, as well as those between other characters. The representation of sexual desire and behavior through intercourse, flirting, rape, and jockeying for sexual power is so pervasive in the novel as to diminish other ways of relating or existing. Second and related to the first, the novel is structured through the logic of Maodi's series of sexual encounters, turning his arousal into a lever that gives birth to a robotic aesthetic sense. Third, the novel cuts the reader off from a sense of historical continuity, presenting the lives of the characters as if they had popped up from a vacuum. Altogether no notion of depth—emotional, psychological, spiritual, or otherwise—exists within the novel's logic as the narrative is flattened and stretched.

The makeover of the countryside into a sexual field is seminal to Mang Ke's novelistic vision, and the first and last paragraphs of the first chapter lay out the transformation from a Maoist emphasis on labor to the new perspective:

> In April of that year, Mai Village, which was on the banks of Daqing Lake, in my eyes seemed like a peasant woman who labors endlessly, always an anxious, unhappy look on her bitter face, her hair always blown about wildly by strong winds off the lake. (Mang Ke 1994, 1)

> Only after I had run off some distance did I stop and look back. At this moment, the line of houses where Mai Feng's house was appeared like a naked woman darkly lying along the riverbank. Was she asleep? I guessed that even if she didn't sleep all night, she could not go without sleep. Was she asleep? I still wondered, could she sleep? (8)

In this first chapter, Maodi braves the dangers of imagined dogs, the possibility of being caught by Mai Feng's mother (who fought the Japanese with swords), and thoughts of her father, a county magistrate (who, we learn in the next chapter, fought Nationalist party leader Chiang Kai-shek), in order to sneak into Mai Feng's room. Although historical references designed to produce awe and respect are present, every myth of the countryside is quickly discharged. Whereas Lu Xun weighed the benefit of awakening the sleeping masses locked in an iron room of ignorance, enlightening them about the conditions of their oppression, Mang Ke's line of village houses is a naked sleeping woman, her only possibility of being awakened coming not from the much-needed enlightenment that would cause the sleeping Chinese masses to awaken from a self-knowledge-starved stupor inside their iron house, as Lu Xun once famously discussed in his preface to "Call to Arms" (Na han), but from sexual pleasure. Under Mang Ke's pen, the countryside, which had once embodied the essence of revolutionary values and became a mystical national site where a transformative schooling of the urban intelligentsia took place, appears as a series of obstacles through which he makes his way to the object of his desire. Maodi recognizes the ideological weight of the history of Mai Feng's mother and father, but he does not exist within a symbolic system that values their accomplishments. He also understands that the village is named after the Mai family and that Mai Feng's father has a relatively powerful position within the political order of the day. Yet neither the historical depth of significance nor the immediate hierarchy of power can absorb Maodi into their symbolic sphere. Like a pinball careening from point to point, Maodi shies away from dangerous spots and propels himself toward the multiple female bodies that populate his landscape.

Maodi's engagement with the peasants and country life does not leave the countryside untouched, although he himself does not instigate any change. Through his liaisons and friendships, the once-revolutionary location becomes saturated with sexual opportunities, metamorphosing into a productive site that adapts itself well to Maodi's thought and behavior. Yet the sexual focus does not begin—as one might imagine it should for a novel written between 1989 and 1993—in an imagined transfer of commoditized urban culture into the once-pristine rural environment but, under Mang Ke's pen, turns out to be indigenous to the countryside. This perspective is merely exposed as Maodi intermingles with his friends and sexual partners. It is revealed in multiple ways, especially through Maodi's impression that his future partners teem with a sexual desire that he can easily tap. Even more significantly, Mang Ke depicts many interactions among peasants as sexual in nature, and sometimes bizarrely so.

The first chapter of *Wild Things* describes Maodi having sex with Mai Feng. The second features him going over the Mai family background, the village situation, and his enforced "brotherhood" with Dachou, who demands a privileged relationship after glimpsing him naked at Mai Feng's house. In the third chapter, the sexual energy bubbling just below the surface of country life becomes the central topic. When production team manager Mai Dazhuang calls Maodi out to work in the fields, Maodi discovers that he is the lone young man working with a group of elderly women and men. One of the women, Xiao Baie, confronts Maodi from the traditional perspective of asking him, a young single man, when he is going to get married, and whether he looks down on country dwellers. This relatively conventional entry into sexual topics—that mentions the real-life cultural and material deficiency of the rural environment—allows Xiao Baie to initiate and sustain unwanted banter about things obscene enough to turn Maodi's ears red and cause the other women to titter. Although it may seem odd that Maodi would find any kind of sexual talk offensive, these older women are not his target population. His embarrassment also could indicate the foundation of traditional morality underlying countryside life, which author Mang Ke frequently invokes, if but briefly and dismissively. The combination of Maodi's unlikely humiliation and the extreme to which the sexual nature of the encounter goes also points to its constructed nature, and the author's desire to push his vision as far as possible.

While ruminating on the hypocrisy of using the Dazhai production model in an area with little good farmland, a perpetual lack of food, and government-supplied moldy corn that turns one's feces black, Maodi witnesses Mai Dazhuang walk up and put his hand on Xiao Baie's crotch:

> Fortunately Mai Dazhuang arrived at just the right moment. When he saw that they were making fun of me, he walked up behind Xiao Baie and grabbed her crotch. At that moment I was liberated, but Mai Dazhuang had shaken the hornets' nest. Xiao Baie turned and let out a shriek, and then she held his arm and called all the other women to pin him to the ground.

> In a moment they had his pants off, and then I saw Xiao Baie's hand fiddle with the thing under the production manager's crotch.
>
> "You want to take advantage, I'll make sure you get your fill!" Xiao Baie's hand and mouth both were moving.
>
> "My god! My god!" Mai Dazhuang did not beg to be let off, but just yelled.
>
> After a while, even without watching I could figure out the results. Otherwise those old women wouldn't laugh so strangely, or jump around like a bunch of ducks hitting the frying pan. (Mang Ke 1994, 18–19)

Both the women and Mai Dazhuang seem to enjoy the sexual encounter, which progresses farther than we might imagine possible under these circumstances. Mang Ke's immediate contamination of the once ideologically pure labor environment by a somewhat perverse sexual encounter could not be more revisionary. In this novel, most of the men and women in the countryside have sordid sexual histories involving various forms of adultery, rape, and sexual revenge for perceived or actual insults. In another example from the novel, one of Maodi's sexual partners, Li Xiaojiu, is a young woman who also has sex with the middle-aged party branch secretary Mai Youcai, a not-uncommon form of behavior. As Maodi states, "Mai village, little Mai village, there were more villages like this on the earth than stars in the sky," implying that this kind of sexual activity goes on all over the country (Mang Ke 1994, 111). In the treatment of this theme, the countryside is not Lu Xun's home of the ignorant and dumb, or Shen Congwen's colorful and mysterious environment, or Zhao Shuli's humorous if ordinary and pedestrian world, or the beckoning site of renewal that the roots-seeking writers depict. Yet much as it did for earlier writers, the countryside here also functions as an instrument that the author makes use of, not as the target of his investigations. Mang Ke is not interested in the countryside in and of itself.

It would be incorrect to state that in *Wild Things* the origin of sexual desire lies in the countryside, since Maodi's overarching interest in sex does not begin there; for that reason, we cannot accuse the author of romancing the rural. The group of sent-down youth with which he lives in Mai village is every bit as sexually interested as are the true country dwellers, and his city friend Peng Wen, also known as Little Scholar (Xiao Xiucai), is no exception. Maodi meets his first girlfriend, Bai Xiaoyi, at Little Scholar's home in the city. Yet neither is sexual desire imported from the city into the countryside. By seamlessly incorporating the countryside into his overarching sexualization of time and space, Mang Ke reconstructs an important and long-standing aspect of revolutionary discourse (the difference between the urban and the rural), a strategy that contributes to the novel's aesthetic flatness. What the countryside does provide is easy mobility and the ability to flutter between two accessible communities of friends and acquaintances. Although Maodi's comment—"Ah, nothing makes you feel that time passes faster than having little to do and living with a woman"—is in reference to his city girlfriend Xiao Baiyi, it applies equally to his experience in the once-holy countryside, where this sentiment is clearly not the proper dream of a revolutionary youth (Mang Ke 1994, 60).

A DISJOINTED HISTORY

We see at least two kinds of significant history in *Wild Things*: revolutionary history and sexual history. Both appear in different guises as they are expressed through the village, the family, or the individual. While sexual history is pervasive and immediate, revolutionary history is shown as disconnected from lived reality, existing more as a false shell of meaning that has little to do with actual relationships, decisions, or behavior.

It goes without saying that neither Maodi nor the other characters have a true belief in revolutionary values; nor do they have an egalitarian social conscience linked to revolutionary idealism, a sense of selflessness, or a concept of serving the people. Cynicism about the revolution is so much a part of these characters and their times as to be unremarked. The first family/individual history to which we are introduced is that of Bai Xiaoyi, Maodi's city girlfriend who eventually makes an appearance in the village, becomes friends with Maodi's main countryside girlfriend Mai Feng, and takes Mai Feng to the hospital to arrange a forced miscarriage when she becomes pregnant. In chapters 5 and 6, Maodi recounts his first encounter with Bai Xiaoyi, who needed a place to stay after breaking up with her coarse, hoodlum-like boyfriend Wang Daan, and approaches her friend Peng Wen when Maodi is visiting.

All of the city characters have families broken apart by the Cultural Revolution, a history that Maodi dutifully if briefly narrates: Peng Wen's father was killed by the "proletariat," and his mother and sister sent to "cadre school" in the countryside. Bai Xiaoyi's parents were branded as capitalists; when she discovered they were not her biological parents as a young teenager, she still refused to disown them and was beaten and nearly raped by a Red Guard, eventually taking Wang Daan on as a boyfriend for protection. This early sexual history—a direct product of the revolutionary environment—is what prods Bai Xiaoyi into a precocious sexual awareness, and it is she, not Maodi, who initiates their sexual encounter by putting her hand down his pants, even though from the beginning Maodi appreciates her alluring face and body and imagines the three of them sleeping in Peng Wen's bed.

And all of this occurs during the Cultural Revolution, when distrust and political paranoia were thriving:

> Maybe it was because I now not only had a girlfriend but also had made love, I felt I had many more worries than before. I could not avoid thinking about things I should think about, or make plans for Bai Xiaoyi and me for the future. Especially after she and I let our desires rage for several days, as the fire of my desire clearly slackened my head slowly cleared, and my anxieties increased. Yes, living at Little Scholar's house, I had to keep my head on. And when was this, anyway? It was when people of every description were "revolting" like crazy, attacking class enemies everywhere. Suspicious, fearful eyes abounded. (Mang Ke 1994, 59)

Revolutionary history, seen here as little more than a cause of fear and anxiety, has become a parody of its once deeply embodied notions of idealism, self-sacrifice, and service to the People. All it is, Maodi notes, is "people hurting people," and his only goal is to wend his way through the streets pasted with slogans encouraging people to "overturn" or "smash" and get to Wang Daan's house so he can lay claim on Bai Xiaoyi (Mang Ke 1994, 59).

Although revolutionary history is hollow in Maodi's life, he still knows of it and notes its former significance, if largely through its failure to impress and its frustrating tendency to cause him concern. Revolutionary history hangs like a shroud, completely disconnected from his life and that of those around him. No one is motivated by the ideals of the revolution, and its lingering, shell-like tenacity, the author murkily implies, may be one motivation behind the serial-encounter model that underlies daily life. The historical disconnect can be seen clearly in another scene, Mang Ke's description of the factional struggle that breaks loose in the village. In chapter 13, Maodi, Dachou, and Bai Xiaoyi—who has joined them in the village—take a boat out on the lake, eventually jumping into the water for a swim. While admiring the tank top clinging to Bai Xiaoyi's body and outlining her full breasts, Maodi is startled by shouts of "Don't move!" A group of some thirty or forty people with guns demands to know the three's affiliation:

> The leader pulled a long face and walked over to us. "Which village are you from?" he asked.
>
> I thought he must be the head, so I said, "Production manager, we are from Mai village."
>
> "Which faction?" he continued.
>
> "What you do mean, 'faction?' No one sent us," I responded, confused.
>
> "I—am asking you which faction!" His voice and appearance were stern.
>
> "We aren't in a faction, not part of any group." Dachou promptly responded for me.
>
> I suddenly understood. "We aren't rebels or loyalists," I quickly added. (Mang Ke 1994, 97–98)

Maodi's initial misunderstanding comes from the dual implications of the word *pai*, which can mean "faction" or "to send (someone somewhere)." He has so little appreciation of the mental context of the revolutionary situation that he fails to understand that the leader is referring to political or revolutionary factions, opting instead for the more common meaning of the word. Unable to figure out which faction is which, and who the enemies are, Maodi goes back to his dormitory to the sound of bullets. The next day he learns that Mai Laozhu was the first person named Mai to die in the fighting, a "fact" that is questioned at the end of the novel.

A later scene pits sexual pleasure against political mobilization more directly. The village broadcast system puts out a call for a meeting, causing a sent-down youth named Dayanr to complain from his bed that he was in the midst of a beautiful dream and "just about to enter" (Mang Ke 1994, 172). The comment produces an exchange of sexual taunts among the sent-down youth in the dormitory, which results in Hu Ren and Ma Nan pulling down Dayanr's pants and masturbating him. Interrupted, they rush to the meeting, where they hear Mai Youcai lecture about the revolutionary class struggle and learn that they will be taking up arms to protect the village against factional strife. When asked if they are rebels or loyalists, Mai Youcai replies: "Of course we are revolutionaries!" (176). The arming of youth destroys the peaceful countryside, and shots and explosions ring out constantly. Maodi and the others are so completely disconnected from political life, however, that they have no idea who is fighting whom or what the various positions represent. The presence of armed fighting most likely dates the novel at the peak of the Cultural Revolution, when most of the factional combat took place. Even so, every reference to ideas or actions that should be comprehensible within a discourse of revolution simply appears as disjointed words or actions that emerge randomly against a background of sexual desire and behavior.

A third history, the history of family life, marriage, social relations within the ordinary context of parents, children, classmates, and work, also is present in the novel, if but in a minor sense. For example, Maodi cannot take Bai Xiaoyi to his house to stay, because he knows his mother will object. Mai Feng's mother asks him what his intentions are with Mai Feng, and now and then asks whether he plans to marry her. The normal path of romantic relationships toward marriage is recognized in these fleeting allusions, but, like the idealism of revolutionary discourse, this discourse has faded to become little more than a structure of meaning that Maodi must dodge as he pursues his sexual encounters. Indeed, the futility and emptiness of revolutionary and familial or kinship histories come together when Mai Feng's mother engages Maodi in an uncharacteristically long discussion:

> "The two of you being friends is no problem, it's okay, it's nothing. But don't let it get out of hand. Xiao Feng (Mai Feng) is still young, and so are you, so you can't just let things happen."
>
> "Of course not! I understand that."
>
> "Hmm, you look like a student who understands the way things are, otherwise why would Xiao Feng be your friend? That girl might have some attitude, but she's not a bad kid, you need to treat her well."
>
> "Of course, I wouldn't treat her bad. Especially since she and I . . ." The warm feeling in my heart almost came out my mouth.
>
> "You and she what?" Mai Feng's mother quickly followed up.
>
> "She said to me that she wants to marry me, no one else . . ." I randomly invented things to say.
>
> "That girl! And you, did you agree to marry her later?"
>
> "Not yet . . . I don't yet dare think about it," I stuttered.
>
> "This is an important matter, you have to think it through." Mai Feng's mother warned me sternly, "If you agree you cannot go back on your word."
>
> "I know that, I know this is important."
>
> "Well," the old woman said, carefully looking me up and down. "Well, we're poor here, do you really want to stay in the countryside?"
>
> "That is Chairman Mao's appeal to us, to take root in the countryside. . . ." (Mang Ke 1994, 209–10)

Maodi has no intention of marrying Mai Feng, and goes on to have sex with Bai Xiaoyi and another woman, Meiqing, as the novel closes in a flurry of sexual activity and fantasy. Yet it is this quotidian reality and the imposition of an older social order, rather than revolutionary history, that eventually reasserts itself toward the end of the novel, with Dachou marrying Li Xiaojiu and Mai Feng's father bringing in police to arrest Maodi.

The novel ends abruptly, and chapter 41 is a comment noting that only two things of importance occurred during that winter. The first was that Mai Feng's father, Mai Wang, died, but not out of anger at Maodi; rather, he drank so much that he fell off the *kang*. The second was that someone named Mai may have fallen through the ice into the lake and died. The odd thing, the villagers kept saying, was that at that time of the year, shouldn't the ice be solid? This reassertion of a pedestrian reality, different from those years when not only the ice but "everything was strange," puts a boundary around the tale of sexual excess, marking it as a product of revolutionary disorder and as most likely at least partially imagined (Mang Ke 1994, 289). Mang Ke's dual histories both are disconnected from this muted but eventually victorious discourse of kinship and daily life, whose reemergence barely warrants notice.

THE AESTHETIC OF FLATNESS

From the first page of *Wild Things,* revolutionary discourse has been gutted, to be replaced by a story of sexual excess, which almost immediately assumes a position as the apparent focus of the story. Yet although Maodi and the other characters appear to be thoroughly taken up by their sexual desires and expressions, it would be a mistake to regard them as sexually obsessed—that is, to interpret them as subjects with a fully developed sexual unconscious and psychologized mind. The encounters that motivate the narrative and Maodi are never presented as interesting, fully embodied, positive ways to live. Sexual desire does not so much torment and engross Maodi—or function as a cause of endless anxiety—as it becomes a narrative vehicle for the displacement of revolutionary history, ethos, and subjectivity. It is within this more instrumental and functional use of sexual desire that we can find the seminal aesthetic principle through which the text unfolds.

As a lever that pushes him from one event to another, Maodi's sexual desire expresses itself not as an all-consuming embodiment, but as a flitting series of encounters that project a near-robotic sensibility. Abandoning any sense of emotional depth that familial relations may provide, and disembodying the once-powerful truth of revolutionary passion, the narrative also refuses to be structured or deepened by the combined emotional, metaphysical, and physical transcendence of a profound sexual bond. It differs starkly, for example, from D. H. Lawrence's 1928 classic *Lady Chatterley's Lover*, where the characters' entire existence is subsumed into a sexual desire that transforms their inner being and is woven through with concepts that imply depth, such as love, mystery, passion, and soul, a concept used liberally throughout Lawrence's work.[6] By contrast, Mang Ke gives us no insight into anything that could be called the "soul" of Maodi, nor does he give us a sense of continuing, invigorating passion. Sexual desire is not an expression of or window into the inner being; inner being does not exist as an underlying concept in the novel. Rather, sexual desire is a surface activity, a series of links that connect Maodi to various other characters and environments. Sexual desire and behavior are not truly transformative to the characters, but produce a network of connections that shoots out in a thin web across the country, spanning and overlaying the city and the countryside. This aesthetic vision of flatness and of a porous surface linked through nodes is a radical revision of revolutionary discourse, which was based on a unified passion that extended all the way from deeply felt emotions out into the most trivial expressions of daily life, from the normative to the punitive. This vision also shows the limits—or creative interpretation—of the more thoroughly sexualized consciousness that would emerge if the creation of a Freudian concept of the mind, or a character formed through a more fully embodied concept of sexual modernity, were the point.

Although Chairman Mao may have wanted the sent-down youth to "take root" in the countryside, instead they bobbed along on its surface, all the while imagining that their labor and passionate ideological desire could form a seamless joint between revolutionary purity and its material and social manifestation, an ideal that Lei Feng so effortlessly projected. *Wild Things* gives the lie to this vision and the philosophies behind it, reducing every encounter to its momentary impact. Emphasis on sexual desire and behavior is a perfect vehicle through which to smash the embodied and subjective revolutionary past, especially as it exists in connection with the holy site of rural China. Although an overarching theme of sexual desire could lead the reader to the deeply tormented, psychologized, sexualized subject, or to the newer sexual playfield of commodification—in this case it creates instead a logic of multiple encounters, producing the web-like structure of the story.[7] Thus absorbed into the aesthetics of surface, the sexual focus easily becomes the anti-depth, anti-revolutionary (and not coincidentally, anti-Freudian) tool through which Mang Ke carries out his vision.

The novel does not solely rely on the *theme* of sexual desire and behavior to express this vision. With very few exceptions—one being the conversation between Maodi and Mai Feng's mother quoted above—the novel moves rapidly from one event, sensibility, and context to another, producing a jumpy sensation that translates the idea of disjointedness into an aesthetic technique. Other than the sexual desire, flirting, taunting, and intercourse that reappear with regularity, there is no meaningful strand to thread events and contexts together. Revolutionary language appears a few times and is discarded. Maodi's worry and concern for the future that are expressed in the translated quote above disappear. The half-teasing, half-cruel culture of the sent-down youth—or any "culture" based on their lives in the countryside—appears only sporadically. Mang Ke dips briefly into familial and individual histories. Petty rivalries and jealousies, attempts to steal food, searching for non-sexual ways to relieve boredom, drinking, verbal jockeying, and fighting all are presented as if they were one sex act after another: engaging for the moment but when finished, in need of rapid replacement. This sense of jerkiness is expressed throughout the novel's short chapters and works well not only with its sexual theme and its revisionary interpretation of rural discourse, but also with its narrative of disengagement. As the reassertion of ordinary kinship bonds suggests, the disjointed histories produce a temporal jolt that is to some extent resolved in the end, if with nothing more than a return to tradition. More important is the web-like structure that covers all available space with no differentiation, implying that there is no opening for a differently imagined future. The revolutionary optimism recouped as hope that we will see in the novels of Wang Xiaobo and Anchee Min simply does not exist.

AUTHORIAL POSITION

Mang Ke's seemingly negative take on the future, as well as the undeveloped characters and jerky narrative, makes it difficult to interpret his standpoint or position and the overall meaning of the novel. Although roots writer Ah Cheng thinks highly of the novel's authenticity, in terms of its position within sent-down youth literature, others simply regard it in the worst case as a failed experiment or in the best case as an unadorned and therefore unliterary representation of the life of a sent-down youth that may indeed possess some truth value:

> Poets cannot necessarily write good novels, but even if they write a bad one, it usually won't be too bad, and its less than attractive parts often make it unique. This is determined by the uniqueness of the poet's individual experience, and is normally the case when the work carries autobiographical traces (Mang Ke's comrade-in-arms Xu Xiao told us that she always wants to "read *Wild Things* as an autobiography, not as a novel"). As a novel taking as its material the sent-down youth, *Wild Things* may be quite authentic, in an unadorned way reflecting the disastrous side of their lives: everything is a mess, the whole thing appears to be a situation where lives have been smashed apart. The main character Maodi and his harem of women (Bai Xiaoyi, Mai Feng, Xiaojiu, Meiqing, etc.) and group of brothers (Little Scholar, Dachou, Thieving Fox [Zei Huli], etc.), with their reliance on that plaything beneath the crotch to while away the time in this desperately poor, wild place—perhaps this does indeed accurately illustrate historical reality. Of course, this novel is not like a mature work. There is not much to say about character development. What can be considered unique is the way the novel reveals the barbarous, remote, coarsely grinding reality of the northern village, along with the "fishy" stench of that dialogue assaulting the nose. I don't really understand life in the northern village (specifically, the Baiyangdian district in Hebei), and am not sure to what extent the reality that the author has penned is accurate. If we completely believe his account, the situation is basically like this: as soon as the big, plain, uncultured girls of Baiyangdian are teased by a chic big brother, they either put their hands in and take out big brother's "thing," or immediately stick out their big white asses. . . . (Zhuang Zhou)[8]

It may be true that the novel is not good literature or that there is some reality to certain aspects of the portrayal—for example, the utter failure of the sent-down youth to "root" in the countryside. A dream sequence, however, give us another angle on the authorial position. Chapter 11 is a disjointed tale of someone crying, a naked woman (Bai Xiaoyi or maybe someone else), sex, orgasms, dirty words, pictures, being overrun by ants, and people dancing and mourning. The disconnected but highly imagistic and sensual language gives us some indication of Mang Ke's larger perspective on the countryside and its literary function.

Although the author of the translated passage above claims that in *Wild Things*, the countryside is easily awakened and sexualized by a stylish young man from the city, the narrative locates the robotic sexual impulse as spread equally across the land. However, much as the dream images of this chapter are artifacts of Maodi's sleeping brain, this countryside also is imagined and produced by the sent-down youth. *Wild Things* does not so much awaken the female fox of a countryside with the city-dwelling sent-down male youth as imply that the mere existence of the sent-down youth presupposes such a place.

In this sense, then, like many writers before him Mang Ke has also both put the countryside to use and, in his own way, extended the intellectual discourse of the rural that runs through 20th-century Chinese literature. His goal is not to tell us something new about peasant life or to project a newly liberated sexual subject. Rather, through dismantling the revolutionary countryside as a site of spiritual origin, intellectual despair, revolutionary passion, or romantic renewal, he aims to attack the consciousness that embodied these values. In the process, he creates a flattened surface aesthetic that coincidentally shatters the country-versus-city theme and binary, one of the most closely held cultural constructs of the century.

INTELLECTUALS, SEX, AND TIME IN WANG XIAOBO'S THE GOLDEN YEARS

> *Chen Xiaoming*: Many writers fear that returning to a narrative of individual experience will result in a lack of depth. In Su Tong's novels, the self is always absent and he does not dare search for the existence of the individual. But when Wang Xiaobo combs through the past of revolutionary times, he does not avoid the existence of the individual. When his writing pushes a man and a woman to the purest state, his novels transcend revolution. Zhang Xianliang's novels go from history to the individual, searching for the individual's place within history; Wang Xiaobo's novels go from the individual to history, and revolution becomes a background.
>
> Wang Xiaobo's inquiries directed at individual existence are nakedly in the open. People always attach a lot of surplus value to sex, but Wang Xiaobo brings it back to a state of purity. Foucault said that sex and money are two sides of the same coin.
>
> *Bai Ye*: I've read so many novels about sex but none of them were as unaffected as what Wang Xiaobo has written.
>
> *Xing Xiaoqun*: Recently I've read several novels such as *Bright Garden* (Wang Xiaobo) but most authors still write about sex as if it testifies to the personality.
>
> *Zhu Wei*: Under Wang Anyi's pen, sex is too authored.

> *Bai Ye*: Sex in *The Abandoned City* (Feidu) also is affected. The sex written by Jia Pingwa is a failure.
> *Bai Ye*: As soon as Wang Xiaobo's novels came out they totally wiped out the other novels that were written about sex.
> *Zhu Zhenglin*: Jia's sex is that of the Chinese gentry, a breath of evil wind, an improper attitude. (Ai and Li 1997, 259–64)

> The sex that Wang Xiaobo writes is ordinary sex, it is mastered without having been taught and skilled without having been learned, it is never lacking and flows and stops naturally . . . This kind of sex is nothing more than a kind of common sense. (Huang Jiwei 1997, 267)

> Among readers, Wang Xiaobo is called a "strange genius" or a "twisted genius." But I feel that his "strangeness" is simply that he is too healthy, and his "twistedness" is just that he is too sincere. . . . For example, his novels about sex are, I think, the best available, at least in contemporary China. He has a very healthy and sincere attitude toward sex, and he makes the reader feel like sex is something that can be treated in a healthy and sincere way. Unlike some writers, he doesn't show sex to be formed out of sentimentality, nor as an expression of lust. Those two things make us feel disgusted. But I think if he were a little more disgusting, then no one would say he is "strange" or "twisted." (Zhou Guoping 1997, 364–65)

The fiction and essays of Wang Xiaobo (1952–97) have become something of a phenomenon in contemporary Chinese culture. While Wang first published stories in 1980, and his novel *The Golden Years* came out in 1992 (published in Hong Kong and Taiwan), he did not become famous until the novel later received a prestigious award, also in Taiwan. Like his protagonist, Wang Er, who is ubiquitous in Wang's fiction, Wang Xiaobo spent some two years as a sent-down youth in Yunnan, from 1968 to 1970; later he worked in a factory for four years before becoming a student at Renmin University in Beijing, where he studied commerce and trade from 1978 to 1982. After teaching for two years, he continued his studies at the University of Pittsburgh, where he received an M.A. degree from the Department of East Asian Studies. Wang was a lecturer in the Beijing University Department of Sociology from 1988 to 1991, after which he became a full-time writer.

Wang's 1997 collection of essays "My Spiritual Garden" (Wode jingshen jiayuan) sparked interest in his work, but *The Golden Years* is generally thought to be his masterpiece.[9] This 1994 novella struck critics with its unorthodox treatment of sexual desire and relations, which in the post-Mao period have become commonplace topics. For some, "it is difficult to imagine that someone like Wang Xiaobo could appear from inside Chinese culture" (Yang Jian 2002, 447). Avoiding total capitulation to the familiar narratives of sex as an indicator of a fallen culture or a slippery slide into decadence, of sexual passion as similar to or emerging out of revolutionary passion, or more recently of sex as part of a new urban or global lifestyle, Wang presents a fresh view that has startled readers.[10] Many critics have tried to come to terms with Wang's experiment, discussing his anti-utopian approach, his black humor, his novel organization of time, his seemingly logical but in actuality absurd constructions, and his clear and direct style. Calling his writing "direct existentialism" or "transcendent existentialism," "ironic and comedic," "free narration," or "satiric and parodic," critics have discussed at length exactly what it is about Wang's writing that has caused such excitement and amazement (Wang Xiaoming 1997, 262; Bai Hua 1997, 259; Ai Xiaoming 1997, 272; Ding Dong 1997).

Although critics have commented on the sex in Wang's writing, the enthusiastic and yet sometimes contradictory intellectual response to Wang's writing also directs us to the question from another angle: through his unorthodox presentation of sexual desire and behavior and his manipulation of conventional emotional motivation, reaction, and response, in what way does Wang's work participate in and alter the debate about modernity in China?[11] In *The Golden Years*, the question centers on how to interpret the character Wang Er: has Wang Xiaobo created an image of freedom and individuality, or has he created a character who cannot be interpreted within those categories, whose existence speaks more to a more elusive working of power through the subject?

In this chapter I show how the implications about modernity that Wang generates by his style are produced through his presentation of time, buttressed by and expressed through his idiosyncratic depiction of sexual relations. Wang's approach also produces a new take on the countryside in the long legacy of rural stories over the revolutionary period. The sexual focus of *The Golden Years* may appear similar to that in the novels of Zhang Xianliang, but unlike Zhang, Wang does not buy into a narrative of internal progress and liberation that his protagonist reaches after once again being put in touch with his sexual power, a male flowering that is the result of a post-revolutionary internal struggle and a means to imagine a future and move toward it. Like many other sent-down youth writers, Wang is not actually interested in the rural, but his instrumental use of the countryside is not as direct or blatant as what we see in Zhang Xianliang's 1985 novel

Half of Man Is Woman (Nanren de yiban shi nüren), where protagonist Zhang Yonglin's journey toward political empowerment can be accomplished only by treating the countryside as a site of sexual rejuvenation, to be disposed of once he reaches his goal. Jia Pingwa's slimy degradation, produced by statist extremism, also is non-evident. The one common theme that Wang Xiaobo makes use of is the concept of sexual activity as being suppressed by the state and thus inherently anti-authoritarian. Even so, as I discuss below, his focus is not on resistance to state control.

The collection *The Golden Years* includes the novellas *The Golden Years, Established at Thirty* (Sanshi erli), *Years Flow Like Water* (Sishui liunian), *Love in the Time of Revolution* (Geming shiqi de aiqing), and *My Yinyang World* (Wode yinyang shijie).[12] The prize-winning novella *The Golden Years,* which was revised several times over a period of twenty years, details the relationship between Wang's ever-present character Wang Er ("Wang Two"), a 21-year-old sent-down-youth working in Yunnan during the Cultural Revolution, and the attractive 26-year-old doctor Chen Qingyang, also a sent-down youth, whose husband is in jail.

The plot is simple and easy to follow, contrasting with many novels by experimental writers from the same period. The novel begins when Chen Qingyang approaches Wang Er to ask for his help in combating the rumor that she is a "worn-out shoe" (poxie) or a promiscuous woman. Thus the sexual theme is established and we quickly learn that the protagonist is speaking from the perspective of twenty years later, looking back over his experience from his present life in Beijing. Several aspects of the story instantly tip us off to Wang Xiaobo's rejection of realism: the excessively ordinary and rather flat language, the straightforward progression without elaborate narration or details, little inner-mind development for the characters, rejection of cause-and-result logic in the characters' responses (especially those of Wang Er), and non-narrative elements like the absurd lists of "proofs" Wang thinks up to prove that Chen is not a worn-out shoe, that he himself exists, that he did not shoot his brigade leader's dog, and so on. From this perspective, the novel closely follows the work of experimental writers, exhibiting extreme attention to issues of language and the construction of meaning, from expressions like "worn-out shoe" through the writing of "confessions" to be turned in to authorities as proof of wrongdoing.

Although every piece of writing about the Cultural Revolution is to some extent a revision that can alter our belief about "what really happened," the novel's rejection of realistic methods and its corresponding attention to language is a clear indication that Wang Xiaobo is not presenting us with a transparent corrective to other Cultural Revolution narratives, that he is not loudly claiming that those stories of violence, suppression, wild and exciting belief followed by disillusionment are false, at least not in the most common sense of the term.[13] Although his story complicates realistic representation, Wang's point is elsewhere, not so much in plot and content as in his language, sense of time, and the relationship between action and understanding.[14] The Cultural Revolution narrative does turn out to be false, but not because it did not occur historically. Rather, Wang's story so thoroughly complicates the logic of revolutionary consciousness that its integrity is challenged.

Several aspects of *The Golden Years* combine to create a unique interpretation of two important and long-held beliefs: that the real can be readily represented, and that the countryside is not only the place but also the time where the real must be spiritually located. The language consistently but subtly defeats narrative expectations, throwing the entire fictional enterprise into an exciting, questionable category, releasing the reader from normative desires, questioning those desires and their ability to express the veracity of the reader's experience, bringing out in each critic a thrilling sense of liberation from his or her consciousness of the past, and drawing sharp attention to itself. The novel marks itself as intellectual by valorizing sensitive appreciation and thought. It refuses intercourse with common methods of understanding history, the past, and the individual, hints at but leaves undeveloped a slight sense of fate, disowns emotion while dissociating itself from coldness and cruelty, and ironically puts forward a peculiar logic that participates in the mild and yet provocative alienation produced by Wang's style. This logic and the novel's refusal to construct an emotional core as a motivation to behavior are what make critics refer to it as *rational*, yet this rationality is developed slowly, with a great deal of ironic humor. Rationality's clarity comes through in the alarmingly direct way that Wang Er pursues his sexual goals, but its limitations are shown both by Wang Er's refusal to confront those who oppose him directly, and by the melancholy of the novel's style.

A focus on sexuality is a crucial tool in this effort because it allows for readily accessible metaphors of exposure, liberation and freedom, delight, and the drive toward life, all of which can be expressed with little direct articulation and can thereby stand as emblems of the author's ontological enterprise. This emphasis nods in the direction of 20th-century norms that situate sexuality at the crux of self-identity, although that alignment is not Wang's goal. Also, sexuality turns out to be an excellent oppositional arena for meaning that functions against both socialist norms of collective identity. Like Mang Ke, Wang rejects the fully psychologized, angst-laden personality.

Despite differences in style and meaning as well as in the overall portrayal of sexual behavior during the Cultural Revolution, Wang's character Wang Er is in some respects the inheritor of Zhang Xianliang's semi-autobiographical character Zhang Yonglin. Although Chen Qingyang participates in their sexual relationship with a level of existential detachment equal to that of Wang Er, she is not granted the same power to project an ontology of time, experience, and intellect. In this respect, Wang Er can be interpreted as yet one more example in a gendered story of intellectual self-questioning within which sexual experience is a male route—successful or not—to knowledge and truth.

And finally, Wang Xiaobo's presentation of sexual desire as almost pastoral in its naturalness provides a striking model of being that in its simplicity and purity appeals to intellectuals. Broadly speaking, *The Golden Years* creates an aesthetic modernity that offers a pleasing and comforting alternative to the stressful politicized Maoist years. In the figure of Wang Er, the author crafts an intellectual model that presents a strongly physical sense of self while simultaneously avoiding the high-pitched emotionalism characteristic of Cultural Revolution mental life. Furthermore, the dully-flowing time that informs Wang Er's consciousness and perception of human interactions produces a seemingly contradictory feeling of distance and intimacy that argues against an interpretation of human relationships as essentially political.

SEX AND YOUTH AND REVOLUTION

"The reason Wang Er and Chen Qingyang make love (and commit a crime) is just that they are young and they want to," writes Ai Xiaoming (1977, 271). It is not hard to see why the direct and unaffected way that Wang Xiaobo describes sexual intercourse has led many critics to find his depiction healthy and beautiful when compared with other literary attempts. Although often imbued with a light lyricism, Wang's writing makes direct reference to legs, penises, breasts, and simply the acts of sex. When Wang

Er is caught and asked to write a self-criticism, what he writes is blatantly non-ideological; stylistically it is curiously similar to the writing of Wang Xiaobo:

> We two had illicit sex for the fortieth time. The place was a straw hut I secretly built on the mountain. If it wasn't the 15th according to the lunar calendar then it was the 16th, anyway the moon was very bright. Chen Qingyang sat on the bamboo bed, the moonlight shining from the door, shining on her body. I stood on the ground and she clutched me around the waist with her legs. We chatted a bit, I said her breasts were not only round but also very regular, and that her navel was round and shallow. All this was good. She said really? I didn't know. Later the moonlight moved away and I lit a cigarette. I smoked half of it then she took it away and smoked a few puffs. She also pinched my nose because there was a local saying which said a virgin boy's nose was hard, but the nose of someone about to give himself up to excessive carnal desire was soft. All this time she lazily lay on the bed, leaning on the bamboo wall. At other times she clutched me like an Australian koala bear, breathing hot air in my face. Finally when the moonlight came in from the window across the door, we parted. (Wang Xiaobo 1994, 24–25)

In *The Golden Years*, Wang Xiaobo almost always reports discussions rather than creating them directly, fostering the impression that an older Wang Er, from the distance of time and place, is describing his earlier interactions, and producing a philosophical impression that directs readers toward dislocation and irony. The directness with which Wang Er relates his sexual exchanges, however, produces a sense of candor, honesty, and truth, because normal emotional effusions and declarations of enduring love—more or less hidden calculations for self-benefit—are absent. Yet the two lovers are not cold to each other. In presenting sexual desire as innate and natural and transcending not only politics but also the normative discourse of love, the author associates sexuality with a rebellious, young, anti-control energy that can be stifled by intervention:

> Whenever bulls were castrated I was present. For most bulls a knife was all that was needed. But for some highly sexed bulls, they had to use the hammer trick, which was to cut open the scrotum, pull out the testicles, and smash them to bits with a wooden hammer. From this point on those operated on only knew how to eat grass and work and nothing else. Even when they were killed, there was no need to tie them up. The team leader who wielded the hammer had no doubt that this operation would be equally as effective on people. Each time he yelled at me: You eggheads, one blow and you would fall in line! According to his logic, the thoroughly red, constantly

erect, foot-long thing on my body was the reincarnation of evil. (Wang Xiaobo 1994, 7–8)

The comparison of docile, castrated bull to human, and the possibility of resistance through an active sexual life—available, perhaps, mostly to those with abnormally large penises—to any kind of taming impulse become even clearer when Wang Er states:

> Of course I had a different opinion than he did. Nothing was more important than this thing, it was equal to my very existence. The sky's color subtly deepened and lazy hued clouds floated across the sky. The bottom half was covered in darkness, the top half still danced in the sun's rays. That day I was twenty-one, I was in my golden years. I had so many hopes. I wanted to love, to eat, in an instant to become a half-dark, half-light cloud in the sky. Only later did I discover that life is a slow beating, people age and with each day hopes vanish, and in the end we become like a bull under the hammer. But when I passed my twenty-first birthday I had no glimmer of this. I thought I would be strong forever and nothing could beat me down. (Wang Xiaobo 1994, 8)

In the scene immediately following this description, Wang Er's friend Le Du is full of envy when he accidentally glimpses Wang's erect penis. We understand immediately that Wang is like an oversexed bull that needs a beating to be made docile. The beating turns out to take place on its own, through the passage of time, however, not through political manipulation.

The author's highlighting of youth connects to a long discourse on youth in communist culture that developed in the 1950s, when the People's Republic of China was also in its own youth; thus it draws the novel toward a charged ideological sphere that addresses the way the collective future is imagined and articulated.[15] Although Wang seems to adopt the view that the very quality of being oversexed contains a germ of resistance to state control, his stylistic handling of this theme injects it with contradiction. Throughout the novel, the commentary of Wang's later self alternates with on-the-spot description, projecting a muted melancholy but also a crucial rejection of melodrama and the high tones of emotional investment. In the construction of youth that is Wang Er, the author issues a triple refusal. We do not find the existential angst of youth that is pervasive in capitalist culture and now readily apparent in China, popping up as the "bastards" of Zhang Yuan's *Beijing Bastards* (Beijing zazhong), invading Sixth Generation film, and appearing in contemporary culture. Neither do we find the naïve excitement and intensity characteristic of youth under socialist culture, or its recent reincarnation in the nostalgia of *no-regrets-for-our-youth* (qingchun wuhui) aging sent-down youth once again celebrating the innocent passions of their early political beliefs.[16] Nor do we find the humanistic, post-socialist youth whose sad desires are the basis of so many characters in realistic or pseudo-realistic stories of the 1980s. If Wang Er is none of these, how can we characterize him, and his relationship with Chen Qingyang?

Wang Er pursues Chen Qingyang not out of any expressed infatuation. We never hear him obsess about his love or lust for her, nor does he torment himself about her response or lack thereof. He does not prostrate himself before her, nor does he force himself on her. Rather, he uses an odd logic, asking her directly, with little banter, flirting, or courtship, if she will have sexual intercourse with him. He develops a humorous explanation of *yiqi*, the code of loyalty generally governing brotherhood, to explain how he thinks their sexual intercourse should take place, and calls it "great friendship" (weida youyi).[17] Throughout the novel, Wang Er pays as least as much attention to his penis or "little monk" (xiao heshang) as he does to Chen Qingyang, giving the impression that he is gazing upon himself more than upon her. Although Chen and Wang Er both proclaim the ugliness of the penis, Wang Er insists loudly to his that it is his one and only enabling power.

As Zhu Zhenglin (1997) writes, however, one must read the novel to get a sense of the low-key and unpretentious charm with which this story unravels, and to appreciate the way in which it quietly rebukes other modes of being. To conduct a long-term sexual relationship on the basis of physical desire that is resolutely neither cynical and angry nor embodied in an emotional expansion of meaning—be it for love or pleasure—is a stark departure from previous models of desire. In steadfastly seeking his aims and luring Chen Qingyang into the mountains, where they can carry on their affair at will, Wang Er uses the strategies of the intellectual. When he hands in his self-criticism, leaders urge him to continue his writing and not bother with other transgressions but simply limit his focus to male-female relations alone; thus, we see that others may also not be as interested in the political discourse as they should be.

But we don't really meet those characters, and we will never know if their interest in his tale is "only lust." Here, Wang Xiaobo seems to imply that most people would be all too willing to trade in their political consciousness for a good erotic novel. But isn't Wang Er's desire "only lust" as well?

As we have seen, most critics do not see any negative, self-serving aspect of lust in Wang Er's behavior but regard it as something healthy and singular. Wang Xiaobo accomplishes this sleight of hand by removing sexual intercourse from its social context of love or lust and by showing the emotional structure that sustains a social interpretation to be false. There is nothing unusual about this strategy; in modern literature all over the world, this kind of knowledge is commonly gained by characters through experience, offering the reader a structure of progress and a way to reflect on his or her own experience. Wang Er, however, understands the normative determination of both sexuality and revolution from the very beginning; when asked by political leaders to write his confession, Wang Er's response is shocking from both perspectives. When confronted by a military representative, who often asks him questions he does not wish to answer, Wang Er remains mute. In the same way, his confession is really no response at all, but a purposeful twisting of the discourses of sexuality and revolutionary consciousness to allow another powerful stance to emerge. From Wang Er's confession, we easily can see why critics find that Wang Xiaobo strips off extraneous elements and reduces male-female interaction to its purest state. The moon, the legs around the waist, the cigarette, hot breath, reported talk that seems to be the most minimalist interaction—what he "confesses" contrasts wickedly with first the well-understood context of a political confession, and second the received understanding of sexual interaction. Wang Er's confession creates not a sense of passion and heat but of leisure and philosophical distance. Throughout the narrative, Wang Xiaobo uses a variety of techniques to heighten the strangeness of Wang Er's responses.

Although it may seem that Wang Er's confession—and thus Wang Xiaobo's fictional effort—is an example of resistance to social norms and state demands, the novel does not promote this interpretation.[18] From the beginning, the writing is infused with a muted sense of melancholy, suggesting that overt resistance is only a secondary concern. Despite the fact that the young Wang Er revels in his youth and the power of his body and gains his alternative, overtly apolitical being within its parameters, the narrating elder Wang Er, with an almost Buddhist-like understanding of the ephemeral nature of life, knows of the "slow beating" that the body suffers, and the degradation of hope that its strength once implied. What brings out the faint sadness of the older narrating Wang Er is this process, and not political or sexual repression, which by comparison is relatively easy to evade. When he and Chen Qingyang meet after many years and with their middle-aged bodies again have sex together, they proceed with familiarity but also with some embarrassment about their declining physical state, particularly on the side of Chen Qingyang. Because the novel does not follow chronological order but flashes between the time in Yunnan, the meeting between Chen and Wang Er twenty years later in Beijing, and philosophical reflections that could belong to the author or Wang Er, it produces a sense of levelness and calm that contrasts with the energy that Wang Er describes himself as feeling when he was young.

The calm, levelness, and melancholy of the narration mediate any notion of direct resistance, as does Wang Xiaobo's pushing of political and ideological issues into the background. Furthermore, because things never change for Wang Er, nor does his attitude or behavior alter the world around him, resistance in its ordinary sense would seem to be the wrong category through which to judge his accomplishments or, correspondingly, those of Wang Xiaobo. Yet the novel takes a strong oppositional position, although for the most part it evades the easily recognized categories of anti-authoritarianism or liberation. Because he does not make use of the us / enemy (wo di) structure that underlies powerful depictions of resistance, Wang Xiaobo avoids a familiar binary that often reifies the opposing elements not only as conceptual entities, but also as an unchanging temporal relationship. It is this expression of the way time functions that both undermines conventional ways of thinking about the revolutionary spirit and elicits the admiration of Chinese intellectuals, who identify with it.

JUST THE WAY IT IS: CHINESE INTELLECTUALS AND TIME PASSING

> Wang Xiaobo has never been satisfied with just telling a story, and always reflects his love of novelistic free form in the telling. And his love of free form can be seen even more clearly in the narrative games he devises. They express the particular experience and feelings of contemporary Chinese people, especially Chinese intellectuals, and convey an overview of the conditions of their existence. This can be seen in a series of works he wrote after returning from the United States. When I say overview, it is because in these works we see a dialogue narrative style in which the narrator freely moves between old and new, Chinese and foreign according to his desires. . . . One key to free form narration is the organization of time. . . . Time is expanded and made complex, and events that are spatially far away are subject to a singular knitting together. . . . Time actually is nothing more than a topic

that has been organized, an unconscious topic. Wang Xiaobo often uses a time-related phrase as the title of his fiction, and this time is branded as that specific time of the collective memory of the Chinese people. (Ai Xiaoming 1997, 273–74)

When Wang Er runs into obstacles, he does not want to struggle or lead the masses to resist. His method is to avoid direct resistance; he won't persist but takes an *okay, whatever* approach toward everything. Basically, however, he does what he wants to do and there's nothing anyone can do about it. He doesn't really care, but it's not a heavy kind of not caring. It's light and carefree. A great deal of his behavior is "low-down," but he has no evil intent and does not wish to harm anyone. You could even say he often does good things and although these good things satisfy the desires of the other party, they are regarded as "bad" by society. In doing these good things he has no clear goals or keen enthusiasm, and of course he won't sacrifice himself for others or give his body to feed the tigers. He has some sense of loyalty and also some hoodlum spirit—and perhaps this hoodlum spirit is for the purpose of dealing with an era also informed by hoodlum spirit. This hoodlum spirit is the product of an age. After a period of properness the era suddenly relaxes for a moment, and then instantly tightens up again. But those who have tasted this flavor and are like this themselves are unwilling to relinquish it.

What kind of a person is Wang Er anyway? Is he an "anti-hero?" An "outsider?" Or maybe a "superfluous man?" Is he a modern "knight errant" or an urban "wanderer?" (He Huaihong 1997, 284–86)

Intellectuals' enthusiasm toward Wang Xiaobo's fiction comes from a number of perspectives, including an appreciation of his sexual honesty, his straightforward descriptions of male and female sexual pleasure, and his elegantly simple language, which avoids obfuscation. Also important are the protagonist Wang Er's personal characteristics, such as his completely non-ideological sense of reality, his privileging of bodily desires, and his subtle humor and irony. As Ai Xiaoming implies, Wang Er's character also seems to indicate or speak to something uniquely Chinese or minimally specific to Chinese intellectuals.[19] He Huaihong points to a particular attitude, an unwillingness to directly confront opposition but a stubborn persistence in gaining one's own desire, an *okay, whatever* attitude that references high moral qualities such as loyalty but also allies itself with a mildly rebellious hoodlum spirit.

What is it about the sense of time that is unique in *The Golden Years*? The novel's refashioning of historical time, along with its take on emotion, determines its peculiar approach to modernity and its position within debates about the Chinese modern. Although there are historical markers—

the existence of sent-down youth, political meetings, confessions—that point to the Cultural Revolution period, in terms of propelling the narrative forward, conventional historical time almost disappears. Wang Er never acts with reference to explicit historical consciousness, nor does he invoke a historical reason for or understanding of someone's behavior or words. One thing that replaces this conventional logic of history is Wang Er's own unique logic of the absurd. Also, the writing suggests that behind Wang Er's behavior lies a sharp discerning intelligence. Wang Er's bright mind translates social discourse into its own humorous and ironic code, which he then uses to create a bubble around him, isolate himself from historicized time, and thereby heighten his sensual and intellectual pleasure. This linguistic process involves wrenching historical time out of its track, halting and reworking it; it is both akin to and gently mocking of the general interpretive work done by intellectuals. In this sense and more obviously because he is a sent-down youth, Wang Er may be understood as a model for intellectuals under various forms of duress.

We also could point to the common complaints heard by and about intellectuals and their social role in Chinese history—that they are weak and rarely stand up to power, that they have persistently refused to take a role of responsibility in relation to the state, instead meekly going along with orders. These reputed qualities have caused a great deal of soul-searching on the topic of intellectuals' complicity during the Cultural Revolution. Or we could take a look at the ivory tower critique often directed at academics, which claims that intellectuals are more interested in the obscure and arcane arguments of their work than in any real-life situation or application or are fully immersed in and protective of what is actually nothing more than a bourgeois life-style at bottom concerned with petty personal pleasures. Both of these criticisms could be targeted at Wang Er, with his *okay, whatever* method of dealing with authority, his stubborn pursuit of his own bodily gratification, and his general rejection of heroism, self-sacrifice, and utopian ideals.

These novelistic confrontations with Maoist demands in both aesthetics and in personality development are relatively easy to locate in *The Golden Years*. But the pleasure of reading the novel, to which so many critics refer, implies that the presentation of an intellectual model through Wang Er, and the twisting of time, are working at a much more subtle level, a sentence-by-sentence displacement of ordinary novelistic concepts and ordinary time. It is remarkable to find that literary intellectuals, whose profession undeniably rests upon analysis and interpretation, deny that Wang's work needs to be analyzed at all, arguing that its meaning can be best apprehended Daoist-like, through direct apprehension:

> When you read the works of modernist Chinese writers, in particular those of several recent experimental writers, they seem involved and abstruse. But *The Golden Years* is not like that, instead providing the pleasure of reading throughout, in every spot. Those seeking the implied meaning of the novel can seek it; yet the value of the work first and foremost comes from the reading itself. Reading intoxicates us, giving a totally new experience of humor and wisdom. We don't need to keep looking for the implied meaning at all. (Ai Xiaoming 1997, 270)

Although it is easy to see that at the level of theme the novel confounds and questions many other more common approaches (particularly that of the experimental writers), this alone cannot explain the anti-intellectual claim that the novel must be experienced, not theorized.

A passage similar to many others in the novel allows us to closely view the way Wang Xiaobo uses time:

> Later I brought someone from the Security Group to investigate the place where we had lived. The little grass hut I had erected on the mountain behind Unit 15 already had a leaky roof and the corn on the ground had attracted many birds. There were a lot of condoms on the ground behind the hut, and these were iron proof that we had lived there. The local people didn't like condoms because, they said, condoms obstructed the flow of *yin-yang* and made you weaker by the day. Actually those local condoms were much better than any I used later, as they were one hundred percent natural rubber. (Wang Xiaobo 1994, 29)

Although the paragraph ostensibly is about the visit of the Security Group representative to the hut for the purpose of tracing the movements of Wang Er and Chen Qingyang, we find out almost nothing about the representative's reaction. Wang quickly shifts to the issue of "proof," a reference to the many absurd proofs he has concocted throughout the novel. This switch to novelistic time and its philosophical connotations is rapid and unmarked. He then switches to the time of daily life and local lore, after which he speedily jumps into "the future" with his seemingly irrelevant evaluation of condoms from the two time periods. In this paragraph, the Security Group representative, who vanishes after the first sentence, represents formal historical time. The reader, set up to expect the usual political discussion of blame and censure or perhaps a flashback to the sexual events that took place in the hut, is pleasantly surprised to find him or herself jerked into another sphere. Before reading the last two sentences, surely no reader expected to run into a comment on the quality of condoms, which in the context would seem to have nothing more than a whimsical relationship to the scene.

Temporal dislocation occurs constantly throughout the story. The reading experience some critics relate is similar to the way that experience under a mind-altering drug is sometimes described; the background disappears, but what is right in front of your face expands and enlarges to fill up your entire consciousness. Time slows down and departs from its normal context, simultaneously opening up and revealing infinite strange and delightful links stretching out like tentacles into as many times and topics as can be imagined. The blandness of daily life becomes the richness of experience. Wang Er's *okay, whatever* actually is not disdain, contempt, or even indifference at all, then, but an attempt to grasp this aspect of lived experience and put it into narrative. It is this challenge to historical determinism in narrative, among other things, that elicits such a strong and positive reaction from the critics, because it allows readers to experience something easily theorized but difficult to directly apprehend. In other words, we expect one thing to lead to another, and Wang confounds our teleological expectations. In the comments of critics, we can see that Wang's presentation of time, sex, and history is richly suggestive to intellectuals seeking to understand their own position in contemporary China. In the next section, I discuss this debate and suggest ways in which Wang's work participates directly in the formation of these understandings.

WANG XIAOBO AND CHINESE MODERNITY

Why does Ai Xiaoming find the kind of time expressed in Wang's fiction to be typical of the collective memory of the Chinese people, or at least of Chinese intellectuals, and how is it related to the Cultural Revolution era? Directly following the passage quoted above, Ai elucidates:

> Time actually is not merely material to be organized, but also an unconscious theme. Wang Xiaobo often uses references to time as his novel's titles. These times are branded as the special times of the collective memory of contemporary Chinese people. During some periods, intellectuals had to explain

> the beating they had taken by claiming that they had been harmed by master magicians from India; in other times, they had to appear to be recalling bitterness or remembering sweetness while engaging in sexual intercourse, or say that the males had been forced to be traitors like the Japanese devils, the females tested with cruel punishment as they willingly were raped. Sadism and masochism in the repressed unconscious mind and perverted sexuality have been analyzed as patterns by Freud. Now Wang Xiaobo has used them in the context of Chinese time and space to expose various bizarre and irrational psychologies in modern Chinese people. (Ai Xiaoming 1997, 274)

Ai implies that Chinese intellectuals always suffer under power; yet they take pleasure in their sufferings, and must use various psychological tricks and metaphors to explain and rationalize their position (274). Using the concepts of sadism and masochism, Ai discusses the complex relations of power in which intellectuals are culturally imbricated. In Ai's view, Wang Er is not so much an indication of this compromised position as he is a running commentary on it, from his humor to his logical language to his direct apprehension and representation of the foot-long red thing on his body.

Arguing that Wang Xiaobo's writing is original and "anti-masses" (fei dazhong), Dai Jinhua finds that ". . . one of the attractions of Wang Xiaobo comes out of his refusal of the 'destiny' that cannot be avoided by intellectuals in the 20th century: he refused to become a 'specialist,' an intellectual in the academy" (Dai Jinhua 2001, 3). This comment is yet another response to the question of how Wang's writing fits into the debates about Chinese modernity, for Dai finds in Wang an example of the organic intellectual who has followed a path that diverges from that of the liberal Western-educated academic intellectual.[20] For Dai, *The Golden Years* is the key to Wang's thinking, and although its expressed sexuality may represent an anti-logical madness characteristic of the Cultural Revolution years, neither sex nor the Cultural Revolution is the real topic of Wang's writing. Wang's novels do not demand psychological analysis to ferret out a sado-masochist complex within the unconscious mind, but rather are in their totality an analysis of power and its workings through history. Dai does not treat sadism and masochism as mental configurations, but rather as metaphors for the historical condition of intellectuals. Sadomasochism may be an apt form within which to describe and represent the rationalizing intellectual's mind as it navigates its way through the treacherous waters of self-benefit and serve-the-people, mandates and taboos. Perhaps Wang Er does present a refreshing manner, an optimistic way to be smart and simply to live under crushing conditions of power and control, a way to be selfish while maintaining integrity, to fully understand what is going on yet still relish pleasure. Dai's emphasis on power implies the importance of position and role, key components in the concept of spirit developed over the century, and especially in revolutionary culture.

Yet what kind of a solution does Wang Er offer? Although I agree with Ai Xiaoming and Dai Jinhua that *The Golden Years* is a discourse on power, it also presents a strong demand for an intellectual modernity with its roots firmly embedded in aesthetic culture. Sexual desire, important as it is, is not simply a discursive spot where Wang Xiaobo can ruminate on power. It also is a site of aesthetic unfolding, or to put it in imagistic language, a hut where the moon shines on vividly naked bodies. To investigate these issues, we can look at the three assumptions about cultural and intellectual work listed by Xudong Zhang (1998, 3) in a recent introduction to contemporary Chinese liberal intellectuals, which I summarize in my words:

1. The state and the people are partners working in tandem to steer and manage the nation.
2. Intellectuals are the moral conscience of the people and have the right to speak for and guide them.
3. Modernity will be achieved through economic, emotional, and aesthetic change rather than political and class struggle.

In *The Golden Years*, the state is at best an irritant that must be pushed aside to make space for life to be lived; at worst it abuses its power. Wang Er, however, never identifies the state as either his primary enemy or his ally. The second assumption, that intellectuals are the moral conscience of the people and must speak for them, experienced a rebirth after the Cultural Revolution, but more recently has been battered by popular culture and commercialism. In the novel, Wang Er does not take this powerful moral position in any overt way, although intellectual moralism informs the novel's stance as a whole. Even if Dai Jinhua's "anti-masses" analysis is interpreted only in the most basic way, she certainly is correct: Wang Xiaobo's writing style is not designed to appeal to a popular audience, and the relative lack of plot and action makes his book an unlikely best-seller. *The Golden Years* not only presents an intellectual model in Wang Er, but also speaks primarily to and about intellectuals. The lack of significant character development in the novel's rural people with whom Wang Er lives and works is remarkable.

As for the third point—that modernity will be achieved through economic, emotional, and aesthetic change rather than class or political struggle—the novel is in full accordance with contemporary notions of change, and a powerful proponent of aesthetic reality. The story's presentation of emotional and aesthetic alternatives is one reason why neo-leftists and liberals alike have found it so fascinating. Wang Er does not acknowledge any mode of direct political struggle, which in his value system is completely useless and passé. Those who do work politically are just waiting for the chance to see Chen Qingyang tied up before them, or to get their hands on Wang Er's narrative of sexual transgression. The sexual theme of the novel presents not just a question of who controls whom, but also a model of deep physical naturalness that can transcend and even symbolically eradicate political crudity.[21] Wang Er's directness in gaining sexual satisfaction, contrasted with his refusal to allow himself to be conventionally emotionally obsessed, in a manner associated with love or lust; the author's creation of a tiny sexual utopia, hidden away from society at large in a mountain hut made of grass, where a fundamental biological interaction can take place in an environment that projects immediacy; the way in which Wang Er's desires color and alter all his other interactions, and even give rise to Chen Qingyang as a smaller ripple of desire flowing out of his larger wave—all of these sexual aspects work in favor of understanding modernity as strongly embodied within aesthetic experience and understanding.

We can better see the contrast if we more intensively compare Wang Xiaobo's approach to that of Zhang Xianliang, and Wang Er to Zhang Yonglin. In Zhang Xianliang's *Half of Man Is Woman*, the protagonist Zhang Yonglin uses his relationship with Huang Xiangjiu as a tool through which to work through his disempowerment under the Maoist leftist excesses of the Cultural Revolution. When he achieves victory over his impotence, he also finds a way to envision a future for himself, and at that point his relationship has served its function and can be discarded. To create as Zhang's partner an unsophisticated woman who cannot possibly understand his philosophical musings or political desires makes his abandonment of her all the more convenient and logical. Sexual intimacy becomes a structure that mimics and encapsulates political life, which still possesses overarching significance for Zhang Yonglin and for the author.

To Wang Xiaobo, however, sexual desire and experience are completely non-instrumental, and he does not even deign to consider the approach of the political life of working on behalf of the general good. Still, this sexual way of being functions only under the larger umbrella of the powerful passage of time and its corollary in Wang Er's attitude of light melancholy, and therefore is not so much a real-life substitute as it is an aesthetics of time, place, and history where alternative ontologies can be imagined. Like time, sexual desire continues, spreading through the past, present, and future; it can be experienced perpetually (if not always at the same intensity), and it thereby offers the protagonist a thread onto which he can clip his radical aesthetic consciousness. Just as the mountain hut allows Wang Er a natural space where he can indulge his sexual desires, the topic of sexuality provides a form accepted in modern society, a structure into which the author can embed his ideas of positive but limited intellectual approach. Like everything else subject to the ravages of time, sexual intercourse is not a tool or strategy through which Wang Er can reach transformative enlightenment; unlike Zhang Yonglin, he does not make any personal progress. Sexual intercourse exists for his benefit, but its power to alter reality is limited by the sadness produced through the passing of time.

Thematically, this portrayal of sexuality lies at the center of Wang Xiaobo's aesthetic vision of life. A more overtly political understanding would imply that behavior at large must be organized, for only through this directness, this demand for a clear recognition of problems and a clear connection between action and result, can power imbalances be addressed and society improved. For Wang Er, the only aspect of his life that he more or less controls is his sexual relationship, and it is here where he transparently lays out a goal, takes steps as he moves toward a positive result, and receives the reward of pure and immediate experience. If Wang Er were to use this sexual relationship as a stepping stone in his political self-cultivation, an impetus to push him along his journey to political reempowerment, Wang Xiaobo's imaginative vision would be similar to that of Zhang Xianliang. By contrast, he presents us with a character whose directedness can be applied only within the realm of sexual relations—and in the larger scheme of things even this sexual pleasure falls victim to an overall lack of control and direction.

However, in *The Golden Years* the focus on aesthetic existence is expressed only weakly through character and theme, and much more strongly through its presentation of time and emotion. The novel's organization, which mimics the kind of modernity Wang envisions in intellectual society at large, makes his plea on behalf of aesthetic transformation particularly powerful. The rendition is forceful partially because Wang avoids political and class struggle, substituting for it a semi-ironic cool, a murky lyricism, and a narrative that twists and turns, delighting the reader with its straightforward sexual descriptions and subtle ingenuity. His refusal to allow his characters to engage at an emotional level also indicates his careful delineation of a thoroughly modern intellectual space. His turn away from emotional excess is not simply a form of avoidance, but a positive movement that aligns Wang Er's intellectual consciousness—and that of the reader—with a new elite aesthetics, a gentle irony that, like Wang Er, escapes overt confrontation with power if at all possible. If confrontation is unavoidable, it is to be mollified through story-telling and off-beat humor.

To understand why this anti-emotional modernity would appear so enticing to Chinese intellectuals, we first must recall the emotional basis of revolutionary passion, which demanded work of the spirit at the most fundamental level of self-construction, and integrated emotion into a chain of loyalty that extended from the person through multiple social units right up to the highest levels of the state. Wang's writing gives not so much as a glimmer of this passion; nor does he allow the appearance of the binary of passion / dejection, which informs so many Cultural Revolution narratives and implies that this history will reproduce itself endlessly. Second, in Wang Er's pursuit of Chen Qingyang the "physical emotion" of sexual desire known as love or lust, which is cleverly manipulated in consumer culture and expressed in many recent novels about decadence or sexual excess, is unrepresented. Although readers can and do hypothesize about the sexual desire that underlies Wang Er's actions and the novel's rationale, the lack of expressions of lust makes them claim that Wang Er's desires are somehow pure and clean. We do not read about Wang Er struggling with sexual desire. This aspect of the novel adds to its anti-emotionalism, and provides a model of an intelligent person who gets what he wants without the debilitating storm and fury of raging emotions.

It is, however, in the presentation of time that the novel unfolds its true bid for an aesthetic modernity. Historically, the time of the novel is the brutal period of the Cultural Revolution, yet Wang Xiaobo's time is a slow-moving, little-changing flow that is tamed by a sense of melancholy and fate. Even scenes that we would suppose to be full of emotion are told levelly and from a distance, granting to time an authoritative adeptness in moderating passion and in creating a sense of the real. Indeed, for Wang Er, the real is nothing other than the body moving through a time that hardly changes, or the passage of time mapped onto the body that does change. Wang Er's life is the organization of undirected time through the body, not a testimony to the pulsing moment aggressively recognized in peaks and valleys, nor the controlled, goal-oriented, directed time of political struggle. Rather, it is a sluggish movement that demands some distance even when Wang Er is totally absorbed.

This kind of time certainly argues against revolutionary consciousness, which must be registered in violently expressed highs and lows. To return to a question I posed at the beginning of this analysis—how does Wang Xiaobo represent the Cultural Revolution?—my interpretation of this slow-moving time is one response. The author does not, however, argue on behalf of reform or the more liberal view of slow change; Wang Er is *uninvolved* with political change, and he discusses anything that could be called *work* only peripherally. Under Wang Xiaobo's pen, the logic of radical change appears as something skimming over the surface of a much more powerful understanding of social life. To see exactly what that understanding is, we must recognize that the novel argues not only against extreme leftism, but also against the idea that power can be resisted. In this sense Dai Jinhua (1998) points toward a valuable understanding of the novel; finding that Foucault rather than Freud is basic to the interpretation of Wang's writing, Dai sees the Foucauldian idea that power relations underlie everything at the root of Wang's thinking (5). I cannot disagree with this interpretation, as Wang Er's mentality is that of someone who from the beginning of the narrative already understands this basic truth. However, although Wang Er knows his life is limited and controlled by his circumstances, he still gets what he wants. Politics—in the direct sense of those in charge of his life, or in the more abstract sense of the many facets of human relations—may get in the way of Wang Er's exploits with Chen Qingyang, but it doesn't change the way he lives his life. Through his depiction of time as flowing slowly through Wang Er, a man only mildly perturbed by political events, Wang Xiaobo has created a forceful alternative intellectual model. Wang Er's distance as he comments on his life, both past and present, his knowledge that the passions of youth are just that and will not result in change, and his sadness as a result of this knowledge—all work to reduce the large and small of politics down to a dull white noise. Wang Er's sense of the world spreads out as he moves through it, modifying all relationships and turning them away from a political interpretation that would see them as a dialectic of exchanges between conflicting positions embodied in passion, expanding his own "twisted" sense of reality. There is no position other than that of Wang Er. Other people and other stances are simply tentacles of his own mind; his consciousness forming the body of the octopus, as he weaves them in and out of the slots where he wants them. Even Chen Qingyang, the only other character into whose mind we delve, often seems like just a pale reflection of Wang Er and his desires.

Wang Er is both engaged and floating, selfish and selfless, intellectual and ordinary. He gets what he wants without killing or coercion. He has a philosophical sense of life and yet appreciates its most sensual forms. He places himself at the center of his universe without dissolving into psychological obsession—this in itself a major accomplishment for the writer during a period when psychological explanations of mental life are proliferating. Wang Er knows his position and role and thoroughly understands the rules, but he gets around them. When critics put aside an analysis of Wang Er's Daoist refusal of social engagement in favor of their own experience of that refusal and the aesthetic, experiential doors it opens through reading pleasure, we have to admire Wang Xiaobo's success. The novel's sadness may contain a bit of regret for the loss of a directly political vision, but also present may be a sigh of relief that takes delight in its ability to find and present a less tumultuous alternative. The *okay, whatever* consciousness of Wang Er, unraveled through a unique sense of time, stands in opposition to the experience of revolutionary subjectivity, which is saturated with passion, fully embodied, and directed by a strong sense of progress for all.

FIVE

Extracting Revolutionary Spirit

Jiang Wen's In the Heat of the Sun *and Anchee Min's* Red Azalea

While it would be difficult to associate an implied emancipation with the disinterested sexual promiscuity put forward by Mang Ke or the philosophical distance of Wang Xiaobo, other writers and filmmakers have represented free sexual relations as both liberating and a symbolic direction for the future. Erotics-as-liberation is not, however, a simple abandonment of the revolutionary past, or a temporal binary in which revolution belongs entirely to the past while sexual desire can indicate the future. In different ways, Jiang Wen and Anchee Min connect sexual desire with the spirit of the revolution, idealistically extracting a powerful essence from the past while throwing away the dregs of official procedure, corruption, and a failure on behalf of the authorities to recognize the inadequacy of policy as it was applied to real-life conditions.

Jiang Wen's 1994 film *In the Heat of the Sun* (Yangguang canlan de rizi), based on a story by Wang Shuo, closely focuses on the main character Ma Xiaojun, a privileged teenager living in a military compound while his parents are off working in the countryside or doing military work. The heyday of the Cultural Revolution is past, and after a brief introduction to Ma's young life, we learn that he already has lost belief in the glory of the revolution. Yet its heroic romanticism lives on, as Ma transfers it into his tryst with Milan during a summer that expands to fill up almost the entire screen time. While recognizing the material and social inadequacy of revolution, Jiang Wen imagines within it an immutable spirit that will lay dormant and spring to life in the future. Here, revolutionary spirit is a bridge to the future, or a powerful gaze that redirects our attention away from the past. The spirit exists not in ideology, which by the summer of 1975 had lost its potency, but in sound, taste, vision, and smell—the recalled sensory experience that the director goes to great length to recreate.

Anchee Min's novel *Red Azalea* (1994), written in English and published in the United States, also suggests that revolutionary spirit—if not the specific and lived ideology of revolution—is mutable in form and location, but constant and liberating in essence. Min merges this spirit with a sexual desire that flourishes through hidden behavior during revolutionary times, when its direct expression is banned. *Red Azalea* distills an imaginary spiritual Maoism, creating it out of and as resistance to political Maoism. Within this context, sexual desire, like spiritual Maoism, becomes the instinctual urge of the individual to fight the dishonesty and duplicity that so often accompanies an aging bureaucracy. Like *In the Heat of the Sun*, *Red Azalea* is directed toward the future, synthesizing aspects of the past and reworking them into a forward look out across the horizon. For Min, revolutionary passion is not presupposed by sexual passion so much as they both are closely aligned within a sphere of the real, the good, and the beautiful.

While both Anchee Min's novel and Jiang Wen's film give expression to a semi-mystical, powerful revolutionary spirit, Jiang Wen provides at least a brief view of a future without it (while implying it may be reborn); by contrast, Anchee Min ends her story with the main characters leaving China for the United States, implying that a spirit-imbued existence cannot be realized within the national or cultural borders of China. As we shall see in Chapter 6, this conclusion is also taken up by He Jianjun in the film *The Postman*. The film goes to an extreme to depict a society that is devoid of spirit, yet is also a place where, without memory or self-awareness, a letter carrier sets out to recreate a positive direction similar to that embodied through a life directed by an ideal revolutionary spirit.

AS YOU WISH IT: JIANG WEN'S IN THE HEAT OF THE SUN

> That square ideographs, each so hard to recall, can actually become a vivid, living picture—how can you not swoon from the seductive power of film. (Jiang Wen et al. 1997, 2)

On September 5, 1994, director Jiang Wen completed the film *In the Heat of the Sun*. Two days later the film was submitted to the Beijing Film Office for evaluation. The office requested seven changes, including alterations in certain terms and in the use of the song *The Internationale* during a scene when the main character beats a boy to near death in an alley.[1] On September 15, Xia Yu (1978–) received Best Actor award at the Venice Film Festival for his portrayal of this main character, Ma Xiaojun; he was the youngest actor ever to receive that award. On October 12, *In the Heat* was shown to over one thousand film and culture specialists and reporters in Beijing. Two days later it was shown to teachers and students from the Beijing Film Academy and Central Drama Institute. Although there were only 1,200 seats available, over 1,700 people crowded in, many sitting on the carpets. On June 1, 1995, the Film Office approved the film for showing to audiences at large, again requesting changes that included modification of the main male character's unruly sexual behavior and once again, decreasing the volume for *The Internationale* during the beating scene.

On June 28, 1995, *In the Heat* debuted in nine Hong Kong theaters, earning four million HK dollars within days, thus becoming one of the top ten earners at the time. It received rave reviews. On August 14 the film was approved for release in the mainland, opening in Shanghai on August 21, first in several prominent theaters for one week and then in some fifty sites, where it played for over twenty days. People stood in line to get tickets, a rare phenomenon for a domestically produced film; over three million RMB worth of tickets were sold. When the film opened in Beijing on August 29, over 4,000 people—almost twice as many as seats were available—crowded into the theater at the Beijing Exhibition Hall. The audience was wildly enthusiastic, and the appearance of Jiang Wen and the actors resulted in long applause. At the Capitol Theater, the film generated more ticket sales than any other since the theater was built, and in Beijing alone the ticket sales topped three million overall (Jiang Wen et al. 1997, 67–84).[2]

Although *In the Heat* made the *Time* magazine list of ten most important films for that year, it did not show widely in theaters in the United States. Some critics attribute its success in China to the way in which the film produces a culturally specific nostalgia, which may be difficult for the non-Chinese film audience to appreciate. In this regard, the film could join other films as well as fiction, poetry, TV series, and advertisements as one example of what Beijing University professor Dai Jinhua (1997) calls "sexually romanticizing the remembrance of revolution and individualizing the writing of history," a film that goes hand in hand with the new consumer society because it "embodies the 'self' and the expression of self" (153–54). Dai argues that this imagined nostalgia is widely prevalent in 1990s China because it creates comfort and stability at a time when people desperately need new links between themselves and society, and the past and the present (160).[3]

The plot of *In the Heat of the Sun* centers on the experiences of Ma Xiaojun, who is about 15 years old in 1975. Ma, who lives on a military base with his parents, hangs around with a group of male friends and one female friend, Yu Beipei, who mysteriously disappears partway into the film and is replaced by Ma's love interest, Milan.[4] With his parents gone most of the time and school taking up little of his attention, Ma is free to do as he wishes. He and his friends get into brawls with other gangs, goof around, and try to meet other girls. Throughout the story, which is narrated in voiceover by Ma's older self (the voice of Jiang Wen), Ma perfects his skill of sneaking into people's homes for the thrill and for the experience of something different. Most of the film takes place in one summer, and it is bracketed by two short sections, one when Ma is much younger, and one when he is much older.

In the Heat of the Sun provides viewers a novel interpretation of the Cultural Revolution, even though the film is set toward the end of this revolutionary high point.[5] The film uses close-ups, romantic classical music, Cultural Revolution music, and sexual display to project the magical sense of creativity that the main character, Ma Xiaojun, finds within himself when his father is sent on military duty and his mother goes to the countryside. The filmmaker was inspired by the fiction of Wang Shuo, whose so-called hooligan literature (liumang wenxue) portrays the lives of young urban no-goods. These predominantly male, alienated city-dwellers may seem to have little in common with the morally charged, hard-working, and ideologically vigilant fictional characters of the Maoist era, but Wang

Shuo and Jiang Wen both show how the attitudes associated with revolutionary romanticism—a fearless disregard for danger in pursuit of victory or heroism, goal-oriented persistence, lyricism in spirit, and loyalty—have infiltrated the consciousness of the young men who hang around in city gangs and have easily been transferred into a semi-revolutionary or, in many instances, blatantly unrevolutionary milieu.[6] Although the revolution itself is dead, its spirit lives on, easily adapted and moved away from its tainted past. *In the Heat* rejects the model story of sent-down youth who are working on behalf of the revolution for the good of the masses, and thus differentiates itself from the valorization of the days of glory, hardship, and finally betrayed true faith that often characterizes Cultural Revolution narratives written by former sent-down youth. Situated in 1975 and centering on a group of boys who no longer believe in overtly revolutionary ideals, the film nonetheless projects a sense that something good can and will come out of this era. Rather than glorifying the past—the innocence and idealism that so often precede disillusionment in sent-down youth memoirs—the film foregrounds an aesthetic, sensual existence abstracted from its time.

Taking advantage of the visual and musical possibilities of the film medium to highlight the logic of revolutionary aesthetics as opposed to socialist ideology and revolutionary spirit as opposed to material obstacles, Jiang Wen depicts a society in which the youngsters already see through the concepts that motivate their parents and teachers, yet still live completely under the control of the daily-life emotive aesthetics that they absorbed from revolutionary culture. Furthermore, Jiang Wen recognizes this narrative—the creation and extraction of emotion-based desire from ideology—as particular to youth, and thus infinitely repeatable, a perpetual but positive state of illusion that can recycle itself endlessly. The film is narrated in a voiceover that belongs to Ma Xiaojun's older self; it is clearly presented as a reordering of the past that is, we are given to believe, part fantasy and part reality. As Dai Jinhua's comments indicate, although some critics find that the film's focus on individual experience ushers in a new age of capitalist pleasure, it is precisely the revolutionary emotive aesthetics, not the new world of consumer goods and material wealth available in modernized Beijing, that creates this half-imagined desire and reminiscence. This new imagination can rewrite the past and provide images all of its own, allowing the burden of history to be lifted. Even more important, however, it nurtures a particular mental state, a creative, utopian *as you wish it* mentality that always looks to the future. The *as you wish it* mentality depends on knowledge from life as it is lived rather than on learned concepts, draws attention to the importance of the memory and understanding that comes from the physical senses of sound, smell, taste, touch, and vision, and insists on the overarching significance of ordinary daily experience. It thus expands the boundaries of what is significant, altering the meaning of a Cultural Revolution, which is generally presented from the perspective of how a clear and much-repeated political ideology produces a deeply rooted faith that eventually is shattered. In essence, the film extracts the revolutionary spirit from the material and political, refines it as an icon of memory and sensation, and redeems and directs it. The most radical aspect of the film is its switch of perspective, as it projects a way of living that looks optimistically to the future.

The film thus revises the Cultural Revolution story, recognizing that revolutionary discourse once was unified through an intact temporal synthesis: with a past to be distanced, a present to be improved, and a future toward which everyone would work. Within this organization, representation of the past is often the most important, as is shown in rituals such as "relating bitterness" (suku, publicly discussing how one was oppressed under pre-revolutionary culture) and self-criticism (ziwo piping, confessing the errors of one's past). Although this unified scheme was powerful and successful in creating revolutionary consciousness, the violence, corruption, and hypocrisy of the Cultural Revolution devastated it, the film implies, and thus another, revised story is needed. One kind of revision is the memoirs of sent-down youth, which provide a wholesale critique through a recreation of the innocence and heartfelt belief that ultimately are destroyed. These stories continue the Maoist emphasis on interpreting the past as the most central act of constructing a present and imagining a future. In such stories, the emotional and spiritual engagement of young revolutionaries is seen as the result of political brainwashing in which youthful emotion and passion were manipulated in a devastating political environment. The inevitable interpretation that this connection produces is that this youthful passion was created falsely and must, therefore, be rejected.

By contrast, *In the Heat* separates the passion of youth from the goals of revolution yet still locates this passion, tinged with mystery, within revolutionary discourse. This innovation is in itself significant, for it allows the viewer to imagine that something good can and should be extracted from those years of violence and fear. Even more important is a structural innovation that is expressed through the mind and actions of the main character Ma Xiaojun. Rather than focusing on and ultimately discrediting the past as the authority for interpreting the present, as sent-down youth memoirs do, here we are encouraged to view from a subtly different angle that privileges the present and the future over the past. This perspective, the film implies, will significantly change the nature of experience.

We see opened a door not so much to the future itself, but more to the point, a way in which an orientation toward the future can become part of one's existential perspective. This is revealed in, for example, the playful self-consciousness shown in the cameo appearances of Wang Shuo, Jiang Wen, and Jiang Wen's friends in the film, in Jiang Wen's fanatic attention to detail and autobiographical authenticity, in the narrating voiceover that warns us not to believe, in the disappearance and reappearance of the character Yu Beipei, and in the direct manipulation of memory and reality in the played-over scenes. A more conventional criticism of the past may have had a similar goal—destroying the past in order to move toward the future, but Jiang Wen's film accomplishes this goal at the level of subjectivity, marking consciousness as a temporal pivot through which this transformation will occur. This provocative tilt is the surprising result of Jiang Wen's interpretation of Wang Shuo's story as sensual experience, of his choice to work against the ordinary sent-down youth narrative, and it is one reason, I suspect, why the film has been so successful in China. The future-facing impetus is projected to the audience most effectively not through a deconstruction of the past as ideologically flawed or empty, but through the film's construction of a sense of possibility, excitement, and spirit in the main character, Ma Xiaojun.

This spirit derives from the heroism revolutionary life exemplifies, and its liberatory potential for all people and nations. We see the damage and hypocrisy that the revolutionary narrative produces, but we also see qualities that can and must be redeemed. For example, the film maintains that a global perspective is and was part of the Communist ideal even during the severely isolated years of the Cultural Revolution. The ultimate goal of socialism was not simply national strength, although this was very important, but the utopian liberation of all humankind; these are sentiments that the voiceover attributes to the young Ma at the beginning of the film. In its transformation of emotions associated with national military heroism and international liberation into a flexible lyrical subjectivity, *In the Heat* grasps the logic of the future—the infusion of life with immediate goals, the ideas of progress, hope, and optimism—and shifts them from a national and global context into a personal, sexual arena, where the idea that *anything can happen* becomes fixed on that first possible kiss. It is in this arena—one often associated with the development of capitalist culture—where the film enlarges the space of possibility and opportunity. Yet there should be no mistaking the original impetus of this revolutionary spirit.

The setting of the film during the wane of the Cultural Revolution in 1975, the age of the main characters (who are too young to have been sent-down youth), and the privileged life within a military compound are the conditions necessary for Jiang Wen to avoid becoming trapped by the common post-revolutionary story of faith followed by betrayal. Jiang Wen is similar to Anchee Min in the way he closely allies the passion of revolutionary romanticism with sexual desire, but he goes farther than Min in depicting the transfer of the future into the film's present. In the film's 1975, the underlying concept—once fully embodied in revolutionary culture—that the future is open and can be created through one's own efforts still exists completely within the boys, but they are already estranged from the ideology of revolution. However, Jiang's reconstruction of the past is complicated by his brief addition of a third time and space. Added to the revolutionary past represented by parents and teachers, and the end-of-revolutionary-concepts but continuing-revolutionary-passion represented by Ma Xiaojun and his friends, we also glimpse an unattractive present: the boys have aged into contemporary businessmen riding in a limousine drinking foreign whiskey. However, as I explain below, their cop-out is portrayed not as their choosing capitalism over socialism, but as a betrayal of the aesthetics and spirit that ordered and gave meaning to their lives when they were young.

They have, in other words, lost the deep significance and pleasure that derived from the spirit of revolution. I do not find the primary meaning of the film to lie in the nostalgia it produces for viewers who went through the Cultural Revolution; however, if we take the perspective of middle age that is briefly represented at the end of the film, the passions of post-yet-still-revolutionary youth could elicit nostalgia. The nostalgia is not, however, for revolutionary ideology, which was already defunct, but for the spirit of its aesthetic life; moreover, this nostalgia is overwhelmed first by the film's central implication, which is that this spirit can be inherited and continued, and second by Jiang Wen's focus on sensation, experience, and subjectivity.

THE SPECIAL CHARACTERISTICS OF YOUTH

> Our dreams are the dreams of youth. That was the story of youth in a nation right in the midst of its own youth. Their passion burned everywhere like fire, and in the flames were fiery loves and hatreds. Now the fire has gone out; its embers still crackle in the ashes. Yet who is to say the passion is really dead? (Jiang Wen et al. 1997, 2)

Appearing in the mid-1990s, along with many other revisionist representations of the Cultural Revolution in film, literature, and music, *In the Heat* rewrites the dominant narrative of trauma, violence, and dislocation. The film does not disregard or completely displace that earlier interpretation but shrinks and limits it, marking it as existing completely within the experience of adults; meanwhile, certain youth—here those who lived relatively free, ideologically unharassed lives in military compounds—had access to a bliss not readily available to the adults. This Cultural Revolution belongs to a youthful group that displaces the political machinations of the older generation—who firmly identified with the orthodox history of the Communist Party that began in 1921—and replaces it with an energy that can be inherited and continued. No longer seen as "ten years of chaos and destruction," as the government has characterized it, the Cultural Revolution becomes a fountainhead of this spirit. This Cultural Revolution is not, of course, *the* Cultural Revolution of the past. Along those lines, although Jiang Wen recognized the autobiographical aspect of the film and the novella on which it is based, he fiercely denied that his film was primarily about the Cultural Revolution:

> Wang Shuo and I have similar backgrounds, we both were kids from military compounds, and we both had a lot of contact with other kids in the area. When I read his story, I was strongly moved. Wang Shuo's story pierced my skin like a needle and the blood shot out with a hiss. . . . In "Ferocious Beasts" I found what at the time I thought was a kind of reality. This reality is subjective. I felt that Wang Shuo had humanely described the process of a youth growing up, and his portrayal exceeded the limitations of the times . . . After I wrote the script, some people misunderstood it to be a Cultural Revolution film, but I had no intention of making a film about the Cultural Revolution. The families, schools, relations between girls and boys of this period—I experienced all of this and wrote it into the script . . . Some of it is from the story, some of it is my own. I'm already unclear about it all but I know that the spirit is there, because Wang Shuo's story gave me a clear grasp on that. (Jiang Wen et al. 1997, 4–6).

The plot unfolds in three time periods: first in Ma Xiaojun's early youth or preteen years at about age 10, second in Ma's teenage years around age 15, and third in his maturity as an adult. The bulk of the film occurs in the second, during one summer of Ma's teenage years. These three periods have implications for the film's perspective on the past, present, and future.

Although there are only a few scenes from Ma's preteen period, they are noteworthy because at this time Ma identifies completely with the entirety—not just the emotive aesthetics or spirit—of the revolutionary discourse. The first scene we see is an upraised hand coming into view at the bottom of the screen, against a blue sky. The hand turns out to belong to a statue of Mao, whose face comes into view next. "In the raging storms of revolution, soldiers' hearts turn toward the sun," we hear, in the first of twenty-some revolutionary songs heard throughout the film. Already we have been given several meanings for "the sun" in the film's title: it is the past under memory (in the voice of the adult Ma, while the initial credits roll); the revolution; glory and heroism; and the national and spiritual leader Mao Zedong. The time is 1969 and Ma's father, with his army unit, has been ordered to Guizhou to stop factional violence. Ma's mother yells at the boy to come down off the perch from which he is observing the dancers in the military send-off. Our first glimpse of Ma shows him differently from the friends with whom he stands: we briefly catch him through the red gauze of a flag, from behind. The view of Ma reddened by the flag hints at his special relationship with revolutionary spirit, which the film will develop as a theme. Ma then joins his mother and father in the back of a truck, which races past a poster of Mao, again with an upturned hand.

Our viewpoint is now from the truck, and trees stream past as we rush forward. Ma gazes up at his father happily and blows excitedly on a whistle, his mother holds him protectively from behind. They smile and point to tanks rumbling below them. The adult-Ma voiceover tells us that the 10-year-old Ma longs for a Sino-Soviet war, because he is certain that the Soviets and the American imperialists will be crushed by the People's Liberation Army, and a new war hero (who is none other than himself) will be created, as his name, "little soldier," suggests. A military helicopter comes in over tall grass that wave in the wind that it makes; our view from below allows the grass to fill up over a third of the screen, creating a close, all-encompassing image of military might and vision. Before Ma's father leaves, the young Ma breaks from his mother's grasp and runs to his father to return the whistle to him. Here Ma is totally identified with his father and his father's mission: revolution, service, and self-sacrifice, all contained within an overarching shell of personal heroism projected by the send-off music and the dancers, and the sense of glory produced by the tanks and planes.

I describe these scenes at length because they show the only time during the span of Ma's lifetime represented in the film when there is complete unification and harmony between the aesthetics and the ideology of revolution. The entire family, indeed the entire community, stands behind the revolutionary effort, and Jiang Wen carefully builds up the scenes to illustrate this confluence. A child who identifies with the colorful flags, the whistle, the tanks and planes, and the idea of heroism, Ma Xiaojun also knows about American imperialism, the Soviet enemy, and national aspirations. As much as is possible for one his age, he represents the Maoist ideal: passionate, with both national and global goals secure in his mind, and sure of his mission. The world lies before him, thoroughly organized through the images and sounds of revolutionary culture. His future is clear.

Our transition to the second time period comes almost immediately, and the dissolution of Ma's revolutionary beliefs is foreshadowed even earlier. Ma's father gets into the plane, and, although the music rises to a crescendo, it is an ancient, bloated piece of machinery belching smoke and noise as it labors its way up into the atmosphere, a hint of the material impossibility of realizing the glorious socialist vision. Soon after, the young Ma Xiaojun, in the same striped shirt, is seen creeping along a wall as he listens to female voices singing about liberated serfs showing gratitude to Chairman Mao. Three girls in school uniforms come into view, practicing a dance in a classroom. A close-up show's Ma's eyes blinking rapidly from outside the window, and the voiceover states that since his father left he has gained great freedom. We are left to infer that with paternalistic control lessened—in other words, with revolutionary unity breaking apart—he is able to see the girls in a different light.

One girl glances at him. There is a sound of breaking glass, and a classroom window shatters. Ma turns to see three boys jump off a porch roof. They are chanting an adolescent rhyme about rubbing poles and rubbing holes. Their playfully erotic rhyme illustrates that a new interpretation has replaced the social harmony of the past that the military send-off dancers represented. The boys run off, with Ma in the chase. When the four friends meet on a pile of dirt, they compete to see who can throw his book bag highest. Ma's bag sails into the sky, the papers and books flying out of it, and when he catches it we see him as a teenager, having graduated from primary school and now living with his buddies on a military base.

Several transformations underlie these scenes. Ma's nuclear family consisting of himself, his mother, and his father has broken apart and been replaced by a group of largely male friends. The surge of heroic, patriotic emotion his younger self felt at the display of dancing, singing, and military force when his father left is now displaced by an interest in the dancing girls themselves, and the girls' revolutionary song is mocked by the dirty ditty of Ma's friends. Significantly, Ma is an observer in both scenes, but only in the second do we see him alone, foreshadowing the break with his friends Ma will experience later in the film as he becomes enamored of Milan.

The substance of the film takes place in the second age-time, when Ma is a teenager. In this time of his life Ma and his friends are completely cynical about the ideology of revolution, and in society at large the unified revolutionary discourse has shattered. There also are suggestions that question the integrity of the past, implying that faith in the revolution never was wholly embodied by its most powerful representative, Ma's father, even during intense times of struggle. As a teenager during the 1940s resistance and fully absorbed by the 1950s national solidification, Ma's father certainly appears to be a good communist. Yet the teenage Ma reflects that his father, who spent the Korean War dismantling American bombs, escaped without a scratch, even though many were killed in this job; Ma's mother suspected that his father actually was hiding out in the mountains rather than fulfilling his duties. This short statement by the voiceover splinters the main symbol of revolutionary unity, and we instantly see a familiar, now-you-see-it-now-you-don't structure, yet one dating from after the Cultural Revolution and not commonly invoked in descriptions of wartime China: the revolutionary discourse is a hypocritical shell, under which hides the manipulative self-interest of individuals and families. In another example, when his mother goes into labor with his brother, the jeep they had available will not start and Ma must enlist his friends to take her to the hospital. His older self comments that as a teenager he understood that this kind of inadequacy in daily life showed how poorly prepared the country was for war, how they would die if actually attacked.

When we compare the Ma Xiaojun in Wang Shuo's short story "Ferocious Beasts" (Dongwu xiongmeng) to the character in the film, we find that in the latter the teenage Ma is much more detached from the authorities around him and from the narratives that they represent. Jiang Wen developed and strengthened Ma's conflict with both his parents and his teacher, which is minor in Wang Shuo's text. In the film, for instance, Ma's mother and father both beat him at different times and for different reasons. Ma's father hits his son because he believes Ma is following the wrong path by getting involved with girls. In the story, rather than physically attacking his son when he finds him with Milan, the father takes the girl into a separate room and gives her a good talking to (Wang Shuo 1995, 300). Also, Wang Shuo's Ma meets Milan's parents and gains their trust and affection, while in the film he avoids contact completely. In this way, Jiang Wen intensifies Ma's conflict with the values of the older generation and demarcates the category of *youth*. Ma's mother is an embittered educator who has been forced to give up her career development to follow her husband as he took up his military duties around the country; she has every reason to be alienated from the revolutionary effort yet cannot in any way publicly show that alienation. She beats Ma because he refuses to take his studies seriously all the while she complains about her own failures, thus merging her anger at him with her personal frustration. Ma's mother links her son to her husband, saying they are both the same in that neither one likes to come home; thus she implies that the wild curiosity and forward motion of the father has been transmitted to the son, saying, "from the young we can see the old" (congxiao kanda). The scenes in the film of Ma's mother crying and bewailing her life are not in the short story, but they add a dimension of realism to Ma's rejection of revolutionary ideology.

Ma's mother (played by one of China's best-known actresses, Siqin Gaowa) is important for another reason. Through the violence directed at her family, we see the day-to-day horrors of the Cultural Revolution as Jiang Wen reconstructs them. This episode occurs directly after what Ma calls the most perfect day of his life: when he carries Milan back to her work unit on his bicycle along an idyllic country road. When Ma arrives at home, he finds his father holding his baby brother and gesturing at him to be quiet. His father whispers something in his ear while his mother sits forlornly on the bed. The scene now switches: the family sit silently on a train, and the voiceover tells us that Ma's maternal grandfather, a wearer of the "four hats" of landlord, capitalist, counter-revolutionary, and Nationalist party member, committed suicide to escape further punishment. He had undergone all of the persecutions common during the Cultural Revolution: house search, physical and mental torture, emotional trauma. Ma Xiaojun comments: "I lived with my grandma and grandpa before I started going to school—I never could understand how he could become a target of the dictatorship of the proletariat, a class enemy." Ma recovers quickly when he returns to Beijing, however, and after this point, he intensifies what his parents condemn as his bad behavior. Thus, though the story of Cultural Revolution suffering and violence is represented in the film, we see Ma Xiaojun existing largely within a different chronicle.

Ma's teacher, another possible role model, is instead portrayed as a laughable example of what education has become as he tries to teach with dry scientific and historical explanations entirely lacking in excitement and inspiration. The teacher is one of the first victims of Ma's new voyeuristic perspective and control; we see Ma viewing him through a telescope as he flirts with a woman and then urinates behind a wall. This weakens the teacher's authority and that of formal education at large. Ma's success in eluding his parents and teacher makes his "escape" from the past and its stultifying influence stark and obvious. Furthermore, his father, mother, and teacher all become examples of how revolutionary ideology, enshrined in bureaucracy and institutions, has eaten away at and corrupted everything that once mattered.

The third time period in the film, presented in black and white, is the brief perspective of the adult Ma, driving in a white Cadillac in modern Beijing with his four friends Yang Gao, Big Ant, and the brothers Liu Sitian (Think-of-Sweetness Liu) and Liu Yiku (Recall-Bitterness Liu). Other than Liu Yiku, who is still dressed in his army clothes, the others all wear Western suits. They pass around a bottle of expensive cognac and fall silent when Liu Yiku, who has been driven crazy fighting in the south, anxiously grabs the bottle and keeps it to himself. Another figure from their past—a mentally disabled boy they call Gulunmu—appears outside, riding his bamboo pole, as always. For the first time in the film, Gulunmu actually says something intelligible, yelling an obscenity at them as they peer out of the car's sunroof. The camera backs away, and a congested scene of modern Beijing takes up the screen.[7]

Our first viewpoint during this time is focused on a good-luck charm picture of Mao Zedong that hangs from the mirror in the Cadillac, and as in the earlier scene with the military truck, we see things from the perspective of the car itself, moving through the busy streets. In this way, Jiang Wen emphasizes the experience rather than the viewing of the experience, as we become part of the moving vehicle. The good luck charm dates from the Mao craze that swept China in the late 1980s and 1990s and reproduced the former leader's face and form on cigarette lighters, clocks, and other paraphernalia, much of it copied from Cultural Revolution models (Dutton 1998, 232–71).[8] Hung on car mirrors, Mao's image was supposed to protect the driver from harm. The huge statue that takes up the screen at the beginning of the movie, when the revolution was still respected, has become a charm, a fetish from a popular culture fragmented into consumer items, which are still endowed with a pan-magical quality.

Bracketed by the overarching, all-important Mao at one end and the shrunken, talisman-like Mao at the other, the teenage years of Ma and his friends expand to fill up the space. Clearly the experience of the teenage Ma is typical only of a few—those who were too young to have been Red Guards participating in the mythologizing or the worst violence of the Cultural Revolution and too young to have gone to the countryside as sent-down youth, yet old enough to know what those experiences were all about. What is the meaning of this emphasis on youth?

Dai Jinhua (1996) interprets the Mao craze and the sent-down youth literature as containing "profoundly complex emotions and declarations" (135). She writes that "what educated youth literature sought was to redeem the self from the calamity, the pillaging, the evil that was history—it was the memory of youth as substitute. Consequently, they tried with near desperation to rip away the memory of their youth from history and the discourse of history" (136). Dai describes sent-down youth literature as fully representing the violence and trauma of the revolutionary struggle itself in the lives of the youth, who either were sent down to the countryside to join the peasants or became Red Guards. Yet her explanation of this generation's desire to rewrite their memory of youth and change their history is relevant to both the story and the film. Extrapolating from her comments, we could regard *In the Heat* as a general statement by those old enough to know about the horror of the Cultural Revolution: we, they claim, would rather think of it as a time of passion characteristic of youth than as a historical calamity.

Along the same lines, in a direct reference to the film, critic Jiang Lei (1997) points out that one of Jiang Wen's contributions has been to help people realize that history can be changed. The tremendous burden that the conventional Cultural Revolution narrative puts on them in its demands for accountability, moral reflection, explanation, and continual angst all can be transformed and even eliminated. While maintaining the overall Cultural Revolution focus (which Jiang Lei calls the "ubiquitous absence") that underlies many films by third, fourth, and fifth generation directors, Jiang Wen has allowed a generation to recover its youthful passion, according to Jiang Lei:

> . . . to say that the Cultural Revolution is a dark page in the lives of thousands and millions of Chinese people is not an exaggeration, but if you grew up in the Cultural Revolution, you never had to go to school, you had those first loves you never really understood, and loyal respect among friends was everywhere, floating in the atmosphere. Listening to *Cavalleria Rusticana* by Mascagni, Jiang Wen lets go of the fatalistic "reflection" of the third generation, the endlessly painful "narrative" of the fourth generation, the energetically thoughtful "allegory" of the fifth generation. He shows us a "situation," an ardent emotion that burns everywhere like a fire, the expression of a stark reality experienced by a bounding life. We feel close to it. (1997, 54)

Further, Jiang Lei adds, under Jiang Wen's direction the Cultural Revolution has metamorphosed from a violent, frightening event that speaks about the essence of Chinese culture to an "opportunity to cut loose," not only for the young but symbolically for the populace at large (54). Thus what formerly belonged only to youth now is made available, in a historically important reconstruction, to everyone.

These insightful interpretations by Dai Jinhua and Jiang Lei are supported not only by the huge screen space Jiang Wen allots to Ma's teenage years, but also by the emotional identification that viewers feel toward the film.[9] Still, Jiang Wen's attempt to, even briefly, represent many narratives—the unified revolutionary discourse, the post-Mao consumer orientation, the standard Cultural Revolution story of suffering, and the simultaneous free and sensual viewpoint of the teenagers—supports his contention that the film is not primarily a historical rewriting. Jiang Wen may be presenting Ma Xiaojun's story as the one that interests him, but the director does not demand that we recognize his version as *the* Cultural Revolution, that we totally pry ourselves loose from the old, burdensome story that casts so much scorn on the entire revolutionary enterprise. Rather, Jiang Wen investigates the revolutionary focus on the importance of proper consciousness while simultaneously valorizing the sensual experience of daily life at its core, separating the significance of subjectivity from ideology and doctrine. Although not everyone has equal access to this spirit, which is concentrated in the young but available only to the selected few, its influence is potentially transformative and widespread. And finally, understanding that the present contains an openness toward the future is one of the most important aspects of the revolutionary spirit.

Film director Huang Jianxin (1954–) alludes to a similar perspective when he comments on the relationship between experiencing the Cultural Revolution as liberation and one's own particular age:

> In 1966 I graduated from primary school, just in time to catch the earth-shattering Great Revolution, a time when the didactic reins of teachers were in the hands of the Red Guards and schools became hotels for their networking. Before the Highest Directive, when Chairman Mao announced that we would resume classes and engage in revolution in that way, we had become a group of wild things. What we liked to do best was to help revolutionary groups distribute propaganda pamphlets, and we didn't worry a bit about what was in them. When I stood on those tall roofs and saw the sky full of dancing paper and thousands of heads scurrying beneath, a sense of greatness was spontaneously generated within me. This feeling was a bit like what I felt later when I read Jin Yong's martial arts novels—I could leap in one jump onto a roof. This was a sort of satisfaction of the imagination . . . History (or should I say the Cultural Revolution) gave me a stretch of good time when I shook off control and grew freely. When I got that, I got my films. (Xie Fei et al. 1998, 57–58)

Huang's comments seem to apply directly to this film, with its many scenes of Ma Xiaojun on the rooftops and his attempt to fly off the smokestack. Huang interprets the Cultural Revolution as a positive time of freedom when creativity was allowed to ferment in form, if not in content; the dancing paper from the rooftops releases not the ideological content of the pamphlets but euphoria, eventually producing the energy and new direction of contemporary film.

At the center of this film's dynamic is this logic of the future—the ability to imaginatively envision a creative route that extends far ahead. The spirit of the future is well nurtured within the revolutionary discourse, picked up and continued by Ma and his friends, but almost disappears in the consumer-capitalist future that the middle-aged men, the limousine, and the cognac represent. The end of the film readily admits to the disappearance of this passionate way of being, a reality recognized by the character Gulunmu, who is shocked into the self-expression of language for the first time.[10] However, it is not only the era that has obliterated this spirit, but also the aging of the film's subjects. As the quote by Jiang Wen at the beginning of this section indicates, this kind of excitement and life force can be reborn continually, because youth always reappears. To identify the Cultural Revolution with the youth of the nation rather than as the expression of Maoist extremism posits a sense of possibility, which can be fomented and fostered in many contexts. Rather than a historical progression of revolutionary ideology that begins in the early 20th century and leads to the Cultural Revolution, Jiang Wen creates an emotional and spiritual intensity and future-oriented direction, possibly endlessly repeating, that rightfully belong to youth.

WHAT HAPPENED TO YU BEIPEI?: MEMORY, SEXUAL DESIRE, AND THE AESTHETICS OF THE FUTURE

Yang Mo's (1914–96) popular novel from the 1950s, *Song of Youth* (Qingchun zhige), is one of the novels Ma Xiaojun tells Milan he has read and enjoyed. In 1959 it was made into a film classic of the same name by Cui Wei (1912–79), who turns the connection between revolutionary youth and passion that the novel investigates into images, movement, juxtaposition, and sound. The film vividly presents images of its heroine, Lin Daojing, as she successfully transforms her self of the 1920s and 1930s from a woman being forced into unwanted marriage by her widowed mother, to a young student seeking knowledge, to a bourgeois wife whose husband wants her to serve him, to an enthusiastic demonstrator who wants to join the revolution for personal glory, and finally to a new Communist Party member who understands the need to serve the people and sacrifice the self, relinquishing heroism. The camera projects this journey by focusing first on Lin's troubled face as she stands alone, and eventually arrives at an image of her leading the masses on toward revolution.[11]

Song of Youth both demonstrates and treads the fine line between working for the people or for one's own self-glory, and the troubled interior of revolutionary heroism. Lu Jiachuan, an ideal male revolutionary who becomes Lin's love object, speaks out against individual heroism, but the individual or hero does not disappear so much as being strengthened by the power of the masses (Ban Wang 1997, 130). Although the characters say one thing, the film does another, wordlessly glamorizing Lin's struggle in very individual terms. Not only is she beautiful and fashionable but she also comes under the loving scrutiny of the camera throughout the film. Many shots of her face full of emotion—anguish, love, desire, and hatred—fill the screen. Her personality is presented as naïve but intelligent, misled but with the possibility of redemption, and her sensitive femininity is highlighted in her movements and expressions. Lin Daojing's revolutionary energy is underwritten by her desire for Lu Jiachuan, a desire that lives on and is intensified after Lu's death by execution.[12] Certainly Lu's death turns the narrative toward a selfless, spiritual desire rather than the chic revolutionary style that also lures her or the possibility of finding pleasure through sexual fulfillment and the joys of bourgeois living. Although these are seen as the alternatives to revolutionary engagement, the film does not posit an original sexual impulse that can be channeled toward revolution so much as a human energy that can be directed anywhere—towards social work, erotic satisfaction, friendship, individual achievement, self-glory, style, and so on.[13]

Song of Youth anticipates themes, visual models, and motifs of *In the Heat of the Sun*: the emphasis on subjectivity shown through close focus on the face of the protagonist; heroism and the desire to fly (voiced by Lin Daojing at a happy moment and Ma Xiaojun as he imitates the character Vasili in the popular film *Lenin in 1918,* and tries to get Milan's attention); the connection between youth and the emotions of revolution; and the motivation of the protagonist by a central fantasy.[14] Yet although *In the Heat of the Sun* references many characteristics of the revolutionary film tradition of which *Song of Youth* is part, the differences between the two films are equally as significant. The heroine Lin Daojing, like the very young Ma Xiaojun, is enamored of the emotive and spiritual content of revolutionary struggle. Unlike Ma, however, she begins with emotional identification and makes her way to ideological understanding. Her identification with individual heroism eventually is modified by her sharp realization of the suffering of peasants. Here, too, she experiences intense emotion, but it is combined with the knowledge that she can help carve out a new future not only for herself, but for the impoverished as well. In order for Lin to ascend to this higher state, she must accept and live by an ethic of self-sacrifice, even to the point of death. Ma Xiaojun follows an opposite course: he begins with a unified consciousness that has fragmented by the time he becomes a teenager (that is, a few minutes into the film), his ideological awareness gone. What remains are the feelings and forward motion he has distilled from his childhood experiences within a revolutionary military family. Ma Xiaojun inherits his energy from the revolutionary tradition fostered by his family and society at large; he redirects it to his relationship with his friends, and to his growing attraction to and then love for Milan.[15] In the earlier film, the "Cui Wei ceremony" propels Lin toward the masses and the film ends with shots of her among them; Ma Xiaojun, however, ends up alone, as his friends block him from leaving the swimming pool from which he tries to escape. The final scene of his teenage years shows Ma floating on his back in the pool. The camera moves to a distance, looking down on him, and he is completely isolated until we see him with his friends at middle age.

Xia Yu, who was not a professional actor when chosen to play the part of Ma Xiaojun, portrays Ma as charmingly shy and mischievous in social relations yet forceful and engaging in his emotions. Jiang Wen cleverly chose an awkward-looking boy to play this part, someone who contrasts with the more conventional tall good looks of his rival, Liu Yiku. As opposed to the character Anchee in *Red Azalea*, who spends half of the text-time trying to be a good Maoist, Ma Xiaojun almost immediately gets past the point of wanting to struggle with the idealistic ideas embodied by the revolution. What ultimately defines him is his privileged access to its spirit, represented and injected into his life in images, narratives, scents, sounds, and songs. The film abounds with references to life as it is lived at the time, implying that the feeling from lived culture now resides in all aspects of existence and is anchored by the slowly developing relationship between Ma Xiaojun and Milan. For Ma Xiaojun, this feeling originates in the revolutionary culture of his youth, whereas for Anchee Min, the revolutionary spirit is fertile, sexual, and primary, as well as trans-historical and mythical.

Jiang Wen's capturing of the revolutionary spirit and turning it into a perspective aimed toward the future are especially apparent in Ma Xiaojun's particular personality trait: a longing to penetrate other people's dwellings and sense their lives. This characteristic connotes the future-oriented subjectivity that reorients the past and opens the present; the idea that *anything can happen* is embodied in a character's desire and translated into behavior. Ma wants to open up the possibility of a new consciousness, a novel perspective on life. When he breaks into other people's homes, he takes nothing other than a few bites of food, the voiceover telling us that he is careful to avoid the designation of *thief*. His goal is to watch, sense, hear, and experience; stealing would alter the forward, freedom-producing significance of his transgressions by giving them a set, and generally negative, meaning. The voiceover tells us that although Ma checks for cash when he enters, he never finds it, and he interprets the lack of cash and electric gadgets, as well as the ubiquitous black and white Soviet-made TV, as indications that the people whose houses he enters are pure and uncorrupted. In this, Ma refers to a Maoist ideal—an absence of desire for material objects—that seems to have been realized in daily life.

A hint of the newly found power that results from his gaze and the breakthrough it represents for the young Ma is shown in an evocative scene at the beginning of the film, when he learns how to alter keys and unlocks a drawer in his parents' desk. What interests him in the drawer are the military badges, which he attaches to his shirt and admires as he struts in front of a mirror, and a condom, which he blows up and bats about the room. These two items mark the poles of a continuum of identity and existence, from the valorization of the revolutionary to the sexual. As the condom floats before us, we see through its transparent sides a photo on the wall of Ma's parents as an enthusiastic young couple. The photo's style dates it to the 1950s, when belief in the power of the revolution and the future of China was largely intact. (We later discover that Ma's younger brother may have been born as a result of the hole Ma puts in the condom-balloon when it deflates.)

These early scenes are devoid of voices, and often even the voiceover of Ma's older self disappears. This absence swells the images' force and augments the existential power of Ma's character. He wants the thrill of living on the edge and narrowly escaping danger. The voiceover tells us that his feeling at being able to unlock forbidden doors and drawers, he believes, must be the same as that experienced by people during World War II, when the Soviet army attacked and won Berlin. This feeling has arisen in Ma from reading novels about war, from listening to and singing lyrical heroic songs, and from viewing revolutionary films. Throughout the film we see many references to such things, and are shown an audience so familiar with the film *Lenin in 1918* that it is able to mouth the lines before they are heard. As in many other scenes, the characters here grasp revolutionary texts, films, and experiences and rework them to produce non-revolutionary meanings. By mouthing the lines along with the actors and laughing at reactions that they have seen many times, they turn the film into an opportunity to act and pretend, thus removing it from its explicit purpose of indoctrination and transforming it into an understated community frolic. In several scenes Ma and his friends strum on guitars and sing mournful Russian folk songs, and they refer to the Ethel L. Voynich's *The Gadfly* (1897) and Nikolai Ostrovsky's *How Steel Was Tempered* (1933), both revolutionary romances, as their common reading material. Revolutionary spirit has survived and become a profoundly emotional expression of inner essence. Ma and his friends also sneak into a showing of *Roman War* (Luoma dazhan), most likely the two-part 1968–69 joint German-Italian-Romanian production directed by Robert Siodmak, Sergiu Nicolaescu, and Andrew Marton. Viewing of the film is restricted (neibu), to be seen only by responsible adults who are interested in seeing it so they can combat decadent culture, but the audience turns out to include most of the families living in the compound. An old official sits with his young secretary in the first row; this, along with the nude blonde shown in the film, acts as an ironic comment on revolutionary moral codes, which allowed those in positions of leadership to view cultural products forbidden to commoners, and another jab at the integrity of revolutionary ideology.[16]

What first interests Ma in Milan is a photo he sees of her on the wall when he sneaks into her family's apartment, not knowing who lives there. It is a chance encounter, yet it also is his choice: Ma's desire to escape restrictions and find access to new ways of living is what opens the door to the possibility of a new world and, quite literally, a novel way of seeing things. Because the film was made at a time when China was undergoing rapid expansion in consumer goods and material desires, it is significant that Ma either rejects or has no access to the road of increased wealth, or stealing—instead following the enrichment he hopes to gain from a simple change of perspective. Yet it is more than a change of perspective, for Ma sees the picture through a telescope he has taken off the wall in this strange house. When he removes the telescope and looks with his bare eyes, the picture is gone. Ma whirls around helplessly, going through this process several times until he finally "produces" the picture on the wall, although it wasn't there a moment before.[17] This now-you-see-it, now-you-don't scene is the first one that clues us in to a secret that the older Ma later admits: he isn't sure any of these events actually occurred. Eventually we learn that the adult Ma has "remembered" a young Ma who has a strong desire to see things from a different angle. For the adult Ma, this finessing of memory provides him with the ability to alter his own past, opening up new possibilities of displacing what may have been a mediocre and routine history with excitement and intrigue.

From the perspective that we the viewers have, however, what we see occurring is the teenage Ma Xiaojun creatively producing his future, not altering his past. From our vantage point at that moment in our viewing, the relationship with Milan occurs, and is the result of Ma's innate desire to gain new surroundings or, quite literally, a new view of the world. When

Ma gets to know Milan better, he insists that there used to be a picture of her in her red swimming suit on the wall, yet she denies that such a picture exists. Later, however, we actually see her at the swimming pool in the same red suit, an appearance that confounds understanding. Our immersion into the actual moment of Ma's encounter—without the benefit of interpretation from the voiceover—parallels the experience Ma himself goes through, and expands the privileging of experiential and sensory meaning that Jiang Wen highlights.

One persistent clue that all is not as it seems is the disappearance of Yu Beipei, a girl who hangs around with the boys at the start of the film. Yu Beipei is a vivacious girl whose thinness contrasts with Milan's plumper body.[18] Before Milan appears, Yu Beipei is the clear object of the boys' sexual attraction; they scheme with her to force a kiss on Ma Xiaojun and leave lipstick on his face, and her flirtatious presence in the boys' shower room results in Yang Gao getting an erection and being mocked and yelled at by the others. As Ma rubs the lipstick off his cheeks, the screen switches to a scene of him dancing with a group of children, all wearing rouge, as they welcome dignitaries in black cars, a quick reference to the revolutionary context. In the first part of the film, Yu Beipei—the only girl in the group of boys—is a significant character. She then disappears from the story until reappearing, without explanation, in the second, revised, non-violent scene of the birthday party for Ma and Liu at the Moscow restaurant. How can we explain her disappearance?

The adult Ma asks: What happened to Yu Beipei? When he swears to tell the truth about what happened, he tells us, he understands how difficult it is to keep one's promise: "It is almost impossible to be honest. Sometimes a smell or a sound takes you back to the past." We then see the boys arriving at the Moscow restaurant again, with Yu Beipei and Milan. The camera shows them happily entering, focuses on a beautiful chandelier, and then on a mural depicting all of China's peoples, Han and minority, happy together. It was under the same picture that the bully of the rival gang (played, in a cameo, by Wang Shuo) was feted, and the top half of the picture features a picture of Mao smiling, with the sun's rays spreading out behind his head.[19] The voiceover states: "Now my head is as clear as the moon. Okay! I'll continue the story, never mind if it's true or false." The birthday party is happy, with no bad feelings, and there are piles of presents, quite a difference from the way the same party was shown earlier, when Ma picks a fight with Liu Yiku over Milan and stabs him repeatedly with a broken bottle. The happy scene switches, and Ma is shown riding his bike outside in a storm. He falls into a hole and screams. He emerges and wanders to Milan's home, yelling her name. When she comes outside, he blurts out that he likes her and then immediately backs off, telling her his bike fell in a hole. She pulls him to her and they embrace.

The question about truth or falseness of the narrative and its revision by the adult Ma is not answered directly; rather, Jiang Wen unravels the truth through subjectivity, feelings, and the sense of things. His answers come in the form of sounds, colors, and fragments of images: Ma Xiaojun's feet twirling his bicycle pedals as he watches Milan flirt with Liu Yiku, Ma emerging black-faced from the smokestack he has climbed to impress Milan, Ma on his knees with his face buried on Milan's bed as if in worship, the dark halls and their opening into a stranger's house, Milan sleeping on the bed while Ma watches her, Ma's back as he rides away from a crying Gulunmu, Milan fingering a telephone cord. Complex questions do not fall under the category of "true" or "false"; rather, Jiang Wen pulls not just the Cultural Revolution, but also experience at large, into a sensory realm. In fourteen or fifteen instances, the camera is focused on feet. The camera foregrounds this unlikely body part, rather than a larger frame. Jiang Wen's aesthetic approach denies the possibility of directly apprehending the reality of any era through investigation of its themes or ideologies or, in this case, even a direct focus on facial expression, which can be blank and unexpressive. On the contrary, Jiang Wen suggests that the whole can be experienced only through its seemingly unrevealing parts, that the subjective truth of the situation must be apprehended indirectly. His focus on feet, which would seem to be a doubtful means of expression, guides us toward many unarticulated realities: Milan's interest in Liu Yiku, which surges through her body and causes her to wrap her feet around the telephone cord flirtatiously; Ma Xiaojun's discomfort at the scene, revealed by the frustrated twirl of his feet on the bicycle pedals. The relative lack of language in many scenes also contributes to the message that the physical experience of life is more powerful than an ideological or intellectual understanding. These aesthetic aspects lead critics to claim that within the context of Chinese films, *In the Heat* has created a new and forceful filmic language (Wang Xue 1996; Dai Jinhua 1999).

Except for a few scenes where they are together, Milan and Yu Beipei occupy different segments of the film, as if their stories are largely exclusive. The older Ma Xiaojun tells us that Milan may be a product of his imagination; she also is a symbolic pivot point for the director's imaginative engagement with revolutionary spirit. Yu Beipei is shown as able to provoke the boys' sexual desires, although her primary role in the group is as "one of the guys." Only Milan has the power to transform Ma Xiaojun's memories into a sublime experience that merges desire, emotion, the sensuality of daily life, and a transcendent spirit that comes out of revolutionary daily life aesthetics.[20] Milan is Yu Beipei transformed by imagination and selective memory that focuses on the sensual subjectivity of a life permeated by revolutionary aesthetics and spirit.

AUTHENTICITY AND THE REAL: WHAT ACTUALLY HAPPENED?

> I certainly did not evaluate this film from the perspective of whether or not it accurately depicted what happened during the Cultural Revolution. . . . The entire life experience, the aesthetic feeling, and the living force of life portrayed all were transformed into a moving energy that accumulated in the shape of the characters. (Zhang Yimou, quoted in Jiang Wen et al. 1997, 70)

> Every day the assistant directors went to middle schools and military courtyards to look for actors, but usually could not find boys and girls who fit the image . . . In my impressions from the times, we were beautiful, pure, and healthy. A friend has kept some photos from that period in black and white, that small kind taken with a 135 mm camera. I realized my impressions were wrong only after seeing the photos. At that time none of us were beautiful, we were dark and thin, our eyes dull, stubborn, maybe even stupid. I thought we were pure, but actually how could we have been pure? So the self of our impressions could not be found. (Wang Shuo 1997, 127)

> The aesthetic world of the film determines its entire characteristics. The color and form of the material is the true story, so even if there is a great deal of fakery and pretending, it still can provide for the audience intimacy and the real. And the real isn't completely naturalistic, because if there is no sublimation, it cannot be called artistic creation. This, I believe, is where Jiang Wen's success lies. With clarity and subtlety, he grasps the hazy mental state and behavior of those times. (Siqin Gaowa 1997, 142)

In his film's lyrical presentation of the Cultural Revolution, Jiang Wen brings out a daily life radically different from the suffering and trauma of conventional understanding. His delimitation of the power of this life to youth, and mostly to boys, simultaneously lifts the burden of history and continues a tradition of granting the control of the cultural narrative to males, who work through a sexual relationship with a woman to arrive at their own self-knowledge and thereby insert themselves as agents into the narrative of cultural progress.[21] Although all the boys in the film exist in the same environment, only Ma Xiaojun—permeated with revolutionary spirit and yet uncontaminated by its ideology, sensitive and awkward, ordinary enough that he will not be captured by any definition of greatness—can grasp the ability to forge a new future out of an old past.

Is it sufficient to state that the import of the film is "Mao was great, we are great too" (Huot 2000, 59)? Or should we regard it as proof of the inexorable "capitalization of culture" that Zhang Yiwu (1998) identifies as central to society in the 1990s:

> Capital starts to become legitimate culture. And a group of commercial films made by Changchun film studies in the 90s express this situation. Their calling cards are luxurious surroundings, fighting, and beautiful women; economic activities are the thread that shows the structural influence of the rise of capital among commoners. And the final symbol of this transformation is Jiang Wen's *In the Heat of the Sun.* This is a film recalling daily life during the Cultural Revolution. But it completely separates itself from the model of persecution and terror that we are used to, showing a subculture composed of a group of youth on the periphery of the dualistic I-live-you-die struggle. It is unrelated to the "grand narratives" of politics and ideology, instead discussing an individual's desire, anxiety, the turbulence of youth, violence without motive, etc. . . . This is a history of the periphery coming to the center. What were once the fantasies of youth, unrelated to politics and ideology, already has become a huge and legitimate memory under postmodern culture. This film is a ritual of victory, the symbol of transformation in a society's structure. That luxurious Lincoln car is nothing other than the rise of a new social force. And this film also uses a method that no one could have imagined to express the imagination of capitalized culture among commoners. (22–23)

Other than the gang encounters there is little "violence without motive" in the film, in that Jiang Wen brings to the filmic surface an intense interest in emotion and tiny changes of the heart, mind, and desire; even so, Zhang Yiwu's comments directing us toward a transformation of social life under the culture of capitalism are insightful. The film does not utterly refuse to represent the grand narratives of politics and ideology, but it shrinks their significance. Other critics have pointed to the development of individuality, the self, or the private life—a process generally associated with culture under capitalism—that is enacted as Ma Xiaojun distinguishes and detaches himself from the group of boys (Dai Jinhua 1997, 153–55; Chen Xiaoming 1997, 135; Li Xun 1996, 61–62). The expansion of sexual desire is a theme in many films and novels, and it coincides nicely with the capitalization of culture among commoners to which Zhang refers. Furthermore, even though the film focuses on Ma's life at a time when he had no interest in material goods, and minimizes or erases the years of his middle years, when he was influenced by wealth and possessions, placing Ma's obsession with Milan at the core of the story may indicate that the film presents a budding focus on the self, a tendency that leads to a middle age in which aesthetic and spiritual values have been replaced by consumer culture.

Even so, central to the critics' interest in the film is not only its rewriting of the Cultural Revolution in terms of themes but also its filmic language, which speaks to a way of defining knowledge that is simultaneously new and old. Knowledge does not have to be learned so much as lived and experienced: this tenet of existential philosophy is inherent in the notion of revolution that gives Ma Xiaojun his inspiration, but it has been lost through corruption and institutionalization. This truth about knowledge unfolds on democratic principles, and is available to those with recognized social positions and those without alike. In terms of Zhang Yiwu's analysis, therefore, the daily lives, desires, and moods of commoners expand in significance, becoming interesting through Jiang Wen's foregrounding of the richness of small movements of the head, foot, hand, and eye. The director's aesthetic method makes the second-by-second transformations significant in and of themselves; in addition, the multiplicity of angles also produces small insights and changes, with shimmering implications at every turn. New perspectives are not only possible but almost mandatory: they exist all around us. The interaction between the ever-changing viewpoints and the deeply felt emotional world—not a simple, historical question of what happened—is what determines the truth of any situation.

Apprehension of the situation is more available to the young, because grand ideological narratives have not unduly corrupted them. Also, the fact that the young reappear generation after generation and are a ready symbol of the future allows Jiang Wen to set forth a utopian vision of possible future reinvigoration by a powerful and youthful spirit. During the Cultural Revolution and more generally under Maoist culture, *youth* was a special category of people who could more purely apprehend and embody the revolutionary spirit. Finally, we cannot ignore the fact that setting off youth as a distinct category has been one of the most successful marketing tools of capitalism, lending a bit more credence to Zhang Yiwu's interpretation.

In directing *In the Heat of the Sun*, Jiang Wen became fanatical about recreating exact details of the Cultural Revolution as they existed in his memory. As he describes it, one of the most important elements he sought to reproduce was the sound of daily life in the military compound:

> I didn't pay any attention to form. For me, most important were the sounds I heard. I was listening to the film, seeing the film. When I was writing the script, it was nothing more than what I had seen and heard during that time. I heard the sounds of the film very clearly, heard how these people talked, heard which songs made up the music, what time the music should start up. I clearly heard the way plastic sandals hit against concrete. And in Milan's house, why did it have to be a wooden floor—I absolutely had to have a wooden floor, even if we had to make it. Because I already had heard and seen all of this. (Jiang Wen 1997, 27)

Thus, Jiang Wen carefully chose the washed-out yellow color of the military uniform worn by Ma's father, re-recorded period songs in monophonic sound because stereo was not available at the time, and required the actors to live together for one month under conditions mimicking those of the Cultural Revolution. In order to get the picture of Milan that "causes Ma Xiaojun to lose his soul," Jiang Wen used four canisters of film, with a ratio of available shots to the one chosen of 23,040 to 1 (Jiang Wen 1997, 36). As He explains, "In the film this picture plays an important role, as everyone has to believe in the change that occurs in Ma Xiaojun after he sees the picture" (36). As this quote illustrates, the director's concern is not to show what actually occurred, but rather to provide a convincing motivation for the subjective changes Ma experiences.

In one shocking scene, the boys and Milan dance to *Swan Lake* in a darkened room filled with hundreds of candles, stuck everywhere and burning brightly. The boys are wearing military uniforms askew—some with jackets but no shirts, hats falling off, and epaulets sticking out. They dance crazily, each doing his individual performance yet all performing together. After Ma Xiaojun and the others sit down to rest, Milan gets up in her olive green pants and white shirt and dances, ballet style, while Liu Yiku accompanies her. As he lights a cigarette and watches, Ma's perspiring face is intense but hard to read, although his interest is obvious.

This is a radical representation that captures some of the film's most important meanings. To interpret the story in terms of what happened may not give us a useful take on the film, but here we can clearly see what didn't happen: very few people were able to dance joyfully and sensually in military uniform during the Cultural Revolution, nor would doing so be even conceivable to many. The dignified loyalty that the military inspired and glorification of struggle, which we see in the scenes where Ma Xiaojun is very young, would prevent most from turning a military uniform into a costume of pleasure. Here, however, this solemnity is not so much disavowed as it is gently and gleefully pushed aside; to twist military garb into something worn for personal and group delight brings out a side of life under revolution not often represented, but it also shows the way to a creativity that will allow for a different future. History once looked at the Cultural Revolution and stopped there, with questions about why, who, and how that had horrific implications for Chinese culture at large and for each person within that culture. Jiang Wen breaks that history, shifting the grounds of apprehension toward a different structure of thought. Most important, he puts forward the hypothesis that the spirit of revolution can be extracted and made to represent all that was good about the past, and can be directed toward the future. The obscenity Gulunmu screams at the middle-aged characters alleges that the revolutionary spirit is dead, but, as the voiceover tells us, it still glows in the embers and may come alive again.

NEVER THIS WILD: RED AZALEA AND THE IMAGINED FUTURE

Anchee Min wrote *Red Azalea* (1994) in English and published it first in the United States.[22] She followed it with *Katherine* (1995), *Becoming Madame Mao* (2000), *Wild Ginger* (2002), *Empress Orchid* (2004), and *The Last Empress* (2007).[23] *Red Azalea* joins a large group of memoirs and fictionalized memoirs, starting with Liang Heng's 1983 *Son of the Revolution,* which are written specifically for Western audiences and emphasize life during the Cultural Revolution. The title of Min's second book, *Katherine,* is the name of an English teacher and history researcher who lives and works in Shanghai during the immediate post-Mao period. The narrative is related from the point of view of one of her female students, and presented as the realistic depiction of a true story. Both *Katherine* and *Red Azalea* highlight sexual desire as the key to personal and national liberation, and both rewrite the

Cultural Revolution or its lingering effects through the lens of sexual desire. *Red Azalea* presents the Cultural Revolution experience as profoundly, if secretly, sensual and erotic. *Katherine* presents it as a time of not only suppression by the state, but also individual psychological repression, and it positions an American woman as the catalyst of and conduit to freedom.

The fact that *Red Azalea* was written in English distinguishes Min's novel from the other novels and films I analyze in this project. In addition, it potentially speaks to many issues, including the author's residency in the United States, censorship in China, the monetary rewards available to Chinese writers who are successful in the West, the demands of publishers, and also the author's perception of her writing and its potential audience. The sexual vision that informs *Red Azalea* is partly related to a concept of the body's desire and its freedom that is widely represented in the West, but also emerges from the post-Mao discourse of sexuality that locates emphasis on sexual representation outside of China, as a form of spiritual pollution that comes from the West. If concerns about contamination from the West of various kinds, which was a major aspect of the Anti-"Spiritual Pollution" Campaign, could be directly expressed in fictional form, *Red Azalea* and *Katherine* would be perfect representatives.[24]

Depending on one's perspective, the West and its promise of libidinal freedom and satisfaction appear as either the ultimate liberation and most-desired future, or as the ultimate corrupter and desecrater of traditional social values. As Geremie R. Barmé shows, recent years have produced both a rash of self-critical, West-promoting texts by Lung-kee Sun, Liu Xiaobo, Long Yingtai, Su Xiaokang, and others, and a strongly nationalistic and sometimes xenophobic attitude that rejects Western ideas, values, and culture. The provocative title of Barmé's (1996) article, "To Screw Foreigners Is Patriotic: China's Avant-Garde Nationalists," illustrates the cardinal role of sexual representation in this relationship.[25] *Red Azalea* and *Katherine* both end with the main Chinese characters leaving for the United States, projecting for the reader an unknown future that exists only because the protagonist wants to flee from a sexually, politically, and personally repressive—yet complex and contradictory—present in China. This Westerly direction, along with many other aspects of the novels, implies that the solution to the repression found in the author's evocative descriptions of life in China lies outside—in both cases, in the United States.[26] It is striking that, to some extent, Anchee Min repeats the same story of struggle, repression, and liberation in sexual freedom in many of her novels, but despite her long residence in the United States, she has yet to write a book that is set outside China. Written for non-Chinese readers and imaginatively interpreting for them the Chinese revolutionary past, *Red Azalea* stands at the juncture between the Maoist past and a future intimately entwined with the West. Rather than displaying the xenophobia that Barmé finds in novels and television shows, the books project the notion of a utopian and modernized future of sexual freedom and expression in the West, which is available to the protagonist through her departure from China, which is presented virtually as an escape.

Min regards sexual liberation as far-reaching and significant beyond the individual, with anti-state resistance as its key ideological meaning and function. She interprets the Chinese revolutionary past using this model, but also distinguishes that past by characterizing sexuality under the revolutionary discourse as a kind of mass emotion. Differentiating a powerful and politically progressive sexual vigor from the suffering that exists under a repressive state Maoism, Min splits revolutionary ideology into two opposite forces. Much as Jiang Wen creates a filmic character in Ma Xiaojun to embody and carry forward the revolutionary spirit, which is envisioned as a future orientation of subjectivity, Anchee Min thematically extracts from the past a potent and utopian energy.

I understand *Red Azalea* and *Katherine* to be part of a tightly related story about the relationship between the Maoist past, a time of confounding excesses and restrictions but a passionate spirit, and an imagined future, in which sexual freedom embodies a general utopian liberation. The relationship between sexual desire and the revolutionary past is much more direct in *Red Azalea*, but because *Katherine* actually features a woman from the United States as one of the primary characters, it gives full expression to the Western, sexually embodied person who actively fights against state control. Katherine exudes a sexual boldness that is almost unimaginable to her students, and she fights and wins a battle against Chinese authorities to adopt and take away from China an orphan girl. Katherine's innate attractiveness, along with her brave struggle on behalf of an unwanted child trapped by bureaucracy, makes her a symbol of vigor, purity, and hope.

By contrast, *Red Azalea* is the story of a girl who enters her teens during the Cultural Revolution and experiences the typical formative events that have come to characterize the "lost generation." Compared with memoirs focusing on the Cultural Revolution that have been published in English, Anchee Min's is a work of fiction, imaginative and closely cut, with little historical background or framework of municipal or village politics within which to interpret the narrative. The most common structure for Cultural Revolution autobiographies is that of an individual at first swept away by and finally resisting a revolutionary tide of political, cultural, and emotional meanings; here, that approach is replaced by a highly subjective stance that features an up-close, sharply sensitive body and mind, seeing and reacting to events in its immediate vicinity. The main character does not tell us how she became such a stalwart revolutionary or clue us into the history that has made her so, therefore, but merely shows herself acting and interacting with those around her, be it her family's chicken, Big Beard, her mother, her brother Space Conqueror, or her female lover Yan.

Similarly, the style of *Red Azalea* is direct and simple, with short, repetitive sentences forming the bulk of the narrative. Min avoids the pitfall of over-explanation of the complicated political meanings that infused everyday life, which is common in Maoist era memoirs written for foreigners. Through her use of short, direct, grammatically simple sentences, the story seems to emerge directly from reality; she avoids not only a confusing history but also the obfuscating veneer of civilization. The story, in other words, presents itself as a real, authentic rendition of something impossibly difficult to represent: the truth of subjectivity under revolutionary culture. What Jiang Wen accomplishes through his focus on sound, sight, and sensation, Min embodies in her textual style. Min embeds the expression of individual subjectivity in a trajectory that moves from the simultaneously individual and mass experience of revolution in China, through the awakening to a powerful desire, to eventually reach the goal of flight to the United States.

In the first few pages of *Red Azalea,* lesbian sexual desire represents the means of emancipation for the protagonist, named Anchee. Yet all forms of sexual behavior, carried out secretly and among people struggling for their own pleasure, act as a dangerous resistance to the all-penetrating control of the Communist state. Anchee's passionate physical relationship with her female lover Yan, Yan's later liaison with the male agricultural worker Leopard, Little Green's sexual intimacy with a fellow sent-down youth, the man who dresses like a woman to get into the women's baths, the woman who pretends to be a man to get into the men's baths and massage men's "sun things," the bath guard who wistfully calls the imposter a "hot thing," Bee OhYang who plays too much table tennis with a male student, Big Tai who seeks girlish-looking men, and Anchee's eroticized exchange with the unidentified supervisor—all represent attempts, successful or unsuccessful, to elude the state's controlling grasp. Much of the narrative's power comes from the strength of its characters' belief in the Communist cause and their complete inability to conduct a direct, face-to-face challenge to power and authority or even to recognize that they are eluding power through their sexual liaisons—though the novel clearly takes that position. In many cases the characters, at least superficially, are completely committed to the revolutionary enterprise, and they compete for honors within this system. Given this dedication, the unstoppable nature of their passion becomes something that wells up from their being; the deeply desiring self, the same self that fights for the revolution daily, longs for emancipation through sexual expression when the revolution does not come through with its promises.

Little Green is the first character to engage in a sexual relationship. Along with Anchee and the others on Red Fire Farm, she was sent down to the countryside to work. Her embroidered underwear, graceful walk, colorful femininity, and braless boldness show that she is ideologically suspect: "a true Communist should never care about the way she looked" (Min 1994, 56). Drawing both male and female interest and jealousy, Little Green is criticized for vanity and becomes a victim of the rivalry for ideological purity between Yan, the party secretary and commander (and Anchee's future lover), and Deputy Commander Lu. Yan and Lu mobilize the entire work corps to go out into the fields at night, where they catch Little Green having sex with a male agricultural worker, also a student sent down from the city. When the worker is executed for rape, Little Green goes insane and eventually drowns.

Min's presentation of Little Green is a preview of her sexualization of all important relationships, not only those between human beings but even those between humans and state goals, national symbols, and ideas. The struggle to interpret Little Green's actions and dress—between the Maoist ideals of social engagement and bourgeois ideas of individual sexual expression—comes down clearly on the side of the latter. It is easy for the reader to see that in Little Green, Min presents femininity and sexuality as suppressed by the revolutionary state. Shortly after Little Green loses her mind, the protagonist Anchee feels sexual desire tearing her apart: "A nameless anxiety had invaded me. It felt like a sweating summer afternoon. Irritatingly hot. The air felt creamy. It was the ripeness of the body. It began to spoil. The body screamed inside trying to break the bondage. I was restless" (Min 1994, 69). Anchee's mind is "no longer the perfect stainless mind" and she begins to fantasize, which leads to her involvement with the clumsy, awkward, endearing, and justice-seeking Commander Yan (71).

Commander Yan is an unflinching and naïve promoter of the revolution who strives to do things right according to revolutionary logic.

The relationship between Anchee and Yan is based on love, admiration, sympathy, and lust. It was Yan who sought out Little Green and her lover, destroying both, but it also was Yan who repeatedly tried to rescue Little Green from insanity. She even catches a hundred poisonous snakes, hoping that by reaching that special number she can bring about a cure—an oddly superstitious and non-revolutionary endeavor. That the inarticulate Yan is unable to manipulate words to her advantage makes her a pure, selfless, and almost abstract proponent of revolutionary passion and behavior. In Yan's enemy, Deputy Commander Lu, Min sets up for us an example of the revolution gone wrong, the revolution disintegrated into self-serving tricks and the malevolent showiness that comes from the exploitation of words.[27] Lu and Yan, both revolutionary leaders, are opposites. Anchee fears that Lu's dislike of her will destroy her through words "that could bury me alive"; Yan, however, "tried not to give expression to a personal grudge—a principle Mao had set for every Party member" (Min 1994, 102–3). When Yan involves herself physically with Anchee, it is the true spirit of the revolution that is sexualized and expressed, and the relationship is carried on in the same room where Lu is reading the works of Mao. Dichotomies of word versus flesh, false versus true, and the like permeate all aspects of the story, with truth and the real always resting on the side of the inarticulate but sensually expressed flesh and the spirit that animates it.

The narrative adequately gives expression to Anchee's respect for Yan's honesty and strength, but what it emphasizes and elaborates on is the raw physical attraction that brings them together:

> She grabbed my hand and pressed it to her chest. She asked me to feel her heart. I wished I was the blood in that chamber. In the hammering of her heartbeat, the rising and falling of her chest, I saw a city of chaos. A mythical force drew me toward her. I felt the blazing of a fire rise inside me. Yan was wearing a thin shirt with a bra under it. The shirt was the color of roots. The bra was plain white. Her bright red underwear added fuel to the fire. As she lazily stretched her body, my heart raged. . . . I could not bear it, the way she looked at me, like water penetrating rocks. Passion overflowed in her eyes. (Min 1994, 130)

Passages such as this one continue throughout, all framed by Yan's attempt, with Anchee's help, to set herself up with Leopard.

The characters sustain their dedication and work discipline for some time, but Commander and Party Secretary Yan, the revolution's stalwart supporter and practitioner, eventually loses faith. The failure of the revolution is evident on the farm, which is one of ten model Communist collectives, none of which make enough food even to feed those who live there, let alone provide food for others in cities or rural areas. The farm's state subsidy is coming to an end, and conditions are only going to get worse. Year by year poverty expands its reach, and Yan loses interest in political study. Revolutionary ardor disappears, to be replaced by the pleasure of physical love, in which Yan and Anchee frequently indulge, and the fear of exposure. Eventually Anchee is selected to try out as an actress, and her relationship with Yan virtually comes to an end, to be replaced by a liaison with the supervisor of the Shanghai film studio where she is assigned to work. A competition corrupted by politicking and manipulation puts Anchee into the loser's position, and another young woman, Cheering Spear, is chosen to play the part of Red Azalea in a revolutionary film under way. With her chance to be an actress destroyed, Anchee is reassigned as a set clerk, a janitorial position in which she has ample opportunity to get to know the ambiguously sexed Supervisor, who is presented to us as a man but—the author reminds us frequently—speaks and looks like a woman. A man / woman who contains within himself not only strong erotic desire but also a yearning for revolutionary passion, the Supervisor faults the model operas for lacking this spirit, which he desperately wants to be the basis of the film *Red Azalea*.

From his initial appearance in the novel, the Supervisor is a contradictory person. He frequently expresses ideologically correct sentiments, but they are much less powerful to him than the subtle erotic exchange between himself and Anchee. As a famous political figure he is constantly under surveillance, but before he leaves for Beijing, he arranges an evening meeting with Anchee in the Peace Park. In the dark, where couples are hiding in the bushes, the Supervisor and Anchee hold each other and kiss, desire racing through their bodies. The identity of the Supervisor becomes increasingly enigmatic—could this female-like man be Chairman Mao's wife, Jiang Qing (1914–91), the Madame Mao of Min's later book by the same name? The Supervisor's extremely high political position is clear. He takes Anchee back to Shanghai when she is chosen to replace Cheering Spear as Red Azalea; in Beijing, there is "a political current that was against him, against the greatest standard-bearer, Comrade Jiang Ching" (Min 1994, 308). The Supervisor's background in acting also corresponds to that of the historical Jiang Qing, who worked on the stage and in film in Shanghai, using the name Lan Ping. The tantalizing hints that the Supervisor is Jiang Qing are all but confirmed near the end of the story, when the Supervisor tells Jiang Qing's tale as that of Red Azalea (the central character in the fictive film), and links himself to the symbolic and essential meaning of the character. Min's decision to represent this character as a man may in part be a reference to the popular critique that Jiang Qing's excessive power and unadorned demeanor made her appear masculine.

The Supervisor draws Anchee's attention to the lovers and masturbators scattered through the park like red azaleas, all "begging for touch and penetration" (Min 1994, 291). Red azaleas—simultaneously the name of Min's book, the title of the fictive revolutionary film for which Anchee auditions, the name of the main character in that film, and a reference to Jiang Qing—serve as a symbol for the transformation of revolutionary into erotic passion or for the purposeful conflation between the two:

> I see the hills of youth covered with blood-colored azaleas. The azaleas keep blooming, invading the mountains and the planet. The earth is bitten and it groans, wailing nonsensically in pleasure-drive. Do you hear it? The passion they had for the Great Helmsman has been betrayed. Oh, how grand a scene! I wish our greatest Chairman could see it. He would be shocked but impotent. . . . (291)

The Supervisor gets Anchee into Beijing and back into the role of Red Azalea, displacing Cheering Spear and her supporter Soviet Wong. Living in obvious wealth and power in Beijing, the Supervisor comes more and more closely to resemble Jiang Qing, and eventually he narrates Jiang Qing's personal tale as a revolutionary love story to Anchee as if it were his own. Anchee is now in her desired role and all seems well, yet problems develop. The year is 1976 and the Maoist revolutionary line is under attack. As the political scene changes, both model operas and the film based on their approach are losing their authenticity; Anchee cannot voice the name "Mao Zedong" that the Supervisor inserts into the play with any kind of true feeling, and she tells him that people will laugh when they hear it (315). Mao dies on September 6, 1976, and Anchee receives the order to return to Red Fire Farm. The Supervisor rescues her and puts her back into a set-clerk position in Shanghai, begging her to live on for the values of Red Azalea—the person of Jiang Qing, the film, the character, and the flower's symbolic meaning.

Red Azalea stands for the unification of revolutionary and erotic desire. The Supervisor tells Anchee that what motivates Red Azalea, who is Mao's wife in the story, is her love for the people, the pain of which must be relieved; behind that, Mao's "love for her faded with the smoke of the roaring cannon" (Min 1994, 320, 325). The Supervisor tells Anchee that Jiang Qing's unfulfilled desire was what created the model operas. She relates:

> He said it was that very same desire that made ancient tragedies stir the souls and foster civilizations. And it was the very same desire that sparked the flame of the Great Cultural Revolution. He stopped and looked around, then said he was a little disappointed that there were not many secretive lovers and masturbators present tonight. . . . He had never trusted the Chinese history books. Because those books were written by people who were impotent of desire. People who were paid by the generations of emperors. They were eunuchs. Their desires had been castrated. (333–34)

By contrasting desire of all kinds with "Chinese history books" and the "generations of emperors" who paid and symbolically castrated people to write them, Min establishes a dichotomy between the state and passion: the state suppresses desire, but passion is natural, creative, and effusive, and is constructing civilizations and inspiring revolutions across the globe. In this passage, desire is expressed locally in the lovers and masturbators in the park, nationally in the Great Cultural Revolution, and globally throughout civilization. The Chinese authorities—be they emperors or those who write official histories or political actors who arrest Jiang Qing and put an end to the Cultural Revolution—are the forces of orderliness and anti-desire.

There are many contradictions in this novel. Anchee and Yan both find themselves emptied of hope and emotionally deadened from years of labor and political indoctrination on the farm. The political scene is riddled with corruption. When the Cultural Revolution is recast as a passionate event that springs from life-giving forces, however, contradictions such as these become insignificant. What Min implies is that though the material and social organization underlying the Cultural Revolution may be defective, what lies behind it is a pure flame of desire that can or should be redeemed. Thus updated and unified through its resistance to state authority, perfect desire, as symbolized by a metaphorical Jiang Qing or a Red Azalea, points away from the past and into the future. The final short chapter shows us what this future looks like. Jiang Qing is arrested and people buy and eat crabs that symbolize her: "She was eaten now" (Min 1994, 335). Taking over is Deng Xiaoping, "one of Mao's Long March cadres" (335). China rises exuberantly, but Anchee, working on as a set clerk in the studio, slides into tuberculosis, loneliness, and abandonment. Even worse, she loses any desire: "I had become a stone, deaf to passion" (336). China is now a place bereft of desire; Anchee's only escape is to leave for America, where she arrives on September 1, 1984. That is the end of the story, and the beginning of an unrepresented future.

DESIRE AND THE MASSES

While recognizing the importance of individual hedonism, 20th century—and in some cases earlier—Western literature also often includes the idea that sexual freedom will produce a society that is both more egalitarian and essentially freer and more authentic, in some abstract and unspecified way. As Rita Felsky (1995) and Linda Grant (1994) have shown and as I discuss in my first chapter, many believed sexual freedom in behavior and representation to be a social and political equalizer, and to contain values that would extend through the personal to the social and political. Anchee Min also associates sexual liberation with political progressiveness, although with a significant variation. The defunct Chinese revolutionary state, Min implies, already has in place a vast egalitarian social structure, but it has lost its spirit and as a result is hypocritical and essentially false. Although recovery of true revolutionary spirit through sexual desire may well have rejuvenating effects, Min does not grant sexual desire the power to revolutionize society in the way that Felsky and Grant describe. This may be because Min portrays Maoism as already having effectively captured the logic of social progress, which thereby needs no further representation; it also may be that Min found it necessary to distance her vision from the extreme leftism of China's actual historical past, and thereby did not want to emphasize the relationship between political progress and sexual desire.

Accounts by radical lesbians and sexual reformers such as Jefferson Poland begin by stating the importance of individual choice in sexual freedom, and see choice as a point from which the sexual revolutionary can build a social force. The theory goes that as more and more individuals come to realize the potential of valorizing sexual desire and behavior, a large-scale social movement that has emancipatory ramifications in foreign and domestic policy will develop. This approach was developed in many directions in the 1960s, at a time when Margaret Mead was publishing in *Redbook* and the American sexual revolution was under way. In California, Herbert Marcuse defined the body as an instrument of pleasure that must struggle against its appropriation by capitalism, and claimed that desire was a revolutionary act (Grant 1994, 138–39). In his book *Do It!*, Jerry Rubin equated sexuality and politics, giving sexuality the overarching conceptual edge by assigning to it a more basic meaning:

> Puritanism leads us to Vietnam. Sexual insecurity results in a supermasculinity trip called imperialism. American foreign policy, especially in Vietnam, makes no sense except sexually. America has a frustrated penis trying to drive itself in Vietnam's tiny slit to prove it is the man. (Quoted in Grant 1994, 139)

Jefferson Poland and the Sexual Freedom League promoted and endorsed prostitution, pornography, and homosexuality, and had a global vision for reforms that led to sexual freedom (Grant 1994, 143). Poland published the magazine *Intercourse* and organized the "Psychedelic Venus Church" to combine the emancipatory potential of drugs and sex (146).[28] A number of other activities and publications, such as the Mitchell brothers' pornographic films and the newspaper the *Berkeley Barb* (which allowed direct advertising for sexual services), evidenced the development of a much more pervasive and influential ideology: that sexuality was a transformative political device capable of liberating people across the globe. Implicit in this sexual revolution was the idea that personal change could lead to political change, and that if sexual relationships could be liberated, so could the relationships of production.

By contrast, Min's representation of a sexual desire that merges into and is inflamed by revolutionary passion is from the beginning a mass emotion. There is no need for unifying political movements (which are reminiscent of state Maoism and thus ideologically corrupt) because this desire, even though it was previously misguided by the revolution, and was eventually hidden under the failure of the revolution, has been continually expressed either individually or in small groups and already permeates Chinese society. Other than the book's readers, only the Supervisor, Min's abstract and nameless unifier of revolutionary and erotic passion who corresponds metaphorically to the radical leftist political figure Jiang Qing, can make visible and link together the "lovers and masturbators" scattered across the horizon. It is the Supervisor's uncanny combination of the spirit of the revolution and the spirit of sexual desire that allows him this mediating position.

Min's eroticism, therefore, is a deep wellspring of passion that is fundamental to the true nature of revolution. In Min's Cultural Revolution, Mao Zedong—once an exemplar of passion—eventually comes to represent its death, while Jiang Qing becomes its embodiment. Sexual desire is a mass sentiment emerging from Chinese revolutionary experience. This kind of cultural nationalism configures desire as coming directly out of the most extreme form of revolution. By separating the revolutionary impulse into the false and stultifying, as represented by Mao, and the true and life-giving, as represented by a mythical Jiang Qing, that is, by separating ideological and cultural Maoism, Min imaginatively depicts the revolution as repressive and liberating at the same time. Under Mao are lined up a number of negative characteristics: excessive concern with form, verbal manipulation, malevolent self-interest, and worst of all a failure to see and promote the true spirit of things.

Min presents Mao as a historical figure, but presents Jiang Qing symbolically in the mysterious person of the Supervisor. This mystification is a necessary fiction if Min wants to develop her eroticized vision, for in it she is able to concentrate a number of qualities that may or may not have much to do with the historical Jiang Qing. On Jiang Qing's side of the binary, we see not only a recognition of the spiritual truth of passion, but also a feminist tendency. On the obvious level, Jiang Qing is rescued from the definition forced on her by those history writers hired by the state. No longer representing the great Communist revolution gone awry due to personal ambition, or the damnable source of ten years of catastrophe for the Chinese nation, she now stands for the true spirit of the revolution. Even more important, this symbolic Jiang Qing is what allows Chinese creative forces to go onward and outward toward the future. In *Red Azalea,* the most significant events at all levels are in the hands of women. Women are the worst and the best. Unlike many Chinese avant-garde novelists, who work out culturally and historically important issues through the minds and behaviors of their male protagonists, here the meaningful processes occur in the consciousness and actions of women.[29] Also, women involved in sexual relationships with men, like Little Green, are more apt to be seen as victims of male aggression than as errant; that being said, they are more available for secret and progressive erotic redefinition than are errant men, who are quickly apprehended by the state.[30]

Ultimately, Min suggests, China's creative revolutionary passion can crystallize in the imagination, but in reality it is gone. Her utopian vision of liberating sexuality is pointed toward the United States, a theme developed more strongly in her subsequent novel, *Katherine. Katherine* takes place after the Cultural Revolution, but concerns the overwhelming revolutionary consciousness that still existed in China during the late 1970s and early 1980s. An American scholar of Chinese history, Katherine comes to China to teach English and do research. Katherine—whose name is rendered as "Kan-si-ren," which in Chinese sounds like "kill a dead person"—is everything the students want to be: bold, outrageous, emotional, full of life, unafraid, and sexy. With her raucous laughter, genuine concern, confident and shapely body, and naïve lack of caution, Katherine becomes a transmitter through which the students come to understand themselves as ruined by the Chinese past: "Do you know that just by standing before us you show us how deformed we are?" (Min 1995, 12). Katherine's perfumed and costumed presence intimates at secret love affairs, and the students dream of being Americans. The novel takes us through the erotic awakening of a Chinese female student, Zebra, from whose perspective the story is told. Like *Red Azalea*, *Katherine* ends when the protagonist gets notice that she will be allowed to emigrate to the United States. With her she takes Little Rabbit, the sickly and discarded little girl Katherine has adopted and tries continually to get out of China.

More clearly than in *Red Azalea*, in *Katherine* Chinese revolutionary passion has no chance of survival, and the lingering aftereffects of its corrupted Maoism have especially destructive meaning for girls. The only route of expression for true revolutionary passion, which contains not only emotional vigor but also a socially progressive attitude, is available through the American visitor, Katherine, who delights in her sexuality and fights to get possession of a female child that no one in China wants. Katherine's vivacious presence teaches the students that the sole way to avoid sensory and emotional death and involvement in corrupting social networks, and the sole way to continue struggling on behalf of the oppressed, is to get out of China. Katherine, who has at least one sexual relationship with an attractive male student, is eventually framed and manipulated by the protagonist's enemies in a local struggle that she does not understand. Branded as a form of "spiritual pollution," Katherine is kicked out of China; only through asking for the help of the powerful American government in the form of a sympathetic congressman does she win the release of Zebra and Little Rabbit.

In *Red Azalea* and *Katherine*, standing between China and the United States but writing for a contemporary American audience, Min transforms the revolutionary experience. One common interpretation of the Cultural Revolution—as nothing more than a time of excessive repression at all levels—is changed under her pen, and becomes a utopian impetus toward a future of freedom located out of and away from China. While it is commonly recognized that during the Cultural Revolution "any indication that fiction, poetry, or drama might include sexual references was enough to have it removed from circulation and its author punished" (Evans 1995, 364), like others in my study Min rewrites the Cultural Revolution as a time of desire. She exploits the contradiction between the social restrictions on sexual behavior and the fact that unorthodox sexual behavior actually did occur, a result of the freedoms given to Red Guards and to students going to the countryside to work, away from their parents and schools. The extent of this behavior is unclear.[31] To say that *In the Heat of the Sun* or *Red Azalea* allows us to imagine the Cultural Revolution differently does not imply that we are to take Min's narrative literally or ignore the significance of the way in which she, along with others, reconstructs the period. Min appears to follow Freud in imagining sexual desire to be at the root of everything. Within this context, her creation of an entire landscape of masturbating, fornicating people has sprung up to replace the standard view of the Maoist period, and her main characters gradually find themselves driven more by desire than by social norms. The emphasis on the social and political arena as the first and most important place for humans to envision the self and invest energy and passion represents, in *Red Azalea*, the discredited if still supple Maoist past.

Yet while the novel pays its respects to a discourse that centers sexual desire as the most mysterious and powerful of all human desires, it intertwines that discourse with themes and aesthetics that are mined from revolutionary discourse.[32] Min aims her imaginative interpretation of the past at an English-reading audience. In the protagonists' flight from China and the overarching sexual framework in both novels, and in the opportunities that the character Katherine presents to her students, Min cuts, chops, and remixes the revolutionary past into a purely future-oriented direction. The contradictions between the realities of revolutionary culture and this utopian sexual idealization are dissolved in this process, and revolutionary spirit is extracted from its unsavory associations, becoming a spirit now free (and perhaps forced) to fly across the sea and root itself outside of the limiting confinement of physical China.

SIX

The Workspace of a New Age Maoist

He Jianjun's The Postman

> Today, who can imagine people giving up their negative freedom to follow a charismatic leader advocating a people's democracy? . . . The age when people would sacrifice their secular happiness for utopian ideals is gone. Now, the opposite holds true: People are willing to abandon any and all ideals in the name of realism.
>
> GAN YANG *1998, 48*

WORK IN NEW ERA CULTURE

More often than not, revolutionary spirit was expressed through one's attitude and behavior toward work, and, as I demonstrated in Chapter Three, the mentality of the worker was a primary site of investigation for the discipline of psychology in the 1950s. As such, work itself must be recognized as a core idea and arena for the unfolding of revolutionary culture, and its deconstruction, along with criticism of both the "model worker" and the concept of work itself, is to be expected in the post-Mao era.[1] Indeed, the worker loyal to the state and motivated by ideas of self-sacrifice and the common good has been replaced by self-centered or simply disengaged working people of all kinds. The very idea of *worker* no longer really fits, because work, which was at the core of the central notion of *serve the people* under Maoism, in more recent representations is no longer at the crux of identity production; rather, it is simply one site among many—and not necessarily the most important one—where the subject is formed. In many cases, emphasis has moved from the work and its results to the subject and its formation and existence in relation to work.[2] Generally this subject, which perhaps by this time could accurately be called a "self," is highly gendered, in a rejection of the Maoist emphasis on non gender-specific labor.

It should not be surprising, therefore, to find that in New Era fiction and film Maoist concepts of work have been prodded and poked, renegotiated, and at times even dismantled. After the death of Mao, writers and film-makers immediately set out to imagine anew the revolutionary or not-so-revolutionary worker and the very idea of work. In the so-called literature of the wounded (shanghen wenxue) of the late 1970s and the early 1980s, the Maoist worker is still represented, but the idealism that sustains him or her has been gutted by the violence of the Cultural Revolution and the corruption of the state. In Wang Meng's (1934–) 1979 novel *Bolshevik Salute* (Buli), for example, in the late 1950s, protagonist Zhong Yicheng actively looks forward to his rehabilitation through labor and gushes romantically about the pleasure and value of hard work:

> Work, work, work! Millions of years ago labor turned monkeys into humans. Millions of years later in China, physical labor was exercising its great strength to purify thinking and create a new soul. Zhong Yicheng deeply believed in this . . . He scooped feces out of latrines. The smell of feces made him feel glorious and peaceful. One bucket after another, he mixed the liquid with earth, feeling from his heart that it was really and truly delightful. (Wang Meng 1989, 100–101)

Zhong recalls the struggle—morning, afternoon, and evening; struggle is a political / military term that describes the extra labor heaped on so-called bad elements. Through the success Zhong experiences in a system that ranks bad elements based on their work, Wang Meng shows that the idea of reforming intellectuals through labor works, so to speak: Zhong's positive attitude and unstinting effort succeed in forging an emotional link between him and the peasants, and a new awareness—indeed, an entire new consciousness—grows within him. Only when party hacks purposefully misinterpret his heroic fight against a fire does Zhong become disillusioned. If only the party were more honest and less corrupt, Wang Meng implies, work could indeed cure intellectuals of real or imaginary attitude problems. Zhong must undergo significant questioning at various phases of contemporary Chinese history; only male characters must undergo such examinations, the females being largely in subservient roles.

Another similar example, which deals with elite rather than strictly manual labor, is Shen Rong's (also Chen Rong, 1935–) 1980 novel *At Middle Age* (Rendao zhongnian). Ophthalmologist Lu Wenting devotes herself heart and soul to her job, eventually suffering a heart attack because of overwork and bad conditions. The author points to party corruption as contributing to the situation, but most of the blame falls on the failure to modernize under party control. In this novel as in *Bolshevik Salute*, the protagonists are true believers in the value of work, and their identities are formed largely within their practice and conception of work.

Shen Rong portrays some work-related problems as gender-based, but she does not bring out these issues as much as does Zhang Jie (1937–). Zhang, in her long novel *The Ark* (Fangzhou), published in 1982, creates a highly gendered work environment in which women are subject to any number of abuses. Despite their hard work and desire to achieve worthwhile accomplishments, there is little chance that her female characters will achieve success in the masculine power context that work is shown to be. Far from being an idealistic realm where the people can be served, work is an arena where male bias against women, corruption, and social prejudice in general can take root and flower.

In his writings about intellectuals sent to work in the countryside, Zhang Xianliang (1936–) pushes aside the lyrical qualities associated with hard labor that Wang Meng exploits, as well as the respect toward work shown by Shen Rong and Zhang Jie despite the bad conditions under which their female characters labor. Zhang Xianliang draws a stark line between physical work and intellectual endeavors, and portrays the latter as much more profound and pleasant. Basically rejecting the Maoist idea of the work-cure, Zhang also shifts the locus of identity construction from labor to sexual relationships and philosophical thought, strengthening a trend that only deepens in the next twenty years. Zhang, however, always ascribes the agency in this redefinition to men; women function as convenient sexual or intellectual catalysts that allow the culturally important males to proceed along their road to self-understanding. Furthermore, he presents the entire process whereby males learn how to gain power through sexuality and intellect as crucial for national renewal. For Zhang Xianliang, as for Zhang Jie, work is gendered at its profoundest levels, but he promotes rather than critiques this gendering.

The most radical deconstruction of work comes with the experimental writers—Yu Hua (1960–), Can Xue (1953–), Su Tong (1963–), Mo Yan (1955–

), and others. In Can Xue's enigmatic *Yellow Mud Street* (Huangni jie), a disturbing shell of socialist work structure remains in place to prick the reader's expectation that some ordinary narrative and social progress may occur. But, although committees meet, leaders convene, and such typical work strategies as procrastination or indecision are in full effect, for him the point is not so much that nothing is accomplished as it is that these strategies are part of a larger set of seemingly unrealistic but strangely logical and real relationships between people in all aspects of life. Again, with the significant exception of the work of Can Xue, the only famous female experimental writer, in the experimentalists' stories the important actors are usually male. For example, Mo Yan's short "Divine Debauchery" (Shenpiao), which is a direct attack on socialist work mores, features a wealthy landowner. Through his aesthetic and spiritual immersion into flowers and his complete disregard for common morality or productive labor, he accomplishes what the socialist system never could completely do: the redistribution of wealth to the poorest in society (Mo Yan 1994).[3] The main character in Yu Hua's "Mistake on the Riverbank" (Hebian de cuowu) is a dedicated policeman who begins to investigate a crime only to slowly lose control over his internal narrative of clues, guilt, cause and effect, and social responsibility. Eventually the idea of work in its entirety disappears from the policeman's mind, which is taken over by a mysterious internal process. In Su Tong's "Wives and Concubines" (Qiqie chengqun) and the Zhang Yimou (1951–) film based on it, *Raise the Red Lantern* (Da hong denglong gaogao gua), work recedes in importance until it virtually disappears, replaced by a sexualized and male-controlled, performance-based, and culturally inherited structure of power and oppression.

In recent years, critiques of work under capitalism have sprung up alongside those of work under socialism. In Zhou Xiaowen's (1954–) film *Ermo*, a peasant woman extracts herself from traditional noodle-making in her village and sets up a modern noodle factory in the city. Her work, once fully integrated into the rural community, becomes focused on a single goal—buying the biggest television set in the village—and in a symbolically significant act, she sells her own blood to get extra money. Zhou exposes the emptiness of the process of narrowing the meaning of work to its exchange value, or the capitalization of work. It is impossible for Ermo to ever really catch up with the images that motivate her: once she buys one, a neighbor instantly proclaims that she will buy a set bigger than Ermo's.[4] Ermo's husband is disabled, so she must do the entrepreneurial work; at the end of the film we see the disturbing image of Ermo awake while everyone else in the room has fallen asleep. Her dull stare at a screen that produces only static implies an intuitive understanding that something has gone wrong, and directs us toward the possibility of budding self-knowledge. Here the director continues a 20th-century tradition of granting heightened awareness to women and other characters on the margins of cultural creation.[5] However, although women can identify problems, social gender restrictions constrain their ability to act effectively on behalf of constructing a viable future.

Recently, young writers also have incorporated work into their projections of a contemporary global lifestyle. For Chen Ran's (1962–) ubiquitous female character Dai Er, work is something of a distracting nuisance that gets in the way of her feelings and thoughts—unless, of course, she can refashion it as part of a new way of living. Generally Chen Ran presents long-term salaried work as restricting: the requirement of set hours and a regular schedule and, most important, the elevation of work goals above those of lifestyle prevent her characters from achieving the freedom and independence they aspire to. The situation, however, is more serious for men, who cannot escape the strictures of responsibility and thus are not as able to live the floating existence as women (Larson 1997a).

THE POSTMAN

One topic of the 1995 film *The Postman* (Youchai), by the sixth generation director He Jianjun (also known as He Yi, 1960–), is urban labor and its gendered meanings.[6] In subtle and in more overt ways, both the theme and the aesthetics of the film depend on a gendered narrative of labor. One important aspect of this gendered story is the film's perspective on generative social space, which is marked as male, not overtly but rather covertly.

In a seemingly contradictory way, the film presents two takes on work. On one hand, it relegates work to a non-idealized sphere that is no different than that occupied, both mentally and physically, by the innocent but alienated city dweller. In this kind of work, women and men inhabit the same world and are separated only by different levels of skill, strength, and normative hierarchy. Work becomes a repetitive, sensual experience of sound and motion, a cynical consciousness, and an attitude of detachment, just as those attributes are part of city life in general. At the same time, work and the workplace carry with them a trace of possibility reminiscent of the idealized work concepts of revolutionary culture, which was a time and place when the revolutionary spirit was completely embodied in the attitude of the worker toward work. Although in the film work is mandatory for everyone, its utopian aspect is open only to the male protagonist, who through this identification takes on the weighty burden of helping others live a correct life.

The film's plot is confusing and it is not always immediately clear who is speaking or acting; the technique, we eventually realize, puts us into a position similar to that of the main character. The film demands some mental detective work on our part since we must put apparently unrelated scenes, people, and words together to form a meaningful narrative. Xiao Dou, a young postal laborer, is assigned to replace Lao Wu, who loses his position as letter carrier in Xingfu (Happiness) District because he has opened and read other people's letters. Shy and awkward, Xiao Dou lives with his sister in a large run-down house passed on to them by their parents, who died when he was young. His sister has a boyfriend, who frequently complains that she must give up this old house so they can get married and move into a modern apartment. She is reluctant to follow this plan as it will leave Xiao Dou behind alone. As Xiao Dou prepares to take over the postal route, a young and attractive female coworker, Yunqing, assists him and, not long after, seduces him.

Xiao Dou immediately follows in Lao Wu's footsteps in more ways than one, opening and reading letters he is supposed to deliver.[7] He goes farther, however; in four instances he tries to intervene in people's lives. The first is that of a woman and a man who are lovers but married to others. Xiao Dou anonymously writes to the man, threatening him with serious but unnamed consequences unless he ends the relationship and leaves all of their correspondence at a prearranged spot for pick-up. The second is the case of a prostitute named Wan Juan, whom a doctor introduces to clients. Xiao Dou visits the doctor after he sees Wan Juan go in, and then goes to see Wan Juan, claiming the doctor sent him. Although she assumes he is there for sex and he does not disabuse her of this idea, he says almost nothing and rushes out before any intimacy takes place. The third instance involves a young couple, who have written suicidal letters to the man's parents. Xiao Dou writes a new letter that describes in sunny terms how everything is fine, and sends it with the pictures originally enclosed in the suicide letter. In the fourth instance, a young drug addict is melancholy and violent over lack of news from his homosexual lover. Xiao Dou, who has been holding the lover's letters, then goes to the youth's apartment, pays the rent so the landlady will allow him to enter, listens to the miserable youth talk about his relationship with his lover and what it is like to be high, and removes some drug paraphernalia when he leaves. He later sees the young man taken out on a stretcher. Previously, Xiao Dou confronted the lover when the latter asked if there were any letters for him, calling him by name and not responding when the surprised youth asked him how he knew his name.

These scenes, unrelated except through the agency of Xiao Dou, present a depressing society chopped into small, isolated, reified units spatially and materially, and therefore mentally and emotionally, a situation experienced equally by the male and female characters. The only healthy way people living in this environment can connect is through organic links developed when they were children—and these eventually fail them—or through the indirect method of letter-writing. Barriers in architecture, work styles, and social habits and at the very level of consciousness are rigidly enforced by various normative structures, and these are what prevent face-to-face communication. Yet people retain a desire for emotionally satisfying relationships with other human beings.

Although the film's portrayal of work is, on the surface, almost opposite to what we find in idealized Maoist images, Xiao Dou's attempt to right what has gone wrong reveals that idealism underlies his concept of what work should be. The seemingly blasé work environment that has replaced the Maoist vision of passion and positive social change is actually a physical and mental *space*—the only one in the film, and one presented with both irony and hope—where positive social change can be conceptualized and put into action. This vision of what work should be, diluted though it is, is inherited as a residue from the long, contradictory discourse of labor under Maoism that included first a glorification, and second a political relationship to authority that demanded a challenge to inappropriate power.[8] The nature of this authority, however, has radically changed and is dispersed into the surroundings, also drawing the viewer's attention to the issue of space. In the film, space is largely the diffusion of authority, making it difficult for any one character to grasp its nature. Because revolutionary spirit is the subjective point through which one determines a relationship to power or those in power, *The Postman* strikes at the heart of subjectivity and agency under the new cultural conditions.

Xiao Dou's job as a postman gives him the opportunity to locate what he finds wrong with society, intervene in personal relationships, and help forge proper connections between people. Although Xiao Dou cannot find a clear authority to challenge, his intervention, ideological in nature, proceeds as if there were one and replaces letter-delivery as his real work. The letter becomes a double-edged representation of the spatial segmentation and inability of people to communicate, and of the hopes that Xiao Dou invests in his work. As the film progresses, Xiao Dou refines his activities, which eventually meet with failure.

The opportunities offered by this special workspace, which is partially imagined and partially remembered by Xiao Dou, are part of a gendered cultural sphere. Xiao Dou is a contemporary anti-hero, an example of the male intellectual now diminished in his abilities and sensibilities, who still takes on the burden of cultural construction and directs his actions toward positive ends. His goal is to act within the space that is the diffusion of authority, and find a place where he can intervene. Women stand in a familiar position, representing first the possibility of a natural life of honest human affection, and second a sexual route that also offers Xiao Dou a path toward increased understanding of his personal and social role. The women characters themselves lack the ability to transcend or even imagine transcending the deadening social limits against which Xiao Dou struggles. The film takes a position on the contemporary debate about Chinese modernity, holding that there is little—but still some—hope for a social life based on revolutionary values to emerge, as long as at least one male actor within this sphere can retain a grasp on his ability to move others toward a positive goal.

THE WORLD DOESN'T SEEM TO NEED US ANYMORE

The film portrays contemporary Chinese society, visually and more generally, as a sensually oppressive set of small boxes. What we first see are slow and gritty shots of run-down apartment buildings as they actually exist in many cities in China. Doors and entryways—foregrounded throughout the film—are blocked by old bicycles, trash, and other items. Paint is fading and falling off, the ground is grimy and dusty, and smog hangs in the air, with four industrial towers in the distance taking up the screen now and then. Colors are brown, beige, dull olive green, and gray. The urban environment is almost completely without charm, and there is not a shred of romanticism in these images.[9] As a laborer, Xiao Dou works with a chain and hoist to install a new mail collection box, a scene that also reappears at the end and anchors the preoccupation with work—physical and mental—that structures the film. Many shots in the post office are close-ups of hands doing their regular work, stamping letters, sorting, filing.

Although Xiao Dou's job at the onset is manual labor, his preoccupation is not the actual work of setting up collection boxes and delivering letters, but rather the more abstract cultural or ideological work of social change; he takes up the demand for cultural improvement directed at males, despite his obvious unsuitability for the role. Close-ups of Xiao Dou heaving the collection box into place, the chains, the weight of iron, and the difficulty of moving the box appear at the beginning and end of the film, and form a frame for the plot. Although here what we see is the resistance of matter in work, we soon discover that the box is not only physically heavy but also endowed with special metaphorical meaning as a spot where a once-removed (not face-to-face) exchange between people takes place.[10] The world-space of human relations in the film has shriveled, it turns out, to the space occupied by this small circular container. The scene thus highlights both the physical labor of work and also its symbolic meanings; furthermore, ideological work is also shown to be hard work. The sharply material images place Xiao Dou's efforts and achievements, questionable though they are, within the context of a long discourse of ideologically meaningful manual labor.

He Jianjun's approach, a kind of dirty realism, shows the grimy city and its dense structures at several points, but never directly implies that it once was otherwise, at least for adults. The camera pans slowly from side to side or top to bottom over blocks of living quarters, lingering there and drawing our attention to their poor condition and deadening regularity, and there are many references to city life as ruins. For example, Xiao Dou and his sister live in a large but dilapidated house that—judging from her constant attempts to get her brother and boyfriend to put on warm clothes—does not have central heating or adequate plumbing and bathing facilities. The boyfriend insists that the furniture in her house is too old and must be replaced with something modern, even though much of it is real wood, the sister protests. In the letter Xiao Dou writes to the old couple in their suicidal son's name, he inquires about plans to tear down the neighborhood where they live.

He Jianjun does not present us with the kind of vibrant world of human connections that once existed in older buildings and the social activities that took place in them (as, for example, in Zhang Yang's 1999 film *Shower*

[Xizao]). Rather, in his frequent straight-on pans across apartment blocks, his centering of doorways leading from one space to another, and in the thematic elements discussed above, he focuses on the division of space into unconnected units and the replacement of the old by the new as an unsettling and unsatisfactory aspects of urban life. However, because the past exists not as any clear history or unified memory that can be manipulated into romance but rather as traces and remnants—the repetition of the orchard story (which I will describe below), the orchard keeper turned fortuneteller, the all-wood furniture inherited from parents, and the soon-to-be destroyed neighborhoods—we can hypothesize that at some point there either was a past different from the present, or that, minimally, there now exists a rapidly fading memory of a time when everyone thought things could, should, or would improve.

Another aspect of this urban fragmentation and disintegration is a mysterious underlying violence that sometimes breaks through the surface. Our first glimpse of it is when Lao Wu is forced roughly into a car and taken away after confessing to opening mail. Shortly thereafter, there is a scene of a man running with several others chasing and yelling at him. Xiao Dou merely observes, making no move toward intervention and expressing no emotion. At Xiao Dou's home, we see the unhappiness of his sister's boyfriend, who is adamant that they must move into the new apartment that is waiting for them. The lack of privacy is obvious, as windowpanes above the doors in the old house provide a visual opening even when they are shut. It is awkward for the couple to interact sexually, with Xiao Dou in the house. We see Xiao Dou listening to them as they make love, and even peering in through the blinds. At the end of the film, there is a mysterious scene in which Xiao Dou's sister is seen crying in the background while her boyfriend yells "Cry! Cry! Can you ever stop crying!" as he kills and chops up a chicken for a meal. The scene again reveals a barely covered hostility and aggression, with no clear explanation.

Other than the relationship between Xiao Dou and his sister, we see very little warmth in human interactions, implying that the depressing environment has affected the consciousnesses of the people who inhabit it and that violence is most likely not unusual. Yunqing seems to be more interested in sexual satisfaction than in any long-term emotional relationship with Xiao Dou; she calmly tells Xiao Dou that her sexual encounter with the post office manager, Lao Liu, six months before was just the same as her encounter with him.[11] At work, Lao Liu compliments Xiao Dou on his work but maintains a distance. At home, his sister's boyfriend offers him a cigarette, but otherwise there is almost no interaction between them. And Xiao Dou fails to make a real connection with any of the people whose letters he intercepts, although that seems to be his goal. Even the party for Xiao Dou's sister and her boyfriend as they prepare to get married, which should be lively and fun, is stilted, and the partygoers complain of the lack of liveliness. Their solution, to take a picture, only reifies the awkwardness of the relationship between Xiao Dou, his sister, and the boyfriend: the shot shows the sister and her fiancé standing next to each other, with Xiao Dou a shadowy presence between them.

The alienation of the characters is obvious, yet no clear cause for it is presented within the film, nor does the film point to any authority responsible for the situation. Although there are a few scenes where the law steps in to enforce social stability, for the most part what we see is a system of normative regulation that, like the repeated pounding of cancellations that is the overwhelming sound of work at the post office, simply reproduces itself. Within society, the film implies, beauty has been overwhelmed and subdued. The routines of daily life and the demands of a large population within a small space could be at fault, but the film does not exactly make that connection either.[12] This portrayal is not unusual in modern film and literature. To bemoan, even subtly, the effects of modernity on human society is a major cultural theme in the 20th century (C. Taylor 1989; Sussman 1997).[13] One thing that makes He Jianjun's film interesting and unusual, however, is its implied connection with, and commentary on, the Chinese revolutionary past in pointing to work as a site where idealistic action can still be imagined—and even, to a small degree and with questionable success, undertaken. Revolutionary spirit lives on, if only in the contorted mental knots of a somewhat hopeless letter carrier.

LATTER DAY CONFUCIAN, NEW AGE MAOIST

What rather quickly becomes clear about Xiao Dou is that by contemporary standards he is almost dysfunctional. Bereft of friends, the only person he is able to talk to is his sister.[14] Their connection—often expressed by chatting about a peach orchard that they frequented as youths, their fear of the orchard keeper, and their failure to taste a peach despite many attempts to steal one—borders on incestuous, and indeed, toward the end of the film, we do see a sex scene, shot from a distance, in which the identity of the two people is unclear. As they lie in bed, and though we are too far away to see moving lips, we hear the sister's voice as she states that she once was in the orchard without Xiao Dou and did taste the peaches after all. It is impossible to tell from watching whether the male partner in the bed is Xiao Dou or his sister's new husband, but her remark seems to be directed at Xiao Dou.[15] The remark about the orchard comes after several similar references at different points in the film, and the statement that neither of them ever tasted a peach is made repeatedly.

The meaning of the orchard is unclear, although the mysterious, exciting, and forbidden context, the reference to a torn skirt and blood running down the girl's leg, the desire for a peach that underlies their visits to the orchard, and the admission of a secret taste all seem to suggest a sexual significance. At the same time, the tale of the orchard is the one story Xiao Dou and his sister love to share, suggesting that the orchard may represent a private, pre-adult, idyllic childhood relationship. Their idyllic childhood days are over, their close relationship is about to end (she is getting married), and Xiao Dou's hitherto-pleasant memory of those times also is destroyed by his sister's revelation. Her admission could be interpreted as a statement that she has had other sexual experiences, or as a betrayal of their special past together.

We do not discover with whom, if anyone, Xiao Dou's sister had a sexual relationship, but another character from the story, the orchard keeper, now is a street-side fortune teller and banana vendor. When Xiao Dou sees the man telling a fortune, he brings himself close and studies the man's face; later the camera focuses on the fortune teller's impassive expression as he reorganizes the bananas in front of him. Because Xiao Dou's sister did taste a peach after all, and because the orchard keeper had supposedly prevented her and Xiao Dou from taking a peach, the film implies a connection: as a child, did the orchard keeper bribe Xiao Dou's sister with a peach to have sexual contact with him?

Thus does Xiao Dou's relationship with his sister, although deeply affectionate for both of them, join the other modern relationships as abnormal by ordinary social standards. In its many sexual references and its sense of scurrying around the issue of sexual relationships, the film picks up a common complaint of the post-Mao days: under Maoism, sexual desire was suppressed by the state and repressed in each person, and this long-lasting suppression is still influential in affecting attitudes toward sex. He

Jianjun recognizes the importance of the topic by proposing a vague sexual motivation behind many events. His main character has sexual difficulties that within psychoanalytical theory would be branded as perversion or repression. For example, he watches his sister bathe through a window. And though he is first afraid when Yunqing kisses him, he soon responds actively and almost violently. Furthermore, three of the situations in which Xiao Dou becomes involved—the extramarital affair, the prostitution and pimping by a doctor, and the drug addict's homosexual relationship—are concerned with sexual relationships that are "illicit," although in the case of the drug addict it is unclear whether Xiao Dou intercedes to "correct" the homosexual liaison or the drug use.[16] The relationship between Xiao Dou and his sister, therefore, is not any different than the others.

Although sexual desire does seem to be behind much of the action and clearly is important in some way, I do not see it as the main target of the director's concern. He Jianjun does not castigate sexual behavior as something that in itself has caused the dilemma; nor is abnormal sexual behavior in the film a clear result of excessive state control, either now or in the past. Even more important, he does not present bringing sexual desire out into the open or centering it as a mandatory part of personal identity as an implicit solution to any problem presented in the film. The film gives us no positive sexual role models to which we as audience could imagine the characters aspiring, and the sexually "progressive" characters are as disturbed as anyone else. The director gives sexual repression as a concept pride of place, but not the power of origination; it is here that his approach differs from that of many other films and novels that center sexual identity as something to be either damned as pollution or praised as liberation.

However, although the director is not making a statement about sexuality that corresponds to these more common interpretations, still sexual relations are clearly of consequence in the film. Their importance lies in several areas. First, sexual relationships are easily invoked as expressions of a more general desire that can transcend sexuality. In this film if anything has been repressed, it is not sexual desire but the idealism associated with a prior society. Indeed, Xiao Dou's tryst with Yunqing shows us what a simple task it is to become sexually involved, and Yunqing's blasé comments about her sexual involvement with Lao Liu indicate no worry about sexual morality or fear of social condemnation. Yet achieving sexual pleasure does not make Xiao Dou happy. We cannot make sense of the sexual desire represented in the film unless we consider it as one theme within the larger concern of Xiao Dou's social role and work, where it can stand in for the ineffable, intangible desires that have been thwarted by cultural change. Sexual desire can encapsulate, represent, and visually express that basic condition.

Second, from the larger viewpoint of gender relations, the film repeats and confirms a conventional aspect of male-female sexual involvement. The relationships that Xiao Dou has with his sister and with Yunqing are similar to the relationships we see between central male characters and women in the films of Chen Kaige (1952–) (with whom director He Jianjun has worked), for instance. For Chen, women always offer redemptive qualities that can help cure personal and social alienation in his forever-seeking male protagonists. For a protagonist to accept this comfort, however, means rejecting the most important male endeavor of cultural reformation and accepting a degree of social feminization that is partially defined by freedom from this responsibility and a corresponding lack of social importance (Larson 1997b).

Along those lines, both Xiao Dou's sister and Yunqing offer him a symbolic and practical way out of his predicament. The sister, on the one hand, embodies an emotional connection that predates adulthood; it was well established before the difficulties so obvious in adult relationships were in place. She also provides a structure for the organization of daily life and its work-related tasks of cooking, eating, and wearing proper clothes. This labor is significant not only in itself, but also in that it presents a larger structure supporting professional work or work on the job, which needs "something to come home to" as a counter-balance. Thus, her defining contribution circumscribes and limits work: it is not socially important so much as it is important for the purpose of sustaining another life, that of family relationships. But if the sister wants to take up her own social role as a wife and transfer these services to her new husband, she cannot continue her relationship with her brother. However, she can offer a replacement for all aspects of her work by finding an appropriate mate for Xiao Dou. In one scene she brings him a sweater she is knitting to see if it fits, and then broaches the idea of his meeting a girl she has chosen. Her physical awkwardness and verbal hesitation as she tests the sweater against Xiao Dou's body shows that she is fully aware of the profound bond her action is breaking. She experiences great difficulty making the offer.

Yunqing, on the other hand, virtually throws herself at Xiao Dou, but her involvement lacks the deep emotional bond inherent in the sister. What Yunqing's presence offers is the potential to redefine labor, and possibly even more significantly than having a loving sister or wife at home. If Xiao Dou were to stay in Yunqing's world, work would not be just something to get away from by going home to a warm and caring environment; it would itself become a site where new physical relationships could be negotiated. The office, in other words, could be redefined as a playground. Physical proximity could allow sexual relations to be smoothly hidden under the movements, gestures, and language of work, which could be both their cover and their necessary condition. In fact, in this model, such actions are not longer simply labor, but become sexual in and of themselves, as the repetitive, pounding throb of the letter stamp in Yunqing's hand indicates. Sexual negotiations and transactions would not have to proceed directly but could be carried out covertly, through speech and acts that ostensibly are part of work. Because of his innocence, Xiao Dou does not realize that Yunqing is attracted to him until she actually approaches. If he were to accept this vision and become experienced in this form of work, it could easily displace both the family-life narrative and the alternative narrative that he has concocted and that plays out through his efforts.

That Xiao Dou has to be torn away from his sister—first by her agency and his passivity in finding him a mate, and second by her admission that their past together has been based on a lie—shows that he is a severely weakened cultural hero. However, he is still strong enough to realize that Yunqing does not offer him what he is seeking, and to take the crucial first step toward putting his idealism into motion. As in Chen Kaige's movies, in *The Postman* the investigation of gender meanings is not central to its goal, although the film is informed by a basic misogyny that insists on the symbolic importance of the gender relations it sets up. The sex of the troubled agent in this fallen utopia is taken for granted; men hold in their hands and minds the power of cultural renewal, and women not only are excluded from this crucially important endeavor but also offer, in various forms, a dangerously alluring temptation that can cause the hero to veer from his track.

The hero must be male, but what kind of a man is Xiao Dou? At many points in the film, Xiao Dou's lack of basic social skills and fundamental inability to articulate his concerns are apparent. When Yunqing invites him out to eat and chat, he replies, anti-socially, "What's there to talk about?" He responds to his boss's compliments on his good work by looking down silently. He runs off without doing anything after entering the prostitute Wan Juan's apartment, and he says almost nothing. And when he visits the drug addict, Zhang Xin, he cannot get a word out of his mouth. Yet within the context of the film, Xiao Dou's dysfunctional nature does not seem too extreme, because the camera, as it slowly moves across cold, gritty streets and shabby, run-down apartments, implies that the entire society is spatially depressing and mentally alienated. Thus, in the sexual encounter between Xiao Dou and Yunqing, when Yunqing comments about sex being the same with him or with Lao Liu, Xiao Dou's response is to wind up a toy elephant in her apartment and watch it go through its mechanical movements, an exact expression of unthinking and unfeeling repetition.

Socially, what makes Xiao Dou a hero is that despite his dysfunctionality, he is motivated by some notion of how things should be. He in no way directly expresses this desire, but we can intuit it from his actions. We see little hope for social improvement, or even any such concept, in the surroundings or the people who live in this society. But in the four cases when he tracks people down and attempts to understand their lives, he creeps out of his observer status to get involved and set right certain perceived wrongs.

In the case of Zhao Zeren, the married man who is having an affair with Qiu Ping, Xiao Dou acts directly, writing to Zhao and urging him to consider several things: the cost of maintaining Qiu Ping's lifestyle, whether or not he could actually make her happy, and other vague but threatening consequences of their relationship. Although the letter is written anonymously, it is quite expressive. It is from this case that we can most directly see Xiao Dou's desire to intervene. He only has the ability to articulate his concerns when he does not confront his targets face-to-face, however, and it diminishes as the film goes on. Yunqing states in one scene that it is hard to understand why people feel comfortable writing to each other but cannot directly state their feelings. Indeed, when Xiao Dou meets with the prostitute Wan Juan, the elderly couple, the drug addict, and the novelist, we cannot discern his rationale for visiting them because he cannot speak out.[17] Without the first case to clue us in, we would have trouble deciphering what Xiao Dou is after.

Still, although weak and inarticulate, Xiao Dou uses the opportunities presented by his work to straighten a society gone awry. His focus on proper relationships—of married adults (the adulterers), of children to parents (the suicidal couple and their elderly parents or parents-in-law), between men and women (Wan Juan and her customers), and between (male) friends—is strongly reminiscent of Confucian values, where these relationships anchor the morality of an entire society. Because Xiao Dou never directly explains his discomfort, we cannot fathom his exact objections to these relationships, but minimally we can see that all of the situations in which he has chosen to intervene to some extent fall outside conventional social morality. His own life is also in this category.

Xiao Dou's sexual interest in his sister would make him a very troubled Confucian indeed. Regarding him as a New Age Maoist, however, does illuminate the film's strange and contradictory notions of gendered work and the relationship of work to social improvement. Anything attractive about work or labor has now been subdued by, first, the same forces that have produced an alienated population and, second, the disappearance of the glorification of work as the backbone of social morality and the expression of the correct spirit in revolutionary culture. Nonetheless, with other social realms—family and sexuality—offering nothing other than diversion, it is work that retains for Xiao Dou the ember of revolutionary values. In other words, when work is sparked by the efforts of a male cultural hero, its lost ability to embody the correct spirit and produce correct moral and spiritual values and a society based on those values is restored. Work is the site through which a social sphere based on correct relationships and the proper spirit can be re-imagined and brought into being. This empowering narrative of work may have been more or less open to both women and men when it was a strong revolutionary discourse, but now that that discourse has faded to the point of disappearing, it requires a male trigger to bring it back to life. Xiao Dou was molded by a revolutionary concept of work and, in turn, tries to mold his non-revolutionary environment to fit this concept. When he cannot imbue his actual job with the revolutionary spirit, he creates a new job for himself that feeds off the old. It also is worth noting that the new capitalist entrepreneurship, with all of its chaotic energy, does not so much as make an appearance—unless we consider the orchard keeper-turned-fortune-teller and fruit vendor, and he in no way represents redemptive possibilities.

The actual situation of workers in China is complex, and a great deal has been written about their savvy and practical understanding of the highly romanticized discourse of the worker under socialism.[18] The attitude of Yunqing, for whom work seems to be nothing more than a way to sustain her life and a space where she can find sexual partners, may illustrate the post-Mao inheritance of decades of worker suspicion toward socialist labor fantasies. In this respect, Lao Liu also is an interesting character, for his attitude toward the workers under him contains a somewhat fatigued vestige of socialist paternalism. For example, he responds in a semi-sympathetic fatherly way toward Lao Wu's transgressions, and urges him to accept the consequences. He uses concerned flattery to get Xiao Dou to help him set up the new mailboxes on a weekend, telling him that he is the only one around who knows how to do it and his services are indispensable. Yet Lao Liu's vacant gaze tells us that he is a lost man, unable to do anything more than simply repeat platitudes that once were living descriptions of the benefits of work.

With the near-total contemporary disillusionment of workers' belief in the glory of labor, it is surprising to find a character motivated by altruistic social improvement. Xiao Dou and his social improvement program are most likely motivated by the ideas of revolutionary culture, and especially the values associated with the model worker. On the website of that most famous of model workers, Lei Feng, there are articles about the Lei Feng spirit, selections from Lei Feng's diary, stories about Lei Feng's life, and much more. Whole-heartedly serving the people and the party, being a mere screw in the huge mechanism of revolution, the emotive intensity of loving and respecting one's job—all these qualities are listed. But it is selections from Lei Feng's diary that most clearly depict the spirit of the socialist worker:

> . . . if you were a drop of water, did you moisten an inch of soil? If you were a ray of sunlight, did you brighten a patch of darkness? If you were a single grain, did you nourish a useful life? If you were the tiniest screw, did you maintain your position in life forever? If you wanted to tell me about certain ideals, did you night and day spread those most beautiful ideals? Since you were alive, did you labor on behalf of those in the future, day by day making life more beautiful? I want to ask you, what have you done for the future? In the reservoir of life, we should not be just endless followers. (June 7, 1958)
>
> Ah, youth, it always is beautiful and good, but true youth belongs only to those who struggle to swim against the current, who labor forgetting the self, who are forever humble. (October 25, 1959)
>
> I must remember: "In work (gongzuo), we must learn from the comrades who have the highest enthusiasm; in life, we must learn from the comrades who have the lowest living standard." (June 5, 1960)
>
> Those who have no thought of themselves but only hold the People in their minds can surely obtain the highest glory and trust. And on the contrary,

> those who have only the self and not the People in their minds shall sooner or later be spat out and rejected by the People. (March 1961)
>
> The most glorious thing in the world—labor (laodong). / The most thoughtful people in the world—laborers. (March 16, 1961)
>
> . . . the People's problems are my problems, to use a bit of my strength to help the People solve their problems is my responsibility, the place where I concentrate my efforts. I am a master, one of the great laboring masses, and conquering any bit of difficulty for the People is my greatest pleasure. (September 11, 1961)

One salient aspect of the Lei Feng myth is the intensity of Lei Feng's feelings for the people, which is brought out in a scene from the 1965 film *Lei Feng*: "At that time the sky was dark, it was pouring rain, the road was sticky with mud, and there was a long way to go, but Lei Feng first and foremost did not think of his own difficulties, but of those of others. He was full of limitless, burning love for the People, and without any hesitation carried the child for the woman and took them to their door" (Yang Guisheng 1965, 3–4). As a model of morality, one of Lei Feng's most essential qualities was his willingness to work on behalf of others (Chen Zhengyang 1990).

These familiar qualities—selflessness and self-denial, serving the People, working hard with no consideration of personal gain, exhaustion, or reward, identifying problems that others have and working to solve them, having no concern about one's own living standards, and believing in a better future and one's own ability to contribute to it—all have a resonance in Xiao Dou's life. Much like an overworked contemporary CEO or a tireless, earnest Party cadre, Xiao Dou takes the office home with him, stuffing his drawers with letters to scan looking for people who need his help. He directs his own activity toward solving the problems he perceives others to have. Rejecting his sister's attempts to find a girlfriend for him and initially, at least, showing little interest in getting involved with Yunqing, Xiao Dou appears to have no desire to improve his own standard of living or to strive for his own pleasures. As he tries to right the incorrect relationships he reads about in others' letters, Xiao Dou is working for a better future for society at large. His latent idealism is expressed in the film not only thematically, but also in a mystical ring of bells that occurs several times throughout the film and stands in marked contrast to the cold and unattractive daily life reality that we see.

GENDERED WORKSPACE AND REVOLUTIONARY SPIRIT

Lei Feng and Xiao Dou are both cultural figures who embody the male responsibility of social improvement and show how work can—and must—be modeled and configured to meet that lofty aim. In contrast to the historical Lei Feng and the image he projected, Xiao Dou has no visible passion nor any clear ideological goal, yet his activities reveal similar ideals. The hidden nature of Xiao Dou's urges has a counterpart in Lei Feng's example as well; indeed, Lei Feng would never have been "found out" had it not been for his diaries, nor Xiao Dou but for the film. After Lei Feng's death, activists wrote and purposely lost diaries that they hoped others would find; although these actions were criticized widely, they may be seen as a performance of political virtue.[19] Likewise in *The Postman*, Xiao Dou's activism is hidden in his work, and he even receives praise from his boss for his excellent performance, much as did Lei Feng—although Xiao Dou's ideological work is not what Lao Liu recognizes.

The film steers clear of several current approaches to cultural expression. Critics have written about the nostalgia of recent years, when the ideals and passions of the revolutionary era have often become disassociated from the violence and fear of the period and taken on an attractive veneer (Dai 1997; Lee 1999, 307–41; Anagnost 1997, 54–56; Xudong Zhang 2000). The slogan "Make a revolution in the depths of your soul," the deep love for the People supposedly felt by model workers such as Lei Feng, the heartfelt loyalty expressed toward Chairman Mao in dances, declarations, and badge-collecting—all speak to an ethic of emotion, desire, and hope, qualities that may be more difficult to find in a consumer society where irony and self-consciousness are of paramount importance. The lack of such an ethic today has produced a nostalgia for what many now remember as pleasant and morally simpler days.[20] It is difficult to envision He Jianjun's film as a nostalgic enterprise, however, because its relentless critique of contemporary culture never allows that nostalgia to emerge. In addition, the film's presentation of the past as a trace rather than as a fully imagined and embodied presence does not lend itself to an interpretation of nostalgia as its primary motivation. Another current topic is the moral decrepitude that comes with capitalist practices.[21] Yet in the film the lure of money and its decadent lifestyle does not entice Xiao Dou or anyone else. Moreover, although we do see in the purloined letters the strong need for human connection, the film does not suggest that some recognizable aspect of society—corruption, greed, power manipulation—has caused people to lose their human essence; nor does it propose a new humanism and subjectivity similar to those debated so actively in the 1980s.[22] Although people have trouble talking to each other directly, in their letters they are full of easily described passion.

Xiao Dou's social intervention cannot be carried on face-to-face because the space available for this kind of direct action no longer exists. Likewise, the space available for any direct human interaction has shrunk, for reasons unclear. Although Xiao Dou has inherited a moral stance and a faint belief in his responsibility to act, the film presents no authority, reason, ultimate cause, or even suspicion of a spot against which he can organize his struggle. In place of the usual bogeys of evil, He Jianjun proposes a spatial logic that restricts human subjectivity—or proposes that the authority inhibiting behavior has diffused into the spaces in which people live. Although this filmic presentation of a problem has obvious relevance to actual urban society in China, where space is at a premium, it is not a realistic portrayal. Indeed, from the point of view of people taking pleasure in their lives and each others' company, and from the perspective of people talking to each other and communicating, the film presents things as much worse than they actually are; in reality, urban spaces with their attractive human energy—malls, discos, bookstores, department stores, sidewalks, theaters, food stalls, restaurants, stadiums, and so on—are always in full swing, but they do not so much as appear in the film. The filming techniques, with their minimal camera movement and close-up attention to the disjointed movements of work, also do not project a sense of realism. The spatial dilemma is expressed in images of real-life separated living units, which are repeated in images of newly constructed apartments at the end of the film, and in the stunted consciousness of the characters.

To imply, as He Jianjun does, that spatial organization determines human consciousness and limits agency, or even any thought of agency, is to gut traditional ideas of authority and diffuse authority into buildings, the ground, images in the sky, and the environment in general. In his vision, as in that of many of the works of experimental writers, a specific History is no longer directly to blame. But in contrast to them, here a material structure is weighing heavily against Xiao Dou's lingering idealism and dooming his project to failure. For Xiao Dou, the body is culturally inscribed, and the mind and heart are culturally inscribed; but even worse, however, there is almost no place not inscribed by this diffusion of authority.[23] When Xiao Dou's actions fall short of helping his targets, and his own relationships with his sister and with Yunqing fail to bring him either motivation or self-understanding, we see that the film neither gives us any authority against which to fight, nor forcefully presents us with any solutions.

The film offers two ways to think of the workspace and the worker as a barely functioning site of spiritual hope—even if hidden, unarticulated, and dysfunctional. On the one hand, in today's China to propose a workplace so seriously compromised must be taken as an ironic smile, the gesture of someone who wants to believe but cannot find a thread on which to hang his faith. By muddying Xiao Dou's idealism with murky issues of sexuality and the idylls of childhood, incest, and revolutionary heroism, He Jianjun hedges his bets and plays to the knowing viewer. No one who has been through the Maoist period and the Cultural Revolution, or even heard the stories of parents and relatives who labored in May 7th Cadre Schools to improve their political standing, could believe transparently and instantly in the curative power of work. On the other hand, He Jianjun—by undermining approaches to understanding the self and society common in recent films and literature, and particularly by placing at the film's center his studied investigation of authority and resistance, so central to 20th-century Chinese cultural discourse—carves out a space in which Xiao Dou's moral activism must be taken seriously. Common sense tells us that the shy and bumbling Xiao Dou, who can almost never directly approach the targets of his altruism and calmly discuss with them the details of and reasons for their situation, should take up his concerned sister's offer of an introduction to a suitable mate and get on with a regular life. Yet he rejects this road, turning his work into a sly new form of *serve the people.*

In beginning this paper with a quote from Gan Yang critiquing Chinese conservatism in the 1990s, I inserted *The Postman* into the contemporary debate on intellectual politics. The debate can be simplified into pro-capitalism and pro-revolution poles that are argued theoretically, historically, culturally, politically, and economically, although the various arguments hardly fit together in a seamless whole, Gan Yang argues (1998). As he states, the multiple aspects of the pro-capitalist line " . . . do not even coordinate well with one another. Rather, *they betray a social mood that relies on tacit agreement*" (italics added) (47). With *The Postman* in mind, I quote a section of

Gan Yang's text that could easily be taken to describe the film rather than the intellectual atmosphere at large:

> In my view, this conservatism is bound to devitalize and suffocate Chinese intellectual life, leaving it epistemologically torpid and regressive. In fact, intellectual ossification, stagnation, and cynicism may already have set in, as evidenced by the publication of *The Last Twenty Years of Chen Yinke.* Full of cultural narcissism and fatalism, this biography evoked widespread resonance and self-pity among Chinese intellectuals. It looks as if Chinese intellectuals have collectively reached a dead end, and all they can do now is to intone mournful elegies for dead masters. (47)[24]

Although *The Postman* is not about intellectuals, it is an intellectual film that makes a proposal about everyday life, work, and the possibility of revolutionary idealism. Projecting a world in which all are resigned to their bleak lives to the point of unawareness of any possible other option, He Jianjun does indeed project "a social mood that relies on tacit agreement." To this bleak resignation, which the film's suffocating editing recognizes as so pervasive that it demands no awareness on the part of the characters, we could say that Xiao Dou offers some relief.

The debate on a possible Chinese alternative modernity often centers on the question of to what extent the revolutionary period should be thought of as integral to the Chinese modern. One approach, promoted by Leo Ou-fan Lee (1999) in his book *Shanghai Modern: The Flowering of a New Urban Culture in China, 1930–1945*, identifies a modernity developing first in Shanghai, later in Taiwan and Hong Kong, and then once again in Shanghai as the concept leaps over the revolutionary period entirely. Another approach has been developed directly by Liu Kang and more indirectly by a number of scholars working in literature, economics, political theory, and cultural theory (Kang Liu 1996; Xudong Zhang 2001).[25] Arguing that revolutionary thought emphasizing equality, engagement, community, and cooperation has had a significant influence on the creation and experience of modernity in China, Liu Kang and others promote greater intellectual awareness of this history and recognition of a lingering commitment to its values in contemporary China. According to Xudong Zhang, the discourse of an alternative modernity or the "Chinese way" maintains as a possibility the promises of equality, democracy, and self-realization for people in China and other places. As such, this vision does not stem from the utopianism of which socialist regimes are often accused, but remains critical of the public withdrawal from ideals of equality and justice in favor of economic progress (Xudong Zhang 2001, 67–68).

The Postman presents us with an example of a bizarre hero who cannot think or act collectively, politically, or even with any clear vision of social improvement or moral right. Yet he develops a plan, and he acts on behalf of the social good and without thought to his own self-benefit. Within the context of the debate on Chinese modernity, what perspective does the film provide? Clearly He Jianjun is very critical of the society that emerged in the mid-1990s. The reforms did not produce prosperity, but a devastated urban environment populated by a people who are almost numbed into dullness and routine. It would never dawn on the characters to resist or even criticize the degradations of their social lives; for them, it is just daily life, and the masses have no awareness of anything else. The possibilities for change have almost evaporated, but they live on in this unlikely hero—not as a psychological trait or as part of a powerful personality, but as a sense of how cultural life should be. The film contributes to a "Chinese way" by holding on to a shred of hope that a social life based on unity, connection, and concern still has a ghost of a chance.

Whether that social life should embrace gender equality at its most basic and generative level, however, is a question the film steadfastly declines to consider, taking for granted the belief that although all have been crushed into the same alienated and un-self-aware routine, which has narrowed their lives and robbed them of meaningful human communication, the power to break through this monotonous worldview resides only in men. Xiao Dou is not a well-developed hero like Lei Feng, but his ability to perceive and act out a story of social improvement is a perspective that no longer exists for women. In *The Postman* we see that the all-important space of social invention is, without question or comment, gendered as male.

Overall, *The Postman* offers an interesting take on the long historical discourse of consciousness, subjectivity, revolutionary spirit, and spiritual civilization. Certainly Xiao Dou, like other members of the strange society depicted in the film, shows all the signs of severe spiritual depletion, and spiritual civilization seems to have disappeared from the face of the earth. The authority of cultural norm no longer exists in publicly recognized morality or ideology, but has been diffused into the spatial environment, turning the consciousness of Xiao Dou into a complex node through which difficult phenomena such as drug use, extramarital affairs, prostitution, and suicide must be filtered and organized for mediation and renewal. Although

Xiao Dou is far removed from actual revolutionary society, he becomes a bizarre spiritual visionary, a contemporary Lei Feng, devoid of the emotion of optimism but directed by its promise, who barely knows what he is doing. The diffusion of authority into space means that Xiao Dou has nothing to hang onto, and unlike the fictional characters Anchee or Ma Xiaojun, Xiao Dou is not motivated by a central love interest or passion. His experience is not related through the voice of an older, more knowing narrator like Wang Er. And unlike Maodi, he does not engage in multiple sexual encounters, although the spatial logic of *Wild Things* shows some similarity to that of *The Postman*. Because his sister, his sexual relationship, and his regular work cannot offer him a spiritual home, he becomes a pure and transparent point of negotiation, transformation, and regeneration.

In other words, Xiao Dou, living in non-revolutionary times, when no one even remembers the concept or importance of spiritual civilization, socially responsible values, or heroic and glorious work, is the most unlikely and in some ways the greatest envoy of revolutionary spirit. Xiao Dou's dour activism implies that recouping the aesthetic lifestyle or the emotive passion of revolutionary romanticism is not possible, necessary, or even desirable. With the possibility of heroism all but gone, what comes to the fore in Xiao Dou is a strong emphasis on the relationships that form the fabric of society. If we strip Lei Feng of the aesthetic and emotive components of revolutionary optimism that according to his diary drove him and also created the myth of Lei Feng, we can see this revolutionary stalwart as doing work that complements what Xiao Dou attempts. Whereas Lei Feng both served as an industrious model in study and work and labored physically to help people solve their daily life problems, Xiao Dou applies himself to the points where through their relationships, people express and enact their moral and spiritual values.

Conclusion

History and Literary Aesthetics in the Study of Modern Chinese Culture

Scholars of modern Chinese literature in the United States, like our colleagues in Western literatures, have for the past thirty or forty years worked under the influence of literary methodologies—critical theory, new historicism, cultural studies, and postcolonial theory—that demand a more historical, political, and contextualized approach than was required in the past, when literature was regarded as philological texts to be mined, from a biographical perspective that tells us about the author, or for its formal and aesthetic qualities. Although those of us working in Chinese literary studies may have come lately to this trend, we by now have succeeded in producing criticism that either explicitly or implicitly questions the value of the autonomous aesthetic and insists on broader contextualization.[1]

The conditions of modern Chinese literary study in the United States, however, are not exactly the same as those of Western literary studies; the differences have resulted in a greater shrinking of literature as an object of study than we see in corresponding fields in Western studies. This tendency is not determined solely by theoretical innovations, but results from interaction between trends in literary criticism and the particular position—

institutional and pedagogical as well as philosophical—of scholars working in modern Chinese literary studies. Indicative of these conditions is the oft-unremarked contextualization of Chinese literature within the larger field of literary studies and academic pedagogy as a literature unknown and unknowable to the extent that, unlike literatures written in Western languages, it can enter intellectual debate only with great difficulty.

Another seldom-recognized, mundane aspect of literary studies requires, simply, that a group of people purporting to be part of an intellectual cohort at least to some extent read the same texts and know the same histories, names, and dates. Intellectual intercourse depends upon these shared points of contact. The failure of Chinese literary studies—and by this I mean the study of Chinese literature—to successfully integrate with the larger field may to some extent be determined by persistent Eurocentrism, but also is formed by the (again mundane) demands of time and resources or, in other words, by both ideological and material concerns. Literary discourse, seemingly democratized, actually works under the same market model as, for example, eBay: all other auction sites are welcome to compete, but economies of scale mean that buyers want maximum exposure to sellers, and sellers want maximum exposure to buyers. Using the same website, speaking the same language, and knowing the same terminology are necessary conditions of any transaction. In approaches to literary study that demand inclusion of multiple literatures and cultures, this problem is often unrecognized and untheorized.

It becomes also "naturally" the case, then, that those literatures that are written in a Western language, along with their critical texts, more easily integrate into general literary study in the United States. This category includes not only the literatures of Europe, but also those of post-colonial cultures where a European language is the lingua franca of the educated. A second group consists of those literatures that have only a modern existence and are preceded by an unrecorded oral tradition, even though they are written in a non-Western language. Because those literatures and their critical commentary emerge from modern history, where developing imperialism, trade, and globalism mean that any number of themes and events will converge, the learning curve is not as steep as it is for those with substantial premodern textual pasts. The most difficult to "know"—to find interesting and necessary to understand—are modern literatures like those of China, which are radically non-Western, written in a non-alphabetic language, and possess a long and complex textual history. The scholarly practice of

Chinese literature criticism and pedagogy is influenced by this deep-seated alterity, which diminishes its presence within the critical and to a lesser extent, pedagogical field.

Is it any wonder that modern Chinese literary scholars working in the United States would respond even more vigorously than their counterparts in Western literary studies to both the theoretical mandates of the field and the true conditions of daily life by decreasing emphasis on the Chinese literary text or abandoning it entirely? A perpetual lack of knowledge about even basic specificities within Chinese literature and culture among both scholars outside the China field and students, along with the historicizing effects of critical trends in literary study, has encouraged the move away from the literary text, to the point that modern Chinese literature has become little more than a branch of historical studies in general. Although this discipline-dissolving tendency is typical of critical theory and cultural studies in many areas, its effect is heightened within modern Chinese literary studies.

This direction may open up new channels of communication with our colleagues in Western literary and cultural studies, but it also has some dire effects. Through our methodology, we deepen the tendency to regard Chinese literature as a special case, and mark Chinese literary study as a field within which foundational theoretical questions are unlikely to emerge. We implicitly support the hierarchy of literary studies that places literatures and literary discourses written in Western languages at the top, turning ourselves into commentators on these studies and carving out for ourselves a deeply subsidiary and derivative position. And as I argue below, we go against the persistent disciplinary strength that despite recent movement toward interdisciplinarity, continues to structure the American university.

Can neoformalism, or a closer focus on the way in which a text produces aesthetic meaning, be useful in rethinking our work? In this conclusion, which maps out the methodology I have used in this study, I argue that the answer is yes. Overall, an essentially historical approach has dampened the influence of our studies, turning them into applications of theory rather than allowing for the possibility of new theories. It has caused us to unwittingly participate in a myth of absolute equality—of texts, events, scholars, histories, traditions, and critiques—that glosses over the existent social and academic hierarchies assigning relative value. Lest anyone imagine that I am proposing that we return to the old days of New Criticism, when the text existed in a social vacuum, I suggest that even with such a refocusing, it is both possible and necessary to retain some of the most important aspects of critical theory, new historicism, and cultural studies. I am not arguing against historicization, but against allowing the logic of historical studies to completely replace aesthetic interpretation, which possesses its own unique ways of producing meaning.

CULTURAL STUDIES AND THE NEW HISTORICISM

In Europe and the United States, literature conceived of as an autonomous aesthetic object has been under attack almost since Kant's *Critique of Judgment* in 1790. More recently, the aesthetic approach to literature has been dissected by both new historicism, which has pulled the rug out from under any proposed value of isolated textual analysis, marking its proponents as old-fashioned romantics, and cultural studies, which leveled the playing field both horizontally and vertically, turning uncritical reference to the old high / low cultural binary into a telltale sign of the unhip. Postcolonial studies pointed out the confluence of aesthetic recognition and power, suggesting that aesthetic analysis either takes power relations for granted, or may even be complicit in maintaining oppression and exploitation through exclusion of aesthetic recognition. The erosion of disciplinary boundaries, a result of critical tendencies of the last half-century, has contributed to the challenge directed toward any implicit or inherent aesthetic judgment of a literary text.

New historicism gained fame through the work of Stephen Greenblatt, whose 1980s scholarship on Renaissance literature put the insights of Michel Foucault and others into a form that revolutionized the study of literature in the United States.[2] Greenblatt's work implied that the historical context of the text and its interaction with other texts and aspects of culture during the time of its production should take center stage in interpretation. New historicism, among other trends, is responsible for putting a nail in the coffin of the elite literary text, for from the perspective of historicity, all texts, events, and practices are equally important and deserving of analysis. To claim otherwise is to fall victim to the obfuscating bourgeois mystification of art, aesthetics, and genius.

Critics of the so-called historicist turn in literary studies, which occurred about the same time as the linguistic or discursive turn in historical studies, have protested the tendency of new historicism to turn literature into a footnote of history. Befuddling to many is the fact that despite their claim that all texts / artifacts are equal, the new historicists tended to spend their time on literary classics or the recognized canon of literary works, digging out subsidiary cultural texts and artifacts to support their interpretation of these canonical texts (Bate 1991, 58: Chandler 2000).[3] Although the critical core of new historicism may contain kernels of contradiction that produce this situation, the reason also may be quite pedestrian: the labor involved in developing a new theoretical position and approach may be best deployed if one works on texts already at least somewhat familiar to one's audience, which will have an immediately understood context within which to evaluate a revisionary methodology. Interpretations and readings of any given text or author's oeuvre, after all, accrue only slowly, and the time and effort required to master those interpretations and readings will go unrecognized if a scholar not only develops a new approach, but also chooses a completely unknown text, especially one written in a little-studied language for which no translation exists.

Cultural studies has provided an even more serious blow to any emphasis on literature, and an attractive model for scholars of modern Chinese literature, for whom it contains not only a method that allows them to join in with their colleagues in other areas, but also a political weapon that nicely overlaps with multiculturalism's critique of Eurocentrism.[4] In her defense of formal analysis as a deeper investigation into the political than what the apparently relevant cultural studies has provided, Elizabeth Maddock Dillon explains how this works, noting that cultural studies, through its construction of the critic as heroically political, thoroughly condemned formal literary criticism as "having no purchase on the facticity of the world" (Dillon 1998, 46). In literary scholarship in the United States, Dillon states, "culture" refers to what lies outside the text, or "*context* in opposition to text" (49). The implication and rhetoric of political commitment, as well as the positioning of the critic as a heroic agent, are what gives cultural studies its power. Concern about political efficacy has pulled critics far away from aesthetic analysis, challenging the very category of literature and, even when the category is allowed, insisting that aesthetic analysis can provide only a limited contribution to the greater and more significant historical and political themes. As Henry Giroux, David Shumway, Paul Smith, and James Sosnoski (1984) claim in their cultural studies manifesto, "In the context of Cultural Studies it will not be appropriate simply to generate idiosyncratic interpretations of cultural artifacts. The most important aim of a counter-disciplinary practice is radical social change."[5] While cultural studies as a field goes much farther than new historicism in its claim to political engagement, both move away from aesthetic analysis.[6]

Cultural studies opened a space for postcolonial studies. With the publication of *Orientalism* in 1978, Edward Said drew attention to the way in which the West had constructed a self-serving vision of Asia and Asians. In her article "Can the Subaltern Speak?," Gayatri Chakravorty Spivak (1988) called attention to the fact that postcolonial studies was made up of Western or Western-trained intellectuals, who tended to reinscribe their own interpretations and concerns on the economically dispossessed, robbing them of a voice and cooperating with imperialism. Both Said and Spivak emphasized the ideological and political in their approaches, and both were strongly concerned with social justice in their critiques. To look at the same problem from another perspective, although postcolonial studies enlarged the geographical space of literary discourse, bringing in—if perhaps problematically—the histories and cultures of countries colonized or formerly colonized by European countries, it paradoxically also expanded the influence of literatures written in European languages. China, never truly colonized, did not restructure its education of elites so that they learned in English, French, or German, and thereby Chinese culture has been only peripherally involved in the postcolonial debate.[7]

THE STUDY OF MODERN CHINESE LITERATURE AND THE TYRANNY OF HISTORY

For many scholars of modern Chinese literature in the United States, cultural studies came as a welcome relief, for it has allowed them to rein in their (tiresome) explanations about writers who are obscure in the West, and to simultaneously integrate their scholarship within the larger trends of the intellectual field. Educated audiences, or scholars who may know a great deal about "theory" and European literary traditions but little about China, are much more willing and able to handle material espoused primarily historically and theoretically rather than with a focus on the specifics of Chinese writers or their novels. For Chinese literary specialists working in the American university, the development of theoretically sound arguments, which is the main benefit of critical theory and cultural studies, became easier when one approached Chinese culture as an example that could fit in with an already well-recognized interpretive trend. Scholarship is more likely to be read by scholars outside the field if the literary text is dealt with quickly and without excessive detail, or is completely abandoned in favor of cultural forms (such as film) that travel more readily.

However, the organization of the university in the United States has been open to the approaches of the new humanities only to a limited degree, a reality that also may partially explain why new historians emphasized canonical texts. American universities basically are divided into disciplines, inter-disciplinary programs, and area studies programs. Despite the challenge to disciplinary purity posed by cultural studies within humanities and social science fields, the most powerful site of the university remains the discipline.[8] In literature this site is generally the English department; even within the larger realm of cultural studies, most scholars are nonetheless first located within a discipline: history, classics, anthropology, philosophy, and so on. Part of the reason for this situation may be simply inertia or the tendency of scholars toward self-reproduction. Another reason could be the depth of specialization within disciplines, which now requires years of dedicated study to master—although from the perspective of the cultural studies scholar, that very specialization is but one manifestation of disciplinary reification. A third reason may be that interdisciplinary work makes little sense unless it is grounded in strong disciplines, which provide enough methodological focus to bring coherence and rigor to the research. Whatever the reasons, disciplines, especially those with a discrete if changing body of foundational texts and a historically developed methodology, have stubbornly maintained a position of strength within the modern American university.

The study of Chinese literature generally has been located in a hybrid department, often a department called East Asian Languages and Literatures—that includes professors teaching language, linguistics, literature, and, more recently, film—or East Asian Cultures / Civilizations, which includes the affiliation of professors whose home departments are history, political science, or another discipline-based field. Some universities also have experimented with large literature departments that include the literatures of many cultures, just as history departments now include professors working in various histories albeit generally with a strong concentration in American or European histories. Because such departments place together literatures and those who study them with little historical or linguistic connection (although such programs may inspire disciplinary strength), they create their own problems, namely the lack of organic connection between disparate cultures and scholars who teach and research in these cultures.[9] By contrast, area or national / cultural language and literature departments offer a compromise between a disciplinary approach and an area study approach; they offer some emphasis on literature as a discipline, and some emphasis on area knowledge in the form of language training. Chinese majors in these departments often pick up other China-related courses, such as history or anthropology, as part of their university general education requirements, thus crafting for themselves an even greater focus on China.

Scholars in departments of Romance or Germanic languages and literatures work under similar situations, but their location within the European tradition links them to other scholars working in Western literatures. Their ability to substantially interact with other literary scholars is greater because they often have a strong understanding of the histories and literatures of not only European nations but also—as I explain above—nations once colonized by European nations, where the language of the educated is a European language. That category includes a great deal of the world: parts of Africa, South America, Mexico, Central America, India, Canada, New Zealand, North America, Australia, Sri Lanka, Bangladesh, Pakistan, and so on. The oft-used category of "non-Western" takes on a narrower meaning when viewed in this context, and it often splits the post-colonial nation into the camps of the educated, who speak a Western language, and the non-educated, who speak an "indigenous" language.

In her recent book on sex and prostitution in China, Elaine Jeffreys (2004) strongly criticizes China scholars for a number of research tendencies, several of which are relevant for my argument in spite of the fact that Jeffreys' main target is not literature specialists, but historians and anthropologists. Jeffreys singles out China scholars' reliance on linguistic skill and special knowledge to gain academic capital and present themselves as the only qualified interpreters of China; their privileging of the native voice that comes through those linguistic channels, often through anecdote; their ready acceptance and promotion of a naïve state-vs.-intellectuals structure; their rejection of the Chinese intellectuals—and texts, reports, or explanations by non-intellectuals—as positivistic and naïve; and their tendency to regard China as a special case. Following research by Gloria Davies (1992, 1998, 2000a, 2000b), Jeffreys criticizes the complex relationship between critical theory and the field of Chinese studies. Davies suggests that the implications of scholarship in Chinese area and language studies are rarely seriously questioned by Chinese scholars, and that within this context, the radical possibilities of critical theory have been tamed by simple application. Taking off from this insight, Jeffreys proposes that reliance on critical theory has caused China scholars to absolve themselves of the need to continually analyze the assumptions of their studies; instead of incitement to radical questioning, critical theory basically has functioned as a tool, "to be borrowed and used" (27). Scholars have tended, therefore, to uncritically reproduce categories and interpretations popular within Western academic circles, while dismissing the analyses of Chinese intellectuals themselves as unsophisticated.

Some contradictions inform Jeffreys's work. For example, she (2004) approves of Rey Chow's claim that cultural studies is correct in its attack on critical theory, that is, that it forces writers to "continue to center on the West" despite its claim to radical heterogeneity—a slight supposedly corrected by cultural studies' emphasis on postcoloniality, race, and power.[10] Jeffreys argues that the relative marginalization of Chow's work within the field of modern Chinese literature / culture is a result of the continued emphasis on digging out knowledge about China—in other words, regarding China studies as an "extended recitation of Chinese language sources or information derived from in-house fieldwork" (65). She also notes, however, that Chow may have marginalized herself through "her desire to be affiliated with the more fashionable and theory-informed fields of postcolonial and cultural studies" (66). Despite what is overall a favorable take on the position Chow has adopted, Jeffreys points out that those who have become known as theorists within Chinese studies have had virtually no impact on the "broader disciplinary space of the new humanities" (66). Finally, while rejecting the claim that critical theory is Eurocentric, Jeffreys questions the "automatic privileging of post-structuralism–deconstruction on the grounds that it is theoretically superior" (27). At the same time, she demands that Chinese scholars deploy critical theory in a way that liberates its radical possibilities.

Although Jeffreys's criticisms are thought-provoking, the contradictions inherent in her work point to thorny problems within the field.[11] Nonetheless, although Jeffreys does not specifically address scholarship on modern Chinese literature, I have taken a short detour through her work because she has directly stated a reality of the field: research on Chinese literature, even by the theoretically savvy, is of little influence in the larger field of literary or cultural theory. From my perspective, this situation is not so much a choice or a misapplication of critical theory as it is the result of confluences that define the field. Although Jeffreys may not be satisfied with the efforts of China scholars, they have indeed followed the model she promotes, imagining that their new methodologies—fully in line with the major directions of intellectual discourse—will liberate the radical political and cultural potential of their research, not to mention gain for them a place within the global intellectual sphere. Inherent in this model is the implicit downgrading of any emphasis on aesthetics as politically useless and therefore trivial. The combination of this theoretical focus and its proclaimed ideology—political efficacy—with the specific conditions of our field has determined the derivative relationship between Chinese and Western literary scholars working in the United States.

NEO-FORMALISM AND THE POSSIBILITIES OF STYLE

The approaches developed through critical theory, which have functioned as a corrective to an emphasis on the internal workings of the text promoted by New Criticism and an earlier yet still active biographical approach to the life of the writer, have radically altered the way we think about literature. Broadly speaking, both critical theory and cultural studies have moved the literary text away from its former definition as a product of genius and an essential aspect of the training of elites, putting it instead within a larger social and ideological context where it now jostles for attention with other cultural practices. They have historicized and shaken up a number of unrecognized but implicitly accepted categories, including not only "literature," but also representations of the nation-state, the dichotomy of the sexes, gender roles, racial stereotypes, and so on.

Nonetheless, scholars recently have begun to question the thorough rejection of aesthetic formalism and challenge the implications of that rejection. While promoting the benefits of cultural studies, some have discussed the practical difficulties of cultural studies as it translates into academic pedagogy and organization within the university, thus speaking to both its underlying premises and the near-impossibility of meeting the challenges it poses. One example of this latter form of scholarship is the collection *Aesthetics in a Multicultural Age* (Elliott, Caton, and Rhyne 2002). In his introduction, subtitled "Cultural Diversity and the Problem of Aesthetics," Emory Elliott (2002) sums up the effects critical theory, new historicism, and cultural studies have had on the humanities: "A new philosophical skepticism has questioned the epistemological foundations of judgment, arguing that all critical standards in the arts are constructed from within certain limited ideologies" (5). Elliott questions whether it is wise or even possible to relinquish any positive notion of the aesthetic, however; instead, he advocates that professors "educate ourselves more fully and energetically in the languages and cultures of those parts of the world whose aesthetic contributions are now understood to be part of the culture of the United States, [so that] we will be much more competent to demonstrate to our students why texts by authors who are of African, Asian, and Hispanic descent are as rich and aesthetically pleasing as they are" (16). I hardly need to point out the practical and theoretical problems with this agenda.

In another article in the same collection, John Carlos Rowe (2002) confronts item by item the various objections to cultural studies, in the process indicating some of the difficulties of the approach. Rowe begins by noting that many scholars criticize cultural studies, "condemning its impossible scope, failure to define its key terms, lack of theoretical self-consciousness, historical ignorance, the 'easiness' of its topics for teaching and research, obsession with 'relevance,' reflex treatment of 'race, class, and gender,' and refusal to read *carefully*" (105).[12] Both Rowe and Elliott single out a central problem of cultural studies in the university: although it provides no criteria for selecting certain literary texts above others, pedagogy makes such selection mandatory. We can easily see that careful inclusion and exclusion is necessary not only in the ten- or fifteen-week course, but also in library purchases and, of course, in research, which is hardly an endeavor that floats free from temporal, political, or economic considerations. A second issue, that of scope, is so overwhelming that Rowe (2002) admits that when he decided to write on a 1854 novel by John Rollin Ridge (also known as Yellow Bird), he found himself "swamped with historical legends, texts, and data from several different historical registers: the history of the Cherokee tribe, its relations with the U.S. government, California in transition from Mexican to U.S. rule, the Gold Rush, Spanish and Latin recyclings of the Murieta legend, and so forth" (109). In short, Rowe comments, whereas the canonical text may imply unjustifiable aesthetic judgments, the noncanonical text demands justification, and "since that justification rarely can be made in terms of the 'universal value' of noncanonical or popular / mass market texts, then the argument must be *profoundly, irreducibly historical*" (109, my emphasis).

Most directly addressing the problems that cultural studies methodology has raised for literary criticism is the previously mentioned Americanist Elizabeth Maddock Dillon (1998), who describes the dilemma in this way:

> I begin with what we might call a bipolar disturbance in literary criticism. Caught between the materialism of cultural studies and the formalism of philosophy, literary criticism is construed, on the one hand, as useless—struck dumb by its lack of purpose in the face of real politics and real bodies—and, on the other hand, as singularly efficacious, the only tool through which to reveal the essentially discursive character of all forms of culture, including bodies and politics . . . This "disturbance," as I've described it, tends to be acted out as a debilitating dialectic: caught between formalism and materialism, literary criticism is left without any ground to stand on. Yet this peculiar bipolarity within literary criticism is intimately linked to the strange status of literature itself. Language becomes recognizably literary at the moment it assumes a rhetorical or formal dimension rather than serving as the invisible conduit of mimetic representation. (46)

Suggesting that we should "examine form as itself culturally enacted or staged," Dillon refers to Fredric Jameson's understanding of form as inseparable from history or materiality and thus the "bearer of political and historical meaning" (47). Arguing that the unifying marker of cultural studies is its rhetoric of political commitment, Dillon shows how alluring the field is to literary critics, who desperately want to avoid banishment to their useless disciplines and exclusion from the "'real' world of politics" (48–49). Yet Dillon directs us back to the formal, aesthetic qualities of the text as the most important element of this task: "the aesthetic may be most political in its formal dimensions, that is, in the forms that it deploys which aim toward the production of coherent political subjects" (67). As I noted earlier in this chapter, Dillon's criticism of cultural studies (in this case, like the New Americanist criticism of Donald Pease and others) is that "politics has been located in the context rather than the text, or alternatively, in the heroic agency of the literary critic," which is expressed as a liberatory political force (67).

In a second study of the relationships between sentimental literature and aesthetics, Dillon (2004) suggests another approach that can mediate between aesthetics and cultural studies: offering a "more thorough-going account of aesthetics as a political and cultural practice" (497). An examination of the history or genealogy of aesthetics hardly amounts to aesthetic or formal analysis but is, rather, the historicizing of the problem of aesthetics;

even so, Dillon's research on aesthetics in Kant and Schiller addresses what she calls a broader contemporary problem: ". . . either the aesthetic assists in breaking free of social structure and is located radically outside of and beyond oppressive social norms, or it covertly functions to enforce normativity by masking the operations of power, helping to lodge ideology in the hearts and minds of docile subjects" (504). In the 20th century, Dillon notes, aesthetics has been thought of as either a form of ideology or a site of emancipation from ideology (516). Without directly coming down in favor of more aesthetic analysis or an approach to aesthetics that somehow breaks free of these limitations, Dillon suggests that this "dream of the outside—of a location beyond social and cultural control" may have an important function within contemporary culture (516).

It is difficult to get around the confusion that Dillon's discussion both identifies and embodies. Today, few would deny that aesthetic forms have political significance. An approach that reads how a literary text produces the believing and acting subject may have no choice but to come down on the side of (1) ideology or (2) emancipation from ideology. But it does not seem too far-fetched to suggest first that, although the aesthetic authority of a text may be socially embedded, it nonetheless functions as an aesthetic text within a specific social and historical environment. Recognizing that the literary qualities of a text may imbue it with the power to influence and create ways of thinking and subjectivities does not equal a belief in the universal aesthetic. Neither does it equal pure ideology or the tracing of either progressive politics or "false consciousness." Whether aesthetic meaning could or should become more central to our work depends on our ability to balance the analytical approaches offered by art and ideology, rather than to side wholeheartedly with one or the other.

MODERN CHINESE LITERARY STUDIES IN THE CONTEMPORARY AMERICAN UNIVERSITY

Taken together, Dillon's two articles provide a strong critique of the ideological underpinnings of cultural studies and offer a way to think about a more concentrated focus on the aesthetics of the literary text. At the same time, her research clearly has been the beneficiary of the historical contextualization demanded by the new historicism and cultural studies. As I consider the position of modern Chinese literary studies within the university today,

I would not wish to give up the advantages critical theory, new historicism, and cultural studies have conferred on the field and on my own reflections about literature, and I clearly have not done so in this highly historical book. The situating of literature within a social and ideological context has led to positive transformations, allowing modern Chinese literature specialists to emerge from their enclosed space of well-trained Sinological experts and opening for them the possibility of interacting with national and international trends in literary studies. While Chinese literature experts have had to modify or at least not press the claim to special knowledge that their linguistic skills and historical / cultural training have provided, they have gained the excitement of participating in literary and cultural debates in much broader environment.

The problem is not that critical theory and cultural studies have been without benefit, but rather, that if they had affected modern Chinese literary studies in the way they have Western literary studies, their influence would have been at least as positive as it has been elsewhere. It is precisely in Western studies, however, that a renewed emphasis on aesthetics, or neoformalism, has been proposed, indicating that even where disciplinary boundaries, the canon, and the very idea of the literary have retained the most strength, critics are dissatisfied with their fields as they have developed. I have argued that the combination of cultural studies with historical disciplinary / area studies developments within the American university and with the radical alterity of Chinese language and culture has inched Chinese literary studies even farther away from aesthetic analysis than is the case within Western literary studies. Although the benefits of the new approaches have been realized, literature as a discipline has lost a great deal of ground, removing from Chinese literary studies one important power base—that of the discipline—within the university.

Although I have welcomed some of the emphasis on the "real world" that cultural studies has provided, I have a few other gnawing doubts about its methodologies, doubts that are relevant to the actual conditions under which we work, both in teaching and in research. First, many or most of the undergraduate students who participate in Chinese literature courses often lack even a basic understanding of what has happened in China over the 20th century, which would seem to be a necessary background to begin a study of literature. Along with the other pressures on the study of literature that I have detailed above, my courses slowly became increasingly historical, encouraged by similar tendencies within the field and aimed at making up for this knowledge deficit. Students read less literature and more "theory," fewer primary texts and more secondary material. Only by abandoning a full explanation of the historical and cultural background of the texts I was teaching have I been able to produce for students the time and ability to fully analyze the literary text.[13]

A second concern is perhaps more far-reaching and significant. Dillon calls into question the imagined / vaunted heroic agency of the cultural studies critic who is responsible for changing the world. While she narrows in on the scholar and teacher, my concern is with the position that cultural studies, with its impossibly wide scope of history and context, constructs for the student. When academic pedagogy goes too far in imagining the world as text, it implies not that formal learning will give students basic tools with which to approach the much more complex, much more befuddling nature of lived reality, but rather that within their studies they are in fact already encountering the world. To take this position to an extreme, such a situation shrinks the world to something much more manageable and comprehensible than it actually is, without recognizing that it is doing so. I have become increasingly dissatisfied with the arrogance of this implication, feeling that a more guarded and less heroic conception of the value and meaning of formal education, along with a recognition of the ultimate density, interest, and complexity of social and material phenomena, would put students in a much better position.

Chinese and Japanese Character List

"90 niandai Zhongguo dianying de kongjian xiangxiang"
90年代中國電影的空間想象
A Q 70 nian 阿 Q 70 年
A Q zhengzhuan 阿Q 正傳
Ah Cheng 阿城
Ai Qing 艾青
Ai Xiaoming 艾曉明
Aiguo xueshi she 愛國學識社
anshi 暗示
Anyi 王安億

Bai Hua 白樺
Bai Xiaoyi 白小藝
Bai Ye 白燁
Baiyangdian 白洋澱
Beijing daxue rikan 北京大學日刊
Beijing daxue xuebao 北京大學學報
Beijing langgang 北京浪綱
Beijing shifan daxue 北京師範大學
Beijing shifan xueyuan 北京師範學堂
Beijing zazhong 北京雜種
benneng 本能
"Biantai xinlixue" 變態心理學
biaoxian 表現
"Bu keneng de yuyan: jingshen fenxi huo xinli fenxi"
不可能的語言：精神分析或心理分析
Buli 布禮

"Butian" 補天
Buzhou shan 不周山

Can Xue 殘雪
"Canqun" 殘春
Cao Richang 曹日昌
Cao Yanming 曹燕明
Cao Zefu 曹澤夫
"Chaoyue xiuzhixin wenhua" 超越羞恥心文化
Chen Daqi 陳大齊
Chen Derong 陳德榮
Chen Fuxing 陳傅興
Chen Guangsheng 陳廣生
Chen Hongmou 陳宏謀
Chen Huang 陳榥
Chen Huangmei 陳荒煤
Chen Jieren 陳界仁
Chen Kaige 陳凱歌
Chen Lifu 陳立夫
Chen Qingyang 陳清揚
Chen Qiwei 陳啓偉
Chen Ran 陳染
Chen Xianghong 陳翔鶴
Chen Xiaoming 陳曉明
Chen Yinke de zuihou ershi nian 陳寅恪的最後二十年
Chen Zhengyang 陳振陽
Chen Zhonggeng 陳仲庚
Cheng Hao 程灝
Cheng Naiyi 程迺頤
Cheng Yi 程頤
"Chenlun" 沉淪
Chi Li 池莉
Chong You 崇有
"Chongdu *Huangjin shidai*" 重讀黃金時代
"Chongshuo *Huangjin shidai*" 重說"黃金時代"
Chu Zhi 楚之
Chuangzao shi 創造社
"Chudu *Huangjin shidai*" 初讀黃金時代

chugoku jin ki 中国人气
"Chunyang" 春陽
Cong shanghen wenxue dao xungen wenxue: wenge hou shinian de dalu wenxue liupai
從傷痕文學到尋根文學：文革后十年的大陸文學流派
"Cong 'xiangtu' dao 'xungen': wenxue xiandaixing de san da liubian"
從"鄉土"到"尋根"：文學現代性的三大流變
Cong xinlixue de guandian kan gexing wenti 從心理學的觀點看個性問題
congxiao kanda 從小看大
Cui Wei 崔嵬

Da hong denglong gaogao gua 大紅燈籠高高挂
Da Mayi 大螞蟻
Da Zhang Jingsheng xiansheng 答張競生先生
Da Zhou Jianren xiansheng 'Guanyu Xingshi de jiju hua'
答周建人先生 關於性史的幾句話
Dachou 大丑
Dai Er 黛二
Dai Houying 戴厚英
Dai Jinhua 戴錦華
Dalu 大陸
Dangdai dianying 當代電影
"Dangdai wenxue zhong de 'chunjie' quxiang yu 'diceng' yishi"
當代文學中的"純"取向與"底層"意識
Dangdai xifang sixiang xianhe: shijiu shiji de sixiangjia
當代西方思想先河：十九世紀的思想家
Dangdai zuojia pinglun 當代作家評論
daode 道德
Dayanr 大眼兒
Deng Ziqi 鄧子奇
Dengzhou shuyuan 登州書院
Di Kaowen 狄考文
dian 癲
Dianying wenxue yuekan 電影文學月刊
Dianying yishu 電影藝術
Ding Dong 丁東
Ding Ling 丁玲
Ding Weiliang 丁韙良
Ding Wenjiang 丁文江

"Diyi shou mengzhong de shige: guanyu Jiang Wen de *Yangguang canlan de rizi*"
第一手夢中的詩歌：慣於姜文的 陽光燦爛的日子
Dongfang zazhi 東方雜誌
Donggong xigong 東宮西宮
"Dongwu xiongmeng" 動物兇猛
Du Weiming 杜維明
Du Yaquan 杜亞泉

Ermo 二嫫

Falun Gong 法輪功
fan jingshen wuran yundong 反精神污染運動
Fan Yuanlian 范源濂
Fang Dongshu 方東樹
Fangzhou 方舟
fanshe 反射
fanxing zhuyi 凡性主義
fei dazhong 非大衆
Fei Min 斐民
Feidu 廢都
"Feizao" 肥皂
feng 瘋
"Fenxi xinlixue" 分析心理學
"Fuluode de yin yishi yu xinlixue" 福魯德的隱意識與心理學
"Fuluote xin xinlixue zhi yiban" 弗洛特新心理學之一斑
Fuluote xinlixue fenxi 弗洛特心理學分析
Fuluoyide xinlixue quanji biaojun ban 弗洛伊德心理學全集標準版
"Fuluoyite ji qi jingshen fenxi de pipan" 弗洛伊特及其精神分析的批判

"Gaige kaifang, tansuo chuangxin: guanyu xin shiqi dianying de lishi jiyi"
改革開放，探索創新：關於新時期電影的歷史記憶
Gao Juefu 高覺敷
"Gao Juefu jiaoshou fangtan lu" 高覺敷教授訪談錄
Gao Qinghai 高清海
Gao Zhuo 高卓
Ge Fei 格非
geming 革命
Geming jingshen xiuyang 革命精神修養
Geming shiqi de aiqing 革命時期的愛情

Geming wenyi yu dazhong wenyi 革命文藝與大衆文藝
Gong Zizhen 龔自珍
gongye xinlixue 工業心理學
gongzuo 工作
Gu Yanwu 顧炎武
"Guan 'lingxue'" 闢"靈學"
"Guanghui de xingxiang" 光輝的形象
Guangming wang 光明网
Guangxu 光緒
"Guanyu wuzhi wenming yu jingshen wenming de jige lilun wenti" 關於物質文明與精神文明的幾個理論問題
"Guanyu Xingshi de jiju hua" 關於性史的幾句話
"Guanyu xinlixue de duixiang wenti" 關於心理學的對象問題
"Guihun youdang de dadi: Lu Xun bixia de nongcun shijie" 鬼魂遊蕩的大地：魯迅筆下的農村世界
Gulunmu 古輪牧
guo 國
Guo Moruo 郭沫若
Guo Xuebo 郭雪波
Guofeng 國風
guohun 國魂
Guomin jingshen zong dongyuan hui mishu chu 國民精神總動員會秘書處
"Guxiang" 故乡

Han Keli 韓藹麗
Han Shaogong 韓少功
Hanshu 漢書
haose 好色
Hattori Unokichi 服部宇之吉
He Chun 何群
He Huaihong 何懷宏
He Jianjun 何建軍
He Jixian 何吉賢
He Yi 何一
"Hebian de cuowu" 河邊的錯誤
Hong Feng 洪峰
Hongdou 紅豆

Honglou meng 紅樓夢
http://past_journal.mnd.gov.tw/
後備部學術季刊/mag64/中共精神動員研究.htm
Hu Qiaomu 胡喬木
Hu Ren 胡人
Huacheng 花城
Huadong shifan daxue Zhongguo xiandai sixiang yanjiusuo
華東師範大學中國現代思想研究所
Huainanzi 淮南子
hualian 化煉
Huang Guangxue 黃光學
Huang Jianxin 黃建新
Huang Jianzhong 黃健中
Huang Jiwe 黃集偉
Huang Xiangjiu 黃香久
Huang Yuanyong 黃遠庸
Huang Zongxi 黃宗羲
Huangdi neijing 黃帝內經
Huangjin shidai 黃金時代
Huangni jie 黃泥街
Huanzhou 幻洲
Hudie de weixiao 蝴蝶的微笑
Huigu xuexi Lei Feng huodong de qiyuan he fazhan
回顧學雷鋒活動的起源和發展
hun 魂

Jia Pingwa 賈平凹
Jiang Guozhong 蔣國忠
Jiang Lei 姜磊
Jiang Qing 江青
Jiang Wen 姜文
jiaoyu ke 教育科
Jiaoyu xinlixue 教育心理学
Jiaoyu zazhi 教育雜誌
Jiefang jun huabao she 解放軍畫報社
"Jieji youai shen" 階級友愛深
"Jiexin shu xueshuo" 解心術學說
Jin Ping Mei 金瓶梅

Jin Yong 金庸
"'Jin Yong ti Lu Xun' re zhengyi, Jin Yong luoxuan Beijing gaokao
"金庸替鲁迅"惹争议 金庸落选北京高中课本
jindai 近代
jing 精
jingshen 精神
jingshen bing 精神病
jingshen bingxue 精神病學
jingshen caifu 精神財富
Jingshen dongyuan 精神動員
jingshen fayu buquan 精神發育不全
jingshen fenlie zheng 精神分裂症
jingshen fenxi 精神分析
jingshen fenxi meixue 精神分析美學
jingshen fenxi xue 精神分析學
Jingshen fenxi yinlun 精神分析引論
Jingshen fenxi yu weiwuguan shiguan 精神分析與唯物史觀
Jingshen fenxi yu Zhong Xi wenxue 精神分析與中西文學
jingshen jingjie 精神境界
jingshen liaofa 精神療法
jingshen shenghuo 精神生活
"Jingshen shenghuo gao yu wuzhi shenghuo—ping Chen Ding tongzhi de xingfu guan" 精神生活高於物質生活— 評陳丁同志的幸福觀
jingshen shengli fa 精神勝利法
jingshen shuairuo zheng 精神衰弱症
jingshen wanneng lun 精神萬能論
jingshen weisheng 精神衛生
jingshen wenming 精神文明
Jingshen wenming cidian 精神文明辭典
jingshen wuneng lun 精神無能論
jingshen wuran 精神污染
"'Jingshen' yao xue, shiqing yao zuo" "精神"要學，事情要做
jingshen yaowu 精神藥物
jingshen zhengtai 精神狀態
Jingshi daxue xinlixue daxue xinlixue jiangyi 京師大學心理學講義

kaozheng 考證
koushi 口失

kuang 狂
Kuang Xinnian 曠新年
Kubota Sadanori 久保田貞則
Kumen de xiangwei 苦悶的象徵
Kuriyagawa Hakuson 廚川白村

Lailai wangwang 來來往往
Lan Ping 蘭萍
Langman qishi: jiyi Wang Xiaobo 浪漫騎士：記憶王小波
Lanyi she 藍衣社
Lao Wu 老吳
laodong 勞動
laodong xinlixue 勞動心理學
Laoji jiuti—xinlixue yidai zongshi Gao Juefu 老驥奮蹄—心理學一代宗師高覺敷
Lei Feng 雷鋒
Lei Feng jingshen 雷鋒精神
"Lei Feng jingshen de daode jiazhi shi yongcun de" 雷鋒精神的道德價值是永存的
Lei Feng shi de yingmo 雷鋒式的英模
Lei Feng xiaozhuan 雷鋒小傳
Li Jianwu 李健吾
Li Jinming 黎錦明
Li Peng 李蓬
Li Tuo 李陀
Li Xiaojiu 李小九
Li Xun 李迅
Li Yinhe 李銀河
Li Zehou 李澤厚
Li Zhi 李贄
Li Zhixi 李之熙
Liang Qichao 梁啓超
Liang Shuming 梁漱溟
"Liang Shuming weiyi de waiguo pengyou—Wei Xiqin" 梁漱溟唯一的外國朋友—衛西琴
liangneng 良能
Liangyuan 亮圓
Lianhe bao fukan 聯合報副刊

Lianhe wenxue 聯合文學
Lin Biao 林彪
Lin Daojing 林道靜
Lin Ruji 林如稷
Ling rou hao (靈肉號)
"Ling yizhi erduo de qiaoji sheng" 另一只耳朵的敲擊聲
linghun靈魂
"Lishi hua yu yuyan: Jiemusun meixue lilun pingxu"
歷史話語寓言：傑姆孫美學理論評析
Liu Chengjie 劉成傑
Liu Jihui 劉紀蕙
Liu Naou 劉吶鷗
Liu Shushen 劉書忱
Liu Sitian 劉思甜
Liu Suola 劉索拉
Liu Yiku 劉憶苦
Liu Zaifu 劉再復
Liumang wenxue 流氓文學
liuyin 六淫
Lixing she 力行社
Lu Erke 禄爾克
Lu Jiachuan 盧嘉川
Lu Jiandong 陸鍵東
Lu Ling 路翎
Lu Taiguang 魯太光
Lu Xun 魯迅
Lü Yin 盧隱
Lun Lei Feng—1963–1990 xue Lei Feng huigu yu zhanwang lilun zhuotan hui wenji
論雷鋒—1963–1990學雷鋒回顧與展望理論座談會論文集
"Lun minqi yu guojia zhi guanxi" 論民氣與國家之關係
"Lun Zhongguo minqi zhi keyong" 論中國民氣之可用
"Lun Zhongguo minzi shuairuo zhi you" 論中國民氣衰弱之由
Lunli 倫理
Lunlixue yu jingshen wenming 倫理學與精神文明
Luoma dazhan 羅馬大戰
luosiding jingshen 鑼絲釘精神

Ma Nan 馬南

Ma Xiaojun 馬小軍
Ma Yuan 馬原
Mai Dazhuang 麥大壯
Mai Feng 麥鳳
Mai Laozhu 麥老珠
Mai Wang 麥旺
Mai Youcai 麥有才
Malisun xuetang 馬禮遜學堂
Maluo shi lishuo" 摩羅詩力說
Mang Ke 芒克
Mangjing 盲井
Manyan 蔓延
"Manzhi huangtang yan" 滿紙荒唐言
Mao Dun 矛盾
Mao zhuxi de hao zhanshi: Lei Feng 毛主席的好戰士：雷鋒
Maodi 毛地
"Maodun lun" 矛盾論
Meiqing 梅青
"Meng zhi yanjiu" 夢之研究
Mengyang xuetang 蒙養學堂
Mi Jiaqi 祕家起
Milan 米蘭
ming 名
minqi 民氣
minzu 民族
minzu jingshen 民族精神
minzu xinli 民族心理
minzu xinlixue 民族心理學
Mo Yan 莫言
Mu Shiying 穆時英

Nahan 吶喊
Nanfang ribao 南方日報
Nanren de yiban shi nüren 男人的一半是女人
neibu 內部
neibu faxing 內部發行
"Nongcun de 'faxian' he 'yanmo': 20 shiji Zhongguo wenxue shiye zhong de nongcun" 農村的'發現'和'淹沒'：20世紀中國文學事業中的農村

nongcun, nongmin, nongye 農村，農民，農業
nongcun shijiao 農村視角

pai 派
Paihuai de youling: Fuluoyide zhuyi yu Zhongguo ershi shiji wenxue
徘徊的幽靈：弗洛伊德主義與中國二十世紀文學
Pan Hannian 潘漢年
Pan Shu 潘菽
Peng Kang 彭康
Peng Wen 彭文
Peng Xiaoling 彭小苓
pi-dou-gai 批鬥改
"Pipan xinlixue de zichan jieji fangxiang" 批判心理學的資產階級方向
"Piping Fuluoyide de sixiang" 批評弗洛伊德的思想
po 魄
poxie 破鞋

qi 氣
Qi Zhirong 祁志榮
Qian Xingcun 錢杏邨
qian xinshi 潛心識
Qian Zhixiu 錢智修
Qian Zhongshu 錢鍾書
Qianxing yishi 潛性逸事
Qilu daxue 齊魯大學
qing 情
qingchun 青春
qingchun wuhui 青春無悔
"Qingchun yongyuan shi meihao de—chongdu *Lei Feng riji*"
青春永遠是美好的—重讀"雷鋒日記"
Qingchun zhige 青春之歌
qingnian 青年
Qiqie chengqun 妻妾成群
qiqing 七情
"Qiren wulun" 齊人物論
qun 群

Ren, a, ren 人阿人
"Ren de zhengque sixiang shi cong nali laide"
人的正確思想是從哪裏來的
ren wei wanwu zhi ling 人爲萬物之靈
ren you xin ling 人有心靈
Rendao zhongnian 人到中年
renge 人格
"Renmin qinwu yuan" 人民勤務員
renshi 認識
Renwen kexue 人文科學
Rong Hong 容閎
Ruxue de sanqi fazhan de qianjing wenti: dalu jiangxue, wennan he taolun
儒學的三期發展的前景問題：大陸講學，問難 和討論

sannong 三農
Sanshi erli 三十而立
Shafei nüshi de riji 沙菲 女士的日記
shanghen wenxue 傷痕文學
Shanxi waiguo wenyan xuexiao 山西外國文言學校
Shao Mujun 邵牧君
shehui 社會
"Shehui xinlixue gaishuo" 社會心理學概說
shen 神
Shen Congwen 沈從文
Shen Heyong 申荷永
shen ming 神明
Shen Rong (Chen Rong) 諶容
Shen Su 申蘇
shenghua 升華
Shengyuehan shuyuan 聖約翰書院
shenjing 神經
shenjing bing 神經病
shenjing shuairuo zheng 神經衰弱症
"Shenpiao" 神嫖
shenti hua 身體化
Shi Yuepi 施約瑟
Shi Zhecun 施蟄存
Shiba Tamotsu 澁江保

Shibao 時報
Shifanguan 師範舘
shijian 實踐
"Shijian lun" 實踐論
shikan hao 試刊號
"Shiren Mang Ke: Wo wan hao wu sun de huo dao xianzai"
詩人芒克：我完好無損地活到現在
Shishuo xinyu 世說新語
shixue 實學
Shōsetsu kara mita Shina no minzoku sei 小说から見た支那の民族性
shuili 說理
Shuimo 水沫
"Shuoshuo shengming de beijing: wenge" 說說生命的背景：文革
Shuwu 書屋
Si Misi 斯密斯
sifa jingshenbing jianding司法精神病鑑定
Siqin Gaowa 斯琴高娃
"Siqu de A Q shidai" 死去的阿Q時代
Sishui liunian 似水流年
siyu 私欲
Song Jiaoren 宋教仁
Song Rushan 宋如珊
Su Tong 蘇童
Subao 蘇報
suku 訴苦
Sun Longji 孫隆基

Tan Sitong 譚嗣同
Tang Dengbo 湯澄波
Tang Qian 唐錢
Tao Jingsun 陶晶孫
Tian Zhuangzhuang 田壯壯
Tian'anmen wange 天安門挽歌
"Ting dang de hua" 聽黨的話
Tongmeng hui 同盟會

Wan Juan 宛娟
Wang Anyi 王安億
Wang Daan 王大安

Wang Er 王二
Wang Er fengliu shi 王二風流史
Wang Jingwei 汪精衛
Wang Jingxi 汪敬熙
Wang Meng 王蒙
Wang Ning 王寧
Wang Ruixing 王瑞興
Wang Shuo 王朔
Wang Shuo wenji 王朔文籍
Wang Tianhou 王天厚
Wang Wanxing 王万星
Wang Xiaobo 王小波
"Wang Xiaobo dizao *Huangjin shidai*" 王小波締造"黃金時代"
"Wang Xiaobo zuopin ji xiaoshuo ji *Huangjin shidai*"
王小波作品及小説集 黃金時代
Wang Xue 王雪
Wang Yangming 王陽明
Wang Yichuan 王一川
Wang Yiren 王以仁
Wang Yunwu 王云五
Wang Zengfan 王增藩
Wei Xichin 衛西琴
Wei Zhong 衛中
"Weida chu zi pingfan" 偉大出自平凡
Weida de gongchan zhuyi zhanshi—Lei Feng
偉大的共產主義戰士—雷鋒
weida youyi 偉大友誼
Wenhua da geming zhong de dixia wenxue 文化大革命中的地下文學
wenming 文明
Wenxin diaolong 文心彫龍
Wenxue yu jingshen fenxi xue 文學與精神分析學
Wenyi gongzuozhe weishenme yao gaizao sixiang
文藝工作者為甚麼要改造思想
"Wenyi gongzuozhe weishenme yao gaizao sixiang—yi jiu wu yi nian shiyi yue ershisi ri zai Beijing wenyi jie zhengfeng xuexi dongyuan dahui shang de jiangyi"
文藝工作者爲什麼要改造思想—一九五一年十一月二十四日在北京文藝界整風學習動員大會上的講義
Wenyi lilun yu piping 文藝理論與批評

wo di 我敵
"Wo shi shei? Fuluoyide yu xiandai Zhongguo de xin zhishifenzi"
我是誰？弗洛伊德與現代中國的新知識分子
Wode jingshen jiayuan 我的精神家園
Wode yinyang shijie 我的陰陽世界
"Women de xingai guannian" 我們的性愛觀念
wu 巫
Wu Hongfei 吳虹飛
Wu Jianguo 吳建國
Wu Lichang 吳立昌
Wu Ma 吳媽
wu yishi 無意識
Wu Zhihui 吳稚暉
Wuxun dazhong zixun zhuangbo youxian gongzi
五旬大衆咨詢轉播有限公司
wuzhi 五志
wuzhi dao jingshen 物質到精神
wuzhi wenming 物質文明

xia yishi 下意識
Xia Yu 夏雨
xian 癇
Xiandai 現代
"Xiandai xinlixue" 現代心理學
Xiandaixing yu Zhongguo dangdai wenxue zhuanxing
現代性與中國當代文學轉型
"Xiang Lei Feng xuexi" 向雷鋒學習
xiang nao wusi de 像鬧五四的
Xiang Peiliang 向培良
"Xiang Zhao Shuli fangxiang maijin" 向趙樹理方向邁進
xiangtu 鄉土
xiangtu wenxue 鄉土文學
"Xianjin shengchangzhe de xinli tedian: lun gongchan zhuyi laodong taidu"
先進生產者的心理特點：論共產主義勞動態度
Xiao Baie 小白鵝
Xiao D 小D
Xiao Dou 小豆
"Xiao Erhei jiehun" 小二黑結婚

xiao heshang 小和尚
Xiao Qian 肖乾
Xiao Xiucai 小秀才
xie 邪
Xie Fei 謝飛
Xie Junmei 謝俊美
Xieta liaowang: Zhongguo dianying wenhua (1978–1998) 斜塔瞭望：中國電影文化（1978–1998）
Ximen Qing 西門慶
xin 心
Xin de lianyi: xiandaixing de jingshen xingshi 心的戀異：現代性的精神形式
Xin ganjue pai 新感覺派
Xin lian'ai guan yu jiating guan 新戀愛觀與新家庭觀
"Xin minzhu zhuyi lun" 新民主主義論
Xin nüxing 新女性
Xin qingnian 新青年
Xin shiji 新世紀
Xin wenyi 新文藝
Xin xinlixue 新心理學
"Xin xinlixue yu jiaoyu" 新心理學與教育
xin zhi fenxi 心之分析
xin zuoyong 心作用
Xinchao 新潮
xing 性
"Xing jiaoyu de jige wenti" 性教育的幾個問題
"Xing jiaoyu de jitiao yuanli" 性教育的幾條原理
"Xing jiaoyu de lilun yu shiji" 性教育的理論與實際
Xing Xiaoqun 邢小群
Xingfu 幸福
Xingge zuhe lun 性格組合論
Xingshi 性史
xingshi hua 形式化
Xingxue juyu 性學舉隅
xingyu bu tiaohe 性欲不調和
Xinhui 楊鑫煇
Xinjie wenming deng 心界文明燈
Xinli 心理

xinli fenxi 心理分析
xinli fenxi xue 心理分析學
Xinli jiaoyu xue 心理教育學
Xinlixue bao 心理學報
Xinli yijie 心理易解
"Xinli zhuanye taolun ren de xinli de shehuixing yu ziranxing wenti" 心理專業討論人的心理的社會性與自然性問題
Xinlixue dagang 心理學大綱
"Xinlixue de zuijin de qushi" 心理學的最近的趨勢
Xinlixue gailun 心理學概論
Xinlixue hui 心理學會
Xinlixue tongshi 心理學通史
Xinlixue tongxun 心理學通訊
xinlixue xi 心理學係
Xinlixue yibao 心理學譯報
xinling 心靈
xinling hui 心靈會
Xinling xue 心靈學
xinti 心体
"Xinzhong yao you bangyang" 心中要有榜樣
Xixiang ji 西厢记
Xizao 洗澡
Xu Jie 許傑
Xu Qinwen 許欽文
Xu Shulian 許淑蓮
Xu Xiao 徐曉
Xuanlian 懸戀
Xuexi Lei Feng fudao cailiao 學習雷鋒輔導材料

Yan Fu 嚴復
Yan Yongjing 顏永京
Yang Gao 楊高
Yang Jian 楊健
Yang Kai 楊凱
Yang Mo 楊沫
Yang Nianqun 楊念群
Yang Xinhui 楊鑫輝
Yangguang canlan de rizi 陽光燦爛的日子

"*Yangguang canlan de rizi*: zai fenlie de xushi beihou"
陽光燦爛的日子：在分裂的敘事背後
"Yao geming de, gen wo zou!" 要革命的，跟我走!
Yao Wenyun 姚文元
Yao Xinyong 姚新勇
Yasuoka Hideo 安冈秀夫
Ye Dehui 葉德輝
Ye Haosheng 葉浩生
Ye Ling 業靈
Ye Lingfeng 葉靈鳳
Ye Qizheng 葉啓政
Yeshi 野事
Yiban 一般
Yibu dianying de dansheng 一部電影的誕生
Yin Hong 尹鴻
yiqi 義氣
yishi 意識
"Yixin xiangzhe dang" 一心向着黨
yixu 意緒
yixue xinlixue 醫學心理學
"Yongsheng zhanshi" 永生的戰士
Youchai 郵差
Yu Beipei 宇北蓓
Yu Dafu 郁達夫
Yu Hua 余華
Yu Tianxiu 余天休
Yuan Gongwei 袁公偉
Yuan Yang'an 袁仰安
Yuan Ying 遠嬰
Yue Daiyun 樂黛雲
Yueshi yu meixue: Ming Qing zhi xiandai Zhongguo wenren de ziwo xingxiang xueshu yantaohui
越世與美學：明清至現代中國文人的自我形象學術研討會
Yunqing 雲清
Yusi 語絲

"Zai Yan'an wenyi zuotanhui shang de jianghua"
在延安文藝座談會上的講話

Zei Huli 賊狐狸
Zeng Xingkui 曾興魁
Zenyang zuoren, wei shi huozhe: xiang Lei Feng tongzhi xuexi
怎樣做人，為誰活着：向雷鋒同志學習
Zhang Ailing 張愛玲
Zhang Dongsun 張東蓀
Zhang Jie 張傑
Zhang Jingsheng 张競生
Zhang Junmai 張君勱
Zhang Mingjuan 章明娟
Zhang Xianliang 張賢亮
Zhang Xichen 章錫琛
Zhang Yang 張揚
Zhang Yiwu 張頤武
Zhang Yuan 張元
Zhang Zai 張載
Zhang Ziping 張資平
Zhao Liru 趙莉如
Zhao Shuli 趙樹理
"Zhao Shuli de wenxue shi yiyi" 趙樹理的文學史意義
Zhao Yan 趙演
zheng 爭
Zheng Boqi 鄭伯奇
Zheng Dongtian 鄭洞天
Zheng Guoen 鄭國恩
zhengyue 正月
"Zhengzhuang—canchi—kongju—Lingwai yizhong guankan de fangfa"
症狀—殘斥—恐懼—另外一種觀看的方法
"'Zhexue' yiming kao" '哲學' 譯名考
zhi 知
zhi 志
Zhi Xiaomin 智效民
zhiqing 知青
zhiqing wenxue 知青文學
zhixing heyi 知行合一
"Zhizhe xixue: yuedu Wang Xiaobo" 知者戲謔：閱讀王小波
Zhong gong jingshen dongyuan yanjiu 中共精神動員研究
Zhongguo jinxiandai xinlixue tongshi 中國近現代心理學通史

Zhongguo qingnian 中國青年
Zhongguo xinlixue shi 中國心理學史
Zhongguo xinlixue shilun 中國心理學史綸
Zhongguo zhiqing wenxue shi 中國知青文學史
Zhonghua shenjing jingshen kexue zazhi 中華神經精神科學雜誌
Zhou Guoping 周國平
Zhou Jianren 周建人
Zhou Xiaowen 周曉雯
Zhou Yang 周揚
Zhou Zuoren 周作人
Zhu Guangqian 朱光潛
Zhu Wei 朱偉
Zhu Xi 朱熹
Zhu Zhenglin 朱正琳
Zhuang Zhou 莊周
Zhuangzi 莊子
Zhuti de suzao yu bianqian: Zhongguo zhiqing wenxue xinlun (1977–1995) 主體的塑造與變遷：中國知青文學新論 (1977–1995)
Zi Xi 慈禧
Zihua xiang 自畫像
zijue nengdongli 自覺能動力
ziwo 自我
ziwo piping 自我批評
"Ziyou de linghun" 自由的靈魂
zuyi 阻抑

Notes

Notes to Chapter One

1. According to psychotherapist Roger Horrocks (2001), "Freud revolutionized modern thought with his conception and development of depth psychology. The word 'depth' is critical here, for Freud postulated a fundamental incoherence in the human being, a division between the surface and what lies underneath—the unconscious" (1).

2. Ellis believed Freud overestimated the centrality of sexual desire, and insisted that it was not the sole root of emotions, ideas, art, and religion. He also could not accept Freud's contention that every dream involved wish fulfillment, and showed how the language slips Freud outlined in *The Psychopathology of Everyday Life* could have their origins in the conscious as well as the unconscious. Ellis accused Freud of uncritically expanding interpretations of adult sex behavior to analyze infantile sexuality, thus obscuring its nature. See Brome (1979, 123–25, 159, 215–16); P. Robinson (1976, especially 1–41); von Krafft-Ebing (1965); and van den Haag (1965). For a study of von Krafft-Ebing's work, especially in the European context, see Oosterhuis (2000).

3. For an excellent web source that introduces early sexual pioneers and maintains an archive about their work, see the Magnus Hirschfeld Archive for Sexuality, maintained by Humboldt University, Berlin (http://www2.hu-berlin.de/sexology/index.htm).

4. After Fliess operated on Eckstein, Eckstein developed serious hemorrhaging, and Freud later discovered that Fliess had accidentally left two feet of gauze in her nasal cavity. However, it is not true, as Breger claims, that Freud interpreted this incident of life-threatening bleeding as sexual in nature (Masson 1985, 133). In fact, Freud states clearly that "we had done her an injustice; she was not at all abnormal . . ." (Masson 1985, 117, letter to Fliess dated March 8, 1895). Yet, in a somewhat contradictory way, Freud continued working with Fliess to develop his sexual theories, and he interpreted Eckstein's spontaneous bleeding at different times as sexual in origin: "I shall be able to prove that you were right, that her episodes of bleeding were hysterical, were occasioned by *longing*, and probably occurred at sexually relevant times [the woman, out of resistance, has not yet supplied me with the dates]" (Masson 1985, 183, letter dated April 26, 1896).

5. For an attack on the entire idea of psychoanalysis or psychotherapy, see Masson (1988), especially chapter 2, "Dora and Freud" (Masson 1988, 45–74). In 1980 Masson, formerly a Freud supporter, was appointed the Project Director of the Freud Archives, and he used his access to restricted materials to throw doubt on Freud's pre-1897 child seduction theories. According to Masson, Freud abandoned these theories not because of a change in his beliefs, but only out of "cowardice in the face of Viennese professional criticism" (Masson 1988, 242). Masson was fired, and the debate became public through Janet Malcolm's book *In the Freud Archives* (Malcolm 1983), which first saw print as two articles in the *New Yorker*. Masson also published the exposé *The Assault on Truth: Freud's Suppression of the Seduction Theory* in 1984. For these controversies and more, see Roazen (2002, 239–58).

6. For the rebuttal that led to a long-term debate in anthropology, see Freeman (1983).

7. See Torrey (1992, 128–213), chapters 6 ("Freud in the Nurseries"), 7 ("Freud in Jails and Prisons"), and 8 ("Philosopher Queen and Psychiatrist Kings: The Freudianization of America"). For the Hegelian undertones in self-help movement concepts such as "self-awareness," "self-actualization," and "consciousness-raising," see D. Robinson (1976, 337–38); Ruitenbeck (1966); and Hale (1971).

8. Turkle (1978) notes that in both the United States and France, disillusionment with political transformation resulted in interest in the spirit and psyche (9–10); she focuses, however, on differences in beliefs and practices about psychoanalysis in the two cultures. Although there are many actual differences between the approach to Freud in the United States and France, I find that in order to make her case stronger, Turkle underestimated the connection between Freud and leftist political belief in the United States. Her comment that since 1968, "a Frenchman often finds a psychoanalyst in places where he might once have expected to find a priest, a teacher, or a physician" (Turkle 1978, 14), could also be true in the United States. For psychoanalytic theory in Great Britain, see Griffiths (1994) and Holmes (1994).

9. Davidson (2001) notes that most of Freud's "discoveries"—infantile sexuality, bisexuality, erotogenic zones—were discussed earlier by Iwan Bloch, Richard von Krafft-Ebing, Havelock Ellis, Wilhelm Fliess, Jean Martin Charcot, and Albert Moll, among others (70–72). However, this history does not detract from Freud's ability to combine and present these ideas in unique ways. Freud went a step further than others in detaching the "sexual instinct" from the genitals and copulation. Davidson (2001) proposes that although this move seemingly set the stage for a further development that would argue against the notion of any sexual activity being by nature perverse, Freud contradictorily "continued to use the idea of perversion" (90). Still, Freud's *Three Essays on the Theory of Sexuality* allowed for the possibility that people could change their mentality, a new perspective on the mind.

10. Reed differentiates between the ontological unconscious of the Romantics and the psychological unconscious, but he points out many precursors to Freud in theory of the unconscious. In the words of Richard Webster (1995), ". . . the Unconscious is not simply an occult entity for whose real existence there is no

palpable evidence. It is an illusion produced by language—a kind of intellectual hallucination" (250). Although neurological researchers recognize that people do things for reasons of which they are not entirely aware, it does not follow that this lack of awareness should be conceptualized as an unconscious fraught with sexual desire and mysterious motivations.

11. According to Jimmie Holland (1976), the influence of Freud within the larger professions of psychology and psychiatry was much greater in the United States than in Germany or Russia, which remained suspicious of psychoanalysis. See also Corson (1976).

12. Eventually psychiatry evolved in directions very different from those of psychoanalysis or even psychology. With a medical background now necessary for practicing psychiatrists, the discipline has come to emphasize the physiology and neurology of the brain, and illness within this context.

13. Crews (1998) contains contributions by some twenty critics of Freud's work and includes well-known cultural figures such as Mikkel Borch-Jacobsen, Stanley Fish, and Ernest Gellner. See also Roudinesco (1997).

14. See Dufresne (2003), chapter 7 ("The Politics of Representing Freud: A Short Account of a Media War, This Time With Feeling") for Dufresne's comments on the 1995 Library of Congress snafu (87–92).

15. For a collection of the work of Szasz's critics and his individual response to each, see Schaler (2004). See Szasz (1959) on the relationship between various psychological disciplines.

16. By 1915, three rival groups with Jung, Adler, and Freud as their leaders functioned within the psychoanalytic movement. Adler argued against Freudian penis envy in women, believing that any such manifestation was "symbolic jealousy of male dominance in society" (Brennan 2003, 229). Jung bypassed Freud's sexual focus, emphasizing extraversion and introversion (231–32).

17. Cushman argues that psychotherapy in the United States rejected Sullivan's centering of the social sphere, instead going down a Freudian path laid out by Melanie Klein's object relations theory. See also Sullivan (1964) and for his general theories, Sullivan (1953, 1954, 1962); Chapman (1976); and Perry (1982).

18. Originally from Sullivan (1946).

19. Cushman develops his theory throughout his book, abstracting it in chapter 1 ("Psychotherapy, the Impossible Bridge") (1995, 1–14). Cushman discusses the differing conditions of psychological theory in Europe, but his study focuses on the United States, where he believes the empty self has been most thoroughly constructed. Although he argues for a more careful contextualization of psychotherapy within the cultural and moral traditions of the country, Cushman is neither naïve about the dangers of that approach and its moralistic tendencies nor entirely critical of psychotherapy as it has emerged in the United States. While he argues along materialist lines, his work is anything but a materialist manifesto. His research is valuable in that it thoroughly shows how many basically Freudian ideas have become accepted and unquestioned not only in psychoanalysis but throughout culture. See also Berger (1965).

20. Ebert (1996) criticizes two of Jameson's books, *The Political Unconscious: Narrative as a Socially Symbolic Act*, and *Postmodernism; or, The Cultural Logic of Late Capitalism*. Although she does not work on Freud directly, Ebert's writing is a comprehensive condemnation of a Freudian sexual theory that removes sexual desire from its social environment and posits it as a hidden motivator.

21. See also Petrovsky (1990, especially 150–89), on Marxist criticism of psychoanalysis and the attempt to develop a Marxist psychology; and Joravsky (1989, especially 233–37 and 419–20). Joravsky's bibliography lists other relevant sources.

22. In Miller's (1998) description of this process, he sympathizes with the psychologists and downplays the ideological issues behind the conflict, stating: "In reality, this emerging systematization of a new revolutionary culture was achieved in large measure by sharpening definitions of who or what was to be included and excluded" (71). Miller also claims that underlying "theoretical discussions, which revolved round the issue of understanding mass behavior, were the fundamental Bolshevik concerns—the desire for control and the need to construct a comprehensive theory capable of justifying that control" (71).

23. Again, Miller (1998) sees the debate as "a far more sinister process" that "amounted to an ideological war against 'Freudianism' in order to delegitimize it completely" (82).

24. Miller (1998) believes that the "distinction is an important one, but Reich was exaggerating its significance in 1929" (91). Many argued with Reich; Moshe Wulff, who had immigrated to Palestine, claimed that Reich was only trying to make his statements acceptable to the authorities in this claim. While it may be true that the attack on psychoanalysis in the Soviet Union was much more comprehensive than Reich indicated, I find his comment prescient in its precise identification of the ability of psychoanalysis to turn itself into a pervasive "view of the world."

25. See also Petrovsky (1990), who traces objections to Freud's pan-sexualism throughout the 1920s and 1930s (157–69). Reimut Reiche's *Sexuality and Class Struggle* (1970) is a manifesto on behalf of the link between class and sexual oppression by someone who participated in the German student movement of the late 1960s. Although Reiche analyzes and supports much of Wilhelm Reich's work, he admits that "in today's context it is difficult to relate quantitatively greater sexual freedom to radical and class-conscious demands, and in many cases this has become historically impossible" (17).

26. For more on Reich and other renegades, see Kurzweil (1989). For a Chinese Marxist discussion of sexual desire and the family, see Fei Min (1949). Fei Min criticizes "free love" under capitalism in chapter 7 (20–23).

Notes to Chapter Two

1. Jingyuan Zhang (1992) believes that Freud's theories had their largest influence in literature during the 1920s and 1930s. Zhang's pioneering work is the first comprehensive book on psychoanalysis in China to appear in English. I am

indebted to this research for both its insights and its list of sources, which structured my initial investigations. See also Liu Jihui (2004). I am grateful to Liu for commenting on an early version of this chapter delivered at Academia Sinica in December 2005, and for introducing me to her work at that time. For a study of Freudian ideas under colonial conditions, see Hartnack (2001).

2. Tang Dengbo evaluated Freud's sexual theories in the context of a mental hospital in Guangzhou, using his investigations to lend support to Freud's sexual theories (Liu Jihui 2004, 138).

3. David Der-wei Wang's (1997) intent is to radically historicize the modern, rejecting it as a "prerequisite to be fulfilled by non-European cultures that wish to catch up to History" (7). His use of the word "repressed" in his title is a play on Freudian and Marxist use of the same term, referring to the "monolithic definition of modernity" that is superimposed on competing voices (20). Rather than interpret the significance of that superimposition, Wang delves into the modernities that were "repressed" through its operation.

4. In chapter 3, "Psychoanalysis and Cosmopolitanism: The Work of Guo Moruo," Shih argues that both psychoanalysis and cosmopolitanism—which appealed to Chinese intellectuals anxious to modernize—assume a universalism of mind and culture, although that universalism is Eurocentric (2000, 96–109).

5. Qicheng Jing and Xiaolan Fu (2001) trace the emergence of "psychological thinking" in China, first to two thousand years ago when philosophers debated human nature, then to Catholic scholastic psychology, to Jesuit missionaries in the 16th and 17th centuries, and finally to modern psychology with information coming into China from Germany, Japan, and the United States. See also Nancy Chen (1999).

6. Lung-Kee Sun (1992) notes that although psychology was introduced as something to assist with teaching, social psychology was often invoked in debates on national character and more generally as part of political discourse.

7. In 1920 Nanjing University and Dongnan University set up departments of psychology (xinlixue xi), both in the School of Education (jiaoyu ke) (Yang and Zhao 1999, 157). My discussion of the late 19th century and early 20th century introductions of psychology is indebted to the comprehensive study by Yang Xinhui and Zhao Liru (1999).

8. For a brief discussion of Confucian valuing of education and social relationships, see Jing and Fu (2001, 408–11). They state: "Confucius believed that, with a common natural endowment as our basis, humans obtained different social traits through learning, and thus education played an important role" (410). Cosmological notions from Buddhism and Daoism also could be relevant, as I later note.

9. See "Kulkosky's Bookmarks for the History of Psychology." Although the philosophical roots of psychology are deep, John Locke (1632–1704) is often considered the founder of empiricism and associationism, which were foundational to experimental psychology. For an argument against the idea that psychology gradually detached itself from a relatively long-term and consistent history of philosophy, see Jones and Elcock (2001), who argue that the conception of philosophy as a unified historical field is a modern invention.

10. The Mengyang Educational Society eventually became Tengchow College (Dengzhou shuyuan) and in 1917, Qilu University (Qilu daxue) (Yang and Zhao 1999, 101–3).

11. In 1983 a copy of the first volume was found in China, with a card inserted in it on which was a message penned by Yan in both Chinese and English, noting that his health did not allow him to finish proofing the second volume. The handwritten copy of volume 2 has not been found. Various terms are used to indicate psychology at this time; *xinling xue*, Yang and Zhao note, may have come from traditional Chinese ideas such as that which Yan repeats at the beginning of his translation: "Humans are the spirit of the ten thousand things" (*ren wei wanwu zhi ling*), or "Humans have heart / mind and spirit" (*ren you xin ling*). According to Yang and Zhao (1999), Yan should be considered the originator of the term *xinling xue*. Haven's *Mental Philosophy* was translated in Japan fourteen years earlier by a title that eventually came to replace *xinling xue* as the preferred modern terminology: *Xinli xue*. G. Stanley Hall mentions Joseph Haven's book as one of a number of texts used to teach mental philosophy, usually during the senior year of college (Yang and Zhao 1999, 94–112).

12. Jing and Fu (2001) discuss another book that also existed in China at this time, *Aspects of Human Nature* (Xingxue juyu) written by William Alexander Parsons (W.A.P.) Martin (Ding Weiliang) (1827–1916), an American missionary who went to Hong Kong in 1850 and then to Ningbo; he moved to Beijing in 1863 and taught in the predecessor to Beijing University. Martin published a number of books in English about China, including *The Chinese: Their Education, Philosophy, and Letters* (1880). According to Beijing University professor Chen Qiwei (2001), *Aspects of Human Nature* was published in 1898 and was about the study of the mind. For a discussion of Martin's translations of international law and the naturalization of Western legal concepts in Chinese, see Lydia H. Liu (1999). See also Girardot (2002), especially "The Strange Saga of Missionary Tradition, Sinological Orientalism, and the Comparative Science of Religions in the Nineteenth Century" (1–16), and "Missionary Hyphenations East and West, 1815–1869" (17–68).

13. The date of publication and publisher of Hattori's lectures are unclear, although a note on the first volume indicates that the Chinese-style volumes were put out around 1900–01; the Western-style bound copy was most likely produced in 1904–6. These lectures are still in existence in a hand-bound, four-volume edition at the Beijing University Library and a Western-style copy at Nanjing University. The first, third, and fourth volumes concern history, ethics, economics, and geography, subjects that were taught by others. The second volume contains the psychology lectures. Song Jiaoren (1882–1913) read the book when he went to Japan to study in 1906, and complimented Hattori on his clear and convincing exposition of cognition (*zhi*), emotion (*qing*), and will (*zhi*). For more on Hattori and Japanese teachers in China in the late Qing and early Republic, see chapter 5, "Japanese Teachers and Advisors in China" (Reynolds 1993, 65–110). Reynolds notes Beijing Normal University president and three-time Minister of Education Fan Yuanlian (1876–1927) as saying, "When the history of Chinese education is

written, and the beginnings of teacher education recounted, page one will have to start with the work of Dr. Hattori [Unokichi (1867–1939)]" (65).

14. Wozniak notes that the book was popular, being republished in Danish eleven times by 1930, at least seven times in German, and seven times in English by 1919. Quotes here are from the Lowndes translation. Wang's translation was based on the English version by Mary E. Lowndes (1891), which was based on the German translation, which was based on the original Danish text. According to Yang and Zhao, *Outlines of Psychology* is the first book on Western psychology translated directly from a Western language into Chinese (Yang and Zhao 1999, 113).

15. Roark was the first president of the Eastern Kentucky State Normal College (which became Eastern Kentucky University), from 1906 to 1909. Although Yang and Zhao mention Roark's work, they do not translate his Chinese name into English. I am grateful to Ruihua Shen for helping me discover his English name.

16. Sun (1992, 237) quotes Charlotte Furth (1983, 322–405).

17. Qian Zhixiu's "Modern Psychology" (Xiandai xinlixue) in *Beijing University Gazette* (Beijing daxue rikan), begins with no. 111 (April 15, 1918) and appears irregularly in subsequent volumes. The journal also bears the Esperanto title *Pekin-Universitato Chiutaga Gazeto* through 1918, although it does not appear in the 1919 copies I have. I could not find a direct reference to Freud, but I do not have access to all of the articles. However, Qian refers to Freud's theories, as I discuss below.

18. In the *Beijing University Gazette*, the dates of these lectures by topic are: the spirit can leave the body (vol. 5, no. 116, April 20, 1918); abnormal psychology (no. 119, April 24, 1918); dream analysis (nos. 120 and 121, April 25 and 26, 1918); hysteria and the subconscious (nos. 123 and 124, April 29 and 30, 1918); and instincts (nos. 129 and 130, May 6 and 7, 1918).

19. See nos. 384, 387, 396, 397, 403, 404, 406, and 408 (May 22 and 26, and June 6, 7, 14, 16, 18, and 20, 1919).

20. The term *xinling*, which had been used to translate "mental philosophy" for Joseph Haven's book, came to be used for "spiritualism," and other terms—namely, *xinli xue*—were picked up to indicate "psychology."

21. Journal articles from this period either have no page numbers or all begin with "1." To find the location of the article in the journal in relation to other articles, consult the table of contents.

22. A close friend of Liang Shuming, Westharp taught at Shanxi Foreign Literatures and Languages School (Shanxi waiguo wenyan xuexiao) and first delivered the content of these articles as lectures there. As an introductory note explains, they were then transcribed and edited for the journal. In 1926, Westharp published *Outline of a Psychology of Collaboration Between the Far East and the Far West* (Esquisse d'une psychologie de collaboration entre l'Extrême-Occident et l'Extrême-Orient). See also Zhi Xiaomin (2004) (accessed November 2005); Lynch (accessed November 2005); and Goldfuss (1993).

23. The English translation of the journal's title is provided in the first issue.

24. Much of the disagreement concerned what constituted instinct, and the relative weight of one instinct versus another. For a helpful analysis that comes directly out of the times, see Bernard (1922). Bernard criticizes Freud's mystical approach and his over-reliance on observational analysis, which lacks a critical perspective; he also attacks the theory of instincts: "It seems hardly necessary to repeat here that there can be no general sex instinct or ego-instinct or instinct of self-preservation. These are abstract value expressions with highly variable and constantly changeable activity content; they are not concrete biological activity units, such as true instincts must be" (355). See also Brown and van der Hart (1998).

25. Jingyuan Zhang (1992, 35) points out that in psychology, behaviorism was much more widely practiced; in education, teachers and theorists were more interested in developing intellectual skills and moral values in students; in philosophy, pragmatism and materialism were the prevalent discourses.

26. One of William McDougall's best-known books is *An Introduction to Social Psychology* (1908). Writing about sentiment, emotions, and innate tendencies, McDougall grounded social behavior in biology and focused on the individual.

27. The reference is to Arthur G. Tansley's 1920 *The New Psychology and Its Relation to Life.* Tansley, a friend of Freud, is known for coining the term "ecosystem." On the complex, Tansley (1920) writes: "Complexes are of all sorts and sizes. Some have a basis in inherited instinct common to all human beings; others are individual and depend primarily on education or experience" (50). Tansley recognizes the "sex complex" as "the largest and the most intense of any of the great universal complexes" but, following Jung, notes that "in the normal civilized man, who is living comfortably above the margin of subsistence, there is a greater or less amount of free psychic energy available which can be turned into any suitable conative channel in which he is able to take an interest—his daily work, sport, a hobby, money-making, politics, religion, social activities of various kinds, and so on. The term *libido* may conveniently be applied to the psychic energy inherent in the great natural complexes, or becoming attached to any individual complex, and discharging itself along the appropriate conative channels" (63).

28. According to Seán Golden, Yan Fu (1854–1921) used the word *qun* (often translated as "herd" or "group") to represent "nation" when he translated works on Darwinism, Social Darwinism, and other social sciences.

29. Bernard (1922) argues that Tansley shows a "tacit recognition of the dominating influence of environment over instinct" in his writing, although he privileges instinct by mentioning it 479 times in this volume, whereas his views on environment are "vague and unanalyzed" (Bernard 1922, 353).

30. Tansley believed that the more civilized a society became, the more likely it was that "primitive sex energy" would be sublimated and "the psychic energy available for employment in channels other than the biosocially necessary ones [would be] greatly augmented, and at the same time the number and variety of these channels [would be] largely increased" (1920, 79–80). In this approach, Tansley provides a model that values education as a positive, civilizing force, arguing against Freud's emphasis on sexual desire: "The Freudian school hold that all

the primitive psychic energy of a child is sex energy in a wide sense, but there is no more warrant for this belief than in the case of primitive man" (84–5).

31. Leary's 400-page dissertation presents a wealth of information about Zhang and the environment in which he worked. Leary relentlessly tracked down sources, and in chapter 7 presents a well-argued interpretation of the conflict between Zhang and his detractors. See also Hsiao-yen Peng (2002), who corrects some erroneous translations and information in Leary's study, and argues that Zhang's position in *Sex Histories* is that of a sexologist rather than an aesthete. Although Peng recognizes the proposition of aesthetic utopia in Zhang Jingsheng's other books, she regards *Sex Histories* as different and more along the lines of Havelock Ellis's work.

32. For comments on the autobiographical form, see Peng Hsiao-yen (2002, 165).

33. For Zhang Jingsheng's translations of Freud's work, see Jingyuan Zhang (1992, 173).

34. These ideas were presented during the discussion of my paper "Who Am I? Freud and the New Intellectual in Republican China" (Wo shi shei? Fuluoyide yu xiandai Zhongguo de xin zhishifenzi) (Larson 2006).

35. The best-known rebuttal of Jameson's argument is Ahmad (1992). See also Wang Yichuan (1996).

36. Yin Hong states: "Sexual psychology, sexual abnormality, and even the unconscious have objective existence, and even when writers have absolutely no knowledge of Freudian theories, their observations, experiences, and imaginings of life can be brought into the their literary visions. To investigate whether these works show the influence of Freudian theory, the most important thing is not whether they describe sex or the unconscious, but whether they can be explained using the viewpoint and method of psychoanalysis" (1994, 43–44). In this instance, I object to Yin Hong's naturalization of concepts such as "sexual abnormality." However, his book conclusively demonstrates the importance of Freudian theory in the work of several important writers and critics of the 1920s and, to a lesser extent, the 1930s.

37. Barlow's first five chapters analyze sexual modernity during the May Fourth period and especially illuminate the fiction and thought of Ding Ling from this perspective. Barlow's comprehensive work illustrates the profound transformation demanded by sexual modernity at every level.

38. For Liu's elaboration of Freud's theories, see chapter 4, "Symptoms—Abjection—Terror: Another Way of Seeing Things" (Zhengzhuang—canchi—kongju—Lingwai yizhong guankan de fangfa) (2004, 89–118).

39. Italicized words appear in their original language. The quote is from Chen Fuxing (1991) in Ye Qizheng (1991) (Liu Jihui 2004, 156–57).

40. Liu Jihui (2004) argues on behalf of the close relationship (or complete identity) between Kuriyagawa's "anguish" and Freud's sexual desire, or "libido," and the author's deployment of Freud's theory that repressed sexual desire can be sublimated into art and literature (Liu Jihui 2004, 132–34).

41. More generally on Lu Xun and psychoanalysis, see Brown (1988a).

42. Animal psychology developed rapidly in China in the 1920s and 1930s, even though connecting human to animal psychology or implying that there was little essential difference presented problems within the debate on eugenics. Early psychological researchers in the West did not all accept the similarity between human and beast. Pierre Janet, for example, believed that psychoanalysis was not only unscientific but also a theory that "equated man with beast" (Turkle 1978, 36).

43. Yasuoka Hideo's *The Chinese National Character in Fiction* (1926) works off the racial theories of the American missionary Arthur Smith (Ch., Si Misi) (1845–1932), whose *Chinese Characteristics* was published in 1894; in 1896 it was translated into Japanese by Shibae Tamotsu as *Chugoku jin ki* (1896). The book was first published as a series of articles in a Shanghai newspaper in the late 1880s and now is often cited as a typical Orientalist work. For more on the debate about national character, see Lydia Liu (1995, 45–76) and Foster (2006, 103–6).

44. This article is in the fourth volume of issue no. 1 (1926), but it came out in 1928.

45. Shu-mei Shih (2001) argues that although Shi Zhecun used the literary strategy of interiority—which developed out of his sense of Western domination a desire to gain equality with the West—to subvert the real, he also believed that his work, which was based not on experience in semi-colonized Shanghai but rather on his relationship to Western modernist texts, was more authentically modern than the work of many other writers (339–43).

46. Liu Jihui (2004) argues that Aubrey Beardsley's decadent graphic style influenced Ye Lingfeng, an artist whose work often adorned the revolutionary literature and criticism of the 1930s put out by Creation Society members, and represented a contradiction: "Chinese cultural discourse contrasted decadent idealist styles or fascist aesthetics with the progressive proletarian spirit, which actually indicates a blind spot in its ideological direction" (165). Commenting on a volume by Peng Kang titled *Revolutionary and Mass Literature and Art* (Geming wenyi yu dazhong wenyi), Liu notes that Guo Moruo chose Ye Lingfeng's image to adorn the volume, showing the connection between revolution and decadence that is typical of fascist aesthetics (177). There is no absolute connection between aesthetic style and politics, however, and Guo could just as easily have regarded Ye's artwork as art nouveau perfectly appropriate to represent the new revolutionary subjectivity.

47. The first dream interpretation clinic in China was opened in 2005, as part of the Shanghai Changning District Mental Health Center ("A Novel Business, Interpreting Dreams," n.a.). According to the article reporting the event, the clinic "takes its theories from Freud, but doesn't discount Chinese medicine, either." The clinic's president comments: "We consider a dream the working of the subconscious rather than a divine portent" as previously believed. See http://www.chinadaily.com.cn/english/doc/2004-03/15/content_314802.htm.

Notes to Chapter Three

1. For a collection of articles about and visual images of the story that extend from its 1921 publication up until 1993, see Peng Xiaoling and Han Keli (1993). For a comprehensive study of Ah Q, the century-long debate he initiated, and his many descendants, see Foster (2006).

2. For information about and discussion of the debate around recovered memory, see the Brown Recovered Memory Project.

3. In an interesting recent development reported in the online discussion group Modern Chinese Literature and Culture (http://mclc.osu.edu/), "The True Story of Ah Q" has been removed from the high school curriculum of a number of Beijing high schools and the martial arts stories of Jin Yong have been added, at least to the teachers' manuals for discussion with students ("Jin Yong Replaces Lu Xun" 2007).

4. According to Heather J. Coleman, Russian Baptists envisioned a revolution of the spirit, and the idea was picked up by a diverse group of revolutionaries such as the Symbolist writer Andrei Bely, the Bolshevik poet Fladimir Mayakovsky, the Russian literary group the Scythians, and Proletkult activists, who "sought to create a new, proletarian culture after 1917 [that] would embrace the notion that political revolution required a subsequent, finishing spiritual revolution" (Coleman 2005, 141). Spiritual revolution was often linked to citizenship and socialism, and Baptist Pavel Pavlov found in the church organization a model of democratization that could be used to resolve class tensions; the rich and poor would consider themselves brothers through a revolution of the spirit (141–42).

5. Hao Chang argues that by the late imperial era, Confucianism expressed a tension between "the ethics of spiritual aspiration and its underlying ontological awareness of the unity of heaven and man," although by the 17th century, the empirical school turned the philosophy toward intellectualism, altering Zhu Xi's emphasis on inner transcendence (29). See also Rodney Taylor (1990).

6. The phrase "order of the soul" comes from Eric Voegelin (1952). Voegelin's *Order and History, Volume One: Israel and Revelation* (1994 [1956]) also is important in Hao Chang's (1993) analysis.

7. I am grateful to Chen Hsiu-fen for her invigorating discussion of my work in Taipei in December 2005 and for providing me with a copy of her dissertation.

8. Vivien Ng (1990) writes about a case in which a doctor working in the late 12th and early 13th century had his assistants use several strategies to influence a mad woman's mind: dressing up outlandishly or as animals, and wolfing down a meal. The fact that some doctors identified emotion or unrequited love as a cause of madness also indicates that they believed it to sometimes have a psychological or mental component, although Ng believes that even these doctors did not conceive of madness as a mental illness (38–51). Nathan Sivin (1995) also argues that it is a mistake to think of madness as a mental illness within the context of Chinese medicine, which did not distinguish between the somatic and the psychological. Martha Li Chiu (1986) finds some examples in the *Inner Classic* that point to mind

and body as separate categories, but never any explicit category of mental illness. See also Ju-K'ang T'ien (1985), who notes that in the 7th century, "emotional imbalance derived from human relations was emphasized as the main factor giving rise to insanity" (73).

9. Charlotte Furth (1999) explains that the "*Inner Canon*'s account of the sexual body followed a rhetorical strategy that was repeated through the ages: the formal relationship of yin and yang itself (here expressed in symbolic numbers) was assumed to explain the relationship of the sexes in a satisfactory way" (46). The importance of this insight is that in classical medicine, gender accounts assign significance not to sexual desire but to reproduction (54–5, 123–46). Furth argues that in looking at traditional Chinese medicine, "we must take account of a social construction that does not privilege erotic pleasure alone over all other possible aspects of the 'sexual'" (126). Therefore, Ye Dehui's (1864–1927) resurrection of Chinese sex manuals was not, as Van Gulik interpreted it, a kind of ars erotica but merely a part of the national building effort in which Ye recognized that Western countries were promoting sexual openness as one significant aspect of modern life (130).

10. Tang (1996) points out that Liang's desire to cultivate the national spirit "means a concentrated, often elitist, effort to consolidate the nation as a self-conscious political unity in order to enable it to participate in the modern world system" (36). Nationalism is inherently relational, since it allows people to identify their position in relation to others (74). See also Tsu (2005), especially chapters 2 ("The Yellow Race"), 3 ("The Menace of Race"), and 4 ("Loving the Nation, Preserving the Race").

11. Sun claims he has found in the May Fourth era "only one instance of 'psychology' denoting the private psyche" (Sun 1992, 258). I doubt the situation is quite this extreme, but I agree with Sun that psychology generally took its meaning from the social context. See also Foster (2006, 19–66).

12. On the traditional metaphysical meaning of *qi* as a vital material force, see Hao Chang (1993, 17). For a discussion of *qi* in Qing China, see On-cho Ng (1993), who argues for a material and social understanding of *qi* and vitalism during the Qing, when "metaphysical criteria of intelligibility" were in decline (55). Many neo-Confucian thinkers linked *qi* closely with *xin*, the heart / mind. According to Huang Zongxi (1610–95), for example, "What is *qi* in heaven is *xin* in man" (46).

13. Chong You complains that Chinese people generally like to stick up only for themselves and have no concept of the nation (Chong You 1904, 6). See also the article "On the Relationship Between the People's Spirit and the Nation" (n.a., 1905), which develops the idea that the key to the people's spirit and thus the strength of the nation is the development of the people's recognition of and love for the larger group; the people's spirit, therefore, will always be valued by the superior person. The second part of this article (also published in *The Times* [Shibao], July 13, 1905) contrasted the development of Chinese civilization with the European enlightenment from the 16th century on. For a discussion of how learning can improve the people's spirit, see Shen Su (1905).

14. In this part of his introduction, Huters discusses research by Yang Nianqun, Xie Junmei, Prasenjit Duara, and Partha Chatterjee. Although Huters recognizes the anxiety produced by the need to both "cherish the nation's history and traditions" and condemn the past, he importantly and I believe correctly objects to the way that in American sinology this anxiety has been interpreted as either psychological trauma or an emotional response—in either case as lacking intellectual content (Huters 2005, 10). For an extended analysis of failure and the sense of failure, see Tsu (2005).

15. Qi Zhirong traces the concept of "spiritual mobilization" as used by Mao Zedong, Deng Xiaoping, and Jiang Zemin from 1950 until contemporary times. Qi argues that the concept and its implementation indicate that "spiritual mobilization" is a kind of method of ideological control institutionalized in party organizations and in education (Qi Zhirong, http://past_journal.mnd.gov.tw [see Chinese character glossary for full citation]).

16. See, for example, the journal *Spiritual Mobilization* (Jingshen dongyuan), a Nationalist party periodical from the 1940s featuring articles by Chiang Kai-shek, Chen Lifu, and others that demand the same self-sacrifice and spiritual loyalty as we see in descriptions of worker's mental characteristics and other texts from the 1950s. The magazine was edited by the National Spiritual Mobilization Committee Secretariat (Guomin jingshen zong dongyuan hui mishu chu), and most of the articles are about developing and sustaining the desire to fight on behalf of the nation.

17. See, for example, Félix Rocquain (1894).

18. For a perspective that argues that although Mao valued the dialectic of theory and practice, his emphasis was on practice, see Womack (1982), who writes: "Ultimately, Mao's justification for ideological commitment is utility" (29). See also Noumoff (1975); and Wakeman (1973), especially "Syncretic Utopianism" (115–36).

19. Keith Michael Baker (1990) shows how the term "revolution" developed in 18th-century France, evolving from being thought of as "extraordinary changes that occur in the world" (as defined in 1690 by Antoine Furetière, and usually used in the plural), to a concept that fully embodied Enlightenment notions of progress and human agency, with active forms such as "revolutionary" and "revolutionize" appearing only after 1789. The new Enlightenment concept of revolution emphasized "a revolution in the human mind," linked cultural change to profound social change, and was globally and universally influential (205–13). I am grateful to Keith for bringing his work to my attention.

20. As I discuss in Chapter 2, the philosopher Li Zehou traced Maoist voluntarism to traditional ontological concepts, especially the harmony between humans and nature that disallowed mind-body dualism and discouraged any attempts to control or conquer nature. See Woei Lien Chong (1999).

21. See also Meisner (1967).

22. Yeo (2002), who links Maoist ideas to Confucianism especially in the area of self-improvement, argues that Maoism is not utopian but anti-utopian, because

it "emphasizes the masses and the uninterrupted revolution of the now" (216). See also Honig (1996).

23. This volume collects Dirlik's articles on Chinese Marxism that were published from 1974 to 2001. For a more complete analysis of the historical conditions under which Maoism was developed and the discourse of national culture, see Dirlik (1997a).

24. See Kang Liu (2005; also 1993). For a defense against interpretations of Mao as an idealist or a plagiarist, see Nick Knight (1990a).

25. Although *jingshen* is not included in her glossaries, for a discussion of this kind of transfer see Lydia H. Liu (1995, especially appendix D, 302–42). Liu does include the term *xinli* for psyche or psychology; *xinli* was used in *The Literary Heart/Mind and the Carving of Dragons* (Wenxin diaolong) and other classical texts (333). For more discussion of modern loan words from Japanese, see Reynolds (1993), who examines a debate over loan words in China in 1957–58 (123–26).

26. Related terms are mental illness (jingshen bing), mental hygiene (jingshen weisheng), psychotherapy (jingshen liaofa), psycho-pharmaceuticals (jingshen yaowu), psychiatry (jingshen bingxue), schizophrenia (jingshen fenlie zheng), psychoanalytical aesthetics (jingshen fenxi meixue), and incomplete mental development (jingshen fayu buquan).

27. This professional difference between *xinli* and *jingshen* is generally but not always true. There are cases where the terms are virtually interchangeable. For example, mental hygiene can be expressed as *xinli weisheng* or *jingshen weisheng*, and psychotherapy can be *xinli zhiliao* or *jingshen zhiliao*. For a list of psychological terms published by the Chinese Academy of Sciences in 1954, see Chin and Chin (1969, 240–60). In his preface to the list, Guo Moruo explains that the list already indicates the reform of the discipline by Marxist ideology and Pavlovian methodology. The study by Chin and Chin is a useful English-language historical introduction to the field as it existed from 1949 to 1966, taking material from *Acta Psychologica Sinica* (Xinlixue bao), published from 1956 to 1966, and beginning again in 1976, and other journals and newspapers. See also L. B. Brown (1981). Unlike Chin and Chin, who work from original documents, Brown, of the School of Psychology at the University of New South Wales, relies on translations by research assistants of articles and papers he collected on two visits to China from 1978 to 1980. His book includes complete translated articles from *Acta Psychologica Sinica*. Brown notes that some researchers in China expressed dissatisfaction about the work of Chin and Chin, which sometimes makes inappropriate comparisons between the research at dissimilar institutions (78). Brown also provides a useful discussion of the history of this journal (183–91).

28. "Individuality" here refers not to personality with no reference to environment or material base, but to individual differences as they develop within the context of the social world. Individuality was difficult to theorize under a system that emphasized collectivity and class. Generally the solution was to categorize individual non-class differences as differences in style and not oppositional to collective qualities. See Xu Shulian (1956, 5–6). This solution proved ineffective in

addressing individual difference, which became a more important part of educational psychology in the early 1960s. See Chin and Chin 1969, 186–99. L. B. Brown (1981) notes that the areas marked out for study at the Psychological Research Institute of the Chinese Academy of Sciences included the three identified by Chin and Chin as well as "psychological and physiological processes," the study of perception, and reflexes in children and animals (84).

29. See "The Psychology Major Discusses the Social and the Natural in the Human Psyche" (1961).

30. In a 1979 interview with psychologist Wu Chen-i, Paul Lowinger asks, "Do you think criticism / self-criticism is a prevention for psychoneurosis or personality disorder?" Wu responds, "Not only prevention, but also curative. You see, we have to educate the patient to recognize or realize their situation and how to improve it, to face reality" (Livingston and Lowinger 1983, 198).

31. Psychological terminology in English also has been imprecise (witness "psychosis" and "neurosis").

32. See Human Rights Watch and Geneva Initiative on Psychiatry (2002). Although Robin Monro is not listed as the official author of this report, the acknowledgments state that it was "researched and written by Robin Munro, a London-based expert on China human rights issues who served as principal China researcher and director of the Hong Kong office of Human Rights Watch during 1989–1998" (Acknowledgments, n.p.). The report includes Munro's 2000 article and several other essays, along with translated documents detailing psychiatric treatment for Falun Gong patients, outlining psychiatric theories, and surveying cases in mental hospitals.

33. "Revolutionary spirit" is ubiquitous in Communist discourse, but also appears in Nationalist texts and speeches. A collection of Chiang Kai-shek's sayings contains numerous examples of the term. See Huang Guangxue, ed. (1967).

34. This volume does not contain page numbers.

35. For a more recent analysis, see Wu Jianguo and Cao Yanming (1982).

36. Speaking of psychology patients, Wu Chen-I in 1979 notes "It seems to me that Mao Tze-tung Thought comes from reality, from real practice, so it teaches patients how to face reality. Revolutionary optimism encourages patients in facing reality. It encourages them after they have lost self-esteem. If you don't believe that you will be able to make change, it's not easy to overcome the many difficulties you must face. Patients need to be armed with revolutionary optimism. Sometimes we speak of a loss of revolutionary face" (Livingston and Lowinger 1983, 200–201).

37. The 1963 *Short Biography of Lei Feng* (Lei Feng xiaozhuan) is organized into chapters titled by reference to qualitative descriptors that capture aspects of Lei Feng's life as he becomes a hero. They include "Listen to the words of the party" (Ting dang de hua), "Greatness comes from the ordinary" (Weida chu zi pingfan), and "Soldier who lives forever" (Yongsheng zhanshi) (Chen Guangsheng 1963). Another version provides "Totally for the party" (Yixin xiangzhe dang), "Class friendship and love is deep" (Jieji youai shen), and "Tireless worker for the people"

(Renmin qinwu yuan) (*Chairman Mao's Good Soldier: Lei Feng* 1978). On the importance of spirit and the relation between spirit and action, see Wang Ruixing (1963).

38. The People's Liberation Army Poster Publisher (Jiefang jun huabao she) also published sets of posters about Lei Feng. See *The Great Communist Soldier—Lei Feng* (1977). The posters I mention are on pages 7, 15, and 23.

39. On Ah Q in the 1980s see Tsu (2005, 125–27). On Lei Feng in the 1990s, see Deng Ziqi and Mi Jiaqi, eds. (1990). This volume includes the speeches of political leaders, articles about Lei Feng, and articles about the movement activities of various work units and schools. Many volumes concerning Lei Feng were published as part of the movement. Most include copies of calligraphy about Lei Feng, beginning with Mao's "Learn from Lei Feng" piece. See also Guo and Li (1990); and Li Zhixi (1991).

Notes to Chapter Four

1. This 2004 article by He Jixian is the first in a series, from a literary perspective, about the "three countryside" (sannong) problem, which is widely discussed today. The three countryside problem refers to the village, the peasant / farmer, and farming / agriculture (nongcun, nongmin, nongye). He Jixian argues that the countryside was "discovered" primarily through "othering" by writers who themselves are not part of the countryside culture they describe. The process of conceptualizing and describing the countryside and its culture inevitably involved simplification and produced the "countryside perspective" (nongcun shijiao) of nativist literature (xiangtu wenxue), and a variety of stances ranging from disdain to admiration, from vilifying to romanticizing.

2. Shen Congwen wrote: "Ever since Mr. Lu Xun started writing fiction that took as its material remembrances of the country village, which readers greatly welcomed, I have gained a great deal of bravery and confidence in my writing" (Chen Zhonggeng 2004, 72).

3. Yang Kai (2004) and others argue against Xia Zhiqing's (C. T. Hsia) mocking critique of Zhao's writing. Yang points out that the 2003 semi-documentary film *Blind Shaft* (Mangjing) is yet another revision of the discourse of the countryside (28–29).

4. For more information on roots writers, see Catherine Vance Yeh (2001, 229–56); Qingxi Li (2000); Song Rushan (2002).

5. A note at the end of the novel states that it was written from 1989 to 1990 and 1992 to 1993 (Mang Ke 1994, 289).

6. Although he criticized Freud's theories in his 1921 *Psychoanalysis and the Unconscious*, Lawrence's vision of sexual passion—as mysterious and profoundly important within the human psyche—is similar to that underlying Freud's work.

7. As Jing Tsu (2005) aptly states, in describing the oft-represented angst of the 1920s and 1930s, "Suffering displayed the emotion of literary modernity. Encom-

passing the nation's demise as well as the individual's tormented sexual identity, suffering provided the common framework in which both the self and the nation could be expressed" (196). Mang Ke does not take advantage of this historically sanctioned way of representation.

8. For a reference to Ah Cheng's opinion, see Wu Hongfei, who states: "His novel *Wild Things* was written based on his experience in the countryside at Baiyangdian. The writer Ah Cheng gives *Wild Things* an excellent rating: 'It is rich, full of vigor, showing the directness and warmth of a group of youth.' Mang Ke was the last of the 'Baiyangdian crowd' to return to the city. Before he left to become a worker, he burned up six years worth of poetry drafts." For more on the Baiyangdian poets, see Yang Jian (1993, 104–9).

9. *The Golden Years* and other works by Wang have recently been translated into English and published as *Wang in Love and Bondage: Three Novellas by Wang Xiaobo*, (2007). The title of the novella *Huangjin shidai* used by the translators is *The Golden Age.*

10. See Ai Xiaoming and Li Yinhe, eds. (1997) throughout for testimonials of many readers about the surprise they experienced when they first encountered Wang's unusual style. As Chen Xiaoming states, "I was rather late in reading Wang Xiaobo's fiction, and the first thing I read was *Love in the Age of Revolution* (Geming shiqi de aiqing) in [the journal] *Huacheng*. I was so shocked" (Ai Xiaoming and Li Yinhe, eds. 1997, 262). Yao Xinyong (2000) proclaims that "The Golden Years is not only radically different from all sent-down youth literature, but also different from all of the styles used in contemporary Chinese literature," but Yao interprets the novel from the perspective of a "repressed structure of feeling" (175).

11. Some of the articles in Ai Xiaoming and Li Yinhe, eds. (1997) directly or indirectly refer to this debate. See also Dai Jinhua (1998). For a discussion of the debate on neo-liberalism and liberalism, see the special issue of *Social Text* entitled "Intellectual Politics in Post-Tiananmen China," ed. Xudong Zhang (1998).

12. The volume I am using is Wang Xiaobo (1994), the first publication from China. The novel was first serialized in *United Daily Supplement* (Lianhe bao fukan) in 1991, when it received a prize. It was first published as a book in Hong Kong in 1992, and the same year it came out in Taiwan as a book. All translations are mine unless otherwise indicated.

13. As Ding Dong (1997) puts it: "The author uses the brightness of humor to bring into the light the pervasive constraints of the period, causing people's spiritual world to leap out from under the historical shadow of tragedy and darkness and making them feel the thrill of liberation. The author purposefully makes the reader feel that this is not the 'truth' of history, but rather is a twisted historical form. That makes us think of the words of one Western writer: 'If we tell you lies, it is because we have to prove to you that the false is true'" (279).

14. Echoing Ding Dong's comments above in an essay entitled "Paper Covered with Wild Words" (Manzhi huangtang yan) (the title is from *The Dream of the Red Chamber* [Honglou meng] and draws attention to the literary technique of embedding various aspects of reality within fiction or within an untrue story), Zhu

Zhenglin (1997) points to the difficulty of treating the plot as a general life during the Cultural Revolution or as a depiction of reality. Furthermore, Zhu finds it impossible to articulate the novel's power through plot-based discussion: "In summing up the content like this it is hard to avoid becoming too simplistic and too coarse, and it lacks accuracy. You have to read the novel, you can't just have someone introduce it to you. Seeing Wang Xiaobo's style, you can quickly see that he has mastered a unique way of narration . . . Unique experience includes unique understanding, and the genius of a writer is to bring it out in unique expression" (282–83).

15. For a discussion of the roots of youth culture in both pre-May Fourth China and in its specific Maoist development in the first twenty years of the People's Republic of China, see Xueping Zhong (1999). Zhong finds ten films that use the word *qingnian* or *qingchun* in their titles and many others that focus on youth. She notes that these films were melodramatic, didactic, and popular, and traces a Maoist change from *qingnian* to *qingchun*, which "became part of a political discourse and youth-oriented popular culture" and suggested identification through youth and a new sense of the self (156).

16. For more on the no-regrets movement see Xueping Zhong (1999, 157–55).

17. Yue Ma (2005) interprets Chen Qingyang's response to Wang Er's overtures as her "being moved by his offer of 'great friendship' and 'personal loyalty' despite her antagonism to physical intimacy" (213).

18. Ding Dong (1997) finds a strong thread of resistance in the novel, commenting: "Sex is the final point of Wang Er's resistance to the outside world. Wang Er says [of his penis], 'In my opinion, nothing is more important than this thing, and it is the basis of my existence.' Just as outside force is an undeniable fact, so is the desire of humans. You do it your way and I'll do it my way. Your lies cannot be reasoned with and my sexual desire likewise cannot be reasoned with. It does not turn on people's will. It's 'ugliness' is to some extent enough to match up against the lies of political power. Chen Qingyang always believes that 'Things that are real must have a reason.' That is exactly why she is tormented; the basic nature of lies is that they cannot be reasoned with" (278). Although I do not totally disagree with Ding Dong's interpretation, I disagree that the emphasis of the story is on resistance. Yue Ma (2005) also feels it would be misleading to read the sexual expression in the novel as a "gesture of political resistance," instead interpreting the novel as satirizing "the idealized association of sexual expression with the freedom of modernity" (212, 214).

19. Here Ai Xiaoming is discussing Wang Xiaobo's works in general, not just *The Golden Years.*

20. Dai makes this argument based on Wang's writing, fully aware that Wang studied in the United States.

21. It is worth noting that Dai Jinhua and others who find in Wang Xiaobo a discourse of power relations often bring in many of his other works, in particular Zhang Yuan's 1996 film *East Palace, West Palace* (Donggong xigong), for which Wang Xiaobo was a writer. In this film a young gay man gets involved with a policeman and begs to be beaten.

Notes to Chapter Five

1. *The Internationale* has been used throughout modern Chinese revolutionary history to inspire greater dedication and fortitude for the Communist struggle. That history makes it a perfect musical reference for ironic commentary as well, as Barbara Mittler (1997) has shown. Zeng Xingkui relates that it was the students' theme song during the Tiananmen Square sit-in, and he brings it into the piece as part of the protest against the 1989 massacre, as "a last sign of the students' will to win" (Mittler 1997, 118). Invoking the song in *In the Heat* to accompany the pseudo-political struggles of the youth gangs is a complex reference to the revolutionary past that suggests many criticisms. The most significant and shocking may be to equate the physical violence of some adolescent boys with the violence of the revolutionary struggle, which supposedly is motivated by ideals of equality and justice.

2. For the information above see Jiang Wen et al. (1997, 67–84). This book includes short essays by the actors and technicians involved in the film's making and an interview with Jiang Wen that details step-by-step the battles he had to gain funding for the film and keep the project alive. It also contains Jiang Wen's reminiscences about his first interest in Wang Shuo's story "Ferocious Beasts" (Dongwu xiongmeng), on which the film is based, along with copies of handwritten notes and scene sketches, the film script, the story, and many pictures of the film in making. For the story, see Wang Shuo (1995). I thank Martin Gieselmann for introducing me to *The Birth of a Film*, and Howard Yuen Fung Choy for lending the book to me for an extended period of time.

3. Dai's (1997) discussion helps us understand why the Cultural Revolution has become an ubiquitous part of popular culture today, invoked in restaurants, music, film, material culture such as teapots and alarm clocks, Mao badge collecting, etc. From this phenomenon, we also may be able to infer one reason why censors allowed the film to be shown in China. Despite being branded as "ten years of chaos and destruction," the Cultural Revolution also involved millions of relatively innocent people, who did their best to live up to its ideals across their daily lives, a reality that the aesthetic revolutionary forms express. Another way of putting this idea is common to governments around the world that wish to criticize the past while retaining the loyalty of the people: the state (at that time) was bad, but the people were good.

4. The film explains that although the correct pronunciation of Yu's name is Beibei, everyone calls her Beipei.

5. For a discussion of the novel and the film, see Huot (2000, 56–60). She states that the privately funded film is the "first film celebration of the Cultural Revolution" in China and points out that it was widely publicized in Beijing, with free t-shirts and other promotional material available (58, 60). Kang Liu (1997a) notes that the film received an award at the Taiwan Film Festival in 1996 (113).

6. For a discussion of Jiang Wen's attraction to Wang Shuo's story, and the autobiographical elements for both the writer and the director, see Jiang Wen (1997).

7. This section of the film originally was much longer, but Jiang Wen decided to cut most of it out, reducing the film's length by almost two hours (1997, 13).

8. Dutton (1998) provides a historical discussion of the Mao fetish throughout Mao's life, during the Cultural Revolution, and after his death (232–71). For a lyrical and revealing discussion of the Mao craze and its significance in terms of social consciousness, see Dai Jinhua (1996).

9. For other references to the emotional reaction the film engendered in viewers, see Dai Jinhua (1999, 413–15). Dai notes that the film was understood as autobiographical and inspired interest in Jiang Wen's early life.

10. Li Xun (1996) notes that Gulunmu's perspective is the same as the film's perspective toward Ma Xiaojun's present life. Li claims that the song played during this black and white segment, titled "Those who have turned their lives around all miss Chairman Mao," is also a rejection of the consumer lifestyle (62).

11. Ban Wang, using research by Dai Jinhua, points out that central to this development are scenes of mass gatherings, which Dai calls the "Cui Wei ceremony," because of their prevalence in Cui Wei's films. Wang also notes the "aspiring for and striving for heroism" that Meng Yue has identified as crucial to the revolutionary film (Ban Wang 1997, 130–31).

12. Ban Wang points out that when discussing *Song of Youth*, "downplaying sexual love does not eliminate its broadly sexual implications or libidinal intensity . . . [The Cui Wei ceremony] may swallow up the particular individual into a 'faceless' collective, but it is also presented as a rebirth of the individual within the community, a reassertion of his or her capacities, identity, and desire . . . It is a fantasy of a total harmony of society and the individual that glorifies these spectacles . . ." (1997, 136).

13. Ban Wang (1997) believes that revolutionary film (in his analysis, *Song of Youth* and *Nie Er*) "sublimates and converts erotic impulses into revolutionary passion" (138), but I disagree with this interpretation. Wang argues that libidinal energy is the most authentic and primary energy, because it implies first that sexual desire can be expressed outside of human social structure, and second that all forms of human life (work, relationships, eating and consumption, art, etc.), which equally demand energy and inspire passion, are secondary to primordial sexual desire. Furthermore, in that this structure repeats the central claim of Freudian psychology, that everything is rooted in the sexual, Wang's interpretation throws more fuel on one of the central 20th-century Western myths of human identity, as I see it.

14. Lin often wears the same white scarf that Milan gives to Liu Yiku (along with a volume of Pushkin's poetry) at the birthday party for him and for Ma Xiaojun at the Moscow restaurant. As Liu wraps it around his neck, someone comments, "Like doing a May Fourth!" (xiang nao wusi de), showing the importance of style, the historical weight that the scarf carries, and Milan's centering of Liu Yiku as her hero. Importantly, the political ideologies of the May Fourth period have disappeared, to be replaced by the aesthetics of the scarf, which testifies to youthful energy.

15. Li Xun (1996) finds that these two endeavors are in opposition and present the viewer with the dichotomy of collective/conformist as opposed to self/individual. For Li, Ma Xiaojun's explosion in the Moscow restaurant is the high point of the film, since it brings to a head these two opposing forces (61). The music that marks the love relationship, Mascagni's *Cavalleria Rusticana*, is heard in the presence of Ma's friends only during the final scene in the swimming pool, when he has alienated Milan with his sexual attack on her and angered his friends. Therefore the loss of the collective and the loss of love become the same thing (61).

16. Another film by this title, directed by Giuseppe Vari, was produced in Italy in 1960. I thank Martin Gieselmann for tracking this film down and sharing the information with me.

17. Zhang Yiwu (1998) describes the shot thus: "*In the Heat of the Sun* has an interesting scene. A boy secretly enters a beautiful girl's room. No one is there, and he uses a telescope to 'gaze' at a picture of the beautiful girl. Everything changes form; the boy gets dizzy and whirls around ceaselessly. The picture becomes a mysterious, vague impression, a point of light turning at high speed" (23).

18. Throughout the film, Ma Xiaojun and Milan joke about her plumpness. In the novel, Wang Shuo (1995) calls Milan well developed, "like a white girl" (273).

19. Author Wang Shuo plays the bully. Jiang Wen, too, has a cameo role in the film, playing the adult Ma Xiaojun in the limousine. The use of cameos shows the director's playfulness and self-consciousness.

20. In a discussion of the meanings of memory in the film, Yomi Braester (2001) comments that Milan first appears in red, with flags on the side of her picture, in a posture often associated with Mao (350–62). Howard Yuen Fung Choy (unpublished paper) notes that the picture of Milan in her home hangs where one would normally find a picture of Mao; thus, Milan has replaced Mao as an object of worship.

21. For an elaboration of this approach in the films of other fifth-generation directors, see Larson (1995, 215–26; 1997b).

22. The title of this section comes from Anchee Min's novel *Katherine*: "We returned to the city and Katherine invited us back to her hut to dance. We were never this wild in our lives, except during the Cultural Revolution when we copied Mao's teachings on the walls" (Min 1995, 106).

23. A number of reviews of *Red Azalea* have been published. They include Polumbaum (1994); Shapiro with Springen (1994); Evans (1994); Tonkin (1993); Shapiro (1994). Many of Min's works focus on life during the revolutionary period, when she was growing up, and they all contain a heavy dose of sexual intrigue.

24. Another book written in Chinese but published in English, by Hong Ying, who lives in England, brazenly sets up sexual behavior as a powerful anti-state expression. In Hong's *Summer of Betrayal* (1997), what represents state power is not the radical leftist government of the Cultural Revolution, but the government that orders the troops into Tiananmen Square in 1989. As the state clamps down on protesters, the young intellectuals on whom the plot centers carry out an orgy

of sexual intercourse, and the protagonist Lin Ying rebelliously confronts police with her naked body.

25. Barmé (1999) has included this article as chapter 10 in his recent book, *In The Red: On Contemporary Chinese Culture*; it ends with a poem written in English by Ouyang Yu titled "Sex Notice": "so instead of boring me let me bore you / with a brand new China-made flute / to play you a tune of starved love / for five thousand years / to flood you with fresh cum / of the Yellow River and the Yangtse / so if you want to come and be my love / call me at sex sex sex plus triple sex" (280). This poem positions a culturally deep sexual power against the life of anger and boredom experienced by Chinese abroad. The English version was originally published in Ianssen and Wang (1996, 106).

26. For an interpretation of *Red Azalea* that differs sharply from mine, see Somerson (1997). Somerson reads the novel as one piece of evidence that transnational feminist theorizing should include issues of sexuality, and she views Min's presentation of desire as an assertion that "women's bodies have desires that cannot be contained through recourse to official ideology" (108). She claims to have moved away from the " 'Western' psychoanalytic framework" that she believes discourages "studies of sexuality in relation to transnational issues" (113), but in her overall approach, and in her valorization of Min's assertion that "women's bodies have desires that cannot be contained through recourse to official ideology" (108), she very much works within the theorization of desire that materialist analyses such as that of Teresa L. Ebert (1996) work against. Somerson argues that the notion of the protagonist "escaping" from China is a Western Orientalist projection (that Min may make use of for the purpose of critiquing it). Although this comment is to some degree insightful, I see the "escape" as a theme developed comprehensively within Min's overarching interpretation of politics and desire in post-revolutionary China. Min's own take on what she is doing is that she is striving for honesty, truth, and the fight against the human evil that the Cultural Revolution embodies: "I believe that humans are born greedy. There's an evil side to it, and if you don't fight it, it may just grow like monsters . . . [it is] this gradual process of how young people are sucked into this giant funnel of insanity. Insanity, little by little gives way to habit. Once you give way to habit, habit gives way to coercion and coercion to sadism. If you study Nazi Germany in the '20s and '30s and communist Russia after Stalin took power—it's the same descent into madness" (Briggs 1998).

27. For an example of an earlier text that also assigns some of the blame for revolutionary excess on the misuse of words, see Wang Meng (1989).

28. See Sam Sloan's extensive website on the Berkeley sexual freedom movement at http://www.samsloan.com/sfl.htm. Sloan notes: "I was President of the Berkeley Sexual Freedom League in 1966 and 1967. I did not found the organization. Jefferson Poland actually thought up the name. However, his was just a publicity stunt. Poland had no actual organization. I also did not organize the first sex orgy. Richard Thorne did that. Thorne looked and talked so much like actor Bill Cosby that I once believed that they were the same person. Thorne disappeared

not long thereafter and changed his name to Ohm. However, I was the first person who organized weekly sex orgies on a regular basis."

29. For a discussion of avant-garde writers and their approach, see Jing Wang (1996); also see the feminist critique of avant-garde writers by Tonglin Lu (1995).

30. I argue that the female writer Chen Ran also situates women in a special position, as more able than men to resist and escape definition by the state, within postmodern culture (Larson 1997a).

31. Harriet Evans notes that Professor Pan Suiming of the People's University in Beijing told her that rape and sexual abuse of women was common during the height of the Cultural Revolution, and that a classified document on this problem was issued. Evans also points out that although the representations of sexuality were not available in openly published form, fictionalized accounts from sent-down students commonly "suggest a range of sexual experiences that had nothing to do with the moral and ideological values of the time" (Evans 1995, 366; 366, n. 12).

32. For a discussion of the "antimodernity" concepts embedded in Chinese Marxist / Maoist modernity, see Wang Hui (1998). Some of the antimodern social practices Wang locates include "fear of a bureaucratic state, contempt for the formalization of legal structures, an emphasis on absolute egalitarianism," and Wang concludes that "inherent in China's socialist modernization experience is a historical antimodernity" (15). Implicit in this analysis is the existence of another "successful" modernity that embodies many of the concepts and practices that Marxism / Maoism has rejected. To Wang's list, we also could add the psychologizing of individual subjectivity—with desire and sexuality at its unconscious center.

Notes to Chapter Six

1. Gotz (1977) notes that "Socialist realism demands positive models, heroes who show the way, who prevail in the ideological struggles as well as physical battles, according to the principles of revolutionary optimism" (91–92). See also Noumoff (1975), who notes that in 1957, "A system was called for integrating physical labour with regular work," the principle being that all cadres had to engage in the same kind of work as ordinary laborers, and only through this kind of institutional resistance could bureaucratization be avoided (181–82). Work was ranked on a scale of least advanced (labor) to most advanced (work), Noumoff explains (182).

2. It is important to note, however, that the Maoist model contained an inherent contradiction between valorizing work, society, and others, and valorizing the self. As the story of Lei Feng shows well, it was all too easy for the revolutionary worker to be put forth as a model in diaries, poems, and images; the following that Lei Feng generated illustrates the fine line between promoting the socialized self and promoting socialism itself.

3. Originally published in *United Literature* (Lianhe wenxue) in 1992.

4. For a detailed analysis of this film, see David L. Li (2001).

5. For a discussion of gender marginalization and aesthetics, see Wendy Larson (2002).

6. Starting in 1982, He Jianjun worked with Chen Kaige and other fifth generation directors on a number of films. In 1988 he began to study film directing, and in 1991 directed the short documentary *Self Portrait* (Zi huaxiang). He directed *Red Beads* (Xuanlian) (also known as *Hongdou*) in 1993, *The Postman* in 1995, *Butterfly Smile* (Hudie de weixiao) in 2001, and *Pirated Copy* (Manyan) in 2004.

7. Xiao Dou has little agency of his own unless a door is opened a crack on his behalf. The first opening is Lao Wu's departure, and the second comes when Yunqing hands him an envelope that has come open and asks him to reseal it. He puts the letter in another envelope and rewrites the address on it. This letter turns out to be the first one that he opens and reads. By calling his attention to the letter, Yunqing has given him an opportunity first to think of reading the letter, and second to open it without detection and without direct deceit, since it was open anyway.

8. In her study of contemporary workers and their concepts of work and of themselves, Lisa Rofel (1999) comments that those raised on Cultural Revolution ideology believe that "struggle against improper authority is the singularly most important activity in life" (176). The Red Guards are perhaps the most extreme example of a group motivated to fight against both conceptual authorities, such as feudal ideas and backward daily habits, and against those who represent authority, such as teachers or local leaders.

9. The only romantic image in the film is of an older couple taking their birds out for a walk. We soon discover, however, that even this happiness is based on an illusion.

10. Several times we see people hesitantly approaching the box to mail letters and pausing, full of trepidation, before they drop a letter into the box.

11. In this scene the camera is focused on Xiao Dou sitting on the floor in his underwear next to Yunqing's bed. He yells out his question, "What was it like that time?" and we hear her disembodied response from a distance. The scene emphasizes Xiao Dou's isolation and Yunqing's lack of emotional connection. At a later point in her bedroom she looks at Xiao Dou and comments about how good she feels, and then moves to caress and kiss him, but we are unsure if Yunqing feels good because she is with Xiao Dou or because she has had a satisfactory sexual experience.

12. Such a sentiment is put into words by the letter from the young suicidal couple: "The world doesn't seem to need us anymore" expresses their lack of a sense of positive social or physical space.

13. As Sussman (1997) writes: ". . . modern Western ideology heightens the moral dilemma, isolation, and play accruing to the self. An increased leeway opened through a more direct engagement with the sources of authority implies greater moral responsibility and added participation in the scenario of an 'ultimate' moral outcome" (81).

14. A lengthy shot of Xiao Dou and his sister talking as they eat is taken from a distance away and a little below, with the camera not moving during the conversation. The monotonous angle contributes to the sense of a general lack of liveliness in relationships, even in this one that is portrayed as more profound than others.

15. I asked director He Jianjun this question in an interview in June 2004, and he told me that the man in bed with the sister is Xiao Dou.

16. The words of the two lovers, which we hear as Xiao Dou reads their letters, refer mostly to their love for each other; thus, it would make more sense that Xiao Dou is intervening because of the sexual relationship.

17. Xiao Dou also writes to the elderly couple, but only in the name of their son.

18. Jackie Sheehan (1998) details a long history of worker activism and uneasy relationships between workers and authorities that spans the entire century. Sheehan also finds that although workers had to negotiate a position for themselves within socialist rhetoric about duties and their vanguard position, they generally took the concepts and ideas with a grain of salt. Practical concerns such as working hours and conditions, wages, living and health issues, and access to various benefits were the motivation behind conflicts between workers and cadres, rather than ideological issues. In his analysis of *biaoxian*, or self-presentation, Andrew G. Walder (1986) finds that ironically, "it is the truly committed who must be the most calculating in their display of commitment . . ." (146), and that there generally is deep resentment against "activists" who constantly try to present themselves as politically correct (166–69). Lisa Rofel (1999) notes that the workers who used "foot-dragging techniques" of resistance, or indirect techniques of subversion, were those who came of age during the Cultural Revolution, because they had developed a politics of authority that encouraged them to challenge improperly used power (174–75).

19. See Andrew Walder (1986) for a discussion of the anger that the blatantly activist approach generated in other workers. It was much safer to gain political recognition through making the chance discovery of a lost diary than through the daily performance of political virtue, which infuriated one's fellow workers.

20. For a reference to this slogan and a discussion of the "Maoist utopian longing for a full and complete life," see Xiaobing Tang (2000, 278–80).

21. A popular example would be Chi Li's 1995 novel *Coming and Going* (Lailai wangwang) and the 1999 television series based on it, which traces the moral downfall of a formerly upright man who had worked as a butcher and studied Mao's writings in his spare time. Jia Pingwa's famous *Abandoned City* (or *Abandoned Capital*) also works along these lines.

22. For discussion of humanism and subjectivity in China, see Liu Zaifu (1999); Jing Wang (1996), chapter 1 on voluntarism and chapter 5 on romancing the subject; Misra (1998), chapter 5. Humanism was proposed as a correction to Maoism throughout the 1980s and into the 1990s. The previously mentioned *Bolshevik Salute* by Wang Meng, although still professing belief in socialism, has an underlying humanist message. Another key literary text in the promotion of humanism is Dai Houying's *People, A, People* (Ren, a, ren) (1999).

23. Jing Wang (1996) describes the pre-experimental roots writers thus: "The body is culturally inscribed but the mind and heart are free" (216).

24. The reference is to Lu Jiandong (1996).

25. Xudong Zhang (2001) contains a number of contributions from the "neo-leftist" position, which argues that "only by including the masses can the success and political-moral meaning of the Chinese Reform be assured" (68).

Notes to Conclusion

1. I first presented the ideas of this chapter at the conference "Methods and Meanings: Regarding Modern Chinese Literature," organized by Xiaobing Tang at the University of Chicago, May 6–7, 2005.

2. For a relatively recent explanation of the new historicism, see Gallagher and Greenblatt (2000). The introduction (1–19) lays out the principles of the approach, and the title of the first chapter ("The Touch of the Real") suggests its epistemological claims. The journal *Representations* was developed to publish new historicist scholarship. Hamilton (1996) positions new historicism within a genealogy that began with Vico and Herder, and was developed as a hermeneutics by Kant and Hegel. The new historicism comes toward the end of this series, eclipsed only by "Postcolonial Stylistics and Postmodern Logic," "Herstory," and "Globalization and the End of History."

3. Chandler (2000) argues (or at least notes that it could be argued) that "this allegiance to the canon was also an allegiance to the critical tradition that shaped the canon . . ." (6).

4. For a discussion of the differences between various kinds of critical theory as they have been expressed and debated in the United States and Great Britain, see Pieters's 2000 review of John Brannigan's *New Historicism and Cultural Materialism.*

5. The work under discussion is "The Need for Cultural Studies: Resisting Intellectuals and Oppositional Public Spheres." Dillon (1998) also discusses the series of articles by Donald Pease in which he argues against disciplinary allegiance and in favor of political engagement, stating that the requirement of the "new Americanist" should be "primary identification with the sociopolitical strategies of social movements, rather than the academic discipline which they practice . . ." (59–61).

6. By "aesthetic" or "formal" analysis, I refer to close reading of the way in which the text produces meaning. "Literariness" is a primary aesthetic component for literature. Aesthetic analysis does not preclude discussion of historical and ideological issues.

7. For a relevant study, see Dirlik (1997).

8. For analysis of the discipline vs. interdisciplinary identity projects, see Wiegman (2002). In a comment on Lisa Lowe's discussion of Asian American studies ("The International within the National: American Studies and Asian American Critique"), Wiegman questions Lowe's optimism about the challenge to the or-

ganization of knowledge that identity studies has delivered, noting that identity studies have not been entirely successful in challenging "the identitarian form of the university's intellectual reproduction in the disciplines" (146). Although such programs aimed to be interdisciplinary and to "overcome the professionalized illegibility between knowledge domains in the university, between, say, the study of literature and language on one hand and political economy on the other," the result has not been entirely successful, with interdisciplinary programs functioning almost entirely as undergraduate study programs (146). As Wiegman argues, disciplinary scholars may find interdisciplinarity liberating, yet "interdisciplinarity is still very much tied to the disciplines where the critical work of reproducing academic intellectual subjects continues to take place" (147). In a further illuminating note, Wiegman states that interdisciplinarity "often protects the disciplines by guaranteeing their proliferation at the site of an object—today so often a minoritized identity—whose social rebellion has engendered it as an object to be known" (154–55, n. 20).

9. The question of why within large universities history is conceived as a department, whereas literature generally is organized through national / linguistic / cultural divisions is too complex for this chapter but raises interesting questions about the assumptions of these categories. Most obviously, literature as a discipline developed out of the study of language, and this connection is still maintained. Even with difficult languages like Chinese, advanced undergraduate students eventually read literature in the original, whereas history departments rarely offer the study of original texts until a student is involved in graduate research, and often even then this original language study is conducted largely within individual research, not as a basis of classroom work. While literature taught as part of a national / cultural unit encourages essentialism in identity, language, and culture, history departments encourage one to imagine that specificity in language and culture should be secondary to an overall historical context.

10. Chow was an early adherent of critical theory (and later, cultural studies) within China studies, bringing in the work of various French and Anglo-theorists. She has been criticized for her reliance on "Western theory," but compared to others working in Chinese studies, her work has gained her the greatest currency within the larger field of cultural studies. However, Chow's approach raises other problems, especially the implication that theory cannot develop outside the West. I have criticized Chow's approach as itself continuing to center on the West (Larson 1997c). As I explain in this chapter, I do not believe cultural studies as a field has adequately addressed this problem of critical theory.

11. Jeffreys's (2004) determination to regard everyone as equal contributors (despite her insistence that other Chinese scholars refuse to recognize hierarchies of knowledge) produces some odd equivalencies, such as that between Michel Foucault and Li Yinhe (68).

12. Rowe (2002) speaks directly to my subject when he notes that his criticism of the "literary history" that he was taught as an undergraduate is "that it was not

sufficiently *historical*, in large part because it failed to take into account the larger political, social, and economic forces involved in such cultural production" (108).

13. One crucial moment of awareness came when an English major in my Modern Chinese Literature course sharply criticized my refusal to engage deeply with the text. His perspective helped me see that the radical difference of the Chinese literary tradition, combined with the developing historicism of the field, had pulled me away from literary analysis and toward a presentation of general cultural and historical background.

Bibliography

Ahmad, Aijaz. 1992. "Jameson's Rhetoric of Otherness and the 'National Allegory.'" In *Theory: Class, Nations, Literatures,* ed. Aijaz Ahmad, 95–122. New York: Verso.

Ai Xiaoming. 1997. "Another Take on *The Golden Years*" (Chongdu *Huangjin shidai*). In *Romantic Knight: Remembering Wang Xiaobo* (Langman qishi: jiyi Wang Xiaobo), ed. Ai Xiaoming and Li Yinhe, 270–76. Beijing: Zhongguo qingnian chubanshe.

Ai Xiaoming and Li Yinhe, eds. 1997. *Romantic Knight: Remembering Wang Xiaobo* (Langman qishi: jiyi Wang Xiaobo). Beijing: Zhongguo qingnian chubanshe.

Althusser, Louis. 1996 [1993]. *Writings on Psychoanalysis: Freud and Lacan.* Trans. Jeffrey Mehlman. New York: Columbia University Press.

Anagnost, Ann. 1997. *National Past-times: Narrative, Representation, and Power in Modern China.* Durham, NC: Duke University Press.

Bai Hua. 1997. "Highlights of a Discussion on Wang Xiaobo's Works and the Novel Collection *The Golden Years*" (Wang Xiaobo zuopin ji xiaoshuo ji *Huangjin shidai*). In *Romantic Knight: Remembering Wang Xiaobo* (Langman qishi: jiyi Wang Xiaobo), ed. Ai Xiaoming and Li Yinhe, 259–64. Beijing: Zhongguo qingnian chubanshe.

Baker, Keith Michael. 1990. *Inventing the French Revolution: Essays on French Political Culture in the Eighteenth Century.* Cambridge: Cambridge University Press.

Barlow, Tani E. 2004. *The Question of Women in Chinese Feminism.* Durham, NC: Duke University Press.

Barmé, Geremie R. 1996. "To Screw Foreigners Is Patriotic: China's Avant-Garde Nationalists." In *Chinese Nationalism*, ed. Jonathan Unger, 183–208. Armonk, NY: M. E. Sharpe.

———. 1999. *In the Red: On Contemporary Chinese Culture.* New York: Columbia University Press.

Bate, Jonathan. 1991. *Romantic Ideology: Wordsworth and the Environmental Tradition.* New York: Routledge.

Bays, Daniel H., ed. 1996. *Christianity in China: From the Eighteenth Century to the Present.* Stanford: Stanford University Press.

Berger, Peter. 1965. "Toward a Sociological Understanding of Psychoanalysis." *Social Research* 32 (spring): 26–41.

Berliner, David C. "The 100-Year Journey of Educational Psychology: From Interest, to Disdain, to Respect for Practice." http://courses.ed.asu.edu/berliner/readings/journey.htm. (accessed December, 2005).

Bernard, Luther Lee. 1922. "Instincts and the Psychoanalysts." *Journal of Abnormal Psychology and Social Psychology* 17: 350–66.

Birken, Lawrence. 1988. *Consuming Desire: Sexual Science and the Emergence of a Culture of Abundance, 1871–1914*. Ithaca, NY: Cornell University Press.

Blowers, G. 2000. "Learning from Others: Japan's Role in Bringing Psychology to China." *American Psychologist* 55: 1433–36.

Bol, Peter K. 2003. "The 'Localist Turn' and 'Local Identity' in Later Imperial China." *Late Imperial China* 24:2 (December): 1–50.

Bonner, Joey. 1986. *Wang Kuo-wei: An Intellectual Biography*. Cambridge: Harvard University Press.

Braester, Yomi. 2001. "Memory at a Standstill: Street-Smart History in Jiang Wen's *In the Heat of the Sun*." *Screen* 42:4 (winter): 350–62.

Brannigan, John. 1998. *New Historicism and Cultural Materialism*. New York: MacMillan.

Breger, Louis. 2000. *Freud: Darkness in the Midst of Vision*. New York: John Wiley & Sons, Inc.

Brennan, James F. 2003 [1982]. *History and Systems of Psychology*. Upper Saddle River, NJ: Prentice Hall.

Briggs, Tracy Wong. 1998. Interview on the World Wide Web. *USA Today* "Bookshelf." June 24.

Brome, Vincent. 1979. *Havelock Ellis, Philosopher of Sex: A Biography*. London, Boston, and Henley: Routledge & Kegan Paul.

Brown, Bruce. 1973. *Marx, Freud, and the Critique of Everyday Life*. New York: Monthly Review Press.

Brown, Carolyn. 1988a. "Lu Xun's Interpretation of Dreams." In *Psycho-Sinology: The Universe of Dreams in Chinese Culture*, ed. Carolyn Brown, 67–79. Washington, DC: Woodrow Wilson International Center for Scholars.

———. 1988b. "Woman as Trope: Gender and Power in Lu Xun's 'Soap.'" *Modern Chinese Literature* 4 (January–February): 55–70.

Brown, L. B. 1981. *Psychology in Contemporary China*. Oxford: Pergamon Press.

Brown, Paul, and Onno van der Hart. 1998. "Memories of Sexual Abuse: Janet's Critique of Freud, a Balanced Approach." *Psychological Reports* 82: 1027–43.

Brown Recovered Memory Project. http://www.brown.edu/Departments/Taubman_Center/Recovmem/ (accessed August 29, 2007).

Brugger, Bill, and David Kelly. 1990. *Chinese Marxism in the Post-Mao Era*. Stanford: Stanford University Press.

Bruner, Jerome. 2004. "A Short History of Psychological Theories of Learning." *Daedalus: Journal of the American Academy of Arts and Sciences* (winter): 13–20.

Cao Richang. 1959. "What Does Psychology Investigate?" *Acta Psychologica Sinica* 4: 244–49. (Translated in full in L. B. Brown 1981, 121–24.)

Cao Zefu. 1964. "Spiritual Life Is Loftier than Material Life: Critiquing Comrade Chen Ding's View on Happiness" (Jingshen shenghuo gao yu wuzhi shenghuo—ping Chen Ding tongzhi de xingfu guan). *Nanfang Daily* (Nanfang ribao) 1:9 (1964): 2. Reprinted in *Ethics* (Lunli) (January–June 1964). Beijing: Zhongguo renmin daxue fushu jianbao ziliao shu kapian she, 1964.

Carpenter, William Benjamin. 1855. *Principles of Mental Physiology, With Their Applications to the Training and Discipline of the Mind and the Study of its Morbid Conditions.* London: J. Churchill.

Chairman Mao's Good Soldier: Lei Feng (Mao zhuxi de hao zhanshi: Lei Feng). 1978. Beijing: Zhongguo qingnian chuban she.

Chandler, David. 2000. " 'One Consciousness,' Historical Criticism and the Romantic Canon." in *Romanticism on the Net* (February). (http://users.ox.ac.uk/scat0385/17ideology.html) (accessed February 2004).

Chang, Hao. 1993. "Confucian Cosmological Myth and Neo-Confucian Transcendence." In *Cosmology, Ontology, and Human Efficacy: Essays in Chinese Thought,* ed. Richard J. Smith and D.W.Y. Kwok, 11–34. Honolulu: University of Hawaii Press.

Chapman, A. H. 1976. *Harry Stack Sullivan: The Man and His Work.* New York: G. P. Putnam's Sons.

Chen Daqi. 1918. "Rebutting 'Spiritualism' " (Guan "lingxue"). *New Youth* (Xin qingnian) 4:5 (May): 370–85.

Chen Derong, trans. 1934. "Theories of Psycho-analysis" (Jiexin shu xueshuo), by John C. Flugel. Shanghai: Shangwu chubanshe.

Chen Fuxing. 1991. "The Impossible Language—Psychoanalysis or Psychological Analysis" (Bu keneng de yuyan: jingshen fenxi huo xinli fenxi). In *The Early River of Contemporary Western Thought: Thinkers of the 19th Century* (Dangdai xifang sixiang xianhe: shijiu shiji de sixiangjia), ed. Ye Qizheng. Taibei: Zhengzhong.

Chen Guangsheng. 1963. *Short Biography of Lei Feng* (Lei Feng xiaozhuan). Beijing: Zhongguo qingnian chubanshe.

Chen, Hsiu-fen. 2003. "Medicine, Society, and the Making of Madness in Imperial China." Ph.D. diss., University of London.

Chen, Nancy H. 1999. "Translating Psychiatry and Mental Health in Twentieth Century China." In *Tokens of Exchange: The Problem of Translation in Global Circulation,* ed. Lydia Liu, 305–30. Durham: Duke University Press.

Chen Qiwei. 2001. "On Translated Names in Philosophy" ("Zhexue" yiming kao). http://www.acriticism.com/article.asp?Newsid=703&type=1005 (accessed May 24, 2006).

Chen Ran. 1995. "The Sound of Another Ear Knocking" (Ling yizhi erduo de qiaoji sheng). In *Hidden Natures, Lost Affairs* (Qianxing yishi), 20–77. Shijiazhuang: Hebei jiaoyu chubanshe.

Chen Xiaoming. 1995a. "The Expansion of Sexual Love, the Self, and Poeticness" (Aiyu, ziwo yu shixing de kuayue). *Dangdai* (June): 45–71.

———. 1995b. "Surpassing emotion: eroticized narrative methods: one literary trend of the 90s" (Chaoyue qinggan: yuwanghua de xushi faze: jiushi niandai wenxue liuxiang zhiyi). *Dangdai* (December): 33–49.

———. 1997. "The Mysterious Other: Postpolitics in Chinese Film." *boundary 2* 24:3 (fall): 123–42.

Chen Zhengyang. 1990. "The Moral Value of the Lei Feng Spirit Is Forever" (Lei Feng jingshen de daode jiazhi shi yongcun de). In *On Lei Feng: 1963–1990 Collected Essays from Looking Back on the Study of Lei Feng and Forward Toward Theoretical Discussion Meetings* (Lun Lei Feng—1963–1990 xue Lei Feng huigu yu zhanwang lilun zhuotan hui wenji), ed. Liu Shushen, 319–26. Beijing: Guofang daxue chuban she.

Chen Zhonggeng. 2004. "From 'Nativist' to 'Root-Seeking': Three Important Developments in Literary Modernity" (Cong 'xiangtu' dao 'xungen': wenxue xiandaixing de san da liubian). *Literary Theory and Criticism* 2 (March): 71–75.

Cheng Naiyi. 1959. "On the Issue of the Target of Psychological Study" (Guanyu xinlixue de duixiang wenti). *Beijing University Academic Journal* [Human sciences] 2: 103–10.

Chin, Robert, and Ai-li S. Chin. 1969. *Psychological Research in Communist China, 1949–1966*. Cambridge: MIT Press.

Chiu, Martha Li. 1986. "Mind, Body, and Illness in a Chinese Medical Tradition." Ph.D. diss., Harvard University.

Chong, Woei Lien. 1996. "Mankind and Nature in Chinese Thought: Li Zehou on the Traditional Roots of Maoist Voluntarism." *China Information* 9:2 / 3 (autumn / winter): 138–75.

———. 1999. "Combining Marx with Kant: The Philosophical Anthropology of Li Zehou." *Philosophy East and West* (April): 120–49.

———. 2002. "Philosophy in an Age of Crisis: Three Thinkers in Post-Cultural Revolution China: Li Zehou, Liu Xiaobo, and Liu Xiaofeng." In *China's Great Proletarian Cultural Revolution: Master Narratives and post-Mao Counternarratives*, ed. Woei Lien Chong, 212–54. Boston: Rowman & Littlefield Publishers, Inc.

Chong You. 1904. "On the Usefulness of the People's Spirit in China" (Lun Zhongguo minqi zhi keyong). *Eastern Miscellany* (Dongfang zazhi) 1 (February 25) (Guangxu year 30, zhengyue, 25th day): 5–7.

Choy, Howard Yuen Fung. "Nostalgific(a)tion: Wang Shuo's and Jiang Wen's Cultural Revolution Romance." Unpublished paper.

Chu Zhi, trans. 1940. *Jingshen fenxi yu weiwuguan shiguan* (*Freud and Marx: A Dialectical Study*, by Reuben Osborn). Shanghai: Shijie chubanshe.

Cloud, Dana L. 1998. *Control and Consolation in American Culture and Politics: Rhetorics of Therapy*. Thousand Oaks, CA: Sage Publications.

Coleman, Heather J. 2005. *Russian Baptists and Spiritual Revolution, 1905–1929*. Bloomington and Indianapolis: Indiana University Press.

Corson, Samuel A., ed. 1976. "A Comparative Look at Soviet Psychiatry." In *Psychiatry and Psychology in the USSR.* New York: Plenum Press.

Crews, Frederick. 1993. "The Unknown Freud." *New York Review of Books* (November 18): 53–66.

———, ed. 1998. *Unauthorized Freud: Doubters Confront a Legend.* New York: Penguin Books.

Cushman, Philip. 1995. *Constructing the Self, Constructing America: A Cultural History of Psychotherapy*, Reading, MA: Addison-Wesley Publishing Co.

Dai Houying. 1999. *People, A, People* (Ren, a, ren). Hefei: Anhui wenyi chuban she.

Dai Jinhua. 1996. "Redemption and Consumption: Depicting Culture in the 1990s." *positions* 4:1 (spring), 127–44.

———. 1997. "Imagined Nostalgia." *boundary 2* 24:3 (fall): 143–62.

———. 1998. "Jokes of the cognoscenti—Reading Wang Xiaobo" (Zhizhe xixue: yuedu Wang Xiaobo). *Contemporary Writers Criticism* (Dangdai zuojia pinglun) 2: 21–34.

———. 1999. *View from the Leaning Tower: Chinese Film Culture 1978–1998* (Xieta liaowang: Zhongguo dianying wenhua 1978–1998). Taibei: Yuanliu.

———. 2001. "Behind Global Spectacle and National Image Making." *positions: east asia cultures critique* 9:1 161–186.

Davidson, Arnold I. 2001. *The Emergence of Sexuality: Historical Epistemology and the Formation of Concepts.* Cambridge: Harvard University Press.

Davies, Gloria. 1991. "The Problematic Modernity of Ah Q." *Chinese Literature: Essays, Articles, Reviews* 13: 57–76.

———. 1992. "Chinese Literary Studies and Post–structuralist Positions: What Next?" *Australian Journal of Chinese Affairs* 28: 67–86.

———. 1998. "Professing Postcoloniality: The Perils of Cultural Legitimation." *Post Colonial Studies* 1: 171–82.

———. 2000a. "Theory, Professionalism, and Chinese Studies." *Modern Chinese Literature and Culture* 12:1: 1–42.

———, ed. 2000b. *Voicing Concerns: Contemporary Chinese Critical Inquiry.* Lanham, MD: Rowman & Littlefield.

de Lauretis, Teresa. 1994. *The Practice of Love: Lesbian Sexuality and Perverse Desire.* Bloomington: Indiana University Press.

Deng Ziqi and Mi Jiaqi, eds. 1990. *A Lei Feng–Style Heroic Model* (Lei Feng shi de yingmo). Beijing: Jiefang jun chuban she.

Dikötter, Frank. 1995. *Sex, Culture, and Modernity in China: Medical Science and the Construction of Sexual Identities in the Early Republican Period.* Honolulu: University of Hawaii Press.

Dillon, Elizabeth Maddock. 1998. "Fear of Formalism: Kant, Twain, and Cultural Studies in American Literature." *Diacritics* 27:4: 46–69.

———. 2004. "Sentimental Aesthetics." *American Literature*, 76:3 (September): 495–523.

Ding Dong. 1997. "Transcending the culture of embarrassment" (Chaoyue xiuzhixin wenhua). In *Romantic Knight: Remembering Wang Xiaobo* (Langman qishi: jiyi Wang Xiaobo), ed. Ai Xiaoming and Li Yinhe, 277–80. Beijing: Zhongguo qingnian chubanshe.

Dirlik, Arif. 1983. "The Predicament of Marxist Revolutionary Consciousness: Mao Zedong, Antonio Gramsci, and the Reformulation of Marxist Revolutionary Theory." *Modern China* 9:2 (April): 182–211.

———. 1997a. "Modernism and Antimodernism in Mao Zedong's Thought." In *Critical Perspectives on Mao Zedong's Thought*, ed. Arif Dirlik, Paul Healy, and Nick Knight, 59–83. Atlantic Highlands, NJ: Humanities Press.

———. 1997b. *The Postcolonial Aura: Third World Criticism in the Age of Global Capitalism*. Boulder, CO: Westview Press.

———. 2005. *Marxism in the Chinese Revolution*. Lanham, MD: Rowman & Littlefield.

———, Paul Michael Healy, and Nick Knight, eds. 1997. *Critical Perspectives on Mao Zedong's Thought*. Atlantic Highlands, NJ: Humanities Press.

Du Weiming (Weiming Tu). 1989. *The Future of Confucianism in Three Periods of Development: Lectures, Debates, and Discussions on the Mainland* (Ruxue de sanqi fazhang de qianjing wenti: dalu jiangxue, wennan he taolun). Taibei: Lianjing chuban shiye gongsi.

Dufresne, Todd. 2003. *Killing Freud: Twentieth-Century Culture and the Death of Psychoanalysis*. New York: Continuum.

Dutton, Michael. 1998. *Streetlife China: Transforming Culture, Rights, and Markets*. Cambridge: Cambridge University Press.

Ebert, Teresa L. 1996. *Ludic Feminism and After: Postmodernism, Desire, and Labor in Late Capitalism*. Ann Arbor: University of Michigan Press.

Ellenberger, Henri. 1970. *The Discovery of the Unconscious*. New York: Basic Books.

Elliott, Emory. 2002. "Introduction: Cultural Diversity and the Problem of Aesthetics." In *Aesthetics in a Multicultural Age*, ed. Emory Elliott, Louis Freitas Caton, and Jeffrey Rhyne, 3–30. New York: Oxford University Press.

———, Louis Freitas Caton, and Jeffrey Rhyne, eds. 2002. *Aesthetics in a Multicultural Age*. New York: Oxford University Press.

Elman, Benjamin A. 2001. *From Philosophy to Philology: Intellectual and Social Aspects of Change in Late Imperial China*. Los Angeles: UCLA Asian Pacific Monograph Series, University of California.

Evans, Harriet. 1994. Review of *Red Azalea*. *The China Quarterly* 139 (fall): 850–51.

———. 1995. "Defining Difference: The 'Scientific' Construction of Sexuality and Gender in the People's Republic of China." *Signs: Journal of Women in Culture and Society* 20:21 (winter): 359–94.

Fei Min. 1949. *The New Concept of Love and the New Concept of the Family* (Xin lian'ai guan yu jiating guan). Shanghai: Shidai shuju.

Felsky, Rita. 1995. *The Gender of Modernity*. Cambridge: Harvard University Press.

Foster, Paul B. 2006. *Ah Q Archaeology: Lu Xun, Ah Q, Ah Q Progeny, and the National Character Discourse in Twentieth-Century China*. Lanham, MD: Lexington Books.

Foucault, Michel. 1990a. *The History of Sexuality: An Introduction*, vol. 1. Trans. Robert Hurley. New York: Vintage Books.

———. 1990b. *The Use of Pleasure: The History of Sexuality*, vol. 2. Trans. Robert Hurley. New York: Vintage Books.

Freeman, Derek. 1983. *Margaret Mead and Samoa: The Making and Unmaking of an Anthropological Myth*. Cambridge: Harvard University Press.

Furth, Charlotte. 1983. "Intellectual Change: From the Reform Movement to the May Fourth Movement, 1895–1920." In *The Cambridge History of China 1912–1949*, ed. Denis Twitchett and John K. Fairbank, vol. 12, 322–405. Cambridge: Cambridge University Press.

———. 1994. "Rethinking Van Gulik: Sexuality and Reproduction in Traditional Chinese Medicine." In *Engendering China: Women, Culture, and the State*, ed. Christina K. Gilmartin, Gail Hershatter, Lisa Rofel, and Tyrene White, 123–46. Cambridge: Harvard University Press.

———. 1999. *A Flourishing Yin: Gender in China's Medical History, 960–1665*. Berkeley: University of California Press.

Gallagher, Catherine, and Stephen Greenblatt. 2000. *Practicing New Historicism*. Chicago: University of Chicago Press.

Gan Yang. 1998. "A Critique of Chinese Conservatism in the 1990s." *Social Text 55* 16:2 (summer): 45–66.

Gao Juefu. 1923. "The New Psychology and Education" (Xin xinlixue yu jiaoyu). *The Educational Review* (Jiaoyu zazhi) 15:10 (October).

———. 1926a, 1926b, 1926c. "An Outline of Social Psychology" (Shehui xinlixue gaishuo). *The Educational Review* 18:3 (March: 1926a); 18:4 (April: 1926b); and 18:5 (May: 1926c).

———. 1934. "Critique of Freud and His Psychoanalysis" (Fuluoyite ji qi jingshen fenxi de pipan). *The Educational Review* 23:3 (March): 1–11.

———. 1986. *History of Chinese Psychology* (Zhongguo xinlixue shi). Beijing: Renmin jiaoyu chuban she.

Gao Qinghai, ed. 1983. *Dictionary of Spiritual Civilization* (Jingshen wenming cidian). Changchun: Jilin University Publishers.

Girardot, Norman J. 2002. *The Victorian Translation of China: James Legge's Oriental Pilgrimage*. Berkeley: University of California Press.

Giroux, Henry, David Shumway, Paul Smith, James Sosnoski. 1984. "The Need for Cultural Studies: Resisting Intellectuals and Oppositional Public Spheres." *Dalhousie Review* 64:2: 472–86.

Golden, Seán. "The Modernization of China and the Chinese Critique of Modernity." http://seneca.uab.es/hmic (accessed August 28, 2007).

Goldfuss, Gabriele. 1993. "Tribulations of a Sinophile in Republican China: The Musician and Pedagogue Alfred Westharp" (Les tribulations d'un sinophile dans la Chine républicaine. Le musicien et pédagogue Alfred Westharp). *Journée de l'Association Française d'Études Chinoises* 12:2.

Goodheart, Eugene. 1997. *The Reign of Ideology*. New York: Columbia University Press.

Gotz, Michael Louis. 1977. "Images of the Worker in Contemporary Chinese Fiction (1949–1964)." Ph.D. diss., University of California, Berkeley.

Grant, Linda. 1994. *Sexing the Millennium: Women and the Sexual Revolution.* New York: Grove Press.

The Great Communist Soldier—Lei Feng (Weida de gongchan zhuyi zhanshi—Lei Feng). 1977. Shanghai: Jiefang jun huabao she.

Griffiths, Phillips, ed. 1994. *Philosophy, Psychology and Psychiatry.* Cambridge: Cambridge University Press.

Guo Xuebo and Li Peng. 1990. *Learn from Lei Feng Educational Materials* (Xuexi Lei Feng fudao cailiao). Beijing: Nongcun duwu chuban she.

Hale, Nathan. 1971. *Freud and the Americans,* vol. 1. New York: Oxford University Press.

Hall, G. Stanley. 1879. "Philosophy in the United States." Originally published in *Mind* 4 (1879): 89–105. http://psychclassics.yorku.ca/Hall/philosophy.htm. (accessed December, 2005).

Hamilton, Paul. 1996. *Historicism: The New Critical Idiom.* New York: Routledge.

Hartnack, Christiane. 2001. *Psychoanalysis in Colonial India.* Oxford: Oxford University Press.

Haven, Joseph. 1862. *Mental Philosophy: Including the Intellect, Sensibilities, and Will.* Boston: Gould & Lincoln.

He Huaihong. 1997. "On My First Reading of *The Golden Years*" (Chudu *Huangjin shidai*). In *Romantic Knight: Remembering Wang Xiaobo* (Langman qishi: jiyi Wang Xiaobo), ed. Ai Xiaoming and Li Yinhe, 284–86. Beijing: Zhongguo qingnian chubanshe.

He Jixian. 2004. "The 'Discovery' and 'Submersion' of the Countryside: The Countryside in the Field of 20th Century Chinese Literature" (Nongcun de 'faxian' he 'yanmo': 20 shiji Zhongguo wenxue shiye zhong de nongcun). In *Literary Theory and Criticism* (Wenyi lilun yu piping) 2 (March): 4–9.

Höffding, Harald. 1891 [1882]. *Outlines of Psychology.* Trans. Mary E. Lowndes. London and New York: Macmillan & Company.

Holland, Jimmie. 1976. "A Comparative Look at Soviet Psychiatry." In *Psychiatry and Psychology in the USSR,* ed. Samuel A. Corson. New York: Plenum Press.

Holmes, Jeremy. 1994. "Meaning and Mechanism in Psychotherapy and General Psychiatry." In *Philosophy, Psychology and Psychiatry,* ed. Phillips Griffiths, 41–54. Cambridge: Cambridge University Press.

Hong, Ying. 1997. *Summer of Betrayal.* New York: Farrar, Straus, Giroux.

Honig, Emily. 1996. "Christianity, Feminism, and Communism: The Life and Times of Deng Yuzhi." in *Christianity in China: From the Eighteenth Century to the Present,* ed. Daniel H. Bays, 243–62. Stanford: Stanford University Press.

Horrocks, Roger. 2001. *Freud Revisited: Psychoanalytic Thought in the Postmodern Age.* Houndsmills, Basingstoke, Hampshire, and New York: Palgrave.

http://edu.sina.com.cn/gaokao/2007-08-23/105798122.shtml (accessed August 29, 2007). This article describes the replacement of Lu Xun's stories by those of Jin Yong in the secondary curriculum in Beijing.

http://www.chinadaily.com.cn/english/doc/2004-03/15/content_314802.htm. (accessed July 23, 2007). This story details the establishment of a dream clinic in Beijing.

Hu Qiaomu. 1952. "Why Do Literary and Art Workers Need to Change Their Thinking?—Talks from the November 24, 1951 Rectification and Study Meeting in Beijing of Delegates in the Literary and Art World" (Wenyi gongzuozhe weishenme gao gaizao sixiang—yi jiu wu yi nian shiyi yue ershisi ri zai Beijing wenyi jie zhengfeng xuexi dongyuan dahui shang de jiangyi). In *Why Literary and Art Workers Need to Change Their Attitudes* (Wenyi gongzuozhe weishenme yao gaizao sixiang), 1–9. Beijing: Renmin wenxue chubanshe.

Huang Guangxue, ed. 1967. *The Cultivation of the Revolutionary Spirit* (Geming jingshen xiuyang). Taibei: Taiwan shangwu yinshu guan.

Huang Jiwei. 1997. "Wang Xiaobo's Creation of *The Golden Years*" (Wang Xiaobo dizao *Huangjin shidai*). In *Romantic Knight: Remembering Wang Xiaobo* (Langman qishi: jiyi Wang Xiaobo), ed. Ai Xiaoming and Li Yinhe, 265–69. Beijing: Zhongguo qingnian chubanshe.

Huang, Martin Weizong. 1990. "The Inescapable Predicament: The Narrator and His Discourse in 'The True Story of Ah Q.'" *Modern China* 16:4 (October): 430–49.

Human Rights Watch and Geneva Initiative on Psychiatry. 2002. *Dangerous Minds: Political Psychiatry in China Today and Its Origins in the Mao Era.* New York: Human Rights Watch.

Huot, Claire. 2000. *China's New Cultural Scene: A Handbook of Changes.* Durham, NC: Duke University Press.

Huters, Theodore. 2005. *Bringing the World Home: Appropriating the West in Late Qing and Early Republican China.* Honolulu: University of Hawaii Press.

Ianssen, Robyn, and Yiyan Wang, eds. 1996. *Footprints on Paper: An Anthology of Australian Writing in English and Chinese.* Sydney: Robyn Ianssen Productions.

Ivanhoe, Philip J. 1990. *Ethics in the Confucian Tradition: The Thought of Mencius and Wang Yang-ming.* Atlanta, GA: Scholars Press.

Jameson, Fredric. 1981. *The Political Unconscious: Narrative as a Socially Symbolic Act.* Ithaca, NY: Cornell University Press.

———. 1986. "Third-World Literature in the Era of Multinational Capitalism." *Social Text* 15: 65–88.

———. 1991. *Postmodernism; or, The Cultural Logic of Late Capitalism.* Durham, NC: Duke University Press.

Jeffreys, Elaine. 2004. *China, Sex and Prostitution.* New York: Routledge Curzon.

Jia Pingwa. 1993. *The Abandoned Capital* (Feidu). Hongkong: Tiandi tushu youxian gongsi.

Jiang Guozhong. 1979. "The Heart / Mind Needs a Model" (Xinzhong yao you bangyang). In *Spring Is Forever Beautiful: Rereading "The Diary of Lei Feng"* (Qingchun yongyuan shi meihao de—chongdu *Lei Feng riji*), 7–11. Shanghai: Renmin chuban she.

Jiang Lei. 1997. "Let's Talk About the Background of Life: The Cultural Revolution"

(Shuoshuo shengming de beijing: wenge). *Film Literature Monthly* (Dianying wenxue yuekan) 312 (May): 51–54.

Jiang Wen. 1996. "Burning dream of youth: notes from the hand of the director of *In the Heat of the Sun*)" (Ranshao qingchun meng: 'Yangguang canlan de rizi' daoyan shouji). *Dangdai dianying* (January 15): 59.

———. 1997. "Recollections in the Sun: The Birth of a Film" in *The Birth of a Film* (Yibu dianying de dansheng), ed. Jiang Wen et al., 1–86. Beijing: Huayi chubanshe.

Jiang Wen et al. 1997. *The Birth of a Film* (Yibu dianying de dansheng). Beijing: Huayi chubanshe.

"'Jin Yong Replaces Lu Xun' Produces Debate: Jin Yong Chosen for High School Texts" ("Jin Yong ti Lu Xun" re zhengyi, Jin Yong luoxuan Beijing gaokao). 2007. http://edu.sina.com.cn/gaokao/2007-08-23/105798122.shtml (accessed November 11, 2007).

Jing, Qicheng, and Xiaolan Fu. 2001. "Modern Chinese Psychology: Its Indigenous Roots and International Influences." *International Journal of Psychology* 36:6: 408–18.

Jones, Dai, and Jonathan Elcock. 2001. *History and Theories of Psychology: A Critical Perspective.* London: Arnold Publishers.

Joravsky, David. 1989. *Russian Psychology: A Critical History.* Oxford: Basil Blackwell Ltd.

Kahn, Joseph. 2006. "Sane Chinese Put in Asylum, Doctor Finds." *New York Times.* March 17, A12.

Kinkley, Jeffrey. 1985. "Shen Congwen and the Uses of Regionalism in Modern Chinese Literature." *Modern Chinese Literature* 1:2: 157–84.

Knight, Nick. 1990a. "Introduction: Soviet Marxism and the Development of Mao Zedong's Philosophical Thought." In *Mao Zedong on Dialectical Materialism: Writings on Philosophy, 1937*, ed. Nick Knight, 3–83. Armonk, NY: M. E. Sharpe.

———,ed. 1990b. *Mao Zedong on Dialectical Materialism: Writings on Philosophy, 1937.* Armonk, NY: M. E. Sharpe.

Kuang Xinnian. 2004. "The Significance of Zhao Shuli's Literary History" (Zhao Shuli de wenxue shi yiyi). *Literary Theory and Criticism* 3 (May): 15–23.

Kubin, Wolfgang. 1982. "Sexuality and Literature in the People's Republic of China, Problems of the Chinese Woman Before and After 1949 as Seen in Ding Ling's 'Diary of Sophia' (1928) and Xi Rong." In *Essays in Modern Chinese Literature and Literary Criticism*, ed. Wolfgang Kubin and Rudolf G. Wagner, 168–91. Bochum: Brockmeyer.

———,ed. 2001. *Symbols of Anguish: In Search of Melancholy in China.* Bern: Peter Lang.

"Kulkosky's Bookmarks for the History of Psychology," http://faculty.colostate-pueblo.edu/paul.kulkosky/401.htm (accessed December, 2005).

Kuoshu, Harry H. 1999. "Visualizing Ah Q: An Allegory's Resistance to Representation." In *Lightness of Being in China: Adaptation and Discursive Figuration in Cinema and Theater*, ed. Harry H. Kuoshu, 17–49. New York: Peter Lang.

Kurzweil, Edith. 1989. *The Freudians: A Comparative Perspective.* New Haven: Yale University Press.

Kurzweil, Edith, and William Phillips, eds. 1983. *Literature and Psychoanalysis.* New York: Columbia University Press.

Kwok, D.W.Y. 1965. *Scientism in Chinese Thought, 1900–1950.* New Haven and London: Yale University Press.

Laqueur, Thomas. 1990. *Making Sex: Body and Gender from the Greeks to Freud.* Cambridge: Harvard University Press.

Larson, Wendy. 1989. "Realism, Modernism, and the Anti-'Spiritual Pollution' Campaign in Modern China." *Modern China* 15:1 (January): 37–71.

———. 1995. "Zhang Yimou: Inter/National Aesthetics and Erotics." In *Cultural Encounters,* ed. Soren Clausen and Anne Wedell-Wedellsborg, 215–26. Aarhus, Denmark: University of Aarhus Press.

———. 1997a. "Women and the Discourse of Desire in Post-Revolutionary China: The Awkward Postmodernism of Chen Ran." *boundary 2* 24:3 (fall): 201–24.

———. 1997b. "The Concubine and the Figure of History: Chen Kaige's *Farewell My Concubine.*" In *From Cultural Critique to Global Capital: Transnational Chinese Cinema,* ed. Sheldon Lu, 331–46. Honolulu: University of Hawaii Press.

———. 1997c. Review of Rey Chow, *Primitive Passions: Visuality, Sexuality, and Ethnography in Chinese Cinema. Journal of Modern Chinese Literature in Chinese* 1:1 (July): 139–43.

———. 2002. "The Self Loving the Self: Men and Connoisseurship in Modern Chinese Literature." *Femininities and Masculinities in China,* ed. Susan Brownell and Jeffrey N. Wasserstrom, 175–97. Berkeley: University of California Press.

———. 2006. "Who Am I? Freud and the New Intellectual in Republican China" (Wo shi shei? Fuluoyide yu xiandai Zhongguo de xin zhishifenzi). Paper presented at conference on Globalism and Aesthetics: The Self-Image of Chinese Intellectuals in the Ming, Qing, and Modern Periods (Yueshi yu meixue: Ming Qing zhi xiandai Zhongguo wenren de ziwo xingxiang xueshu yantaohui). Institute of Chinese Literature and Philosophy, Academia Sinica, Taiwan, December 7–8.

Leary, Charles. 1994. "Sexual Modernism in China: Zhang Jingsheng and 1920s Urban Culture." Ph.D. diss., Cornell University.

Lee, Leo Ou-fan. 1999. *Shanghai Modern: The Flowering of a New Urban Culture in China, 1930–1945.* Cambridge: Harvard University Press.

Li, David L. 2001. "'What Will Become of Us If We Don't Stop?': *Ermo*'s China and the End of Globalization." *Comparative Literature* 53:4: 442–61.

Li Qingxi. 2000. "Searching for Roots: Anticultural Return in Mainland Chinese Literature of the 1980s." In *Chinese Literature in the Second Half of the Twentieth Century: A Critical Survey,* ed. Pang-yuan Chi and David Wang, 110–23. Bloomington: Indiana University Press.

Li Xun. 1996. "*In the Heat of the Sun*: Behind the Splintering of Narrative" (Yangguang canlan de rizi: zai fenlie de xushi beihou). *Dangdai dianying* (Beijing) (November 15): 60–62.

Li Zhixi, ed. 1991. *Looking Back on the Origin and Development of the Movement to Study Lei Feng* (Huigu xuexi Lei Feng huodong de qiyuan he fazhan). Shenyang: Baishan chuban she.

Lin, Tsung-yi. 1985. "The Shaping of Chinese Psychiatry in the Context of Politics and Public Health." In *Mental Health Planning for One Billion People*, ed. Tsung-yi Lin and Leon Eisenberg, 3–37. Vancouver: University of British Columbia Press.

Liu Chengjie, Wang Tianhou, and Zhang Mingjuan. 1958. "The Psychological Characteristics of Progressive Producers" (Xianjin shengchangzhe de xinli tedian: lun gongchan zhuyi laodong taidu). *Beijing University Academic Journal* (Beijing daxue xuebao) [Human sciences (Renwen kexue)] 4: 39–51.

Liu Jianmei. 2003. *Revolution plus Love: Literary History, Women's Bodies, and Thematic Repetition in Twentieth-Century Chinese Fiction.* Honolulu: University of Hawaii Press.

Liu Jihui. 2004. *Perverted Heart: the Psychic Forms of Modernity* (Xin de lianyi: xiandaixing de jingshen xingshi). Taibei: Maitian chuban.

Liu, Kang. 1993. "Subjectivity, Marxism, and Culture Theory in China." *Social Text* 31 / 32: 114–41.

———. 1996. "Is There an Alternative to (Capitalist) Globalization? The Debate About Modernity in China." *boundary 2* 23:3: 193–218.

———. 1997a. "Popular Culture and the Culture of the Masses in Contemporary China." *boundary 2* 24:3 (fall): 99–122.

———. 1997b. "The Legacy of Mao and Althusser: Problematics of Dialectics, Alternative Modernity, and Cultural Revolution." In *Critical Perspectives on Mao Zedong's Thought*, ed. Arif Dirlik, Paul Healy, and Nick Knight, 234–63. Atlantic Highlands, NJ: Humanities Press.

———. 2005. "The Predicament of Marxist Revolutionary Consciousness: Mao Zedong, Antonio Gramsci, and the Reformulation of Marxist Revolutionary Theory." In *Marxism in the Chinese Revolution*, ed. Arif Dirlik, 125–50. Lanham, MD: Rowman & Littlefield.

Liu, Lydia H. 1995. *Translingual Practice: Literature, National Culture, and Translated Modernity—China, 1900–1937.* Stanford: Stanford University Press.

———. 1999. "Legislating the Universal: The Circulation of International Law in the Nineteenth Century," in *Tokens of Exchange: The Problem of Translation in Global Circulation.* ed. Lydia H. Liu, 127–64. Durham, NC: Duke University Press.

———, ed. 1999. *Tokens of Exchange: The Problem of Translation in Global Circulation.* Durham, NC: Duke University Press.

Liu Shushen, ed. 1990. *On Lei Feng: 1963–1990 Collected Essays from Looking Back on the Study of Lei Feng and Forward Toward Theoretical Discussion Meetings*

(Lun Lei Feng—1963–1990 xue Lei Feng huigu yu zhanwang lilun zhuotan hui wenji). Beijing: Guofang daxue chuban she.

Liu Zaifu. 1999. *On the Composition of Personality* (Xingge zuhe lun). Hefei: Anhui wenyi chuban she.

Livingston, Martha, and Paul Lowinger. 1983. *The Minds of the Chinese People: Mental Health in New China.* Englewood Cliffs, NJ: Prentice-Hall, Inc.

Low, Barbara. 1920. *Psycho-Analysis: A Brief Account of the Freudian Theory.* New York: Harcourt, Brace, & Howe.

———. 1927. *Psycho-Analysis: A Brief Account of the Freudian Theory Freudian Psychology* (Fuluote xinlixue fenxi). Trans. Zhao Yan. Shanghai: Shangwu chubanshe.

Lowe, Lisa. 1998. "The International Within the National: American Studies and Asian American Critique." *Cultural Critique* 40 (fall): 29–47.

Lu Jiandong. 1996. *The Last Twenty Years of Chen Yinke* (Chen Yinke de zuihou ershi nian). Beijing: Sanlian shudian.

Lu, Junhua. 1981. "Ah Q's Spiritual Victory: The Philosophical and Psychological Implications." *Social Sciences in China* 3: 21–60.

Lu Taiguang. 2004. "Vast Land Where Ghosts Wander: The Village World Under Lu Xun's Pen" (Guihun youdang de dadi: Lu Xun bixia de nongcun shijie). *Literary Theory and Criticism* 2 (March): 16–22.

Lu, Tonglin. 1995. *Misogyny, Cultural Nihilism, and Oppositional Politics: Contemporary Chinese Experimental Fiction.* Stanford: Stanford University Press.

Lynch, Catherine Alfred. "Liang Shuming's Turn in the 1920s." http://chinese-thought.unix-vip.cn4e.com/modules.php?name=Content&pa=showpage&pid=334. Institute of Modern Chinese Thought and Culture Research of East China Normal University (Huadong shifan daxue Zhongguo xiandai sixiang yanjiusuo). (Accessed November 2005).

Ma, Yue. 2005. "Wang Xiaobo: The Double Temptation of Revolution and Sexual Allurement." *Concentric: Literary and Cultural Studies* 31:2 (July): 201–21.

Magnus Hirschfeld Archive for Sexuality. Humboldt University, Berlin: http://www2.hu-berlin.de/sexology/index.htm.

Maher, Michael, S.J. 1900. *Psychology: Empirical and Rational.* London, New York: Longmans, Green.

Malcolm, Janet. 1983. *In the Freud Archives.* New York: Alfred A. Knopf.

Mang Ke. 1994. *Wild Things* (Yeshi). Changsha: Hunan wenyi chubanshe.

Mao Zedong. 1986. "Where Does Correct Thinking Come From?" (Ren de zhengque sixiang shi cong nali laide), ed. Editorial Committee of the Documents of the Central Chinese Communist Party (Zhong gong zhongyang wenxian bianji weiyuan hui), 839–41. Beijing: Renmin chubanshe.

Marcuse, Herbert. 1966 [1955]. *Eros and Civilization: A Philosophical Inquiry into Freud.* Boston: Beacon Press.

Martin, William Alexander Parsons. 1880. *The Chinese: Their Education, Philosophy, and Letters.* Shanghai: Hanlin Papers.

———. 1898. *Aspects of Human Nature* (Xingxue juyu). Shanghai: Guangxue hui.

Masson, Jeffrey Moussaieff. 1984. *The Assault on Truth: Freud's Suppression of the Seduction Theory*. New York: Farrar, Straus & Giroux.

———. 1985. *The Complete Letters of Sigmund Freud to Wilhelm Fleiss, 1887–1904*. Cambridge: Belknap Press, Harvard University Press.

———. 1988. *Against Therapy: Emotional Tyranny and the Myth of Psychological Healing*. New York: Atheneum.

McDougall, William. 1908. *An Introduction to Social Psychology*. London: Methuen.

Meisner, Maurice. 1967. *Li Ta-chao and the Origins of Chinese Marxism*. Cambridge: Harvard University Press.

———. 1982. *Marxism, Maoism, and Utopianism: Eight Essays*. Madison: University of Wisconsin Press.

Meyer, Catherine, Mikkel Borch-Jacobsen, Jean Cottraux, and Didier Pleux. 2005. *The Black Book of Psychoanalysis—How to Live, Think and Get on Better Without Freud* (Le livre noir de la psychanalyse: Vivre, penser et aller mieux sans Freud). Paris: Editions des Arènes.

Miller, Martin A. 1998. *Freud and the Bolsheviks: Psychoanalysis in Imperial Russia and the Soviet Union*. New Haven: Yale University Press.

Mills, Harriet. 1977. "Lu Xun: Literature and Revolution—From Mara to Marx." In *Modern Chinese Literature in the May Fourth Era*, ed. Merle Goldman, 189–220. Cambridge: Harvard University Press.

Min, Anchee. 1994. *Red Azalea*. New York: Berkeley Books.

———. 1995. *Katherine*. New York: Riverhead Books.

Misra, Kalpana. 1998. *From Post-Maoism to Post-Marxism: The Erosion of Official Ideology in Deng's China*. New York: Routledge.

Mittler, Barbara. 1997. *Dangerous Tunes: The Politics of Chinese Music in Hong Kong, Taiwan, and the People's Republic of China Since 1949*. Wiesbaden: Harrassowitz Verlag.

Mo Yan. 1994. "Divine Debauchery." Trans. Andrew F. Jones. In *Running Wild: The New Chinese Writers*, ed. David Der-wei Wang with Jeanne Tai, 1–12. New York: Columbia University Press.

Munro, Robin. 2000. "Judicial Psychiatry in China and Its Political Abuses." *Columbia Journal of Asian Law* 14:1 (spring): 1–125.

Ng, On-cho. 1993. "Toward an Interpretation of Ch'ing Ontology." In *Cosmology, Ontology, and Human Efficacy: Essays in Chinese Thought*, ed. Richard J. Smith and D.W.Y. Kwok, 35–58. Honolulu: University of Hawaii Press.

Ng, Vivien W. 1990. *Madness in Late Imperial China: From Illness to Deviance*. Norman and London: University of Oklahoma Press.

Ni Chung-fan. 1957. "A Preliminary Criticism of the Behaviorism of J. B. Watson." *Acta Psychologica Sinica* 1:2: 194–200.

Norman J. Girardot. 2002. *The Victorian Translation of China: James Legge's Oriental Pilgrimage*. Berkeley: University of California Press.

Noumoff, Samuel J. 1975. "The Philosophic Basis of the Theory of Social Transformation in China." Ph.D. diss., New York University.

"A Novel Business, Interpreting Dreams." http://www.chinadaily.com.cn/english/doc/2004-03/15/content_314802.htm. (Accessed July 23, 2007.)

"On the Relationship Between the People's Spirit and the Nation" (Lun minqi yu guojia zhi guanxi), part 1. *Eastern Miscellany* 6 (July 1905) (Guangxu year 31): 121–23; part 2, *Eastern Miscellany* 9 (October 1905) (Guangxu year 31): 183–85.

Oosterhuis, Harry. 2000. *Stepchildren of Nature: Krafft-Ebing, Psychiatry, and the Making of Sexual Identity.* Chicago: University of Chicago Press.

Osborn, Reuben. 1937. *Freud and Marx: A Dialectical Study.* New York: Equinox Co-operative Press, Inc.

———. 1965. *Marxism and Psychoanalysis.* New York: Dell Publishing Company.

Ostrovsky, Nicolai. 1959 [1936]. *How the Steel Was Tempered.* Moscow: Foreign Languages Publishing House.

Pearson, Veronica. 1995. *Mental Health Care in China: State Policies, Professional Services and Family Responsibilities.* London: Gaskell.

Peng, Hsiao-yen. 2002. "*Sex Histories*: Zhang Jingsheng's Sexual Revolution." In *Feminism/Femininity in Chinese Literature*, ed. Peng-hsiang Chen and Whitney Crothers Dilley, 159–78. Amsterdam: Rodopi.

Peng Xiaoling and Han Keli, eds. 1993. *Seventy Years of Ah Q* (A Q 70 nian). Beijing: Beijing chubanshe.

Perry, Helen Swick. 1982. *Psychiatrist of America: The Life of Harry Stack Sullivan.* Cambridge: Harvard University Press.

Petrovsky, Arthur. 1990. *Psychology in the Soviet Union: A Historical Outline.* Trans. Lilia Nakhapetyan. Moscow: Progress Publishers.

"Philosophy in the United States" [1879]. Originally published in *Mind* 4: 89–105. http://psychclassics.yorku.ca/Hall/philosophy.htm. (Accessed December, 2005).

Pieters, Jürgen. 2000. "Past, Present and Future: New Historicism versus Cultural Materialism." http://www.iath.virginia.edu/pmc/text-only/issue.100/10.2.r_pieters.txt. (Accessed February, 2004).

Polumbaum, Judy. 1994. "The Cultural Contradictions of Communism" *The Women's Review of Books* 11:8 (May): 1–4.

"The Psychology Major Discusses the Social and the Natural in the Human Psyche" (Xinli zhuanye taolun ren de xinli de shehuixing yu ziranxing wenti). 1961. *Beijing University Academic Journal* [Human sciences] 4: 42–41 (begins on 42, ends on 41).

Qi Zhirong. "Research on the Spiritual Mobilization of the Chinese Communists" (Zhong gong jingshen dongyuan yanjiu). http://past_journal.mnd.gov.tw (see Chinese character glossary for full citation). (Accessed May 2, 2006).

Qian Xingcun. 1993 [1928]. "The Dead-and-Gone Era of Ah Q." In *Seventy Years of Ah Q* (A Q 70 nian), ed. Peng Xiaoling and Han Keli, 70–81. Beijing: Beijing chubanshe.

Qian Zhixiu. 1914. "Research on Dreams" (Meng zhi yanjiu). *Eastern Miscellany* 10:11 (April).

———. 1918–19. "Modern Psychology" (Xiandai xinlixue), *Beijing University Gazette* (Beijing daxue rikan) 114 (April 18, 1919); 5:116 (April 20, 1918); 119

(April 24, 1918); 120, 121 (April 25, 26, 1918); 123, 124 (April 29, 30, 1918); 129, 130 (May 6, 7, 1918); 384, 387, 396, 397, 403, 404, 406, 408 (May 22, 26, June 6, 7, 14, 16, 18, 20, 1919).

Queen, Sarah A. 2001. "Inventories of the Past: Rethinking the 'School' Affiliation of the *Huainanzi.*" *Asia Major* 14:1: 51–72.

Quinney, Anne. 2004. "Psychoanalysis Is on the Couch: France Celebrates Freud in 2000." *French Cultural Studies* 15:2: 114–26.

Radicalesbians. 1991. *For Lesbians Only: A Separatist Anthology.* London: Radical Feminist Lesbian Publishers.

Ratner, C. 1970. "Mental Illness in the People's Republic of China." *Voices: Journal of American Academy of Psychotherapists* 14:4: 80–84.

Reed, Edward S. 1997. *From Soul to Mind: The Emergence of Psychology from Erasmus Darwin to William James.* New Haven: Yale University Press.

Reiche, Reimut. 1970. *Sexuality and Class Struggle.* Trans. Susan Bennett. New York: Praeger.

Reynolds, Douglas R. 1993. *China, 1898–1902: The Xinzheng Revolution and Japan.* Cambridge: Council on East Asian Studies, Harvard University.

Rickard, John S. 1999. *Joyce's Book of Memory: The Mnemotechnic of Ulysses.* Durham, NC: Duke University Press.

Roark, Ruric N. 1895. *Psychology in Education; Designed as a Text-book, and for the Use of the General Reader.* New York: American Book Company.

Roazen, Paul. 2002. *The Trauma of Freud: Controversies in Psychoanalysis.* New Brunswick, NJ: Transaction Publishers.

Robinson, Daniel N. 1976. *An Intellectual History of Psychology.* New York: MacMillan Publishing Company.

Robinson, Paul. 1976. *The Modernization of Sex: Havelock Ellis, Alfred Kinsey, William Masters and Virginia Johnson.* New York: Harper & Row.

———. 1993. *Freud and His Critics.* Berkeley: University of California Press.

Rocquain, Félix. 1894. *The Revolutionary Spirit Preceding the French Revolution.* Trans. J. D. Hunting. London: Swan Sonnenschein & Co.

Rofel, Lisa. 1999. *Other Modernities: Gendered Yearnings in China After Socialism.* Berkeley: University of California Press.

Roudinesco, Elizabeth. 1997. *Jacques Lacan: Outline of a Life, History of a System of Thought.* Trans. Barbara Bay. New York: Columbia University Press.

Rowe, John Carlos. 2002. "Resistance to Cultural Studies." In *Aesthetics in a Multicultural Age,* ed. Emory Elliott, Louis Freitas Caton, and Jeffrey Rhyne, 105–20. New York: Oxford University Press.

Rowe, William T. 2001. *Saving the World: Chen Hongmou and Elite Consciousness in Eighteenth-Century China.* Stanford: Stanford University Press.

Ruitenbeck, Hendrik. 1966. *Freud and America.* New York: Macmillan.

Schaler, Jeffrey A., ed. 2004. *Szasz Under Fire: The Psychiatric Abolitionist Faces His Critics.* Chicago and La Salle, IL: Open Court Publishing Company.

Seelow, David. 2005. *Radical Modernism and Sexuality: Freud/Reich/D. H. Lawrence and Beyond.* New York: Palgrave Macmillan.

Shapiro, Judith Shapiro. 1994. "Counterrevolutionary Sex: A Chinese Author's Memoir of Forbidden Love During the Cultural Revolution." *New York Times Book Review.* (February 11), sec. 7, p. 11.

Shapiro, Laura, with Karen Springen. 1994. "This Girl's Life." *Newsweek* 123:15 (April 11): 76–77.

Sheehan, Jackie. 1998. *Chinese Workers: A New History.* New York: Routledge.

Shen Heyong. 2000. "Record of a Discussion with Professor Gao Juefu" (Gao Juefu jiaoshou fangtan lu). In *Long Kicking Steed: The Honorable Professor Gao Juefu and One Era of Psychology* (Laoji jiuti—xinlixue yidai zongshi Gao Juefu), ed. Ye Haosheng, 192–99. Nanjing: Nanjing daxue chubanshe.

Shen Su. 1905. "On Why the Chinese People's Spirit Is Weak" (Lun Zhongguo minzi shuairuo zhi you). *Eastern Miscellany* 8 (September) (Guangxu year 31): 154–56.

Shih, Shu-mei. 2001. *The Lure of the Modern: Writing Modernism in Semicolonial China, 1917–1937.* Berkeley: University of California Press.

Siqin Gaowa 1997. "Discussing Jiang Wen from the Perspective of the Film *In the Heat of the Sun.*" In *The Birth of a Film* (Yibu dianying de dansheng), ed. Jiang Wen et al., 141–44. Beijing: Huayi chubanshe.

Sivin, Nathan. 1995. *Medicine, Philosophy, and Religion in Ancient China,* 1–19. Hampshire: Variorum.

Sloan, Sam. "The Sexual Freedom Movement in the 1960s." http://www.samsloan.com/sfl.htm. (Accessed August 10, 2007).

Smith, Arthur. 1894. *Chinese Characteristics.* London: Fleming H. Revell.

———. 1896. *Chinese Characteristics* (Chūgokujin kishitsu). Trans. Shiba Tamotsu. Tokyo: Hakubunkan shuppan.

Somerson, Wendy. 1997. "Under the Mosquito Net: Space and Sexuality in Red Azalea." *College Literature* Special Issue 24:1 (February): 98–115.

Song Rushan. 2002. *From Literature of the Wounded to Root-Seeking Literature: Schools of Mainland Literature in the Ten Years After the Cultural Revolution* (Cong shanghen wenxue dao xungen wenxue: wenge hou shinian de dalu wenxue liupai). Taibei: Xiuwei zixun.

Spivak, Gayatri Chakravorty. 1988. "Can the Subaltern Speak?" In *Marxism and the Interpretation of Culture,* ed. Cary Nelson and Lawrence Grossberg, 271–313. London: Macmillan.

Stocking, George W., Jr. 1966. "Franz Boas and the Culture Concept in Historical Perspective." *American Anthropologist* 68: 867–82.

Sullivan, Harry Stack. 1946. "The Cultural Revolution to End War—An Editorial on the Second William Alanson White Memorial Lectures by Major-General G. B. Chisholm." *Psychiatry* 9: 81–87.

———. 1953. *The Interpersonal Theory of Psychiatry.* New York: W. W. Norton.

———. 1954. *The Psychiatric Interview.* New York: W. W. Norton.

———. 1962. *Schizophrenia as Human Process.* New York: W. W. Norton.

———. 1964 [1944]. "The Illusion of Personal Individuality." In *The Fusion of Psychiatry and Social Sciences,* ed. H. S. Perry. New York: W. W. Norton.

Sun, Lung-Kee. 1992. "Social Psychology in the Late Qing Period." *Modern China* 18:3 (July): 235–62.

———. 1996. "Fin-de-Siècle in the May Fourth Era." In *Remapping China: Fissures in Historical Terrain*, ed. Gail Hershatter, Emily Honig, Jonathan N. Lipman, and Randall Stross, 194–209. Stanford: Stanford University Press.

Sussman, Henry. 1997. *The Aesthetic Contract: Statutes of Art and Intellectual Work in Modernity*. Stanford: Stanford University Press.

Sutton, Donald S. 2000. "From Credulity to Scorn: Confucians Confront the Spirit Mediums in Late Imperial China." *Late Imperial China* 21:2 (December): 1–39.

Szasz, Thomas S. 1959. "Psychiatry, Psychotherapy, and Psychology." *AMA Archives of General Psychiatry* 1 (November): 455–63.

———. 1960. "The Myth of Mental Illness: Foundations of a Theory of Personal Conduct." *American Psychologist* 15: 113–18.

———. 1978. *The Myth of Psychotherapy: Mental Healing as Religion, Rhetoric, and Repression*. Cambridge: Oxford.

Tang Qian. 1960. "Critiquing Freud's Thought" (Piping Fuluoyide de sixiang). *Beijing University Academic Journal* [Human sciences] 1: 115–22.

Tang, Xiaobing. 1996. *Global Space and the Nationalist Discourse: The Historical Thinking of Liang Qichao*. Stanford: Stanford University Press.

———. 2000. *Chinese Modern: The Heroic and the Quotidian*. Durham, NC: Duke University Press.

Tansley, Arthur G. 1920. *The New Psychology and Its Relation to Life*. London: G. Allen & Unwin; New York: Dodd, Mead.

Taylor, Charles. 1989. *Sources of the Self: The Making of the Modern Identity*. Cambridge: Harvard University Press.

Taylor, Rodney. 1990. *The Religious Dimensions of Confucianism*. Albany: State University of New York Press.

T'ien Ju-K'ang. 1985. "Traditional Chinese Beliefs and Attitudes Toward Mental Illness." In *Chinese Culture and Mental Health*, ed. Wen-Shing Tseng and David Y. H. Wu, 67–81. Orlando, FL: Academic Press, Inc.

Tonkin, Boyd. 1993. "Reds in Bed." *New Statesman and Society* 6:275 (October 22): 41.

Torrey, E. Fuller. 1992. *Freudian Fraud: The Malignant Effect of Freud's Theory on American Thought and Culture*. New York: Harper Collins Publishers.

Tsau, Shu-ying. 2001. "'They Learn in Suffering What They Teach in Song': Lu Xun and Kuriyagawa Hakuson." In *Symbols of Anguish: In Search of Melancholy in China*, ed. Wolfgang Kubin, 441–69. Bern: Peter Lang.

Tsu, Jing. 2005. *Failure, Nationalism, and Literature: The Making of Modern Chinese Identity, 1895–1937*. Stanford: Stanford University Press.

Turkle, Sherry. 1978. *Psychoanalytic Politics: Freud's French Revolution*. New York: Basic Books, Inc.

van den Haag, Ernest. 1965. "Introduction." In *Psychopathia Sexualis: A Medico-Forensic Study*, 7–19. New York: G. P. Putnam's Sons.

Veneigem, Raoul. 1983 (1979). *The Book of Pleasures* (Les livres des plaisirs). London: Pending Press.

Voegelin, Eric. 1952. *The New Science of Politics.* Chicago: University of Chicago.

———. 1994 [1956]. *Order and History.* Vol. 1: *Israel and Revelation.* Baton Rouge: Louisiana State University Press.

von Krafft-Ebing, Richard. 1965 [1886]. *Psychopathia Sexualis: A Medico-Forensic Study.* New York: G. P. Putnam's Sons.

Voynich, Ethel L. 1906 [1897]. *The Gadfly.* New York: Henry Holt & Company.

Wakeman, Frederic, Jr. 1973. *History and Will: Philosophical Perspectives of Mao Tse-tung's Thought.* Berkeley: University of California Press.

Walder, Andrew G. 1986. *Communist Neo-Traditionalism: Work and Authority in Chinese Industry.* Berkeley: University of California Press.

Wang, Ban. 1997. *The Sublime Figure of History: Aesthetics and Politics in Twentieth Century China.* Stanford: Stanford University Press.

Wang, David Der-wei. 1997. *Fin-de-siècle Splendor: Repressed Modernities of Late Qing Fiction, 1849–1911.* Stanford: Stanford University Press.

Wang Hui. 1998. "Contemporary Chinese Thought and the Question of Modernity." *Social Text* 55 (summer): 9–44.

Wang, Jing. 1996. *High Culture Fever: Politics, Aesthetics, and Ideology in Deng's China.* Berkeley: University of California Press.

Wang Jingxi. 1920. "The Most Recent Trends of Psychology" (Xinlixue de zuijin de qushi). *The Renaissance* (Xinchao) 2:5 (May): 889–902.

Wang Meng. 1989. *Bolshevik Salute: A Modernist Chinese Novel.* Trans. Wendy Larson. Seattle: University of Washington Press.

Wang Ning. 2002. *Literature and Psychoanalysis* (Wenxue yu jingshen fenxi xue). Beijing: Renmin wenxue chubanshe.

Wang Ruixing. 1963. "Study 'Spirit,' Do Things" ('Jingshen' yao xue, shiqing yao zuo), *How to Be a Person: Who to Live For: Learn from Comrade Lei Feng* (Zenyang zuoren, wei shi huozhe: xiang Lei Feng tongzhi xuexi). Tianjin: Tianjin renmin chuban she.

Wang Shuo. 1995. "Ferocious Beasts." In *Works of Wang Shuo* (Wang Shuo wenji), 248–332. Beijing: Huayi chuban she.

———. 1997. "Remembering *In the Heat of the Sun*" (*Yangguang canlan de rizi* huiyi). In *The Birth of a Film* (Yibu dianying de dansheng) ed. Jiang Wen et al., 126–30. Beijing: Huayi chubanshe.

Wang Xiaobo. 1992a. *The Golden Years* (Huangjin shidai). Taibei: Lianjing chuban shiye gongsi.

———. 1992b. *The Romantic History of Wang Er* (Wang Er fengliu shi). Hong Kong: Fangrong chubanshe.

———. 1994. *The Golden Years* (Huangjin shidai). Beijing: Huaxia chubanshe.

———. 2007. *Wang in Love and Bondage: Three Novellas by Wang Xiaobo.* Trans. Hongling Zhang and Jason Sommer. Albany: State University of New York Press.

Wang Xue. 1996. "The First Poem in the Dream: On Jiang Wen's *In the Heat of the*

Sun" (Diyi shou mengzhong de shige: guanyu Jiang Wen de *Yangguang canlan de rizi*). *Contemporary Film* 1 (January): 63–64.

"Wang Yangming (1472–1529 CE)." N.d. *The Internet Encyclopedia of Philosophy.* http://www.iep.utm.edu/w/wangyang.htm. (Accessed April 4, 2006).

Wang Yichuan. 1996. "Historicity and allegory: Analytical Critique of Jameson's Aesthetic Theory" (Lishi hua yu yuyan: Jiemusun meixue lilun pingxu). *Contemporary Film* (Dangdai dianying) 2: 41–49.

Wang Zengfan. 1979. "'Those for the Revolution, Come with Me!'" (Yao geming de, gen wo zou!). In *Youth is Forever Beautiful: Rereading Lei Feng's Diary* (Qingchun yongyuan shi meihao de—chongdu *Lei Feng riji*), 79–83. Shanghai: Renmin chubanshe.

Wang Zheng. 1999. *Women in the Chinese Enlightenment: Oral and Textual Histories.* Berkeley: University of California Press.

Webster, Richard. 1995. *Why Freud Was Wrong: Sin, Science and Psychoanalysis.* New York: Basic Books.

Westharp, Alfred (Daniel). 1926. *Outline of a Psychology of Collaboration Between the Far East and the Far West* (Esquisse d'une psychologie de collaboration entre l'Extrême-Occident et l'Extrême-Orient). Beijing: La Politique de Pékin.

Wiegman, Robyn. 2002. "Difference and Disciplinarity." In *Aesthetics in a Multicultural Age*, ed. Emory Elliott, Louis Freitas Caton, and Jeffrey Rhyne. New York: Oxford University Press.

Womack, Brantly. 1982. *The Foundations of Mao Zedong's Political Thought 1917–1935*. Honolulu: University Press of Hawaii.

Wozniak Robert H. "Harald Höffding: *Outlines of Psychology* (1882; English 1891)." In *Thoemmes Continuum: The History of Ideas*, http://www.thoemmes.com/psych/hoffding.htm. (Accessed May 24, 2006).

Wu Hongfei. "The Poet Mang Ke: I Have Lived, Perfectly Intact, Till Now" (Shiren Mang Ke: Wo wan hao wu sun de huo dao xianzai). Beijing langgang. http://news.sina.com.tw/articles/13/55/12/13551268.html. (Accessed January 24, 2006).

Wu Jianguo and Cao Yanming. 1982. "Some Theoretical Issues Concerning Material Civilization and Spiritual Civilization" (Guanyu wuzhi wenming yu jingshen wenming de jige lilun wenti). In *Ethics and Civilization* (Lunlixue yu jingshen wenming). Tianjin: Zhongguo lunli xuehui, September 11, preliminary issue (shikan hao) restricted distribution (neibu faxing): 21–22.

Wu Lichang. 1987. *Psychoanalysis and Literature in China and the West* (Jingshen fenxi yu Zhong Xi wenxue). Shanghai: Xuelin chubanshe.

Wuxun dazhong zixun zhuangbo youxian gongzi (listed in English as the Public Information Company), http://www.leifeng.com. (Accessed April 2006).

Xie Fei, Zheng Dongtian, Huang Jianzhong, Tian Zhuangzhuang, He Chun, Huang Jianxin, Shao Mujun, Zheng Guoen, Dai Jinhua, and Yuan Ying. 1998. "The Opening of Reform, Investigation of new Creativity: Historical Memories of the New Era Film" (Gaige kaifang, tansuo chuangxin: guanyu xin shiqi dianying de lishi jiyi). *Contemporary Film* (Dangdai dianying) 6 (November): 45–65.

Xu Shulian. 1956. "Looking at Individuality from the Perspective of Psychology"

(Cong xinlixue de guandian kan gexing wenti). *Chinese Youth* (Zhongguo qingnian) 15: 5–6.

Y. 1920. "A Few Words on the New Psychology of Freud" (Fuluote xin xinlixue zhi yiban). *Eastern Miscellany* 17:22 (November 25).

Yang Guisheng. 1965. "Glorious Image" (Guanghui de xingxiang). *Film Art* (Dianying yishu) (January): 3–4.

Yang Hui. 1998. "Contemporary Chinese Thought and the Question of Modernity." *Social Text* 55 (summer): 9–44.

Yang Jian. 1993. *Underground Literature of the Cultural Revolution* (Wenhua da geming zhong de dixia wenxue). Jinan: Chaohua chubanshe.

———. 2002. *History of Chinese Sent-Down Youth Literature* (Zhongguo zhiqing wenxue shi). Beijing: Zhongguo gongren chubanshe.

Yang Kai. 2004. "The Direction Toward 'Purity' in Contemporary Chinese Literature and 'Base' Consciousness: Speaking from the Question of Whether Zhao Shuli is 'Popular Literature'" (Dangdai wenxue zhong de 'chunjie' quxiang yu 'diceng' yishi). *Literary Theory and Criticism* 3 (May): 24–29.

Yang Xinhui. 2002. *On the History of Chinese Psychology* (Zhongguo xinlixue shilun). Hefei: Anhui jiaoyu chuban she.

Yang Xinhui and Zhao Liru, eds. 1999. *History of Psychology in Early Modern and Modern China* (Zhongguo jinxiandai xinlixue tongshi). Vol. 2 of *A Comprehensive History of Psychology* (Xinlixue tongshi). Jinan: Shangdong jiaoyu chuban she.

Yao Xinyong. 2000. *Transformation and Creation of Subjectivity: New Theories on Chinese Sent-Down Youth Literature (1977–1995)* (Zhuti de suzao yu bianqian: Zhongguo zhiqing wenxue xinlun [1977–1995]). Jinan: Jinan daxue chubanshe.

Yasuoka Hideo. 1926. *The Chinese National Character in Fiction* (Shōsetsu kara mita Shina no minzoku sei), Tokyo: Shuhokaku shuppan.

Ye Qizheng. 1991. *The Early River of Contemporary Western Thought: Thinkers of the 19th Century* (Dangdai xifang sixiang xianhe: shijiu shiji de sixiangjia). Taibei: Zhengzhong.

Yeh, Catherine Vance. 2001. "Root Literature of the 1980s as a Double Burden." In *The Appropriation of Cultural Capital: China's May Fourth Project*, ed. Milena Dolezelova-Velingerova and Oldrich Kral, 229–56. Cambridge: Harvard University Asia Center.

Yeo, K. K. 2002. *Chairman Mao Meets the Apostle Paul: Christianity, Communism, and the Hope of China.* Grand Rapids, MI: Brazos Press.

Yin Hong. 1994. *Wandering Spirit: Freudianism and Twentieth Century Chinese Literature* (Paihuai de youling: Fuluoyide zhuyi yu Zhongguo ershi shiji wenxue). Kunming: Yunnan renmin chuban she.

Yin Jinan. 1995. "Zhongguo nanxing de 'Nüxing zhuyi'" (The feminism of Chinese men). *Dushu* 8: 136–38.

Yu Tianxiu (Yu Tinn Hugh). 1922a. "Psychoanalysis" (Fenxi xinlixue). *Journal of Chinese Psychology* (Xinli) 1:1 (January): 83–85.

———. 1922b. "Psychoanalysis" (Fenxi xinlixue). *Journal of Chinese Psychology* 1:2 (March): 1–5.

Yu, Ouyang. 1996. "Sex Notice." In *Footprints on Paper: An Anthology of Chinese and English Language Writers Working in Australia*, ed. Robyn Ianssen and Yiyan, 106. Sydney: Robyn Ianssen Productions.

Yuan Gongwei. 2005 [1953]. *The New Psychology* (Xin xinlixue). Shanghai: Guangxie shuju.

Zha, Jianying. 1995. *China Pop: How Soap Operas, Tabloids, and Bestsellers Are Transforming a Culture.* New York: New York Press.

Zha Xiduo (Zha Jianying). 1994. "Youse yanjinglide xiyangjing"—Beijingrende Niuyue meng" (Looking at the west through colored glasses—Beijing people have New York dreams). *Jiushi niandai yuekan* (The nineties monthly) 2: 16–17.

Zhang Jingsheng. 1926a. *Sex Histories* (Xingshi). Beijing: Beijing youzhong chubanshe.

———. 1926b. "A Response to Mr. Zhou Jianren's 'A Few Words On *Sex Histories*' " (Da Zhou Jianren xiansheng 'Guanyu *Xingshi* de jiju hua'). *In Common* (Yiban) 1:3: 434–36.

Zhang, Jingyuan. 1992. *Psychoanalysis in China: Literary Transformations, 1919–1949.* Ithaca, NY: East Asia Program, Cornell University.

Zhang Renli. 1997. "Introduction." in *The Birth of a Film* (Yibu dianying de dansheng), ed. Jiang Wen et al., 1–6. Beijing: Huayi chubanshe.

Zhang Xianliang. 1992. *Three love novels by Zhang Xianling* (Zhang Xianliang aiqing sanbuqu). Beijing: Huayi chubanshe.

Zhang Yiwu. 1994. "Post new era Chinese films: a fragmented challenge" (Hou xin shiqi Zhongguo dianying: fenlie de tiaozhan). *Zhongguo dianying* 4: 12–35.

———. 1998. "Spatial Imagination in Chinese Films of the 90s" (90 niandai Zhongguo dianying de kongjian xiangxiang). *Contemporary Film* 2 (March): 16–23.

Zhang, Xudong. 1998. "Intellectual Politics in Post-Tiananmen China." *Social Text* 55 (summer): 1–8.

———. 2000. "Shanghai Nostalgia: Postrevolutionary Allegories in Wang Anyi's Literary Production in the 1990s." *positions* 8:2 (fall): 349–88.

———. 2001. "The Making of the Post-Tiananmen Intellectual Field: A Critical Overview." In *Whither China? Intellectual Positions in Contemporary China*, ed. Xudong Zhang, 1–78. Durham, NC: Duke University Press.

Zhang, Yingjin. 1996. *The City in Modern Chinese Literature and Film: Configurations of Space, Time, and Gender.* Stanford: Stanford University Press.

Zheng Sili. 1994. *Chinese sex culture: a thousand-year knot* (Zhongguo xing wenhua: yige qiannian bujie zhi jie). Beijing: Zhongguo duiwai fanyi chuban gongsi.

Zhi Xiaomin. 2004. "Liang Shuming's Only Foreign Friend—Alfred Westharp" (Liang Shuming weiyi de waiguo pengyou—Wei Xiqin). Guangming net (Guangming wang). http://www.gmw.cn/content/2004-07/27/content_64175.htm. July 26. (Accessed November 2005).

Zhong, Xueping. 1999. "'Long Live Youth' and the Ironies of Youth and Gender in Chinese Films of the 1950s and 1960s." *Modern Chinese Literature and Culture* 11:2 (fall): 150–85.

Zhou Guoping. 1997. "Free Soul" (Ziyou de linghun). In *Romantic Knight: Remembering Wang Xiaobo* (Langman qishi: jiyi Wang Xiaobo), ed. Ai Xiaoming and Li Yinhe, 364–68. Beijing: Zhongguo qingnian chubanshe.

Zhou Jianren. 1922. "The Theory and Actuality of Sex Education" (Xing jiaoyu de lilun yu shiji). *The Educational Review* (Jiaoyu zazhi) 14:8 (August).

———. 1923. "Some Principles of Sex Education" (Xing jiaoyu de jitiao yuanli). *Educational Review* (Jiaoyu zazhi) 15:8 (August).

———. 1926a. "A Few Words About *Sex Histories*" (Guanyu *Xingshi* de jiju hua). *In Common* (September): 114–18.

———. 1926b. "Responding to Mr. Zhang Jingsheng" (Da Zhang Jingsheng xiansheng). *In Common* 1:3: 436–40.

Zhou Zuoren. 1926. "Some Problems in Sex Education" (Xing jiaoyu de jige wenti). *Educational Review* 18:5 (May).

Zhu Guangqian. 1921. "Freud's Unconscious and Psychology" (Fulude de yin yishi yu xinlixue). *Eastern Miscellany* 18:14 (July 25).

Zhu Zhenglin. 1997. "Paper Covered with Wild Words" (Manzhi huangtang yan). In *Romantic Knight: Remembering Wang Xiaobo* (Langman qishi: jiyi Wang Xiaobo), ed. Ai Xiaoming and Li Yinhe, 281–83. Beijing: Zhongguo qingnian chubanshe.

Zhuang Zhou. 2000. "Qiren wulun." Part 2, Novels and Plays. http://www.xys.org/xys/ebooks/literature/essays/qirenwulun3.txt. Originally published in *Bookroom* (Shuwu) 10. (Accessed January 24, 2006).

Index

Note: Figures are indicated by *f* following a page number.